Internal Marketing

The term *internal marketing* was coined originally in the 1970s for a management approach to building and retaining service delivery competence. Today, the term has been applied to a broader range of management and social interests. By bringing together a multi-disciplinary set of contributions from leading writers in the field of service marketing and management, this volume represents a much-needed resource of the current 'state of the art' research and conceptual development in internal marketing. Comprising new theoretical and empirical work, and case studies based on a wide range of sector and industry applications, *Internal Marketing* identifies key themes and issues, including:

- a social model of marketing
- a human resources management perspective
- marketing and service management
- quality management
- organisational development
- corporate identity, image and reputation
- corporate communication

Richard J. Varey is a specialist in the communication perspective on management. He is Director of the Corporate Communication Research Unit and Associate Head of School responsible for Research at the Graduate School of Management at the University of Salford.

Barbara R. Lewis is Professor of Marketing at the Manchester School of Management. Her teaching and research interests are focused on the marketing of services, and in particular service quality issues. She is co-author of *Services Marketing: A European Perspective*.

Internal Marketing

Directions for Management

**Edited by
Richard J. Varey
and Barbara R. Lewis**

London and New York

First published 2000
by Routledge
11 New Fetter Lane, London EC4P 4EE

Simultaneously published in the USA and Canada
by Routledge
29 West 35th Street, New York, NY 10001

Routledge is an imprint of the Taylor & Francis Group

Typeset in Baskerville by Taylor & Francis Books Ltd
Printed and bound in Great Britain by Biddles Ltd, Guildford and King's
Lynn

British Library Cataloguing in Publication Data
A catalogue record for this book is available from the British Library

Library of Congress Cataloging in Publication Data
Internal marketing : directions of management / edited by Richard J.
Varey and Barbara R. Lewis.
     p.cm.
Includes index.
1. Marketing–Management. 2. Marketing channels. 3 Market
segmentation. I. Varey, Richard J., 1955- II. Lewis, Barbara R.

HF5415.13 .I577 2000
658.8'02–dc21

                                                        00–022193

ISBN 0–415–21318–5 (pbk)
ISBN 0–415–21317–7 (hbk)

Contents

Illustrations

Contributors

Pervaiz K. Ahmed is currently the Unilever Lecturer in Innovation at the University of Bradford Management Centre. Previously he has been a Lecturer in Strategic Management in the Department of Economics and Management at Dundee University, a Lecturer in Business Policy in the Huddersfield University School of Business and Lecturer in Marketing Research at University College, Aberystwyth. His main research interests are in new product development, globalisation strategies, strategic issues in the implementation of TQM and corporate culture.

David Ballantyne teaches relationship marketing, services marketing and logistics management at Monash University, Melbourne. He is also a Visiting Fellow at the Centre for Relationship Marketing and Service Management at Cranfield University, UK. He is co-author of *Relationship Marketing: Bringing Quality, Customer Service and Marketing Together* (1991), which was the first text published internationally on this rapidly evolving marketing and management approach to improving business performance. He is a past director of the Total Quality Management Institute of Australia and has held senior executive positions in marketing research, public relations and strategic marketing in the financial services industry. His current research interests include the quality of external customer relationships, internal networks and knowledge generation as a competitive resource.

James G. Barnes is Professor of Marketing in the Faculty of Business Administration, Memorial University of Newfoundland, Canada, where he served as Dean from 1978 to 1988. He has presented more than fifty papers at national and international academic conferences and has published more than thirty papers in refereed journals, including the *Journal of Consumer Research*, the *Journal of Advertising Research*, the *Services Industries Journal* and *Psychology and Marketing*. He serves on the Editorial Review Boards of the *International Journal of Bank Marketing* and the *International Journal of Customer Relationship Management*. He has published six textbooks as author or co-author, including *Fundamentals of Marketing*, now in its eighth edition and *Understanding Services Management*. His research interests and specialities include services marketing, service quality, and consumer relationships. Dr Barnes is also Executive Chairman of the Bristol Group, an integrated marketing communications and information consultancy, with clients throughout Canada and in the United States and Europe.

Leonard L. Berry holds the J.C. Penney Chair of Retailing Studies, and is Distinguished Professor of Marketing and Founding Director of the Center for Retailing Studies at Texas A&M University. A former national president for the American Marketing Association, he is author of *Discovering the Soul of Service* and *On Great Service*, and co-author of *Marketing Services* and *Delivering Quality Service*, published by the Free Press. Dr Berry received the 1996 Career Contributions to Services Marketing Award from the American Marketing Association. He also has twice been recognised with the highest honours Texas A&M bestows on a faculty member: the Distinguished Achievement Award in Teaching (in 1990) and the Distinguished Achievement Award in Research (in 1996). He serves on the board of directors of several publicly traded companies.

Sara Carter is Reader in the Department of Marketing at the University of Strathclyde. Her main research area is in the issue of small firms and entrepreneurship. She has undertaken a number of research studies on the small firm sector, including projects financed by the Department of Employment and Shell (UK) Ltd, the Economic and Social Research Council, the European Union, Scottish Enterprise and Glasgow Development Agency. Her publications include a book *Women as Entrepreneurs* (Academic Press, 1992), an edited reader *Enterprise and Small Business: Principles, Practice and Policy* (Pearson Education, 2000) and several articles in academic and practitioner journals.

Ian Chaston is part of the research Group for Organisational Learning at Plymouth Business School. He has previously published *Managing for Marketing Excellence* (1990), *Customer-Focused Marketing* (1993) and *New Marketing Strategies* (1999).

Peter A. Dunne is a graduate of the Masters of Business Administration program at Memorial University of Newfoundland. He holds an Honours Bachelor of Science degree in Psychology from Memorial University. He has worked for several years in management positions with a large Canadian bank. His research interests lie generally in services marketing, with a particular emphasis on the impact of technology on customers' perception of service quality.

Jean-Paul Flipo is Professor in the Ecole de Management de Lyon (France), in the field of marketing and management of service organisations. He was also visiting professor at York University of Toronto (Canada), at ESADE of Barcelona (Spain) and HEC Lausanne (Switzerland). He has published several books in French on service management and some contributions in books written in English. He is also past executive vice-president of the French Marketing Association and he is partner in a service company co-founded in 1987 in Lyon.

Susan K. Foreman joined the Marketing Faculty at Henley in 1990 and is currently the Marketing Faculty Group Leader. She teaches on MBA programmes and executive courses. Her MSc is in marketing, which she gained at the Manchester School of Management at UMIST. Her PhD research, in the area of transaction costs economics and marketing, is from Henley/Brunel University. Her current research and consulting interests are in the areas of internal marketing, services marketing and transaction costs approaches to marketing theory.

Audrey Gilmore is a Reader in Marketing at the University of Ulster at Jordanstown, Northern Ireland. Her teaching and research interests are in services marketing, marketing management, managerial competencies, networking and marketing in small and medium sized enterprises (SMEs). Her current research involves collaborative studies with the University of Monash, Australia and the University of Orebro, Sweden on SME managerial decision making. She is joint editor of the *European Journal of Marketing*.

Evert Gummesson is Professor of Service Management and Marketing and Research Director at the School of Business, Stockholm University, Sweden, and a management consultant. He has been featured in the *Journal of Retailing* as one of the international pioneers of services marketing. His latest book is *Total Relationship Marketing* (1999).

William E. Halal is Professor of Management at George Washington University, Washington, DC. An authority on emerging technologies, he has published *The New Capitalism* (1986), *Internal Markets* (1993), *The New Management* (1996), *The Infinite Resource* (1998) and *21st Century Economics* (1999). He is a member of the board of the World Future Society.

Lorrie A. Hecker is Marketing Director and project leader at the New York offices of The Marketing & Communication Agency.

Frank Hoffmann is research assistant with the Services Management group of the Catholic University of Eichstaett in Ingolstadt. His current research interests focus on the question of how business television can help to fulfil special internal communications requirements of companies with field representative structures, such as insurance companies or building societies.

Gillian Hogg spent six years as a manager in the NHS after graduating with a degree in English. She joined Stirling University as a research assistant in 1992. Her PhD was on the management of quality and standards in professional services, and her present research interests are in the area of the management and marketing of services. She is currently Senior Lecturer and Director of the MSc programme at the University of Strathclyde in Glasgow.

Barbara R. Lewis is Professor of Marketing and head of the marketing group at the Manchester School of Management, UMIST. Her teaching and research is in the services sector, where her research activities relate to customer care and service quality, and areas of recent focus have included assessment of determinants of service quality, intra-organisational issues, internal marketing, and service failure and recovery. She has published over one hundred journal articles and conference papers, was founder editor of the *International Journal of Bank Marketing*, has edited special issues for a number of marketing journals, and currently serves on the editorial board of several prominent journals. She is a co-author of *Services Marketing: A European Perspective* (Prentice Hall, 1999).

Peter Mudie is Lecturer in Marketing at Napier University Business School. His research interests are in consumer education and critical aspects of marketing. He is the author of *Marketing: An Analytical Perspective* (Prentice- Hall); and *The Management and Marketing of Services*, 2nd Edition (Butterworth-Heinemann).

A. Parasuraman is Professor and holder of the James W. McLamore Chair in Marketing at the University of Miami. He teaches and researches in the areas of services marketing, service quality measurement and improvement, and services marketing strategy. He has received many distinguished teaching and research awards and has written numerous articles in journals such as the *Journal of Marketing, Journal of Marketing Research, Journal of Retailing* and *Sloan Management Review*. He is a former editor of the *Journal of the Academy of Marketing Science* and serves on the editorial review boards of five other journals. Dr Parasuraman is the author of *Marketing Research* and co-author of *Delivering Quality Service: Balancing Customer Perceptions and Expectations* and *Marketing Services: Competing Through Quality*.

Mohammed Rafiq is Senior Lecturer in Retailing and Marketing at the Business School, Loughborough University. His current research interests are in the areas of retail space allocation modelling, shopping centre development and marketing, international retailing, internal marketing and services management.

Bernd Stauss is Professor of Business Administration at the Department of Business Administration of the Catholic University of Eichstaett in Ingolstadt, where he holds the first German Chair of Services Management. He has published several articles on services marketing, total quality management in service companies, customer satisfaction and internal marketing. He has recently published books on quality management, service quality, complaint management and service orientation at universities. His current research interests are in customer satisfaction, customer retention and regain management.

Kevin Thomson is Chairman of The Marketing & Communication Agency Ltd, Marlow, England; a Fellow of the Chartered Institute of Marketing;

Senior Research Fellow with the Open University Business School; and an Accredited Business Communicator with the IABC. He has published *The Employee Revolution* (1990), *Managing Your Internal Customers* (1993) and *Emotional Capital* (1998).

Richard J. Varey is Director of the Corporate Communication Research Unit and Associate Head of School (Research) in the Graduate School of Management, University of Salford, England. He is a member of the editorial boards of the *Journal of Communication Management* and the *Journal of Marketing Communications*, and book reviewer for *Corporate Communications: An International Journal*. He is currently writing *Corporate Communication: A Relationship Management Perspective* (forthcoming 2000), and *Marketing Communication: A Contemporary Introduction* (forthcoming 2001).

Paivi Voima has a Master of Economic Sciences degree from the Swedish School of Economics and Business Administration, Helsinki, where she is presently a doctoral student with Professor Christian Grönroos working and publishing in the area of internal marketing. She has previously been a consultant with Andersen Consulting and an assistant and project manager at the Swedish School of Economics and Business Administration. She is a part-time marketing manager at Extor Limited.

Preface

Internal marketing, the application of marketing management to the corporate organisation, was first suggested in the late 1970s. Since then it has been adopted widely in management and marketing.

This collection of new essays by an international group of leading scholars was commissioned in recognition of the importance, after two decades of developments, of contemporary reflection on, and synthesis in, the conception of internal marketing. We have encouraged intellectual trespassing in various traditional disciplines in order to reflect on marketing thought in a 'new management' among otherwise closed knowledge domains (often with competing claims).

In particular, we have surfaced a communication perspective that has not featured strongly in most of the literature to date, and feel justified in doing this as explorers and missionaries. Our quest is not for a single closed definition; we are not seeking to resolve the problem of 'confusion' in thinking about this management approach. In fact, we will inevitably add to the chaos. But, we believe that this may catalyse further thought and effort and that this will be a productive enterprise. This is, then, a feast of ideas and orientations, rather than a 'concept-controlled diet'.

Each subject studied by mankind has, until relatively recently, been treated more or less as an isolated area; each discipline developing its own theories and understandings, with generally little connection with the findings of studies in other fields of knowledge. The tendency to divide already separate fields of study into increasingly smaller portions has led to gaps in our overall knowledge of human behaviour, and greater synthesis can serve our needs.

For more than half a century, through the work of a number of notable people (for example, Ludwig von Bertalanffy (1969) and James Miller (1978)), areas of study have become less isolated so that their respective theories and understandings are now more integrated. Some common principles and properties of widely different phenomena have been revealed by the interdisciplinary study known as general systems theory, a way of looking at the world that sees an interconnected hierarchy of matter and energy. The basic theme of the systems approach is that all phenomena are related in some way. Accordingly, everything is seen as part of a system. Following a major study, Miller (1978) concluded that all living systems are composed of sub-systems that take in, process and put out matter, energy or information, or combinations of these. He identified nineteen critical sub-systems that seem to characterise all living systems, including corporations and societies. We see internal marketing as a sub-system of management, which itself is a sub-system of human interaction in social systems.

In a comprehensive review of published discussion of internal marketing (Varey, 1996) a narrow conception based on a managerialistic/mechanistic notion of marketing as a directive and promotional/expressive/reproductive tool of managerialistic self-interest and exploitation was revealed. There had been much debate around the question of defining internal marketing, but little reflection on the characterisation and premises assumed for adoption. An analysis of the components of the internal marketing framework, conducted by revisiting the sub-concepts (such as marketing, market, etc.), suggested considerable scope for a more holistic framework that could transcend the fragmenting specialisation.

For some time, the specialisation that arose with capitalism had separated thinkers when knowledge should arise in the wide community of thinkers, in an evolving pluralist ecology of knowledge. The proliferation of knowledge sub-cultures prevents the formation of a single expressive tradition that can speak to all. Sociologist Daniel Bell (1976) sees this as a basic weakness in society, as many are excluded (often for political reasons). Bell also raised the recognition that a new relationship of, and for, production and consumption arises in the emerging service economy in which encounter or communication between people is central. Communication inquiry and management has come of age.

This book is structured around the evolving context for managing work and emerging organisational forms. We examine the competencies required for managing in contemporary environments, before putting communication and service delivery under the spotlight. Some new developments in thinking are suggested, before re-orienting marketing thinking on the basis of contemporary communication theory. We conclude with a summary of the themes, issues, perspectives and contributions offered by each author.

Bill Halal raises the emerging context of market-based management where market structure and forces enter the organisation of business enterprise more fully. Evert Gummesson shows that there are many relationships in the new organisational forms, and all are important to the rising perspective of relationship marketing. David Ballantyne takes this further, showing that the corporation is a network of service-oriented relationships.

Jean-Paul Flipo raises some political aspects of management that must be considered carefully in trying to adopt an internal marketing approach to business management. Audrey Gilmore highlights managerial competencies, whilst Ian Chaston examines the development of corporate competencies for servicing customers. Sara Carter and Gill Hogg examine a mechanism that implants internal marketing with the necessary link into business performance. Susan Foreman reviews the economic thinking underlying the adoption of internal marketing and offers a clarification.

Bernd Stauss and Frank Hoffmann apply a 'communication gap' analysis to internal communication and examine Business TV as an internal marketing channel for necessary communication. Kevin Thomson and Lorrie Arganbright reflect on several consulting projects and some recent surveys to identify the impact on business performance of engaging people more fully with the business. Leonard Berry and Parsu Parasuraman take a look back at their classic 1992 article and find that their views are now even more pertinent to service management. Peter Dunne and James Barnes explore the question of whether or not the human resource management function can develop through internal marketing to meet contemporary business challenges.

A synthesis of two models of internal marketing is provided by Mohammed Rafiq and Pervaiz Ahmed, whilst a complementary internal relationship marketing framework is explained by Paivi Voima. Lest we forget in our theorising that people are at the heart of social endeavours, Peter Mudie brings attention back to some critical social concerns, drawing in voices that have not been included in the debates on the applicability of marketing for corporate management.

Richard Varey identifies the need to broaden the conception of internal marketing, and highlights the fundamental problem of outmoded communication theory as the basis for most discussion on marketing, internal marketing and marketing communication. Finally, we, the editors, attempt to distil the lessons of this book into an agenda for further developments.

So, then, we offer up an intentionally eclectic menu, but please do not fear duplicity in our motives. We have commissioned a diverse range of perspectives and points of view to produce a pluralistic presentation. We offer contributions from this group of leading Western scholars and commentators from their perspectives of Australia, the British Isles, Canada, Finland, France, Germany, Sweden and the USA. Some do not agree. Indeed, we have assembled a number of lenses through which to examine the problems of contemporary management of business enterprise. We hope that we have raised some significant provocations, and that this combination of authors and their work will catalyse (or provoke) evolutionary forces further.

Richard J. Varey
Salford

Barbara R. Lewis
Manchester
September 1999

References

Bell, D. (1976) *The Cultural Contradictions of Capitalism*, New York: Basic Books.

Bertalanffy, L. von (1969) *General Systems Theory*, New York: George Braziller.

Miller, J.O. (1978) *Living Systems*, New York: McGraw-Hill.

Varey, R.J. (1996) 'A Broadened Conception of Internal Marketing', unpublished PhD thesis, Manchester School of Management, UMIST.

Acknowledgements

This book would, of course, not have appeared had the contributors not participated. For their efforts and ideas, we are most appreciative.

Stuart Hay (formerly of Routledge) and Michelle Gallagher at Routledge patiently championed this project into print.

Joe and Pat Varey, and Alec Smalley, never voiced any desire to become expert on internal marketing. Nevertheless, they have lived with us through this project. For their patience, thank you.

Part I

Context

1 From hierarchy to enterprise

Internal markets are the foundation for a knowledge economy[1]

William E. Halal

Introduction

During the 1990s decade of Capitalism Triumphant, we heard constantly about the evils of central planning and authoritarian control. Yet the prevailing corporate structure remains a centrally-managed hierarchy, albeit adorned with a few gentle touches and good intentions. Despite recent claims about empowerment, teams, networking, and other progressive management concepts, this was also a decade of harsh downsizing, top-down change, and extravagant executive pay. Beneath the rhetoric, little is really different.

The problem is that we need flexible dynamic organizations, but the concepts in currency today simply cannot get us there. We usually have meager measures of performance below the level of major divisions, so it is hard to know if empowered people working in teams actually create value or destroy it; the result is little sound basis for ensuring accountability or allocating resources effectively. Further, without some form of decentralized control, major decisions must still be made by top management, thus reducing operating managers to bureaucrats rather than entrepreneurs. Many advocate just allowing employees the freedom to be more flexible, but unguided freedom soon becomes anarchy.

Other concepts that purport to replace the hierarchy suffer from the same limitation. There is the federal organization, the boundaryless corporation, the learning organization, the agile company, the spider's web, and so on. These ideas may encourage a more fluid variation of hierarchy, but they do not answer the questions raised above. The issue remains: how can an organization be designed as a true bottom-up system that permits spontaneous creativity while maintaining some form of coherent control?

Fundamentally, this problem will resist solution as long as we continue to think instinctively of management within a hierarchical control framework. Major corporations comprise economic systems that are as large and complex as national economies, yet they are commonly viewed as private firms to be managed by executives: moving resources about like a portfolio of investments, forming global strategies, restructuring the organization, and setting financial targets. How does this differ from the central planning that failed in the

Communist bloc? Why would such control be bad for a national economy but good for a *corporate* economy? Can *any* fixed structure remain useful for long in a world of constant change?

Top-down management may be working temporarily, but it is not going to withstand the massive changes looming ahead as relentless hypercompetition drives open a frontier of new products, markets, and industries that nobody really understands. A knowledge-based global order is emerging rapidly, yet the bulk of useful knowledge lies unused among employees at the bottom and scattered outside office walls among customers, suppliers, communities, and other stakeholder groups. Andrew Grove, former CEO of Intel, put it best: "The Internet is like a tidal wave, and we are in kayaks" (Grove, 1996).

Downsizing, for instance, seems to make sense from a capital-centred view, but the knowledge held by employees comprises 70 percent of all corporate assets! (Stewart, 1996). To put it more sharply, the economic value of employee knowledge exceeds all of the financial assets, capital investment, patents, and other resources of most companies. Today's downsizing highlights the inability of most corporations to really use their most valuable resource: the knowledge and creativity residing in the minds of employees.

The solution is a fundamentally different approach that harnesses the talents lying dormant in people. While Fortune 500 dinosaurs downsized by three million employees during the 1990s, smaller firms and new ventures upsized by creating 21 million new jobs. This salient fact shows that the key to vitalizing organizations is to bring the liberating power of small enterprise inside of big business.

In short, we need to shift the locus of power from top to bottom, to think of management in terms of enterprise rather than hierarchy. This may sound revolutionary, but today's revolution is as dramatic as the Industrial Revolution. We tend to hear the Information half of the Information Revolution but to ignore the Revolution half. Just as the idea that Communism might yield to markets seemed preposterous a few years ago, similar change is needed in big corporations: "Corporate Perestroika". Robert Shapiro, CEO of Monsanto, put it this way: "We have to figure out how to organize employees without intrusive systems of control. People give more if they control themselves" (Shapiro, 1997).

This introductory chapter reports the results of my studies focusing on hundreds of examples of internal enterprise being used to solve problems directly, creatively, and quickly. Pay-for-performance plans are being expanded to form self-managed units that are held accountable for results but free to choose their co-workers, leaders, work methods, suppliers, and generally "run their own business" as they think best. Line and support units are being converted into profit centers that buy and sell from each other and from outside the company, converting former monopolies into competitive business units. MCI, ABB, Johnson & Johnson, Hewlett-Packard, Lufthansa, and other companies have developed fully decentralized bottom-up structures that form complete "internal market economies" with hundreds of autonomous business units (Halal *et al.*, 1993). These internal enterprises may buy and sell to other units within the company, compete with one another, and even work with outside competitors.

The same trend can be seen in "reinventing government" and introducing competition into education (Osborne and Gaebler, 1992).

It takes only a little imagination to extend these trends to the point where the logic of free markets governs rather than the logic of hierarchy. The concept of internal markets has profound implications because it shifts the source of knowledge, initiative, and control from top to bottom, thereby providing the same benefits of external markets: better decisions through price information, customer focus, accountability for economic results, and as much entrepreneurial freedom as possible. One of the central implications is the need for "internal marketing" between internal enterprises – the subject of this book.

Yes, markets are messy, but they are also bursting with creative energy; roughly like the Internet, our best model of self-organizing market systems. Nobody could possibly control the Internet's complex activities, yet by allowing millions of people to pursue their own interests, somehow the system grows and thrives beyond anything we could imagine.

In the final analysis, only a new form of management based on enterprise can meet the challenges lying ahead in a knowledge economy. The vague hope that participation, team spirit, inspiring leadership, and other worthy but limited ideas can co-ordinate tens of thousands of people into truly dynamic, entrepreneurial organization is little more than pious wishing. Mayor Steve Goldsmith of Indianapolis reports that he struggled for years trying today's popular management methods, but nothing really changed until he turned the city's departments into self-supporting units competing with outside contractors.

Principles of internal markets

It has become a cliché to note that business schools are notorious for their poor management. Mine was no exception. An especially irksome problem was getting the copy centre to work properly. Professors thrive on paper, yet we could not seem to get copies made in less than a week. We knew that our local Kinko's could get them done in a day, but we would have to pay. Since the copy centre was free, we kept using it despite bad service. In fact, that is one reason why the service was bad: we overused this free good, clogging the system. Repeated attempts to get the copy centre to improve its operations, and the faculty to curb their excessive usage, had little effect.

The problem was that we were relying on a hierarchical assignment of tasks that were too complex for this approach. We needed good service. We needed faculty accountability. We needed a copy centre manager who was motivated to help us. We needed a choice of providers. In short, we needed a market.

After much argument, we asked the copy centre manager (let's call him Art) if he would like to turn the operation into "his own business". He could still use the school's copiers and facilities to serve the faculty's needs, but his income would be based on a percentage of the profits. The departments would get his old budget and could use it to either patronize Art or other copy centres. Art had an entrepreneurial streak, so he welcomed the opportunity.

Well, everything changed within days. A few people went to Kinko's, which got Art thinking about how to improve operations. And having to pay now, the faculty carefully considered whether or not they really needed a hundred copies of their latest tome. Our copy centre's service soon matched Kinko's, Art became a celebrated hero, and the problem was solved – by an internal market.

This little story illustrates the power of a dramatically different concept that has been emerging quietly for years to realize the ideal of internal enterprise. To move us beyond the confining logic of hierarchy, an entrepreneurial management framework has been defined by Jay Forrester, Russell Ackoff, Gifford and Elizabeth Pinchot, and myself (Forrester, 1965; Ackoff, 1981; Pinchot and Pinchot, 1994; Halal *et al.*, 1993), that views organizations as markets – "internal markets".

Internal markets are *meta*structures, or processes, that transcend ordinary structures. Unlike fixed hierarchies or centrally-coordinated networks, they are *complete internal market economies* designed to produce continual, rapid structural change, just as external markets do. Although only a few companies have implemented this idea as yet, Table 1.1 shows fairly wide acceptance of some key features, and the examples in the display on pp.7–8 demonstrate various approaches that have been used.

Table 1.1 Adoption of internal market practices (sample = 426 corporate managers)

Practice	Not practiced (0–3)	Partially practiced (4–6)	Fully practiced (7–10)	Mean (0–10)
Line units are treated as semiautonomous enterprises that have control over their own operations and keep most of their revenue	38%	20%	42%	4.9
Staff and support units (HRD, Legal, IS, etc.) are treated as profit centers that obtain revenue by selling their services to other units	73%	8%	19%	2.5
Line units are generally allowed to buy products and services from any organization, inside or outside the company	37%	18%	45%	5.2
Staff and support units are generally allowed to sell their services to any organization, inside or outside the company	62%	12%	26%	3.3
Apart from proprietary secrets, employees have access to central information systems that contain all available company information	30%	24%	46%	5.6

Source: Halal, *The New Management* (Berrett-Koehler, 1998).

Principles of internal markets

1   *Transform the hierarchy into internal enterprise units.* Rather than depart-
    ments, "internal enterprises" form the building blocks of an internal
    market system. All line and staff units are transformed into enter-
    prises by becoming accountable for performance but gaining control
    over their operations, as an external enterprise does. Alliances
    between internal enterprises link corporations together into a global
    economy.

2   *Create an economic infrastructure to guide decisions.* Executives design and
    regulate the infrastructure of this "organizational economy," just as
    governments manage national economies: establishing common
    systems for accounting, communications, incentives, governing poli-
    cies, an entrepreneurial culture, and so on. Management may also
    encourage the formation of various business arrangements that exist
    in an economic system: venture capital firms, consultants, distributors,
    and so on.

3   *Provide leadership to foster collaborative synergy.* An internal economy is
    more than a *laissez-faire* market, but a community of entrepreneurs
    that fosters collaborative synergy: joint ventures, sharing of tech-
    nology, solving common problems, and so on among both internal
    and external partners. Corporate executives provide the leadership to
    guide this internal market by encouraging the development of various
    strategies.

Exemplars of internal markets

Johnson & Johnson's 168 separately chartered companies form their own
    strategies, relationships with suppliers and clients, and other business
    affairs. CEO Ralph Larsen says the system "provides a sense of
    ownership that you simply cannot get any other way."
Motorola uses autonomous units that compete with one another to
    produce the most successful products in America. One manager said:
    "The fact that I may conflict with another manager's turf is tough
    beans. Things will sort themselves out in the market."

Cypress Semiconductor defines each business unit as a separate corporation and support units from manufacturing subsidiaries to testing centers sell their services to line units. The CEO, T.J. Rodgers, says "We've gotten rid of socialism in the organization."

Merck & Company has been rated the top Fortune 500 company because researchers pool their efforts in projects they choose, merging talents and resources into a new team. The CEO said: "Everybody here gravitates around a hot project. It's like a live organism."

Clark Equipment survived Chapter 11 by requiring all business units with a staff of 500 people or more to become self-supporting enterprises. Within months, staff decreased by 400 positions, costs were reduced across the company, and sales moved upward.

Alcoa revitalized a bureaucracy by converting all units into suppliers or clients that were free to conduct business with outside competitors. This dose of economic reality doubled productivity, and support groups brought in outside business.

Xerox is transforming itself from a functional hierarchy into an internal market composed of nine independent business units, each including dozens of self-managed teams. Teams and business units are held accountable for performance and rewarded with bonuses.

Koch Industries has grown from a small firm to one of the largest private corporations in the world as a result of its system of "market-based management." The CEO, Charles Koch, defines all corporate functions in terms of market equivalents.

Matsushita allows its research labs, product groups, and sales units to choose who they prefer to work with. The result is intense internal competition to develop successful products.

Semco has thrived in the turbulent economy of Brazil by forming dozens of internal enterprises called "satellites." The CEO, Ricardo Semler, says "Semco has abandoned traditional business practices [to] the discipline of our own community marketplace."

Halal *et al.* (1993)

People are sceptical, initially, about internal markets because the idea breaks so sharply from the hierarchy. At first, the notion seems fraught with conflict, and it is certainly true that internal markets incur the same risks, turmoil, and other drawbacks of any market system. But, these doubts occur precisely because the concept represents a dramatically different logic. By grasping the central idea that an internal market replicates an external market, the behaviour of such a system becomes almost self-evident.

As market forces replace hierarchical controls, the release of entrepreneurial energy produces roughly the same self-organizing, creative interplay that makes external markets so advantageous. Experience shows that solutions to difficult problems emerge far more quickly and almost spontaneously, permitting a rush of economic growth that can rarely be planned by even the most brilliant managers of hierarchical systems.

Markets can be chaotic, but they are spreading around the globe because they excel over the other alternative – central planning – whether in communist governments or capitalist corporations. In both nations and organizations, planned economies are too cumbersome to cope with a complex new era, while free enterprise – either internal or external – offers an economic philosophy able to produce adaptive change rapidly and efficiently.

The three central principles shown in the display above are now described more fully, illustrated by the experiences of companies that my colleagues and I have studied and worked with.

Transform the hierarchy into internal enterprise units

Rather than think of "divisions," "departments," and other hierarchical concepts, the logic of internal markets transforms line, staff, and all other units, into their entrepreneurial equivalents – an "internal enterprise," or what the Pinchots call an "intraprise." This change may require creative re-engineering of existing structures, but it is usually feasible if an external or internal client can be identified, and that is almost always possible, as will be shown. An AT&T manager reported: "We link internal suppliers with internal and external customers."

Units are converted into intraprises by accepting controls on *performance* in return for freedom of *operations*. Hewlett-Packard (HP) is famous for its entrepreneurial system that holds units accountable for results but gives them wide operating latitude. As one HP executive described it, "The financial controls are very tight, what is loose is how [people] meet those goals." This sharply focused understanding enhances both control *and* freedom to provide two major strengths:

1   All units are accountable for results.
2   Creative entrepreneurship is encouraged.

There is wide agreement that performance evaluations should include customer satisfaction, product quality, and other measures to ensure a realistic balance to avoid over-emphasizing short-term profit. Managers are then held accountable through incentive pay, stock plans, budget allocations, or outright dismissal. The ideal arrangement is to treat each unit as a small, separate enterprise, free to manage its own operations. It is important to allow all units the freedom to conduct business transactions both inside and outside the firm. Without that freedom, managers are subject to the bureaucracy of central controls, internal monopolies, and other drawbacks of a planned economy.

Although the decentralization of line units is well-known, the display on pp.

10–11 shows how the concept is being applied to staff units, manufacturing facilities, information system (IS) departments, R&D, marketing and distribution, employee work teams, starting new ventures, government, and even the CEO's office. This reminds us of the key principle for creating internal markets: all market functions should ideally be replicated within organizations. Raymond Smith, former CEO of Bell Atlantic, described the logic (Kanter, 1991):

> We are determined to revolutionize staff support, to convert a bureaucratic roadblock into an entrepreneurial force. Staffs tend to grow and produce services that may be neither wanted nor required. I decided to place the control of discretionary staff in the hands of those who were paying for them…line units…The most important thing is that spending for support activities is now controlled by clients.

Converting hierarchical functions into entrepreneurial equivalents

Support units. IBM converted its Human Resource Development division into an autonomous business, "Workforce Solutions," which sells its services to IBM units and other companies. The Federal Government is breaking up the monopoly of the General Services Administration and the Government Printing Office by allowing line agencies to patronize other suppliers.

Manufacturing. Alcoa treats its manufacturing units as "internal job shops" that produce goods for internal and external clients. IBM, DEC, NCR, and other companies are selling their excess plant capacity by "contract manufacturing" for other firms. A spokesman for the U.S. Department of Commerce said: "Manufacturing is becoming a service function. Plants are making different products for different companies in different industries."

Information systems. Rather than have the information systems (IS) department impose its choice of equipment on users, companies such as Brown-Foreman and Sunoco allow users to choose between the company's IS office and outside competitors. In the U.S. Government, the FAA, the DoD, and other agencies are forming "information utilities" that charge internal clients for computer time, electronic mail, and other IS services.

Research and development. In order to use research funds more effectively, Bell Labs, Phillips Electronics, and Esso Canada are converting their R&D departments into profit centers that sell research services to line units and outside clients. Instead of relying on the debatable allocation of resources from the top of a hierarchy, the value of research is then determined by the willingness of profit-center managers to pay for the results.

Marketing, logistics, and service. Marketing, logistics, and customer service units can be reorganized into the internal equivalent of distributorships that handle the full line of a company's products for some region to provide integrated service. Johnson & Johnson established common customer units that provide all sales and distribution services to outside retailers.

Work teams. Market principles can be carried to the grassroots by organizing workers into self-managed profit-centers. A paper-making company helped loggers form teams that were paid for the amount of timber they produced, thereby eliminating the need for job classes, performance evaluations, foremen, and other complex systems. Loggers became keenly motivated because they could "run their own business" and they earned more, while management was pleased with the higher productivity and lower overhead.

New ventures. Scores of companies have set up venture capital systems that welcome business proposals from any employee (an intrapreneur) to start a new venture, which is then nursed into life in a business incubator. Twelve states now allow teachers, parents, and administrators to form "charter schools," and a dozen others are moving toward the concept.

The CEO's office. When James Rinehart was CEO of Clark Equipment, he redefined the CEO's office as a profit center in which revenue was derived from assets invested in business units (similar to a venture capital firm), and from a portion of sales (like a "tax" by the "corporate government"). This concept establishes a logical relationship between the CEO and operating managers. Like any profit center, the CEO must keep the costs charged to managers down and the value they receive up to add value to these "clients."

Government. Internal markets are entering government as city, state, and federal bureaucracies are converted into enterprises. Mayor Steve Goldsmith of Indianapolis reports that years of TQM and reengineering had little impact on reining-in costs. Upon outsourcing functions to private suppliers and allowing city departments to compete with their external counterparts, costs typically dropped by half or more. One city manager voluntarily decided to abolish his department because it made more sense.

Halal *et al.* (1993)

Figure 1.1 illustrates the internal market that results from "privatizing" an organization with product, functional, and geographic structures. The heart of the system consists of new ventures spun off by product divisions to become independent business units that develop products or services. Functional support units are profit centers that sell their assistance to other units or external businesses. Geographic areas are also profit centers, distributing the full line of products and services to clients in their region. The network of business relationships formed by the intersection of these product, functional, and regional units comprises the internal market economy.

From this view, the organization is no longer a pyramid of power but a web of changing business relationships held together by clusters of internal enterprise – as in any market. This system may appear radically different, but it represents simply an extension of the trend that began decades ago when large corporations decentralized into autonomous product divisions.

Create an economic infrastructure to guide decisions

With operational matters transferred to internal enterprises, executives focus on designing an infrastructure of performance measures, financial incentives, communication systems, an entrepreneurial culture, and other corporate-wide frameworks. This infrastructure then guides decisions by market forces instead of by administrative fiat. The behaviour of this market system is then regulated,

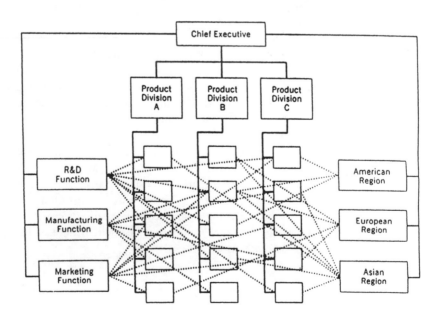

Figure 1.1 Example of an internal market organization

monitored for weaknesses and failures, and corrective changes are made to improve its performance.

When Alcoa moved to an internal market economy, its managers soon realized that, previously, decisions had been based on faulty estimates of costs and revenues. Like many corporations, the finances of operating units were pooled into larger divisions, absorbed by corporate overhead, and otherwise not identified accurately for individual units. Upon converting all units into autonomous enterprises with their own profit and loss statements, the newfound awareness of actual costs and revenues immediately altered decisions in more realistic directions. AT&T realized the same benefits when its large groups were divided into forty or so profit centers to highlight their individual performance. "The effect was staggering," said James Meehan, the CFO.

A striking example of the power of incentives to change behaviour can be seen when converting staff units into profit centers. In the typical organization, IS services are provided free to line units, with the predictable result that people waste resources carelessly. Stories abound of line units demanding multiple copies of huge computer printouts that are never read, of overseas offices equipped with international telephone lines used by clerks to call home in the U.S.A. every day. But when presented with monthly bills by the IS department, there is a marked change in attitude, causing line managers to select less costly systems that often provide better service as well (Halal, 1992). Conversely, giving line units the freedom to choose among competing IS sources causes these internal suppliers to shape up equally fast.

There is also a need to instill the subtle norms of a social system. MCI learned that an internal market must be augmented by an entrepreneurial culture that stresses individual initiative, embracing change, and supporting employees. The MCI culture constitutes a commonly understood, informal, management system that guides working together effectively. Since this system exists in the minds of people rather than in cumbersome written policies, it is far more flexible because it is a shared idea. MCI employees and the company are one and the same, allowing quick agreement on a new product, organizational change, and other complex undertakings.

The impact of these various aspects of infrastructure illustrates the crucial need to design organizations as complex, interacting systems. As Jay Forrester and Peter Senge point out, managers today must become organizational *designers*, in addition to *operators*, by creating a new class of adaptive, high-performing, intelligent organizations (see Halal *et al.*, 1993, chaps 3 and 5).

Provide leadership to foster collaborative synergy

This model of entrepreneurial management raises tough questions about the role of executives and the very nature of corporations. If an organization is no longer a fixed, centrally-controlled, structure but a fluid tangle of autonomous units going their own way, what gives it an identity that makes it more than the sum of its parts? What is best for the individual units, and for the organization as a whole? How does this array of business units differ from an ordinary market economy? Why should they remain together at all? In short, what truly *is* an entrepreneurial corporation, and how should it be managed?

Internal enterprise does not mean that corporations are balkanized into warring camps. The role of executives shifts to designing these self-managed systems and providing leadership to unify diverse interests into a strategic whole, a "corporate community." CEOs may give up much of their formal authority in a market system, but they lead by ensuring accountability, resolving conflict, encouraging cooperation, forming alliances, providing inspiration, and other forms of strategic guidance that shape this system into a more productive community. One of Hewlett-Packard's great strengths is that its executives guide by persuasive leadership rather than fiat. The former CEO, Lewis Platt, said, "In HP, you really can't order people to do anything. My job is to encourage people to work together, to experiment" (Deutschman, 1994).

Johnson & Johnson (J&J) encourage coalitions of business units that serve everyone better. J&J's 166 separate companies retain their fierce autonomy because it "provides a sense of ownership that you simply cannot get any other way," says the CEO, John Larsen. But the company's big clients, Wal-Mart, Kmart, and other retailers want to avoid being bombarded by sales calls from dozens of J&J units. The CEO's solution was to urge his operating managers to pool such efforts into "customer support centers" that operate as internal distributorships to coordinate sales, logistics, and service for each major retailer.

Such examples illustrate the resolution of two opposing sets of difficult demands. Modern executives must permit operating managers entrepreneurial freedom to gain their commitment, creativity, and flexibility. Yet, they must also avoid disruptive conflict, needless duplication, and unnecessary risk. A market can provide this combination of freedom and control, but not by remaining a *laissez-faire* system. Leadership is essential to reconcile these opposing demands into a synergistic corporate community that adds net value to its internal enterprises.

Indeed, without the creation of net value there is little to justify uniting business units into a larger parent organization. Hierarchical organizations may contain units that *destroy* value, but this is not apparent because the internal economic behaviour of the system is masked by its bureaucratic structure. Studies also show that roughly half of corporations would increase value by simply being broken up into their individual business units, which highlights the ineffectiveness of present corporate control systems (see, for example, Pasternack and Viscio, 1998). An internal market strips away all this bureaucracy by regarding each unit as an enterprise, setting the stage for more realistic management.

Thus, an internal market is not simply a *laissez-faire* economy, but a *guided* economy, a vehicle for reaching common goals that is more effective than either a *laissez-faire* market or an authoritarian hierarchy. As these principles show, corporate executives guide an internal market by designing an economic infrastructure, setting policies to regulate the system, resolving critical issues, sharing valuable knowledge, and encouraging cooperative strategies. These benefits create the synergy that adds value that outside enterprises, working alone, cannot match.

The flowering of enterprise

A market structure does not *assure* effective management, but it is an essential starting point. Talented people, inspiring leadership, clever strategy, and other factors are also necessary, but these are secondary causes. The Russians are highly educated, talented people with a wealth of resources, yet their economy was trapped in an archaic system for decades.

A similar problem faces managers in capitalist societies today. Capable, well-intentioned people working in corporations, governments, and other institutions are trapped in outmoded hierarchical structures. This impending shift to a market form of organization presents similar challenges and opportunities to those posed by the restructuring of socialist economies. What are the implications of this profoundly different philosophy?

The advantages and disadvantages

Naturally, internal markets incur the same disorder, risk, and general turmoil of external markets, but they also permit some compelling advantages. The creative destruction of markets may unleash reservoirs of energy, but this energy can turn into anarchy if not guided into useful paths. Conversely, hierarchical control may avoid this disorder, but it also inhibits creative freedom. The design of organizational structures, therefore, requires balancing the pros and cons of hierarchy versus enterprise. As shown in Table 1.2, the organization's environment determines which approach is best, which then fixes the type of accountability, motivational system, and culture needed, as well as the corresponding advantages and disadvantages.

Table 1.2 Balancing control versus freedom

	Hierarchical Control	*Market Freedom*
Environment:	Stable, simple	Turbulent, complex
Accountability:	Supervision	Performance
Motivation:	Security	Reward, challenge
Culture:	Efficiency	Enterprise
Disadvantages:	Bureaucracy	Disorder, risk
Advantages:	Order, equity	Client focus, innovation, adaptive change

Economists argue that hierarchies are superior because markets produce transaction costs in searching for alternatives, managing financial transactions, and so on. But the Information Revolution is reducing transaction costs, and decreased overhead and gains in innovation can offset any cost increases. Western Airlines eliminated 500 management jobs, and the resulting decrease in bureaucracy saved huge costs and improved performance. Studies by Thomas Malone at MIT show that decreasing IT costs "should lead to a shift from [management] decisions...to the use of markets" (see Williamson, 1975; Clutterback, 1982; Malone *et al.*, 1989).

Many think that markets increase conflict as units pursue different goals and compete for resources. However, experience shows that market systems can *resolve* the abundant conflict that persists now. Peter Drucker observed that conflict within corporations is *more* intense than conflict between corporations, largely because decisions are often imposed arbitrarily and the choices, if any, are minimal, so relations are usually fraught with tension and misunderstanding. In a market, however, decisions are clearly defined, voluntary, and selected from a range of options, providing a rational basis for sound working relationships that can replace office politics with openly-reached agreements.

Even the troublesome aspects of internal markets can represent useful organizational adjustments. Is a manager in a free market organization unable to staff his unit? In the outside world this means that working conditions are poor. Are some units suffering losses? A market would let them fail because they do not produce value. Do differences in income exist? Wage inequalities can motivate good performance, and they urge poor workers to shape up. Thus, what appears to be disorder in a market is often vital information about economic reality that should be heeded.

Although markets are superior under most conditions today, there are no perfect organizational designs and there are infinite ways to organize a market system. We should hold no illusion that some universal structure can be applied in an all-encompassing way. Internal markets are no panacea. They are not useful in military operations, space launches, and other situations requiring close coordination of thousands of people and intricate plans, not in other routine operations facing a relatively simple, stable environment.

Thus, organizations will have to trade off the costs and gains of each approach. The prudent executive will combine varying degrees of hierarchical control and market freedom to find that mix which best suits his/her organization.

Living with market systems

The drawbacks of enterprise seem especially severe now as mergers, bankruptcies, layoffs, and other changes are ending corporate loyalty and generally making work life more traumatic. If internal markets introduce more of the same, how will we tolerate working in market organizations?

These turbulent changes are unavoidable because the world is in the throes of massive economic restructuring that exerts two major demands: accountability for performance in order to survive, and creative entrepreneurship to adapt to chaotic change, the two major strengths of internal markets. This explains the new role now emerging for individuals in a fast moving, temporary society. Whereas it made sense to treat people as *employees* in a hierarchical economy, an internal market system requires people to assume the role of *entrepreneurs.*

Thus, the former paternalistic employment relationship in which people were paid for holding a *position* is yielding to a "self-employed" role offering people an *opportunity.* The old "work ethic" is becoming an "enterprise ethic" that values the freedom and self-reliance, and rewards and risks that form the complementary rights and responsibilities of entrepreneurship. In fact, these are the roles preferred by the majority of businesspeople today (Leinberger and Tucker, 1992; Kotter, 1995).

In many cases, an internal market is *less* harsh. By decentralizing responsibility to self-managed units, the demands of a turbulent economy can be resolved better through voluntary layoffs, growing the business, tolerating lower rewards, or other local solutions. Self-management, thereby, permits constant, small adjustments to the ebb and flow of market forces, avoiding the large periodic crashes that now result from executives having to bear this unreasonable burden alone.

For instance, a market organization can help make TQM, downsizing, reengineering, and other forms of restructuring more successful. Just as any external business can manage its affairs better without government interference, these approaches are likely to work best if they originate voluntarily from autonomous units held accountable for serving their clients. If managers could treat units as internal enterprises that benefit from their performance, they will almost invariably improve operations beyond the expectations of top management. Ralph Larsen, CEO of J&J, says, "Managers come up with better solutions and set tougher standards for themselves than I would impose" (O'Reilly, 1994). In place of forced downsizing, for instance, this bottom-up approach produces self-initiated right-sizing throughout the organization: "self-sizing."

Letting go

It is useful, at this point, to summarize the conclusions presented in this chapter:

1   As economies become more complex, they must be self-managed by entrepreneurial systems operating from the bottom-up.
2   Present management concepts are limited because they are largely modifications of the top-down hierarchy.
3   A different perspective based on principles of enterprise is evolving to create complete internal market economies that are designed and managed in a similar way to external market economies.
4   Internal markets are not appropriate in all cases, but they are best for most organizations today because they offer the dynamic qualities needed to navigate a complex world.

Transforming organizations into market systems is formidable because it involves a profound upheaval, somewhat similar to the transformation of socialism to market economies. Experiences of companies that have made this transition offer some guidelines, as shown below. The CEO described how ABB created the system described in the second display below: "We took our best people and gave them six weeks to design the restructuring. We called it the Manhattan Project" (Taylor, 1991).

Guides to reorganizing into market systems

The following guidelines were derived by examining the experiences of companies that have successfully transitioned to internal market systems:

- Learn about the concept of internal markets to gain a solid grasp of the possibilities and the problems involved.
- Start small in some limited part of the organization with willing, enterprising volunteers who will see it through.
- Provide thorough training in the business skills needed to succeed in a market environment.
- Plan the change collectively and sketch out a realistic vision of how it will work.
- Prepare people by shaping an entrepreneurial culture.
- Most importantly, give the reorganization top priority.

ABB'S internal market for a global corporation

Percy Barnavik, the CEO of Asea Boveri Brown (ABB) corporation, has been described as "moving more aggressively than any CEO to build the new model of competitive enterprise." He described his firm's structure as follows:

A confederation of entrepreneurs: "We are a federation of national companies...a collection of local businesses with intense global coordination."

Multidimensional structure: "Along one dimension, ABB is structured into 50 or so business areas operating worldwide. Alongside this structure sits a country structure of 1,200 local companies that do the work of business areas in different countries."

Decentralization: "Our managers need well-defined responsibilities, clear accountability, and maximum degrees of freedom. I don't expect them to do things that hurt their business but are good for ABB. That's not natural. We always create separate legal entities to allow real balance sheets with real cash flow and dividends. Managers inherit results year to year through changes in equity."

Support units as profit centers: "You can go into any centralized corporation and cut its headquarters staff by 90%. You spin off 30% into free-standing service centers that perform real work and charge for it. You decentralize 30% by pushing them down into line organizations. Then, 30% disappears through reductions."

Small internal enterprises: "Our operations are divided into 4,500 profit centers with an average of 50 employees. We are fervent believers in decentralization. People can aspire to meaningful career ladders in units small enough to be committed to."

A strategic information system that unites the firm: "We have a glue of transparent, centralized, reporting through a management information system called Abacus."

Employee entrepreneurs: "I don't sit like a godfather, allocating jobs. What I guarantee is that every member of the federation has a fair shot at the opportunities."

Facilitating leadership: "Real communication takes time, and top managers must be willing to make the investment… meeting with the company CEOs in an open, honest dialogue."

Taylor (1991)

In the late 1980s, when computer companies had become bloated, Hewlett-Packard (HP) restructured to avoid the bureaucracy that swamped IBM. "We had too damn many committees. If we didn't fix things, we'd be in the same shape as IBM is today," said David Packard. HP dismantled unneeded controls to renew its belief that each division should be a self-managed enterprise. Former CEO John Young endorsed the development of radical new products, such as HP's first desktop printer that competed with the company's existing products, which would have been heresy at IBM. Today, the LaserJet line accounts for 40 percent of HP's sales. HP was valued at one-tenth of IBM in 1990; through this skillful blend of enterprise and support, HP is now worth about as much as IBM.

Hewlett-Packard's internal market system

Hewlett-Packard has become the second largest American computer maker by creating an entrepreneurial organization that allows it to lead constantly in technological innovation. HP's profits grow at an annual rate of 30 percent, and the bulk of sales come from products that are less than two years old. Although management may not think of their organization as an internal market, it contains most elements of the market model.

Decentralized structure: The company's 96,000 employees are organized into small, global, cross-functional units that never exceed 1,500 people, creating a decentralized, constantly changing structure that produces thousands of products.

Internal enterprises: Each unit is an enterprise that "owns its business." Units plan their own strategy, work with their suppliers and customers, reinvest their profits in the unit, and have their own financial statements. "Our profit-and-loss statement is like any other small company," said one unit manager.

Internal competition: Units are accorded almost complete freedom to manage their affairs as they feel is best, including competing against other HP units and doing business with HP competitors. For instance, the HP laser printer competes with the ink-jet printer, and another unit choose to buy millions of chips from a competitor because they were priced lower than HP's chips. Said one manager, "We don't feel an allegiance to any other part of HP. We feel an allegiance to our customer."

Internal cooperation: Units also cooperate when it is useful by offering the benefits of their experience, sharing technology, organizing joint ventures, and so on. "I've never seen anyone say no if you ask for help," said one manager.

Facilitating leadership: The CEO and other corporate executives avoid making operating decisions that intrude on unit autonomy, but focus instead on facilitating cooperative relationships, offering advice, holding units accountable, and providing leadership. "The best I can do is bring people together and hope they mate," said Lewis Platt, the former CEO.

Deutschman (1994)

Although corporations such as these are using some market mechanisms, managers do not yet generally understand the broader concept of an internal market economy. The CIT survey in Table 1.1 shows that most corporations do not allow profit centers to keep their revenue, they impose limits on outsourcing, and support units are rarely profit centers. The result is that, throughout large companies, business units strain against corporate bureaucracies that burden operations with excessive overhead and monopoly power (for a good analysis of the problem, see Cantoni, 1993). Managers in the CIT survey reported: "We can't use outside sources if a product or service is available inside;" "I know of no company where staff units are nothing but profit drains; they are the most sacred of cows." So, there is a long way to go before we realize the potential of internal market freedoms.

In the final analysis, a market form of organization seems almost inevitable because it offers the only way of adapting to an age where harnessing knowledge is the key to coping with constant, rapid change. Instead of relying on the heroic but risky judgement of executives to move the organization in some wholesale direction, the units of an internal market feel their way along like the cells of a superorganism possessing a life of its own, producing a constant stream of adaptive change. The central conclusion of today's exploding interest in the science of chaos and complexity is that complex systems adapt best when they are organized into networks of numerous small, autonomous units, thereby producing spontaneous order out of chaos.

The knowledge society lying ahead will present more complex intricacies than we can imagine, and much less control. This unpredictable nature of the modern world can be managed only by a local form of intelligence that guides average people to meet complexity where it begins: at the grassroots. Information technology will provide the communication for this system, and markets will provide the economic foundation.

Many will think this challenge is too enormous, but that is what we thought about changing the Soviet Union. The move to market organizations seems likely to roll on because internal markets offer the same powerful advantages that inspired the overthrow of Communism: opportunities for personal achievement, liberation from authority, accountability for performance, entrepreneurial initiative, creative innovation, high quality and service, ease of handling complexity, fast reaction time, and flexibility for change. Imagine creative managers, engineers, and workers being turned free to launch myriad ventures, all guided by top management teams that provide a supportive infrastructure and inspiring leadership. Yes, many of these ventures would fail, but many more would thrive to create a new breed of dynamic, self-organizing institutions. Here are three simple but bold actions that highlight proven ways to mobilize the corporation:

Link resources to performance. Rather than using budgets and other crude controls that are unrelated to results, link resource allocations to economic and social value created by units.

Allow units total freedom. Allow all units almost total operating and strategic freedom, including the right to buy and sell from partners both inside or outside the firm.

Replace downsizing with self-sizing. Let units handle their own staffing rather than impose layoffs. That is, "self-sizing" instead of downsizing.

Why would tough-minded executives yield control over these crucial matters? Because they can lead an organization where everyone shares the responsibility for success. Today's executives must shed their old role as captains of commerce to become "economic gardeners" of these organic systems. They must develop organizations that guide business behaviour more effectively, organize people into self-managed units, and assist in forming collaborative relationships to resolve the old conflicts between workers and managers, sellers and buyers, and all the other divisions we can no longer afford.

Leaders can no longer force people to do any of these complex tasks any more than gardeners can force nature to produce what they want. Gardeners are attentive to the subtle signs of need in their garden. They must provide the right amounts of water, light, and nutrients and then lovingly allow plants to grow as they should. In other words, they must let go. Bob Kuperman, CEO of Chiat/Day, described this new role as follows:

> Basically, our organization is now a living thing with a life all its own. Management can support it and guide it, but not control it. If you let it design itself, it takes off and people use their best possible abilities. We've got to make this succeed because the old way doesn't work anymore.
>
> (Halal, 1998)

This vignette illustrates that letting go of our tenacious need to control can release the abundant entrepreneurial talent now languishing beneath the layers of today's bureaucracies. The first step is to recognize that organizations must be understood, designed, and managed as market economies in their own right.

Notes

1   Earlier versions of this chapter appeared in *Internal Markets* (New York: John Wiley & Sons, 1993) and *The New Management* (San Francisco: Berrett-Koehler, 1998).

References and further reading

Ackoff, R. (1981) *Creating the Corporate Future*, New York: John Wiley & Sons.
Cantoni, C. (1993) *Corporate Dandelions*, New York: Amacom.
Clutterback, D. (1982) "The Whittling Away of Middle Management," *International Management*, November, 10–16.
Deutschman, A. (1994) "H-P Continues to Grow," *Fortune*, 2 May.
Forrester, J. (1965) "A New Corporate Design," *Industrial Management Review* 7(1): 5–17.
Grove, A. (1996) "A Conversation with the Lords of Wintel," *Fortune*, 8 July.
Halal, W.E. (1992) *Fee-For-Service in IS Departments*, International Data Corporation.
—— et al. (1993) *Internal Markets: Bringing the Power of Free Enterprise INSIDE Your Organization*, New York: John Wiley & Sons.
—— (1998) *The Infinite Resource*, San Francisco: Jossey-Bass.
—— (in progress) *Corporations in transition*, George Washington University.
Kanter, R.M. (1991) "Championing Change: An Interview with Bell Atlantic's CEO Raymond Smith," *Harvard Business Review*, January–February.
Kotter, J. (1995) *The New Rules: How to Succeed in Today's Corporate World*, New York: The Free Press.

Leinberger, P. and Tucker, B. (1992) *The New Individualists*, New York: HarperCollins.

Malone, T. *et al.* (1989) "The Logic of Electronic Markets," *Harvard Business Review*, May–June.

O'Reilly, B. (1994) "J&J is on a Roll," *Fortune*, 26 December.

Osborne, D. and Gaebler, T. (1992) *Reinventing Government*, Reading, MA: Addison-Wesley.

Pasternack, B. and Viscio, A. (1998) "The Centerless Corporation," *Strategy and Business* 12(3): 10–21.

Pinchot, G. and Pinchot, E. (1994) *The End of Bureaucracy and the Rise of the Intelligent Organization*, San Francisco: Berrett-Koehler.

Shapiro, R. (1997) "Growth Through Global Sustainability," *Harvard Business Review*, January–February.

Stewart, T. (1996) "Trying to Grasp the Intangible," *Fortune*, 2 October.

Taylor, W. (1991) "The Logic of Global Business," *Harvard Business Review*, March–April.

Williamson, O. (1975) *Markets and Hierarchies*, New York: The Free Press.

Part II
Structure

2 Internal marketing in the light of relationship marketing and network organizations

Evert Gummesson

Introduction

Internal marketing – as the term implies – is the opposite of or a supplement to external marketing. It requires a boundary between a company and its market and wider environment. However, a series of current business phenomena cause confusion in the drawing of organizational boundaries. Companies are increasingly understood as networks of relationships with fuzzy and variable boundaries to their customers, suppliers and others, as well as to society at large. As a result, internal marketing becomes a troubled concept and we need to pose the question: has it got a future? This chapter will discuss the consequences of new realities of marketing and organization and the need to view internal marketing in a new light.

Vanishing boundaries

Current marketing terminology usually reserves internal marketing for the application of marketing management knowledge – which was originally developed for external marketing – on the 'internal market', that is the employees. The purpose is to get employees in tune with existing conditions and procedures as well as with major changes – such as a revised business mission after a merger – thus making them better equipped to handle the external marketing.

The internal marketing concept emerged from services marketing. Its concern was to get everyone who was involved in service encounters – the front line or contact staff – to perform better in the interaction with customers. The use of the concept has broadened beyond services and become accepted terminology in all types of organizations. This generalization from service companies to manufacturing companies is well justified, as it is now mainstream knowledge that services are significant in all types of business activity.

Internal marketing assumes a demarcation line between the inside and the outside of an organization. What happens to internal marketing if this assumption is relaxed? To some extent, it has already been relaxed by the gradual introduction of a market economy inside the organization:

- *The company has become an internal marketplace.* Through decentralization and the establishment of profit centres, corporations have gone from internal planned economies to internal market economies. Today, organizational units are partially competing, selling and buying between each other. Sometimes profit centres are incorporated and enjoy autonomous legal status and high independence. Sometimes they are business areas, divisions, or units with varying names; they have limited autonomy but are basically responsible for their financial results. Compared to the concept of internal marketing which emerged around 1980, the profit centre organization started as a trend in manufacturing industries in the 1960s and the trend has proven sustainable. The idea was subsequently adopted by private service industries and later by government agencies.
- *Employees have become internal customers.* The internal customer concept is often ascribed to the founder of Toyota, who said as early as in the 1950s: 'The next process is your customer' (Lu, 1985: viii). It has become established in quality management that employees are internal customers to one another. An employee's ability to influence and satisfy the needs of others inside the organization is considered an antecedent to external customer satisfaction. Only if internal customer relationships work can the quality of the outcome be excellent, thus creating satisfied, or even better, delighted external customers.

The advent of two recent realities of management – relationship marketing and network (or virtual) organizations – is shedding an even sharper light on the ambiguity of organizational boundaries, challenging the viability of the inside–outside divide. We will now look into the properties of these two phenomena and their interdependence and effect on internal marketing.

Relationship marketing

Definition

There are many definitions of relationship marketing, most of them stressing the need to develop long-term relationships with customers and sometimes other stakeholders (see, for example, Morgan and Hunt, 1994; Grönroos, 1996). Relationship marketing is often contrasted to transaction marketing, the one-shot deal with a short-term perspective (Jackson, 1985).

My concept, *total relationship marketing*, will be used as the starting point for treating relationship marketing (Gummesson, 1999a). The major difference between the majority of relationship marketing definitions and total relationship marketing is that the latter is more comprehensive. In this chapter, I will review internal marketing in the light of certain elements of total relationship marketing and its link to network organizations.

In its most generic form, I define relationship marketing as 'marketing seen as relationships, networks and interaction' or 'marketing based on interaction within a network of relationships'. In the broadest sense of total relationship marketing, all management, the whole society, and even life itself, form networks of relationships within which we interact in our roles of business executives, employees, consumers, citizens and human beings (Gummesson, 1999b).

The relationship marketing credo

The credo of relationship marketing embraces a series of properties and strategies. These were originally designed with the customer–supplier relationships in mind, and most of the writings in relationship marketing are limited to that dyad. It will, however, be obvious that they are equally applicable to internal relationships:

Collaboration. The core contribution from relationship marketing is its emphasis on collaboration. In a narrow sense it comprises the collaboration between customer and supplier. This has always been a practical necessity for services and for the development, production, marketing and purchasing of complex products in business marketing. Its practice, however, is often unprofessional and guided by legal-bureaucratic values and lack of empathy. Its introduction in theory and education is long overdue. Although collaboration was advocated by Alderson in 1965 (and possibly by others) as necessary in a functioning market economy, it did not arouse general interest. Today, several sources independent of relationship marketing stress collaboration (see, for example, Solomon, 1992; Mattsson and Lundgren, 1992–93; Brandenburger and Nalebuff, 1996). Collaboration is the very reason for forming an organization; you collaborate inside and compete outside. In total relationship marketing you both collaborate and compete, inside as well as outside the organization.

Long relationships. A series of studies claim that the longer the relationship with a customer, the higher the profit will be. This is primarily due to two effects of customer loyalty: reduced marketing costs when fewer customers defect; and increased 'customer share' or 'share of wallet' (a higher share of the customer's purchase of a product or service goes to a single supplier). Long relationships are also needed inside the organization. Reichheld (1996) claims that high turnover of employees, downsizing and early retirement – which have characterized the 1990s – deprive the organization of human intellectual capital, including internal and external relationships.

Win–win. Effective collaboration in a long-term relationship can only take place if the parties feel like winners, or at least that they gain from the relationship and that it is their best option under current circumstances. It requires each party to think of the other party as a partner rather than as an adversary. Short term street-smarts and excessive greed, which are characteristic of much marketing practice and internal manoeuvring, have no place in relationship marketing. Internal win–win relationships – when employees feel they are working in a company that gives them something back such as reasonable salary, encouragement and development potential – boost motivation and performance.

Joint value-creation. Partners in collaboration create value together. The traditional view is that value is created by the supplier; it is referred to as value-added and follows Porter's popular value chain. The value constellation or the value field

(Normann and Ramirez, 1993; Duncan and Moriarty, 1997) as well as relationship marketing and network organizations all say differently; value is created in a network of relationships of stakeholders. In the traditional sense, consumption is destruction; according to the dictionary the word consumption even means 'a wasting disease, esp. pulmonary tuberculosis'. But, for the consumer the product or service is adding value only when it is consumed and used, and for services the production, delivery and consumption are in part concurrent events. It is trivial to say that organizational tiers and units with their special skills and functions should work in concert, but we know that often they do not.

Each customer is an individual. The traditional marketing management approach is mass marketing. Customers are treated as statistics, decimals, and averages of grey masses, whether it is a large general mass or a smaller mass segment. Mass promotion and mass distribution are said to be cost-effective, and it is considered too costly to treat customers, especially ordinary consumers, as individuals. Relationship marketing addresses each customer as an individual which is distinctly epitomized in the expression one-to-one marketing (Peppers and Rogers, 1997). Employees are also individuals and it is not commendable to treat them as anonymous members of crude segments such as blue collar or white collar workers, old or young, male or female, or manufacturing, accounting or sales departments.

Market, mega- and nano-relationships

The total relationship marketing concept identifies thirty relationships ('the 30Rs') which include stakeholders as well as properties of relationships (Gummesson, 1999a). The relationships appear in three overriding categories. First, *market relationships* exist in the market proper, embracing relationships between a company and its customers, own suppliers, intermediaries and competitors. They can be characterized as being close, distant, interactive, electronic, face-to-face, or many-headed to mention a few examples.

However, market relationships are not isolated from other relationships in the environment. *Mega-relationships*, forming the second category, appear on the societal level. They have an impact on marketing but go beyond the market. Among them are relationships to governments, politicians and civil servants through lobbying; social relationships based on birth, friendship and club membership; and the mass media relationship.

The third category is *nano-relationships*, existing on the organization level. They are the focal point of interest for internal marketing and internal marketing is defined as one of seven nano-relationships. They concern relationships between employees, between tiers in the organization and between functional specialities. In a similar vein, the relationship marketing concept by Christopher *et al.* (1991) identifies internal markets (the organization and its staff) and employee markets (from which employees are recruited and promoted) as two of its six markets; and Morgan and Hunt (1994) use the term internal partnerships to encompass employees, functional departments, and business units.

A nano-relationship view of internal marketing is underscored in the conclu-sions from a case study of a bank (Ballantyne, 1997: 354): 'Internal Marketing is a relationship development process in which staff autonomy and know-how combine to create and circulate new organizational knowledge that will chal-lenge internal activities which need to be changed to enhance quality in marketplace relationships.'

The three categories of relationships are – as all categories in social life – fuzzy entities with a core and broad boundaries that gradually merge with the boundaries of adjacent categories. What the company is depends on the perspective and the context. In services marketing, the customer is part of production and delivery. Nano-relationships merge with market relationships and mega-level regulatory authorities are involved in manufacturing and service delivery. For example, airline personnel collaborate on an ongoing basis with passengers, travel agencies, competing airlines, air traffic control, customs, secu-rity staff, and others. Where should we draw the border between the airline and its external environment?

In the next section, the concept of network organizations – coming not from marketing but from organization theory and practice – will add further to the analysis.

Network organizations

Definition

We are increasingly accepting that organizations are dynamic processes in networks rather than well-structured hierarchies and functional silos. According to Weick (1979: 88) organizations are relationships and interaction:

> 'Most "things" in organizations are actually relationships, variables tied together in a systematic fashion…The word *organization* is a noun, and it is also a myth. If you look for an organization you won't find it. What you will find is that there are events, linked together, that transpire within concrete walls and these sequences, their pathways, and their timing are the forms we erroneously make a substance when we talk about an organization.'

While Weick describes a relationship approach to the inside of an organization, Badaracco (1991: ix) describes the transition from the closed and well-defined corporation – the citadel – to a network interacting with its environment:

> Firms were…islands of managerial co-ordination in a sea of market relation-ships. But this is an outdated view. Companies are now breaking down barriers which, like the Berlin Wall, have endured for decades. Their managers are now working in a world that consists not simply of markets and firms, but of complex relationships with a variety of other organizations.

Handy (1990: 87ff) has proposed the *shamrock organization* as a metaphor for the different roles in a company. A shamrock normally has three leaves. These symbolize three types of human resources: the *employees*, those who work with the core activities of the company; the *suppliers* who supplement the corporation with resources; and the *part-time employees and temporary workers* who provide human resource flexibility. But a special shamrock may have four leaves, the fourth being the *customers*. In the service management literature, customers have long been treated as temporary employees during service production, delivery and marketing processes. The customers are the professional representatives of the need and use of the service and their presence is usually required for the performance of the service.

These descriptions are all in the spirit of network organizations, also referred to as virtual or imaginary organizations. An imaginary organization is '...a system in which assets, processes, and actors critical to the "focal" enterprise exist and function both inside and outside the limits of the enterprise's conventional "landscape" formed by its legal structure, its accounting, its organisation charts, and the language otherwise used to describe the enterprise' (Hedberg *et al.*, 1997: 13). Whereas the concept of virtual organization is usually associated with information technology (IT), the concept of imaginary organization is broader and stresses both IT and human aspects. Furthermore, imaginary organizations are imagined, they are images and not physical objects. They are what people perceive them to be depending on the vantage point from which they are being observed and lived. A company is not the same for the chief executive as it is for accounting staff (spending most of the time in the office), a salesperson (spending most of the time in the offices of customers), or the investor (comparing stock quotations on a computer screen). Imaginary organizations need a special type of leader – an 'imaginator' – who can lead in today's complexity, fast pace of change and hypercompetition.

Practical implications

Network organizations are bigger than they look on paper. Their core can be small, yet they can engage huge resources in their network of alliances, personal contacts, and outsourced activities. Amazon.com is not a big bookshop if we count the number of employees or books in stock, but it is the world's largest bookshop if we look at the sales volume. It breaks the boundaries of conventional industries; it is not primarily in the book business. Its core capital is its network of relationships, particularly the customer base to whom they will also sell music and other products. Its unprecedented high value on the stock exchange (US $20 billion in the summer of 1999) does not bear relation to its profits and tangible assets. Its value is based on expectations for the future; its value is imagined.

Although suppliers are not employees, the boundary between suppliers and own employees is fuzzy. Subcontractors and cottage industries have a long history in manufacturing. They provide flexibility, add resources when sales peak, but cost nothing when sales drop. The 'knowledge industry' employs intellectuals who need to be organized, but the industry is strategically dependent on free intellectuals such as authors and reviewers. The former are officially part of the organization, the latter are part of the external network. The search for the organization of the knowledge-based company partly concerns the form of affiliation for those who generate revenue: employment, full-time or part-time work, ownership or shared ownership, and legal design. Financial and tax considerations may influence the structure. Freelance workers are common in journalism, the performing arts, and among consultants and craftsmen. A freelancer can have his or her own firm which can grow through partnering or employees. Companies that rent temporary secretaries and other staff, such as the international Manpower, are growing rapidly as a consequence of increasing outsourcing of internal services. Computer consulting firms have often earned the major share of their revenue from renting programmers on long-term contracts.

An interesting observation is that while relationships between suppliers and customers are becoming closer, relationships between employers and employees are becoming looser and more flexible (Root, 1994). The first part of the observation is in the spirit of relationship marketing, the second in the spirit of network organizations.

Hierarchical boundaries v. unbounded networks

Network organizations share their core characteristics with relationship marketing: they are unbounded networks of relationships within which interaction occurs.

The traditional way of approaching marketing and organization in textbooks and education leads us astray. The books often look like nostalgic albums with black and white picture postcards from the industrial society: factories with smoky chimneys, mass manufacturing, huge companies, hierarchies, and clearly defined roles and positions. Surely this exists and will continue to exist, but it is not the only or even dominating part of business. We have come to a point where the new – which is often old but newly uncovered – is commencing to be visible and is developing with more zest. It is the outcome of the service society, the information society, the knowledge society, the post-industrial society, the post-modern society, the experience society – all dimensions of what I prefer to name the *value society*. Services, information, knowledge or whatever are only means to create value, not ends.

The literature treats internal marketing within a formal boundary context and rarely challenges the existence of the inside–outside of the company. However, Varey (1995: 51), who suggests a model where internal marketing is part of an integrated customer-oriented management model, says that the model '…does not assume the pre-existence of structures of organization…'. The balance between internal and external focus is also discussed by Gummesson (1999a) and Lings (1999).

Figure 2.1 shows internal marketing in the hierarchical, well-delimited organization. The internal marketing activities are in-bound and directed to the

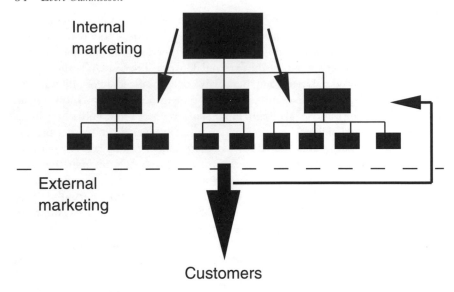

Figure 2.1 Internal and external marketing and their interdependence in the traditional
        well-delimited hierarchy

Source: Gummesson, 1999a: 212

personnel. External marketing is out-bound but can also impact the employee
market, which is shown by the arrow to the right. For example, advertisements
for a company sometimes attract the employee's attention more than they attract
the consumer's attention, and if the chief executive is interviewed on television
employees watch with particular curiosity.

Internal marketing in networks is more complex and fluid than in the hierarchy. Not only must own staff be reached, but also other actors within the
company's network. Figure 2.2 shows the principal structure of a network of
relationships in which we can interact. The terms external and internal lose their
absolute properties. They become contingent on the conditions of each specific
business situation. The black nodes in the figure represent the core competence
or 'the focal enterprise' around which networks exist. What is internal is a matter
of perception, and the distinction is not of crucial interest. What is crucial,
though, is that everyone is reached and influenced by pertinent information.

Two cases of internal marketing

Two successful cases of the implementation of internal marketing will be
presented next. The first is from Ericsson, a global supplier of telecom systems
and equipment. The second concerns Carlshamn, a factory in Sweden making
oil-based food products.

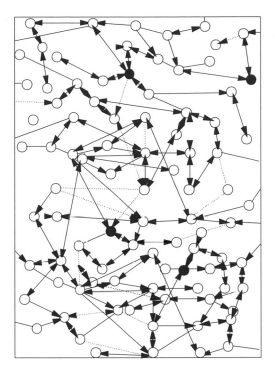

Figure 2.2 The firm immersed in a complex network reality of nano, market and mega
relationships; it is a network-based organization

Source: Gummesson, 1999a: 212

The Ericsson case

Ericsson has implemented several cases of internal marketing, to change their
traditional approach to quality (Gummesson, 1987). The following case is from a
business area that produced electronic components to Ericsson's telephone
equipment. There was a need for a certain amount of in-house design and
manufacturing to protect and develop the core competence and to secure the
supply of strategic components. The company took a decision to exploit its
knowledge on the external market. The internal customer base was too small to
secure future development, and the business area was too sheltered to be really
progressive and cost-effective. After a long life of internal deliveries without
competition, the business area was required to prove its ability to meet the
competition from other manufacturers, among them the successful Motorola.

A transition to a more business-like and market-oriented culture was called for and
internal marketing was *one* contribution to gradually establishing a new culture.
Organizational culture is a complex phenomenon which is not easily changed or
managed. Internal marketing alone rarely accomplishes a change but it can be
supportive of change.

After a survey of possible means of reaching out to the personnel, a publication was developed to explain the new situation. It was inspired by a Scandinavian Airlines (SAS) publication which became a role model for other companies. It was an unsophisticated brochure with short sentences and simple drawings which presented essential facts and strategies.

In internal marketing, as in everything else, management commitment is crucial. It was important for the head of the business area and his divisional managers to show that they stood behind the message. Although a brochure is cost-effective in the mass marketing sense that it physically reaches everybody at a low per capita cost, it is cost-ineffective in the sense that its message will persuade few people. In direct mail to the external market a response rate of five per cent or even less can make a campaign break even. However, it is not enough if five, twenty-five or seventy-five per cent of the staff think and behave in conformity with a new mission; the aim is one hundred per cent.

A relationship marketing approach was chosen, stressing interactivity and physical presence. After discussions and tests it was concluded that the best way would be to appear in person, even if that would take time. How do you do this with 2,000 people working in three towns far apart? Fifty-six appearances by the head of the business area and his management team were called for. Most executives would claim they could not spare the time. In this case, the business area head understood the necessity of presence and kept his promise to be there. He met everybody, most of them seeing him for the first time, and only missed half an hour at one occasion; it was when the King visited the factory.

Groups of a maximum of forty employees participated in half day programmes which ended with lunch or dinner with management. Considering that many of them worked shifts, several programmes had to be performed at night, ending with coffee and cake. The management team presented ongoing changes and made comments followed by the participants working in groups around a number of themes with a subsequent plenary discussion. The brochure was distributed as documentation only when the participants left; it was not the core of the internal marketing, it was just a part of an interactive event.

The Carlshamn case

The mission of the Carlshamn factory of only supplying consumer co-operative stores was broadened to include sales to all types of retailers. Considering predictions about future market conditions, management determined that this change was necessary in order to retain market share and gradually expand.

A major organizational restructuring was being implemented and the problems of informing and influencing everyone were massive. The purpose of internal marketing in this case was similar to that of Ericsson, but the solution was very different.

At Christmas all employees were given a special edition of Trivial Pursuit, one of the world's most loved quiz games. Of the 2,000 questions in Trivial Pursuit, 500 were substituted. The new questions either concerned local issues of general interest or were specific to company issues, for example, 'How many small soap bars for hotel rooms does the subsidiary in Stavanger, Norway, produce in one year: 2, 4, or 6 million?' and 'Which are the two most important ingredients in our margarine?'

The game was a hit. Employees played it over Christmas, in their spare time. That was also the idea; it was handed out during the last hours before the Christmas holiday. This way, its messages also reached family members and friends. Other people, including local citizens, customers, and suppliers asked for the game after it made the news in the local paper and radio station. Although each game was costly to produce, the company was generous in giving it away.

Comments

The Ericsson case is an example of directing the internal marketing to employees in the traditional well-defined sense, that is to nano-relationships alone. In the Carlshamn case, the internal marketing activity reached beyond the nano-relationships and had a positive mega and market communications effect.

Why did these two cases turn out well? Internal marketing can be based on personal and interactive relationships as well as on mass marketing. Traditional ways of internal mass marketing – such as the distribution of formal memos and internal magazines – are insufficient; they are often routinely performed and build more on bureaucratic principles and wishful thinking than on professional marketing and communications know-how.

In these two cases and within the spirit of relationship marketing, the internal marketing was interactive, had its focus on the individual, and aimed to explain a new win–win situation. The internal customer was an individual participant, not just a statistic in a target group.

Electronic and human relationships in internal marketing

Everything today is affected by IT. Relationship marketing and network organizations are commonly presented as children of IT, in particular of computer databases and the new infrastructure created by internet, e-mail, voice mail, and mobile phones. This is not the whole truth; both relationship marketing and network organizations have been around since the dawn of business. IT, however, changes certain rules of the marketing and organizational game and invents new games. Consequently, a discourse on the role of IT in internal marketing is called for.

By the *electronic relationship* is meant all types of relationships, networks and interaction through computers and telecom. It will be compared with the *human relationship* which is essentially face-to-face contact. The electronic relationship offers *high tech*, the human relationship offers *high touch*.

The total relationship marketing and network structures have a counterpart in IT through *internet* (the limitless network reaching each and everyone, a new infrastructure on nano-, mega-, and market levels), *intranet* (a network on the nano-level, accessible only for those working within a formally defined organization), and *extranet* (a network accessible for selected partners such as major suppliers and club member customers, primarily belonging to the market level).

The technology itself is only of avail when put to constructive use. The role of managers as well as operating procedures change, as much information is available on the 'net'. Despite this, both when internal marketing is used in major changes and to maintain operating quality, personal contact is critical. High tech will never make the need for high touch obsolete.

When it comes to daily ongoing operations that are not emotionally loaded, intranet is highly efficient. Hallowell (1999) points out that the increasing use of e-mail and voice mail inside companies can alienate employees from each other and from the organization: 'The irony is that this kind of alienation in the workplace derives not from lack of communication but from a surplus of the wrong kind.' The *human moments* are disappearing and with them physical presence and emotional and intellectual attention. Management by e-mail is replacing management by walking around; internal electronic relationships become more frequent than internal human relationships; and the distant relationship takes precedence over the close relationship. Using e-mail and intranet in a sensitive context, such as blaming an employee for something that went wrong, causes personal and organizational stress. The fact that intranet is a potentially interactive medium is no consolation. There is often delayed interaction, and written text – being completely devoid of body language – is perceived differently from face-to-face interaction with instant feed-back.

IT has gradually influenced the structures and processes of companies. IT can help to glue together activities which are taken from different parts of an organization, from different legal units with different owners, and from different geographical locations. IT can mean enhanced ability to act and reduced cost of customer contact. This may be the overture to a new type of company where the future possibilities of electronics are now being explored: databases with rapid access to customers, networks of rapid communication, and rapid dissemination of new knowledge.

Two cases of the manufacture of musical instruments from two centuries far apart will be compared to demonstrate the differences and similarities between electronic 'space relationships' and the physical 'place relationships'. The Yamaha case is mainly based on Wikström *et al.* (1998: 14–16), and the Stradivarius case mainly on Badaracco (1991: 79–81).

The Yamaha keyboard case

Among other things, IT has led to the spawning of customer discussion groups or newsgroups where product and service development takes place, competing or collaborating with the supplier. One such case is Yamaha.

Yamaha learnt that some hundred musicians had formed a spontaneous discussion group on the Internet. The company logged in to the group and found that the musicians were discussing the pros and cons of keyboard manufacturers and how they themselves could improve their instruments.

This was a novel type of customer-to-customer interaction built on a novel network. The interaction was not dependent on physical presence of the participants, nor of knowledge about one another. Yamaha saw the possibility for direct contact with a customer niche with the Internet as the enabler. They offered the discussion group access to their R&D department of thirty people. The customer-to-customer network now merged with a supplier-to-customer network.

When the discussion group began to ask intriguing questions about such matters as the re-welding of electronic circuits to new processors, the R&D department could not cope. Yamaha had to admit that they did not have the time nor competence to answer. One hundred customers and users had outwitted the supplier R&D specialists and designers. Traditional production-oriented logic would claim that the R&D people were the experts with the superior knowledge. The case points to the fact that user knowledge can be extensive and that it is difficult for large global firms to access this knowledge.

Three impediments to this type of access can be identified. One is mental: companies do not believe customers to be knowledgeable, or customers do not engage in expressing their thoughts, one reason being that customers do not trust the supplier to be genuinely interested. The second is physical: it is difficult for the supplier to find those customers who are knowledgeable and willing to share their knowledge, and it is difficult for the customer to find the right person to speak to in the supplying organization. Third, much of customer knowledge is developed through customer-to-customer interaction and not through a single individual. The Internet now offers a technically feasible solution to access customer knowledge. This knowledge is deeper and more valid than the knowledge furnished by conventional market research techniques such as postal questionnaires, personal interviews, focus groups, or consumer panels.

The Stradivarius violin case

Let us move from electronics to acoustics, from the twenty-first century virtual marketspace to the physical marketplace three centuries ago.

Stradivarius built violins with a sound quality and beauty that has not been surpassed since. The excellence in quality is explained not only by the skills of the master in using tools, wood, and varnish but also by his network within which others developed raw material, designed violins, experimented with new strings, invented techniques for treating wood, composed music, bought his instruments, and played on them.

Stradivarius worked in Cremona, Italy, where there was a century-long tradition of building violins. He was the student of the master Nicolo Amati, and after Stradivarius's death in 1737 his two sons successfully continued the business. Everyone was there physically – Stradivarius, his suppliers, his end-users, his master, his successors – and they all knew each other. They were embedded in the physical environment of a small Italian town.

Comments

The two cases embrace both internal and external relationships and the borderline between them becomes immaterial. They show that interaction in network organizations applied equally well in the old craft's local operation as it applies in today's high tech global corporation. The difference is that IT has wiped out the limitations of physical closeness and offers global space closeness. The similarity is that both are dependent on high touch – but through different media. Stradivarius had a high touch face-to-face relationship with his network. The Internet offers a high tech infrastructure, but we are beginning to discern a new type of high touch through high tech. The relationship is not the same in cyberspace as in Cremona, but it is there, and we have yet to learn how to handle it.

Summing up: the future practice of internal marketing

The boundaries between a modern business, its markets and society – that is between the nano-, market and mega-relationships – have gradually become blurred. A first phase was that companies went from being planned economies to become partly internal market economies through the introduction of profit centres; and the notion of employees having to satisfy the needs of each other to achieve quality, treating each other as internal customers. A second phase is emerging from two new management realities, total relationship marketing and network organizations. IT has added the technical dimension of a new infrastructure for communication.

All these developments demand collaboration across traditional boundaries. My conclusion may then sound like a paradox: internal marketing has a future! The reason is that internal marketing adds to an integrated view of marketing as it is otherwise easy to forget the importance of the knowledge and commitment of *all* personnel for successful external marketing. The same view is expressed in quality management and it clearly stands out in the modern quality awards such as the European Quality Award: all pieces of the organization and its interaction with the market and society are engaged in joint-value creation. If one piece is missing, the outcome will be unsatisfactory quality.

Finally, let me suggest the following guidelines for the practice of internal marketing:

Use the internal marketing concept as a perspective and a direction for marketing. An internal perspective – a pair of eyeglasses which only allows us to look inwards on nano-relationships – forces us to notice other things than when deploying an out-bound market and mega perspective. In order to apply different perspectives, we do not need to define clearly what is outside and inside the company, but can let it be contingent on the situation.

Follow the relationship marketing credo. Collaborate with your employees; aim for long-term relationships; propose win–win situations; create value together; and treat employees as individuals. Use these strategies with consideration of both high tech and high touch aspects.

Make sure that implementation is systematic and dedicated. Marketing efforts – internal as well as external – often stumble on the implementation being too superficial and weak. I have previously claimed that 'The ability and strength to execute a decision is more crucial for success than the underlying analysis' (Gummesson, 1998: 242). A message should, of course, be well thought-out and honest, and its method of dissemination be designed creatively to fit a specific situation. The internal marketing plan is a useful tool – and companies should put serious effort into it – but nothing has actually happened until the effect is shown in action and financial results.

References

Alderson, W. (1965) *Dynamic Marketing Behavior*, Homewood, IL: Irwin.

Badaracco, J.L. (1991) *The Knowledge Link: How Firms Compete through Strategic Alliances*, Boston, MA: Harvard Business School Press.

Ballantyne, D. (1997) 'Internal Marketing for Internal Networks', *Journal of Marketing Management* 13(5): 343–66.

Brandenburger, A.M. and Nalebuff, B.J. (1996) *Co-opetition*, Boston, MA: Harvard Business School Press.

Christopher, M., Payne, A. and Ballantyne, D. (1991) *Relationship Marketing*, Oxford: Butterworth-Heinemann.

Duncan, T. and Moriarty, S. (1997) *Driving Brand Value*, New York: McGraw-Hill.

Grönroos, C. (1996) 'Relationship Marketing Logic', *Asia-Australia Marketing Journal* 4: 7–18.

Gummesson, E. (1987) 'Using Internal Marketing to Develop a New Corporate Culture – The Case of Ericsson Quality', in Congram, C.A., Czepiel, J.A. and Shanahan, J.B. (eds), *Services Marketing: Integrating the Competitive Advantage*, Chicago: American Marketing Association; also in *Journal of Business and Industrial Marketing* 2(Fall): 23–8.

—— (1998) 'Implementation Requires a Relationship Marketing Paradigm', *Journal of the Academy of Marketing Science* 26(3): 242–9.

—— (1999a) *Total Relationship Marketing*, Oxford: Butterworth-Heinemann.

—— (1999b) 'Total Relationship Marketing: Experimenting with a Synthesis of Research Frontiers', *Australasian Marketing Journal* 7(Autumn): 72–88.

Hallowell, E.M. (1999) 'The Human Moment at Work', *Harvard Business Review*, January–February.

Handy, C. (1990) *The Age of Unreason*, Boston, MA: Harvard Business School Press.

Hedberg, B., Dahlgren, G., Hansson, J. and Olve, N-G. (1997) *Virtual Organizations and Beyond: Discover Imaginary Systems*, London: John Wiley & Sons.

Jackson, B.B. (1985) *Winning and Keeping Industrial Customers*, Lexington, MA: Lexington Books.

Lings, I.N. (1999) 'Balancing Internal and External Market Orientations', *Journal of Marketing Management* 15(4): 239–63.

Lu, D.J. (1985) 'Translator's Introduction', in Ishikawa, K., *What Is Total Quality Control? The Japanese Way*, Englewood Cliffs, NJ: Prentice-Hall.

Mattsson, L.-G. and Lundgren, A. (1992–3) 'En paradox? – konkurrens i industriella nätverk', *MTC-kontakten* 22: 8–9.

Morgan, R.M. and Hunt, S.D. (1994) 'The Commitment-Trust Theory of Relationship Marketing', *Journal of Marketing* 58(July): 20–38.

Normann, R. and Ramírez, R. (1993) 'From Value Chain to Value Constellation', *Harvard Business Review*, July–August: 65–77.

Peppers, D. and Rogers, M. (1997) *Enterprise One to One*, London: Piatkus Books.

Reichheld, F.F. (1996) *The Loyalty Effect*, Boston, MA: Harvard Business School Press.

Root, P.H. (1994) 'Relationship Marketing in the Age of Paradox: What Do We Know? What Do We Need to Know?', presentation at the *14th American Marketing Association Faculty Consortium*, Emory Business School, Atlanta, GA, USA, June.

Solomon, R.C. (1992) *Ethics and Excellence*, Oxford: Oxford University Press.

Varey, R.J. (1995) 'Internal Marketing: A Review and Some Inter-disciplinary Research Challenges', *International Journal of Service Industry Management* 6(1): 40–63.

Weick, K.E. (1979) *The Social Psychology of Organizing*, Reading, MA: Addison-Wesley.

Wikström, S., Lundquist, A. and Beckérus, Å. (1998) *Det interaktiva företaget*, Stockholm: Svenska Förlaget.

3 The strengths and weaknesses of internal marketing

David Ballantyne

Introduction

I have for 20 years, off and on, puzzled about the nature of the internal organisation of marketing and the difficulties this poses for marketing as a function in achieving its avowed external or customer oriented goal. So for me, what is often called the 'implementation' gap is my reference point for *internal marketing*. I discuss working through what to do about this in this chapter.

My own understanding of internal marketing was profoundly influenced by a customer service improvement programme in which I was directly involved. A large retail bank had established the programme in Australia in the late 1980s. For three years, I headed up a customer service group whose job it was to make it happen.

In an earlier exploration of this banking case (Ballantyne, 1997), I described how cyclical patterns of internal work activity developed which gave internal marketing its energy and structure. Also, *internal networks* of willing staff volunteers emerged, as if on cue. Their interaction and collaboration led to the discovery and circulation of new knowledge.

I am still awed by these internal networks of relationships and how, in a more generally applicable sense, they might contribute to achieving external marketing goals. In my banking case, it started with an ambitious idea to put 'customers first', ratified at board level. This gave legitimacy to working in staff teams on changes to internal policies and processes that would facilitate better customer service. Also, this cross-functional-team based activity and its effects helped raise the *customer consciousness* of other employees not directly involved. Internal networks emerged first as a communication conduit, but then became a potent force for change in their own right.

My experience of internal marketing comes down to this. It is a strategy for developing relationships between staff across internal organisational boundaries. This is done so that staff autonomy and know-how may combine in opening up knowledge generating processes that challenge any internal activities that need to be changed. The purpose of this activity is to enhance the quality of external marketing relationships.

However, while this kind of definition has face validity, it does not explain the 'how' of everything. Nor does it signal the strengths and weaknesses of the concept. In this chapter, I intend to subject my banking study to further examination and, in so doing, suggest a synthesis of some of the competing concepts most commonly associated with the term 'internal marketing'.

This chapter is the result of inductive and theory generating research. My synthesis of internal marketing as both strategy and application is supported by a broad range of theory and practice, some of which falls outside the traditional boundaries of the marketing discipline.

Market orientation

My point of departure for internal marketing is *market orientation*. By all means let us use the term market(ing) orientation, but like Brown *et al.* (1996: 680), I mean 'orientation' as a sense of a direction and not as an operationalisation of the marketing concept.

In my banking study, market orientation was evident in the choice of an internal communications logo, 'Customer First'. The strategy was that customer service improvement would lead to better customer relationships, more retained customers and thereby complement the organisation's marketing activities. Overall, this would contribute to better long-term profitability. However, as the strategy was approved at board level, the linear logic is better expressed in reverse order, starting with profitability, and working back from that to the point where someone has to 'do something' at the nadir point, where internal marketing begins (see Figure 3.1).

The marketing department was actively involved in designing market research to find the critical customer service issues, but the direction of the strategy was in the hands of a small customer service group set up to facilitate the change in orientation. This group reported directly to the general manager, branch banking.

The first head of the group had been recruited, 'from outside', and she had an unusually appropriate background in marketing and organisational behaviour. The group composition also had a strong marketing and human resource management background. At the time, it seemed that people had been recruited

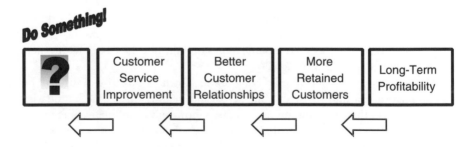

Figure 3.1 'Customer First': linear logic

Source: Ballantyne (1997)

from everywhere, a strange group of bedfellows. On reflection, what they shared was a common commitment to make 'Customer First' work, whatever their individual motives and personal histories.

Market orientation was evident in the idea to involve staff in making the kinds of internal changes to policies and procedures that could be linked to market place performance that external customers would value. This involves more than traditional marketing skills. The more orthodox marketing approach to try to change staff attitudes by formal communications alone was rejected as superficial and unidirectional. The customer service group's activity continued for five years without a break and ended midway during the protracted recession of the 1990s. The customer had become the 'problem' rather than the solution (Ballantyne, 1997: 363–4).

If marketing is primarily a disciplinary synthesis for creating customer value and understanding exchange behaviour, the point of view I want to adopt here, it must operate within a broad web of social and economic interactions. In this sense, marketing is a guiding philosophy of the organisation, and is not confined merely to the marketing department (Hooley *et al.*, 1990). Of course, there is often a rather weak spread of marketing ideas and techniques across the functional divisions of firms, and this is sometimes thought to explain a lack of organisation-wide marketing orientation. However, the problem could be a lack of sufficient marketing tools as much as a lack of spread in the use of existing marketing tools.

Certainly, marketing as a synthetic discipline (Baker, 1993) has made a virtue of absorbing points of view and techniques from other disciplines. I would assert that the belief that we have a discipline called marketing is sustained not by the evidence of its subject matter but by its usefulness. In a similar vein, Popper (1962: 67) has said that:

> We are not students of subject matter but students of problems. And problems may cut right across the borders of any subject matter or discipline.

At the level of strategy implementation, a recurring issue for debate is whether or not marketing, as a department, really needs more *cross-functional* authority. However, such a course is likely to stimulate more internal conflict than solutions. In my banking study, for example, it was very clear that the customer service group would have to be a catalyst for change, rather than attempt to ride roughshod over the authority of other departments. To critique McKenna's call to marketing action (1991), marketing is *not* everything because not everything is or could or should ever be functional marketing activity. Yet, everything *is* marketing in the sense that organisational outputs are designed for and delivered to the markets.

So it is that *control* of customer oriented action within organisations remains problematic. Internal marketing has remained a puzzle rather than a solution over the last twenty years because marketing has swept its cross-functional ambivalence under the carpet, as we shall see.

What does internal marketing mean?

There is renewal of interest in the marketing literature as to what internal marketing might mean and what activities it might embrace. However, there is no agreed conceptual framework that explains the managerial scope of internal marketing, whether broad or narrow (Grönroos, 1994; Ballantyne *et al.*, 1995; Rafiq and Ahmed, 1995; Varey, 1995). Is there a convergence of view forming? I see some evidence for this. A brief historical review illustrates.

Grönroos (1981) emphasised open two-way communications and effective coordination of tasks between front line and support staff with a view to getting more *motivated* and *customer conscious* staff at all levels of the firm. His objective was to focus the internal work effort to meet the needs of external customers.

Berry (1981, 1983) advocated treating employees as *internal customers*, an idea trialed in the 1950s by Japanese quality managers. Berry added a further marketing dimension by viewing employees' jobs as if they were *internal products*. What underlies this formulation is marketing exchange expressed in hierarchical terms between employers and staff. As a clear point of difference, the earlier Japanese formulation emphasised the link between internal customers and internal suppliers, so staff would know how each contributed to the work of the other, in non-hierarchical *quality chains*, with links all the way to the external customer (Oakland, 1989: 4).

Japanese quality logic later became identified with Total Quality Management (TQM) and emphasises cooperation and obligation as a motivator. The TQM idea is to empower cross-functional staff teams to work on improving the everyday work processes in which they are involved. I believe this to be an important distinction.

Berry's logic is that organisations need employees who are satisfied with their job products in order to have satisfied customers. This staff satisfaction/customer satisfaction link is also emphasised by George (1977, 1990) and others. Later, Berry and Parasuraman (1991: 162) cautioned that barriers to performance occur when parts of the organisation act 'without cohesion or a unified spirit', limiting contact employees' ability to perform. Berry and Parasuraman (1991: 151) also emphasised treating staff the way you would want them to treat customers in the expectation that this will encourage 'effective marketing behaviour'. A contrasting perspective is that staff satisfaction with their work will be positively related to customer satisfaction when that work is *customer oriented* (Ballantyne, 1997: 356).

Taking another tack, Piercy and Morgan (1991) recommend the development of strategies that apply external (4Ps) marketing techniques to internal (employee) markets. However, this would seem to give rise to difficulty in practice, as the legitimate roles of marketing and other functions overlap within the organisation. Collins and Payne (1991), recognising the ambiguity of managerial overlap, made a case for the transfer of marketing thinking to the HRM domain. What seems to have been overlooked here is the utility of deploying some HRM thinking in the marketing domain, especially those aspects of organisational behaviour and learning.

Ahmed and Rafiq (1995) seek to avoid task and functional ambiguity by setting the boundaries for internal marketing more tightly. They propose a multi-stage schema built around 4Ps with three strategy levels (direction, path, action). Using the 4Ps as an implementation method is also recommended in Piercy and Morgan (1991) and Piercy (1995). Ahmed and Rafiq, in delimiting the internal marketing concept as they do, seek to get back to *marketing-like* techniques (1995: 34). The irony is that this was a phrase used earlier by Grönroos to create more developmental latitude (1990: 223). Grönroos makes his position very clear: 'total management of marketing has to be an integral part of overall management... *market-oriented management* is what it's all about' (1990: 152).

Finally, Ballantyne *et al.* (1995) broadened the domain of inquiry with the following definition:

> Internal marketing is any form of marketing within an organisation which focuses staff attention on the internal activities that need to be changed in order to enhance external market place performance.

The idea here is that internal marketing is legitimised by its purpose, by its *market orientation*, not by choice of methods.

Internal marketing: a long and winding road?

The dominant lines of thought emerging from the literature are that internal marketing is a strategic approach to challenging both the attitudes and behaviour of staff towards an understanding of the centrality of the customer. The term 'customer consciousness' is appropriate here. As to how this might be achieved, it might mean a 4Ps approach turned inward to staff, or it might mean 'whatever it takes' to improve both customer consciousness *and* marketplace performance within one coherent activity-based agenda.

Influencing staff motivation might mean pursuing one or both 'employee as customer' logics. First, that staff satisfaction is embedded in the notion of *receiving* job-products and, second, that satisfaction of a deeper kind comes from *partici-pating* in the reappraisal of internal activities where outcomes impact on customer perceived performance (Ballantyne, 1997: 356). A third, and limited, alternative is to turn a marketing communications strategy inward, given non-problematic goals, such as new product information or routine changes in staff training.

What is evident is that different authors postulate different means to achieve similar marketplace ends. However, there is very little empirically based evidence in the literature to suggest how internal marketing actually develops or motivates customer conscious employees, or contributes to external market performance.

I can find only four empirical contributions. First, there is Gummesson (1987), a case study of the early stages of a programme of culture change which focused on the effectiveness of exchanges between internal suppliers and internal customers. Second, Ahmed and Rafiq (1995) illustrate their marketing-like 4Ps schema with a case study of how an insurance company communicated to staff a major change in its product mix strategy. Third, Hogg *et al.* (1998) present the early results from a tracking study of customer focused culture change that improved top down and bottom up communications. Fourth, Ballantyne (1997) described a banking study in service improvement, under further review in this chapter. The definition of internal marketing, grounded in this banking case, is as follows:

> Internal marketing is a relationship development process in which staff autonomy and know-how combine to create and circulate new organisational knowledge. That will challenge internal activities that need to be changed to enhance quality in market place relationships.
>
> (1997: 354)

My analysis leads me to the conclusion that there are, essentially, two categories of internal marketing activity, at two levels. Each of these involves interaction between people and resources across departmental boundaries. They are:

Transactional level (didactic)

- One-way communications (monologue)
- Knowledge circulation (new product information, skills training, etc.)

Relational level (interactive, collaborative)

- Two-way communications (dialogue)
- Knowledge discovery (quality improvement, team-based learning, etc.)

The first level represents the 4Ps 'didactic' methods school of internal marketing. The second represents the relationship-based 'collaborative' school. I have framed this second level to exclude coercive methods more appropriate at the didactic level. A combination of activities at both levels would run the risk of being covertly manipulative.

As to the categories, communications can be seen as a monologue, or as dialogue. As a one-way street, or two-way. The second category is knowledge, which is circulated explicitly, or generated through interaction as a reciprocal to dialogue. There is no strict cause–effect instrumentality intended between dialogue and knowledge. However, I would argue that the will to create new knowledge leads to dialogue and, in turn, the will to dialogue generates new knowledge (Ballantyne, 1999).

Recurring cycle of activities

Any observer tries to formulate and recognise patterns in events, the recurring nature of some happenings, and reflects on possible consequences of one happening on another.

I want now to return to my banking case for an elaboration and an explanation of these themes. I will describe the recurring cycle of internal marketing activity that emerged, which was underpinned by internal relationship development. These recurring cycles made possible the translation of external customer requirements into operational forms.

First, I want to represent the sequential incidents, or more correctly the *critical incidents*, that contributed to customers' service improvements (Ballantyne, 1990) and, second, extract the main patterns of *learning behaviour* that account for those incidents.

Turning the wheel

In the banking study, 'turning the wheel' meant service quality improvement, and all the events and incidents on the way. The cycle of activity reveals the critical incidents (Figure 3.2). The sequence began with performance evaluation, using extensive qualitative/quantitative market research. This enabled customers to tell the bank what was essential to their requirements and in what areas they sought improvement.

Next came a diagnostic review phase. This required staff review groups to interpret and resolve the critical customer service issues. As preparation for that

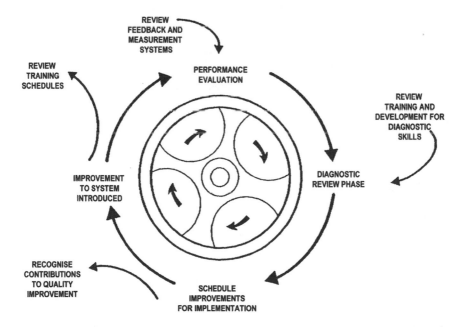

Figure 3.2 Turning the wheel of quality improvement– continuously
Source: Ballantyne (1990)

task, training and development was provided in group-dynamics and diagnostic problem solving skills. Each diagnostic group comprised from three to five members, and all were volunteers. In the first round, this was conducted as a centralised activity with forty staff working together, representing staff from all over Australia. Later, the team concept was successfully spread through thirty-plus regions with twenty or so volunteers working together in each region on three-monthly term projects, many for more than one 'spin' of the wheel. Later again, the learning and knowledge gained was codified as problem solving heuristics and regularly deployed in branches as a customer 'code breaker', under the facilitation of the branch manager.

Next came scheduling improvements, which involved making formal recommendations for implementation. This meant making choices between options on a cost–benefit basis and seeking approvals from the appropriate line authority. Formal reports were prepared and presentations made and successes celebrated.

When improvements to systems were introduced, recognition and rewards were given to those involved under a 'key contributor' programme. As a consequence of customer focused research and working through to achieve changes to systems and policies, training schedules could then be altered and improved. Periodically, market research feedback instruments were reviewed and new customer data obtained to take the wheel of quality improvement on a new trajectory.

Selecting sequential incidents, and then narrowing down to critical incidents, is always open to review as theory and in practice. These particular incidents were selected because they were both recurring and consequential. Certainly, there are always environmental contingencies and internal barriers that must be dealt with in specific cases in different ways (Piercy, 1995: 34). Such constraints are time and place-related and tend to hide a mix of social, technical and structural elements that are difficult to determine a priori.

Patterns of learning behaviour

Following the organisational learning insights of Senge (1990), I now see that this cycle of activity and its 'critical incidents' can be reframed as a pattern of *learning behaviour* which might occur within any organisational setting. Senge describes this kind of behaviour as a 'reinforcing circle' wherein feedback accelerates and recalibrates the direction of change (Senge 1990: 80–4).

Thus the recurring cycle of internal marketing (Figure 3.3) is a theoretical abstraction derived from reframing the empirical events of my banking case. This pattern of activities corresponds well with an earlier attempted formulation (Ballantyne, 1997: 355). In addition, the new concept fits well with the relational (collaborative) perspective of internal marketing, defined and discussed earlier in this chapter.

Distinct phases and modes for internal marketing are now clearly revealed. These are as follows:

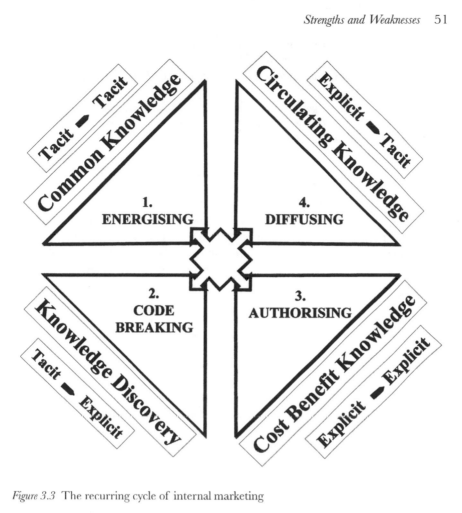

Figure 3.3 The recurring cycle of internal marketing

Energising: seeking and receiving the willing commitment of staff to work towards a given goal within or outside the boundaries of their job descriptions.   Katz and Kahn (1966) remind us that 'energy renewal comes directly from the organisational activity itself' . What people felt is explained by what they wanted to achieve. In the banking case, highly focused work on customer service improvement was a chance to do something really worthwhile; something that touched the dominant values of many who volunteered. As most volunteers were front line staff, it was also a chance to improve the procedures that constrained them personally in dealing with customers. Again, some would have joined up for the glory. If there was any one defining characteristic of all these volunteers it was that they agreed passionately with the 'customer first' purpose and were strong willed enough to want to participate in spite of doubts and fears about the magnitude of the task and their ability to do it. We might say that they had a combination of strategic intent and commitment. What became very clear in the 'diagnostic skills' workshop experience, that propelled every new group into action, was that alone they could do nothing and that only by working together could they learn from each other what they needed to know. This was the source of their strength and, through trust in each other, this was the source of their common knowledge.

Code breaking: translating known customer requirements into an agenda for detailed changes in production or delivery systems by utilising personal resources of 'know-how'. The right steps in intuitive, experientially-based, work cannot be known in advance. Discovering and uncovering operational solutions to customer problems is *customer consciousness* in action. In the banking case, customer focused problem solving work increased participants' sense of self-worth and purpose, and it stretched their capabilities. Bringing personal know-how to the surface, in small problem solving groups, was a necessary part of confirming the validity of personal experience and gaining the confidence to challenge entrenched internal policies and procedures. Such autonomy at work, and the defence of it by the bank's customer service department, was difficult for competitors to comprehend from their watchtowers, let alone to copy.

Authorising: making choices between options on a cost–benefit basis and gaining approvals from the appropriate line authority. Dealing with dysfunctional processes that cross over departmental borders requires explicit knowledge, advocacy and listening skills. Making the case for internal changes, especially those that seem to impact negatively on certain staff or powerful sections of management, may need to be put again and again. This requires a well-documented argument for changing the particular process or policy and an understanding of the broader context in which it operates. In the banking study, what was helpful was access to non-routine channels of knowledge provided by a growing network of participants at all hierarchical levels of the organisation.

Diffusing: circulating new knowledge across department borders. Any organisation has legitimate hierarchical divisions that tend to constrain interaction across internal borders and these distort two-way communications. Circulating new knowledge is more than mere message making. What people do and not what they say (and I would here emphasise training programmes) are also 'messages' whose meanings must be negotiated in dialogue (Steiner, 1999).

Each identified activity is a part of a pattern of learning behaviour embedded in everyday business chaos. Each activity is complementary and contributes to the cyclical 'spin' from one to another. In this sense, they are interrelated and provide a measure of structure one to another. Each mode of activity contributes something to the whole.

In Ballantyne (1997), the term *border crossing* is used where I now see two parts, 'authorising' and 'diffusing'. In this, I follow the guidance of Max Weber who, in his scientific work, took the view that concepts in the social sciences never stand as final, exhaustive, or definitive accounts of complex reality. Instead, they are logical simplifications to be used as *heuristic devices* against which reality might be compared and measured (Jary and Jary, 1991: 550).

The learning cycle repeats itself, from phase four back to phase one, otherwise there is no continuous learning. Dixon (1999) cautions that learning is not the accumulated knowledge of an organisation (its intellectual capital), but it is the continuous 'construction and reconstruction of meaning'.

Knowledge generation as the reconstruction of meaning

It is now necessary to discuss knowledge generation in the context of the learning behaviour model already presented (Figure 3.3). Internal marketing is seen as a knowledge-generating process with the intended purpose of producing external marketplace outcomes. Each phase of the learning cycle represents a different kind of gain in knowledge. To take each phase in turn:

'Energising': the sharing of common knowledge. Tapping into the tacit and subjective insights of employees and bringing those insights to the surface of organisational life is the source of new knowledge (Nonaka and Takeuchi, 1995). In the banking case, this was facilitated in a workshop environment where small staff groups could explore the meaning of their work experiences and personal insights. What is at issue here is the willingness of employees to pass on what amounts to their working knowledge, which Nonaka calls *know-how*. This is represented in the learning behaviour model (Figure 3.3) as a movement from *tacit to tacit*, a sharing of common knowledge under conditions of trust.

'Code breaking': the discovery of new knowledge. The intention here is to go beyond merely deploying working knowledge in a given task. The move is from *tacit to explicit* knowledge in the diagnostic task of understanding the underlying meaning of customer needs and how to convert that into operational solutions (see Figure 3.3). For this 'discovery' to begin, there is a requisite need for personal commitment from those participating, that is their trust in the organisation and the value they see arising out of their participation (Ballantyne, 1999).

Nonaka (1991) introduced a Japanese management perspective to Western management thinking which is insightful. He uses the term *redundancy* to illustrate how knowledge is created and understood. 'Redundancy' in this sense does not mean obsolescence but refers to a necessary information overlap between departments or associated business units. It starts with recognising the struggle there is to articulate anything from the tacit level to the explicit level. Nonaka (1991: 102) recommends a staffing overlap between departments. This, of course, is contrary to the supposed virtues of 'down-sizing'. However, the point of real interest here is that such a strategy demands frequent and deeper dialogue between departments. This is because managers and other employees are placed in 'overlapping' work situations that challenge employees to re-examine what they take for granted.

Authorising: obtaining cost–benefit knowledge.   This is a task familiar to every organisation and requires no special comment. The movement here is from *explicit to explicit* knowledge between departments. In the context of internal marketing, dialogue between departments leads to new understandings and these feed back into further dialogue.

Diffusing: circulating knowledge.   Circulating new knowledge is not just a matter of processing objective information (with technologies such as data mining and data warehousing). The movement here is from *explicit to tacit* knowledge as new knowledge is circulated and transferred back into training programmes, policies and procedures.

In summary, I take the view that internal marketing is a mode of organisation for *generating knowledge* within a firm. I see the boundaries of shared knowledge to be stable only when defended by cultural assumptions. The banking case illustrates this. The shift to market orientation and 'customers first' meant that the logic of existing organisational knowledge was reframed, seen from a different perspective. Thus, new knowledge was indeed 'discovered' in a new patterning of the verities. Much of what we call new knowledge occurs in this way, which is to say we are constantly caught up in a process of new pattern recognition. There is no final 'stable state'.

Catalysts, coalitions and constellations

I will now conceptualise the *internal network* organisation that grew to support the internal marketing effort in the banking study. Separate roles of catalyst, coalitions and constellations became important. In its totality, the role of the network was to generate and facilitate knowledge transfers of value to the host organisation (Ballantyne, 1997: 361).

Over five years, recurring cycles of energising, code breaking, authorising and diffusing behaviour gained mass, one cycle giving rise to another, supported by the head office customer service department. It is appropriate to think of this central team function as a catalyst. Their strategic intent and commitment was critical. Every communication they made was an implicit promise to be confirmed in interactions, otherwise credibility was at risk (Ballantyne *et al.*, 1991: 209–10).

Staff coalitions emerged, in head office departments, and their role was to provide advocacy and information across hierarchical borders. Likewise, in the regions and branches there were constellations of internal marketing activity. Their umbilical cord to the catalyst was necessary at first, but less so as time went on. The term *constellation* is borrowed from Wikström and Normann (1994) as it seems apt to talk of a great number of stars in clusters and patterns. I see them now as *customer conscious* coalitions and constellations, a network organisation *within* a host organisation (Figure 3.4a). As long as the lines of authority between the board, top management and the catalyst team remained, the network was

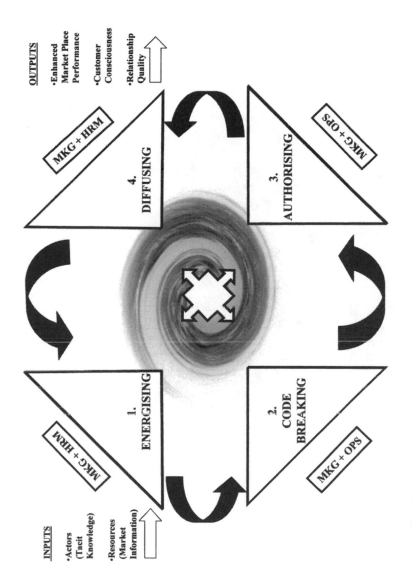

INPUTS
•Actors
(Tacit
Knowledge)
•Resources
(Market
Information)

OUTPUTS
•Enhanced
Market Place
Performance
•Customer
Consciousness
•Relationship
Quality

MKG + HRM

1.
ENERGISING

2.
CODE
BREAKING

MKG + OPS

3.
AUTHORISING

4.
DIFFUSING

MKG + HRM

MKG + OPS

Figure 3.4a Interaction within networks of relationships

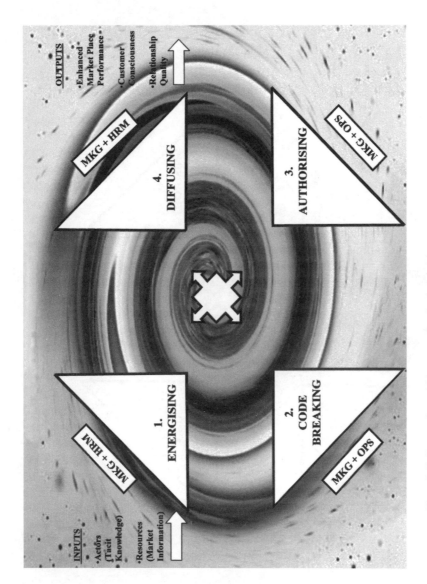

INPUTS
• Actors (Tacit Knowledge)
• Resources (Market Information)

OUTPUTS
• Enhanced Market Place Performance
• Customer Consciousness
• Relationship Quality

1. ENERGISING
MKG + HRM

2. CODE BREAKING
MKG + OPS

3. AUTHORISING
MKG + OPS

4. DIFFUSING
MKG + HRM

Figure 3.4b Interaction within networks of relationships

legitimised. Their ability to challenge activities that needed to be changed increased as the network grew (Figure 3.4b).

Ultimately, external factors began to impinge. The global 1990s economic recession hit Australia and businesses were faltering. Customers who were part of the new solution became part of the new problem. Two years into the recession, and after five years of putting 'customers first', the strategy and structure were wound back and the catalyst disbanded.

Relationship development and trust

Trust is often conceived as a behavioural intention. Reliance is placed on another person or thing in relation to some hoped for or expected outcome. There may be some risk involved, or faith (as in 'blind' trust), or some confidence in the other as a consequence of past experience, or as a condition of the norms of that relationship (Ballantyne, 1999).

In my judgement, the kinds of behaviours found in internal marketing (see Figure 3.3) are deeply enabled by *trust*. That is to say, trusting in oneself and containing one's anxiety and, at the same time, trusting others through interactive experience. The *interdependence* of participants, a condition of effective group performance, becomes in part a consequence of dissolving boundaries of mistrust, one to the other, and between wider coalitions, one to another. In the banking case, it was the implicit task of the head office catalyst team to create the conditions, environmental settings and workshops where this behaviour might be exemplified and experienced.

The perspective of institutional economics on 'trust' is tightly constraining as it has been argued that *risk*, not trust, is 'exactly suited' to describing the calculative behaviour of economic actors (Williamson, 1993). This view is popular in the marketing literature possibly because of its calculative rigour (Cowles, 1996: 35). Yet, it does not provide a guide to behaviour in internal marketing situations, in situations where institutional norms provide no protection. You need to trust before you can take risks together. In the banking case, we faced risks involved in interacting in trust in unfamiliar situations without 'institutional safeguards'. Trust was viable because it was necessary between participants forming new relationships.

The network organisation of catalyst, coalitions and constellations maintains its knowledge generating 'spin' (Figures 3.4a, 3.4b), in part, because of the constancy of its purpose and its privileged legitimacy. The catalyst gives protection from predators and provides creative space for volunteer teams to work with autonomy and in trust, enfolded within rounds of routine business activity. Collaboration with specialist departmental stakeholders enables each department to discover how to have their goals met on a common path. Dialogue and knowledge generation emerge as parallel processes, two sides of the one coin. Tacit knowledge of participants and market research information provides renewable inputs. Customer orientation, internal relationship quality and enhanced market facing policies are the most likely outputs.

Regrets? Too few to mention

I will conclude with a simple question: is internal marketing viable?

First, traditional marketing-like methods are sometimes viable. For example, when marketing is turned inward it may communicate effectively changes that do not cross over departmental authority lines. These are *transactional* aims in terms that have been used earlier.

Second, when there are *relational* methods, the stakes are higher, as are potential marketplace rewards. To begin, business unit legitimacy helps. CEO or board level approval is an advantage but not a reason for holding back. It might be adequate enough to begin strategy implementation if the next senior officer in line fully supports the team catalyst. Things might get better along the way. On the other hand, it helps to be aware that there will always be organisational constraints and rival agendas, which may require a deviation from course. In terms of guiding theoretical concepts, starting up a recurring cycle of learning behaviour must generate new knowledge (Figure 3.3). How much knowledge is generated depends, in the end, on the specific situational opportunities and constraints.

Third, internal networks of relationships will support and nurture internal marketing activity. The phrase 'interaction within networks of relationships' (Figures 3.4a, 3.4b) is a guiding principle. Gummesson (1999) used this phrase to describe any aspect of relationship marketing. I see it as equally applicable for *internal* relationship marketing because it opens up the possibility of the new.

Fourth, internal marketing is unlikely to succeed as a stand alone departmental effort. Marketing may, indeed, provide leadership but the recurring cycle of activities demand collaboration between departments. 'Energising' and 'diffusing', as new patterns of learning behaviour, require cooperation from HRM at least, and code breaking and authorising require the support of operational departments (see Figures 3.4a, 3.4b).

The strength of internal marketing is its strategic intent coupled with the will to do it, as well as trusting and being trustworthy. As interdependencies within relationships grow, a sense of obligation to achieve an explicit purpose also grows. Thus, actions are explained by their results. Its weakness is the limited marketing toolbox that blinds us to the fact that with collaboration, across departmental borders, new knowledge and interdisciplinary tools are available.

My hope is that my explanatory journey through one single banking case may open up the marketing toolbox to new conceptual tools. What constrains this most of all, in my view, is a functional and transactional sense of marketing's role. In relationship marketing, concerns about 'marketing-like' activities no longer apply as rigidly as before because collaborating across boundaries is the means to mutual exchanges of value. The boundaries are where you want them to be.

References

Ahmed, P.K. and Rafiq, M. (1995) 'The Role of Internal Marketing in the Implementation of Marketing Strategies', *Journal of Marketing Practice: Applied Marketing Science* 1(4): 32–51.

Baker, M.J. (1993) 'Editorial', *Journal of Marketing Management* 9: 215–16.

Ballantyne, D. (1990) 'Turning the Wheel of Quality Improvement, Continuously', *International Journal of Bank Marketing* 8(2): 3–11.

—— (1997) 'Internal Networks for Internal Marketing', *Journal of Marketing Management* 13: 343–66.

—— (1999) 'Dialogue and Knowledge Generation: Two Sides of the Same Coin in Relationship Marketing', *2nd WWW Conference on Relationship Marketing*, http://www.mcb.co.uk/services/conferen/nov99/rm/paper3.html.

Ballantyne, D., Christopher, M. and Payne, A. (1991) 'A Pathology of Company Wide Quality Initiatives: Seven Prescriptions for Failure', *Fifth Annual Conference of the British Academy of Management*, Bath, September; revised in Payne, A. (ed.) (1995) *Advances in Relationship Marketing*, London: Kogan Page, 205–19.

—— (1995) 'Improving the Quality of Services Marketing: Service (Re) Design is the Critical Link', *Journal of Marketing Management* 2(1): 7–24.

Berry, L.L. (1981) 'The Employee as Customer', *Journal of Retail Banking* 3(March): 25–8.

—— (1983) 'Relationship Marketing', in Berry, L.L., Shostack, G.L. and Upah, G.D. (eds), *Emerging Perspectives on Services Marketing*, Chicago: American Marketing Association, 27–8.

Berry, L.L. and Parasuraman, A. (1991) *Marketing Services: Competing through Quality*, New York: The Free Press, 152.

Brown, S., MacLaren, P. and Stevens, L. (1996) 'Marcadia Postponed: Marketing, Utopia and the Millennium', *Journal of Marketing Management*, 12: 671–83.

Collins, B. and Payne, A.F.T. (1991) 'Internal Marketing: A New Perspective for HRM', *European Management Journal* 9(3): 261–70.

Cowles, D.L. (1996) 'The Role of Trust in Customer Relationships: Asking the Right Questions', *Australasian Marketing Journal (formally Asia-Australia Marketing Journal)* 4(1): 31–41.

Dixon, N. (1999) *The Organizational Learning Cycle*, 2nd edn, Aldershot: Gower Publishing.

George, W.R. (1977) 'The Retailing of Services: A Challenging Future', *Journal of Retailing* 53(3): 85–98.

—— (1990) 'Internal Marketing and Organisational Behaviour: A Partnership in Developing Customer-Conscious Employees at Every Level', *Journal of Business Research* 20(1): 63–70.

Grönroos, C. (1981) 'Internal Marketing; An Integral Part of Marketing Theory', in Donnelly, J.H. and George, W.R. (eds), *Marketing of Services*, Chicago: American Marketing Association, 236–8.

—— (1982) *Strategic Marketing and Management in the Service Sector*, Bromley: Chartwell-Bratt, 38–40.

—— (1990) *Service Management and Marketing: Managing the Moments of Truth in Service Competition*, Lexington, MA: Lexington Books.

—— (1994) 'From Marketing Mix to Relationship Marketing: Towards a Paradigm Shift in Marketing', *Asia-Australia Marketing Journal* 2(1): 9–29.

Gummesson, E. (1987) 'Using Internal Marketing to Develop a New Culture: The Case of Ericsson Quality', *Journal of Business and Industrial Marketing* 2(3): 23–8.

—— (1999) 'Total Relationship Marketing: Experimenting with a Synthesis of Research Frontiers', *Australasian Marketing Journal* 7(1): 72–85.

Hogg, G., Carter, S. and Dunne, A. (1998) 'Investing in People: Internal Marketing and Corporate Culture', *Journal of Marketing Management* 14: 879–95.

Hooley, G.J., Lynch, J.E. and Shepherd, J. (1990) 'The Marketing Concept: Putting the Theory into Practice', *European Journal of Marketing* 24(9): 7–24.

Jary, D. and Jary, J. (1991) *The Harper Collins Dictionary of Sociology*, New York: Harper Collins.

Katz, D. and Kahn, R.L. (1966) *The Social Psychology of Organizations*, New York: John Wiley & Sons, 14–29.

McKenna, R. (1991) 'Marketing is Everything', *Harvard Business Review,* January–February, 65–79.

Nonaka, I. (1991) 'The Knowledge-Creating Company', *Harvard Business Review,* November–December, 96–104.

Nonaka, I. and Takeuchi, H. (1995) *The Knowledge Creating Company: How Japanese Companies Create the Dynamics of Innovation*, New York: Oxford University Press.

Oakland, J.S. (1989) *Total Quality Management*, Oxford: Butterworth-Heinemann.

Piercy, N.F. (1995) 'Customer Satisfaction and the Internal Market', *Journal of Marketing Practice: Applied Marketing Science* 1(1): 22–44.

Piercy, N. and Morgan, N. (1991) 'Internal Marketing: The Missing Half of the Marketing Program', *Long Range Planning* 24(2): 82–93.

Popper, K. (1962) *Conjectures and Refutations*, New York: Harper & Row.

Rafiq, M. and Ahmed, P.K. (1995) 'The Limits of Internal Marketing', in Kunst, P. and Lemmink, J. (eds), *Managing Service Quality*, London: Paul Chapman Publishing, 121–32.

Senge, P.M. (1990) *The Fifth Discipline: The Art and Practice of the Learning Organisation*, New York: Doubleday.

Varey, R.J. (1995) 'A Model of Internal Marketing for Building and Sustaining a Competitive Service Advantage', *Journal of Marketing Management* 11: 25–40.

Wikström, S. and Normann, R. (1994) *Knowledge and Value: A New Perspective on Corporate Transformation*, London: Routledge.

Williamson, O. (1993) 'Calculativeness, Trust and Economic Organisation', *The Journal of Law and Economics* 36(1), part 2, 485–6.

Part III

Management/ competency

4   Effectiveness implies leaving myths aside

Jean-Paul Flipo

Introduction

Over the past fifteen years, the marketing function in firms has developed, as external markets have become more and more open and competitive. Nowadays, the need for 'customer orientation', the strategic importance of the marketing function, the existence of 'part-time marketers', and so on are issues that are no longer disputed.

A myth is not something which does not exist, or has never existed. It is just a partial view of reality, or even a detail, which is amplified and magnified in order to make up social representations that support one or several political intents. It is the reason why myths are, generally speaking, positive, idealistic, morally defensible, 'politically correct'. Most of the time, as put by Lévi-Strauss (1958), myths are intended to reconcile, in believers' minds, contradictory, conflictual, or paradoxical views on a reality. Breaking free from myths does not mean destroying them, but assessing their actual nature and role and, for a manager, to make sounder decisions, rooted in objective reality, in order to manage it more successfully.

Now internal marketing, as literature shows, is largely a myth. At best, it is a very ambiguous concept with many different meanings; at worst it is something coined to manipulate a firm's personnel. It is a myth whose role is precisely to reconcile contradictory perspectives, in a holistic sense. Firms can be run only if co-operative behaviour is developed amongst all their main stakeholders, namely shareholders, providers, clients and personnel, and it is the primary task of the general managers to enhance and maintain this co-operative behaviour. But, this task is intrinsically difficult because, in human organisations, conflict may arise permanently, simply because every stakeholder tries to gain more from a given situation in relation to his power position. This holistic perspective of the firms' management seems to be absolutely necessary to explain the role of myths in internal marketing.

Using this perspective, here we are going to try to overcome contradictions or misleading perceptions of the internal marketing concept. For that, we choose to stick to firms' real practices, in order to give orientations that are essentially pragmatic.

In the first part of this discussion, we will give briefly the conceptual framework on which our reflection is grounded, together with the basic perspective illustrated here, i.e. a strict parallel between external and internal marketing, in order to better understand players' behaviour. This will allow us to present an updated concept of internal marketing, which could open new avenues for management practices.

In the second part, we will draw on the perspective presented before a revisited view of internal marketing, as regards the big issues that are currently debated: how to boost change and innovation within the firm, whether empowerment is necessary and in what form, how to make the famous marketing wheel work (internally and externally), and so on. This discussion is not intended to apply only in service companies, but this type of firm remains our basic reference, for which internal marketing is more relevant than in any industrial firm.

A political view of marketing practices

Amongst the numerous possibilities for defining internal marketing (Varey, 1995), we will retain here, as mentioned, that which represents the holistic approach, which is at the same time 'political', in the sense that it is through one's power that every stakeholder tries to obtain the best advantage from a given managerial situation (Cyert and March, 1983; Flipo, 1983). Basically, marketing happened to appear inside firms not only (and in many cases, not at all) as a 'managerial philosophy', but also as a set of tools to counter the rising power of customers (Bagozzi, 1979; Arndt, 1983). Now, the latter was triggered by political decisions of liberal nations, which decided on liberalisation and globalisation of the local economies. In consequence, the whole functioning of liberal societies has tended to become more and more 'market-oriented'. For the firms, that means that every stakeholder can choose, under the market perspective, the best 'offer' in the market, thus installing a permanent instability in given situations. Shareholders may sell and buy daily, providers may sell to one firm one day and favour another the day after, personnel may be laid-off abruptly without real managerial justification (managers included), customers tend to be less and less loyal to their providers, etc.

Hence, the concept of internal marketing retained here is the following: a managerial perspective which is aimed at taking advantage internally of the competitive forces shaping the markets, while enhancing co-operative behaviour inside the firm in order to face growing customer power. The myth of internal marketing is intended to reconcile this contradiction.

Internal marketing is no more than the application in the internal arena of a generalised marketing concept, which can be applied, as everybody knows, to 'purchasing marketing', 'shareholder marketing', and obviously to 'customer marketing'. The main issues boil down to how to make the firm's main stakeholders loyal, in a world in which individualistic and opportunistic behaviour is promoted, and the other way round: how to take advantage of possible favourable market situations, while risking the loss of some co-operative behaviour? The holistic view gives a perspective which presents all marketing practices as a general managerial orientation that makes a permanent adjustment possible, like a sort of osmotic pressure, of the different stakeholders' market conditions (Flipo, 1984). Let us examine the concrete consequences of this view.

Today the main goal of internal marketing is to benefit internally from the virtues of external competition. Literature on internal marketing stresses the importance of improving co-operative behaviour amongst employees. Here, we should like to go a stage further.

External competition, which justifies external marketing, results in making the customer more demanding, more powerful *vis-à-vis* the providers. In the logic of competitive markets, competition must be introduced in the internal arena, because it puts personnel in a situation in which everyone must strive to be able to deal with these demanding customers: the best employees will achieve that, and will make the customers loyal to the company. The worst performers will not succeed and, as in the external competitive markets, the weakest will be obliged to quit their jobs. The general situation becomes the following: the weakly performing employees mentally assimilate the external constraint so well that they understand on their own that they are no longer in the right place. If not, management makes them understand that, through indirect messages meaning that they are no longer 'competitive' or, according to a concept which appeared recently, 'employable'. This is what can be called, according to Courpasson (1995), the 'soft constraint'.

Does this contradict the views presenting internal marketing as a way to 'satisfy internal customers'? Not at all, insofar as it is applied to chosen employees, whose selection was based fundamentally on their ability to integrate this constraint *positively*. Positively means that these people are proud to be the best in their category, are willing to strive to maintain their 'competitive advantage', and know what the tools are for achieving that: co-operation with selected colleagues, training, general commitment towards the employer, amount of personal work, arrangements about their personal life, etc. In a word, they want to take advantage for themselves of what is said for marketing practice in general: market opportunities. This is the best way to maintain their employability, even in case they lose their job in an economic world in which, as everybody knows, 'flexibility' is a basic orientation.

However, perfect competition does not exist in reality: why? The general opinion of academic economists about this issue consists of arguing that there is, as a rule, specifically in human sciences, a gap between theory and practice which stems from the fact that concepts cannot grasp and stand for all the idiosyncratic aspects of concrete situations.

However, if we observe the general marketing behaviour of firms, one can offer another explanation which refers to a *political* behaviour of these firms. Concretely, companies often try to secure a good, or tenable, competitive stance, not only by striving to be better than competitors, but also by avoiding coping directly with competition. The reason why is the following: competition is largely perceived as being good for the economy in general, but often too risky for a firm in particular. Moreover, competition has strong positive effects (increasing general wealth), but represents a permanent threat for companies which happen to make awkward, or simply unlucky, decisions in a world in which market complexity and openness create a permanent high level of risk.

Nowadays, global economy is led by financial markets, which obviously have a behaviour of risk avoidance. Hence, managers are 'governed' so that they take advantage of competition when it is possible, and avoid competition when the risk incurred seems too high. This is the explanation for this apparent paradox: as deregulation develops, so does competition avoidance, and risk avoidance, simultaneously.

Consequently, the current expertise of a marketing manager is equally concerned with struggling face-to-face in the competitive arena, and protecting the firm against possible competitive threats, by the means of carving out market niches, building up politically induced entry barriers, lobbying for more advantageous regulation (or deregulation which leaves room for special arrangements), building alliances, mergers and acquisitions which lead to market domination, etc. These practices are largely observable in the contemporary liberal economy.

In other words, the 'comparative advantage' perspective, nowadays, offers many more satisfactory explanations of realities (Hunt and Morgan, 1995) than the neo-liberal one, which is supported by economists who seldom know the day-to-day running of the firms. Moreover, the multiple possibilities of influencing the markets pertain to a political perspective of management which finds many fields of application in marketing.

Consequences for internal marketing.   If we transpose the observations presented in the first part of this discussion concerning marketing practices to the internal market, we will be able to find a list of implications for internal marketing, notwithstanding that both 'markets' are not comparable in every aspect.

Can employees be 'customers'?

Definitely yes, as can be any of the members of the firm's 'coalition', to the extent that it means that the organisation must offer them the minimum conditions and advantages, in the hope of getting in exchange their co-operative behaviour, or eliminating concerns of possible conflicts. However, it does not go beyond that, i.e. consideration for the philosophical aspects of running a 'human' company is extremely rare, as well as considering the customer the same way: as an end in himself or herself. The only end in itself that exists today in companies is *profit*, and the shareholders or owners give delegation to the CEOs to make their financial interests prevail over any other consideration. So, internal and external customers are given only 'limited' satisfaction, that may also come from their mere mutual co-operative (i.e. commercial) behaviour.

What are the effects of 'pure and perfect' competition?

This concept cannot exist internally either. This means that legal and cultural rigidities prevent the internal market from being totally free. As it is in the interest of firms to boost competition amongst employees, the internal marketing strategies will have to take into account these constraints, and benchmark these internal conditions with those of competitors, in order to check if it does not represent a competitive handicap. If so, one can distinguish two cases. Firstly, when the handicap comes from overcost, the companies are led to boost competition amongst employees, internally to eliminate the weakest, and/or externally in order to decrease costs: delocalisation has become a banal managerial decision. Secondly, when the competitive handicap does not stem from cost, but from an inappropriate organisation, companies are used to boosting co-operative behaviour on the part of employees, in order to re-engineer, restructure, innovate, etc. Both are possible at the same time (for example, downsizing practices, followed by delocalisation).

Are there common strategic practices between external and internal marketing?

Among several commonalities whose explanations are too substantial to develop here, we wish to mention a particular one. As products and services are marketed through symbolic and imaginary attributes, so are the companies themselves to their employees. Myths, heroes, edifying stories, mission in society, links with societal myths, the ideal image of the firm, social and power status of employees within the firms, customer orientation, the latest fashionable management concepts, etc., are used to knit daily the imaginary dimension of the firm. For example, when a manager presents his firm as being the *compelling place to work, to shop and to invest* (Rucci *et al.*, 1998), first he underlines the commonalities of the three concerned markets (making an explicit reference to the famous 'service profit chain' of Heskett *et al*, 1997), respectively of employees, customers and shareholders. Second, he magnifies what he believes to be the competitive stance of Sears in the U.S.A., *the* leader, a statement which is not only based on figures, but also as the company which leads the practices of all mass distributors. In that case, Sears is 'compelled' to boost the corporate image, because of previous difficulties with all these constituencies, in the early 1990s, which resulted in a massive lay-off of employees (several thousand people). Generally speaking, the creative ideas that are used for advertising, enhancing the corporate image, are also used internally. The difference is that internal customers know much more of the reality than do the external customers, which means that internal credibility is more difficult to achieve.

How is the political behaviour of employees to be expressed?

Indeed, this behaviour is to be expected, so that personnel are able to cope with the internal competitive pressure, these practices being modelled by the external marketing ones, presented before. Many authors underline the fact that it is necessary, for the firm to run smoothly, that all the constituencies adopt a co-operative way of working, thus building loyalty to the company. The 'service profit chain' (Heskett *et al.*, 1997) is a concept which tends to demonstrate that everything which goes against co-operation is detrimental to the company. This is, to a certain extent, a tautological assertion. The real issue is the fact that human social behaviour is *always simultaneously co-operative and conflictual* (at least potentially). A large number of social scientists (or novelists...), have for long put forward and largely illustrated this view.

In consequence, designing and defining an internal marketing strategy today is more complex than ever, as it reflects the external complexity of markets and human behaviour in modern societies which, being more open and freer than ever, are more open to political, individualistic and opportunistic behaviour.

Consequences for internal marketing management

Some recommendations will now be presented, based on the previous analysis. Basically, the 'liberal' society functions according to a permanent selection of the fittest, which means that success is linked to the adaptation of human behaviour to the conditions of the markets, be they internal or external. Many authors assert that these market conditions have become *inhuman* (Garten, 1997), insofar as globalisation is also a sort of world war, in which the fate of rank-and-file workers (or 'soldiers') has little weight, compared to the financial and commercial stakes. Has the scope, or the nature, of internal marketing changed in the current economic environment?

We assert that it can still exist, and represent a true competitive weapon, provided that management practices are not limited to a balance of power game facing employees. Consideration for the human aspects of work and economies seems required, or at least a minimum consideration, for the ethical issues involved. This is not contradictory with what was presented in the first part of the discussion: internal marketing must deal first with the forces that shape modern markets, which means selecting and managing the fittest people, and in so doing exert a traditional hierarchical coercive power (for the conflictual aspects of human behaviour). It must simultaneously show a very open and pro-active co-operative side, which is typical of internal marketing.

Let us now deal with the key issues of modern management, related to competitive advantages.

Managing management credibility

Personnel who are able to cope with demanding customers will turn out to be demanding themselves *vis-à-vis* their managers; they want to benefit more from their greater contribution to the marketing success of their employer. It is not only a question of financial benefits (although it is an important aspect), but also they are able to assess the value delivered by management in the marketing success of the firm, and challenge the managers if they do not meet their legitimate requirements. Consequently, management must be at the highest level of expertise in order to face a higher level of management issues, whose aim is to create trust, which entails commitment and loyalty amongst selected personnel. Obviously, a high rate of turnover amongst executives is a very bad situation for credibility. Now, the current frantic thrust towards mergers, acquisitions, alliances, re-engineering and downsizing, which entail a high degree of instability amongst executives and management in general, represents true handicaps. For the personnel, how can they be committed to a company that changes frequently and without warning its owner(s), CEO, middle management, allied parties and so on? If internal marketing is to be recognised as a powerful competitive asset, it must be taken into consideration, together with financial and political arrangements that are dealt with at the highest level of the enterprise (or even outside this enterprise, by shareholders who do not know, and do not care, what it represents in concrete terms). How can a manager require sales personnel to work on developing customer loyalty, if he or she is placed in an unstable position?

Another crucial aspect of credibility refers to what is known in the human resource management field about reciprocal individual consideration, fairness, clarity of decisions, the balance between what is demanded of employees and the way they are rewarded. There is nothing new about these issues.

Managing limits to internal competition

In order to contain political behaviour of employees, it is in the best interest of firms to recognise that employees need protection. Indeed, internal competition results not only in eliminating the least fit, it also instils a climate of rivalry between individuals, specifically amongst people who cannot perform at the same level because of innate personal qualities. 'Our employees are the best' is evidently a myth, a contradiction in terms, a motto that can only be put forward in advertising for the external corporate image. How to cope with these inevitable internal inequalities is another challenge for managers, given that a high rate of personnel turnover is not an asset for a firm. Remember the complex issue already mentioned: a firm must always give employees effective inducements for co-operation, as well as maintain amongst them a fair competitive atmosphere. The ideal situation is merely altruistic: co-operation as well as conflict is directed only to the greater competitiveness of the company as a whole, which means that all the constituencies of the firm are in a 'win–win–win–win…' game. Unfortunately, altruism is not a sentiment shared massively by people: in the current economic game, individualism and opportunism are encouraged and, consequently, everybody tries to gain more than others.

Now, if managers want to control the internal competitive side of personnel behaviour, they must put limits to it. The fundamental assertion of economists, according to which competence is the only criterion through which individual employees must be assessed, can be challenged. Human links, relationships, feelings, sympathy, pleasure in working together, collective solidarity for a project, etc.; in short, all that may be a necessary ingredient to maintain a positive state of mind, or even enthusiasm, inside the firm, must be cultivated, included at the expense of mere competence. An example is given by the famous soccer teams. It is not always the best teams intrinsically that win; human factors make the difference. What can be said of individuals is valid for internal services as well: in a world in which employees know less and less of what the limits of their company are (Gummesson, 1996), the imaginary concept of it must be also managed, but this is all the more difficult as the real limits of the firm are constantly challenged for reasons of renewal of arrangements concerning collective or individual competences.

Dealing with an updated 'internal marketing mix'

Compared with the situation that prevailed in the early 1980s for employees, the current one is undoubtedly less beneficial. The product 'job' (Flipo, 1986) is more demanding in terms of workload, stress, flexibility, and so on, and no better in terms of internal status and amount of human or material resources. Salaries at best have stagnated and, further, unemployment has dramatically developed even in wealthy countries. The 'internal market' is less and less attractive for employees, but is accepted as such given the external constraint, or threat, of no job. Hence, internal marketing needs more sophisticated methods in order to maintain job attractiveness: creating perceived value that costs little or nothing, or is tied to the creation of improved financial results. This is the reason why imaginary gimmicks are so popular amongst firms (which, in particular, create pride to belong to them), but they also employ managers who develop true leadership and humane qualities, or encourage employees to become shareholders. However, in many industries, as mentioned before, managers are dependent on external market conditions, which impose internal practices on all firms that want to be competitive. For example, in the hotel industry (namely big international chains), the employment conditions are particularly bad. According to Hartline and Ferrel (1996), for example, low levels of wages for a long period of service (including unpaid overtime), revolving work schedules including nights, little prospect of career progression, etc., break the famous relationship between job satisfaction and better individual efficiency.

The element 'communication', in the marketing mix, is the only one that can compensate for the unfavourable work conditions. Then the aim is to create a positive climate, a 'fun' atmosphere, but which can only be triggered by employees themselves. It is beyond managers' power to create it directly, although it is possible for them to create the conditions that enhance this climate.

What about 'empowerment', in this perspective?

One of the most popular fashionable gimmicks is 'empowerment'. Undoubtedly, the word sounds like an altruistic decision: giving employees consideration, a certain degree of independence and so on. All the managers who support, or practise, empowerment, present it first of all as a human (and even humanist) revolution (Wetlaufer, 1999). Their sincerity cannot be challenged, but the competitive and conflictual conditions of the markets imply that strict limits are given to this autonomy (even if the latter is greater than before). More importantly, we can state that a firm's control, audit, and reporting are much tighter than before in order, first, to avoid enduring local problems, and second, to have tools available that allow top managers to assess permanently the 'competitiveness' of the local executives or employees.

In this perspective, empowerment may be interpreted also as a myth: personnel whose job is at the front desk facing customers need to be empowered for evident reasons to be able to respond to customer demands, which are constantly growing. But, in no way does it correspond to a true *internal* empowerment: having internalised the competitive constraints and the strategic thrust of their employer, employees fully depend on the latter for their jobs, for fair reward, and to maintain their internal status. Having a comprehensive and consistent set of internal values and practices is more important than giving local autonomy. So, empowerment is just for external use, and of little importance with regard to the internal hierarchical structure. Moreover, recent management tools (for example, micro-computers) make it possible to control rank-and-file personnel 'softly'. It is no longer necessary to watch people (as did a foreman, for example). A daily listing shows in a flash the best and the worst performers, and people who fall into the middle ground.

Installing empowerment on the internal side of the firm undoubtedly develops competition amongst employees, all the more if controlled individual or collective results are published. As put by Beirne (1999), 'Available empirical studies provide clear evidence that empowerment schemes generate tensions and encounter difficulties which regularly result in failure'. And failure means loss of credibility of management. The fact is that, beyond a limited number of success stories, empowerment, every time it is evaluated as a panacea, fails (Shapiro, 1995; Argyris, 1998). The real current challenge for internal marketing is the one we are going now to deal with: change and innovation management.

Change and innovation management

The permanent need for change and innovation (enhanced by competitive pressure) is another constraint to which personnel are subjected, another element which can destabilise and sometimes upset individuals. It is clear from the earlier discussion that employees are prone to react to it through a behaviour of risk avoidance, as do managers facing external risks. How to control this behaviour is essentially a question of knowledge of possible political behaviour of employees:

what triggers risk avoidance, and what are their possible strategies that could block change? Anticipating personnel's reactions is the best way to maximise the chances of success, the same way as external challenges are faced by marketers. 'Resistance to change' is not necessarily a reflex amongst corporate personnel, but anxiousness about it is felt more and more: so, the reasons for anxiousness must be discovered, in order to be removed.

First of all, the destabilising effect of change disturbs the established order, which is considered as being viable, and puts in place a supposed new order in which the relative individual or collective stances are no longer the same. Who is winning (and who is losing) with respect to status, quietness, influence, power, money, etc., in that change and, consequently, what kind of possible compensation must the 'losers' be offered by management?

Second, how are the players likely to appropriate the change as planned by managers? There is necessarily a gap between the two: the organisation is not just a mechanical tool for an economic purpose but it is, first of all, a human community which has its own autonomous regulatory practices (beyond management control). Anticipation is difficult here, because the main persons concerned are not themselves knowledgeable about that, but following step by step through an open dialogue the way it is put in place can be a useful method.

Third, scepticism is felt very frequently by employees, about the aim of change, as well as the means selected to achieve the project. This scepticism will be all the deeper when it concerns partly a reduction of means or, worse, includes 'downsizing', which is often the case. The most frequent consequence is the fact that change is only lived as a constraint, which reduces considerably the range of its expected positive effects.

Fourth, how are the inherent risks of innovation shared (Stuart, 1998)? Possible failure may stem from a problem of internal misconception, internal poor implementation, or externally relating to customers or competitors, and so on. It is a popular 'game', amongst firms, to seek out the people, or department, responsible for a failure. Management should recognise the 'systemic' origin of a failure, which does not mean that the excess in the opposite sense is acceptable. The faults or mistakes must be isolated considering at the same time the actors and the system (Crozier and Friedberg, 1977).

One of the main results of a positive internal climate is to ground human relationships on trust, but trust can only exist if it is cultivated every day. Coping with the latter challenges allows managers to show that innovation and change can benefit the whole enterprise, and achieving successful changes is as important as, and largely necessary to, succeeding in the external market.

Double-bind with external marketing issues

Several databases concerning markets in the most developed countries show that the general rate of satisfaction of external customers is declining, or at best stagnating, in spite of well-known efforts achieved in product or service quality management (Fornell *et al.*,1996; Fournier *et al.*, 1998). As an explanation, the general reaction of managers consists of saying 'the customer demands progress more rapidly than we can follow, in spite of our commitment to improve endlessly what we market'. But the product or service marketed is no less than the product or service fabricated by the personnel, and will always be so. The machines, be they more and more sophisticated and numerous, cannot function without the human factor behind and around them.

Coping with real internal marketing issues is probably the best way to reverse this negative trend, at least to the benefit of the companies that choose it, given that current practice is so poor. Indeed, many articles concerning internal marketing stress the fact that few application examples are given, and often the same ones are cited again and again (Varey, 1995). In a business environment in which 'survival of the fittest' is a natural instinct, internal marketing has much work left to do to gain acceptance in most firms. Academics and practitioners must strive to continue to substantiate the real competitive advantage it represents, one of the few whose scope also concerns long range perspectives.

Conclusion

Living dangerously on a day-to-day basis is by no means a comfortable situation for a company, or for an individual: both struggle for economic life, the latter inside the environment of the former. Coping with a competitive environment, be it external or internal, demands a very high level of management performance, in order to maintain trust amongst all the constituencies of the firm (Mayaux and Flipo, 1997). By addressing the real issues and stakes concerning personnel acting in a competitive context, internal marketing allows managers to maintain a fair balance between them.

Many facts show that this fair balance is threatened by the overpowering influence of shareholders: it is experienced at the expense of personnel and, consequently, of customers. The most frequent strategy used by firms to manage these imbalanced situations consists of using myths that are intended to fill the gaps between the ideal situation and the real one. The worst situation would be that managers get deceived by their own manoeuvres, or let themselves be deceived by societal myths that support idealised images of bewildering realities.

References

Argyris, C. (1998) 'Empowerment: the Emperor's New Clothes', *Harvard Business Review*, May–June: 76, 98–105.
Arndt, J. (1983) 'The Political Economy Paradigm: Foundation for Theory Building in Marketing', *Journal of Marketing* 47(Fall): 44–54.
Bagozzi, R.P. (1979) 'Towards a Formal Theory of Marketing Exchanges', *Special AMA Conference Proceedings on Theory in Marketing*, Phoenix, AZ, February, 32–9.
Beirne, M. (1999) 'Managing to Empower?: A Healthy Review of Resources and Constraints', *European Management Journal* 17(2): 218–25.

Courpasson, D. (1996) 'The French Deposit Bank: Managerial Professions between Ratio-nalisation and Trust', in Morgan, G. and Knight, D. (eds), *Deregulation and European Financial Services*, London: Macmillan, 66–85.

Crozier, D.M. and Friedberg, E. (1977) *L'acteur et le système*, Paris: Seuil, 325–48.

Cyert, D. and March, F. (1983) *A Behavioural Theory of the Firm*, Englewood Cliffs, NJ: Prentice-Hall, 114–27.

Flipo, J.-P. (1983) 'Pouvoir et Marketing', *Revue Française de Gestion* 42 (September–October): 90–9.

—— (1984) *Le management des entreprises de services*, Paris: Les Editions d'Organisation, 19–34.

—— (1986) 'Service Firms: Interdependence of External and Internal Marketing Strategies', *European Journal of Marketing* 20(8): 5–14.

Fornell, C., Johnson, M.D., Anderson, E.W., Cha, J. and Bryant, B.E. (1996) 'The American Customer Satisfaction Index: Nature, Purpose and Findings, *Journal of Marketing* 60 (October): 7–18.

Fournier, S., Dobscha, S. and Mick, D.G. (1998) 'Preventing the Premature Death of Relationship Marketing', *Harvard Business Review*, January–February: 42–51.

Garten, J.E. (1997) 'Can the World Survive the Triumph of Capitalism?', *Harvard Business Review*, January–February: 144–50.

Gummesson, E. (1996) 'Relationship Marketing and Imaginary Organisation: A Synthesis', *European Journal of Marketing* 30(2): 31–44.

Hartline, M.D. and Ferrell, O.C. (1996) 'The Management of Customer-Contact Service Employees: An Empirical Investigation', *Journal of Marketing* 60 (October): 52–67.

Heskett, J.L., Sasser, W.E. and Schlesinger, L.A. (1997) *The Service Profit Chain: How Leading Companies Link Profit and Growth to Loyalty, Satisfaction and Value*, New York: The Free Press, 17–38.

Hunt, S.D. and Morgan, R.M. (1995) 'The Comparative Advantage Theory of Competition', *Journal of Marketing* 59 (April): 1–15.

Lévy-Strauss, C. (1958) *Anthropologie structurale*, Paris: Plon, 175–210.

Mayaux, F. and Flipo, J.P. (1997) 'Services Marketing: Nothing to do without Trust', in Bidault, F., Gomez, P.-Y. and Marion, G. (eds), *Trust: Firms and Society*, London: Macmillan Business, 121–32.

Rucci, A.J., Kirn, S.P. and Quinn, R.T. (1998) 'The Employee-Customer-Profit Chain at Sears', *Harvard Business Review*, January–February: 82–98.

Shapiro, E.C. (1995) *Fad Surfing in the Boardroom*, Reading, MA: Addison-Wesley, 81–92.

Stuart, F.I. (1998) 'The Influence of Organizational Culture and Internal Politics on New Service Design and Introduction', *International Journal of Service Industry Management*, 9(5): 469–85.

Varey, R.J. (1995) 'Internal Marketing: A Review and Some Inter-Disciplinary Research Challenges', *International Journal of Service Industry Management* 6(1): 40–63.

Wetlaufer, S. (1999) 'Organizing for Empowerment: an Interview with AES's Roger Sant and Dennis Bakke', *Harvard Business Review*, January–February: 111–23.

5 Managerial interactions of internal marketing

Audrey Gilmore

Introduction

There is little doubt that the role of marketing management is undergoing change (Grönroos, 1990; Gummesson, 1991). In recent times, many organisations have been emphasising 'partnerships' and 'networking' in their interactions with other firms (Ford, 1990). Consequently, the role of marketing is changing within the context of the organisation, with more emphasis on 'partnering' within the organisation, teamwork among members and sharing of responsibility. Indeed, marketing management may occur in companies without boundaries; where suppliers are not outsiders; internal functions begin to overlap and blur; and all staff are integral to the service delivery. This clearly has an effect on the management of internal 'customers'.

The influence of the more recent theoretical developments, such as relationship marketing, and a re-emphasis of networking, interaction and total quality management theories (the 'hot topics' of the 1990s), undoubtedly have had an influence on, and contribute to, the importance of internal marketing in practice. Although many previous approaches to internal marketing have had considerable success in improving some organisations' external activity, the problem of achieving a holistic, organisation-wide, action-oriented implementation of internal marketing still remains.

Initially, this discussion will provide a definition of internal marketing in the context of managerial interactions, consider the organisational context of internal marketing and the barriers which impede its successful implementation. The second part of the discussion will consider how internal marketing can be operated, developed, and sustained within an organisation through the fostering and development of management competencies, specifically in the context of inter-organisational networking and relationship development.

Definition of internal marketing in the context of managerial interactions

The term 'internal marketing' has been widely used in organisations. However, the term is often used loosely to describe many different managerial initiatives aimed at improving the effectiveness and efficiency of organisational resource application. The use of the term 'marketing' in this context does not simply mean the application or performance of marketing activity. More specifically, it means a focus on marketing concepts and theories that can be adopted for application to managing the organisation of efforts to meet the needs of the internal customer (employee), so that they in turn can understand and value the philosophy of providing satisfaction for the external customer.

Internal marketing evolves from the idea that employees represent an internal (or first) market within the organisation. This market needs to be educated and informed about the organisation's mission, the benefits of its products and services and the expectations of its customers. The rationale for this is that successful 'marketing' to this group will contribute significantly towards achieving ultimate collective success in the delivery of all marketing activity to external customers. Thus, the overwhelming purpose of internal marketing is to 'involve' employees in the organisation's mission and strategic direction, and to help them understand and value the corporate objectives. In so doing, it will achieve a 'balance' between operational efficiency and management objectives.

Gummesson (1991) writes that internal marketing can be practised at different levels within an organisation and with its suppliers and networks. For example, it can occur within the customer–supplier relationship; in the application of marketing know-how to personnel; in the activities which focus on encouraging a company to be marketing-oriented; and in the marketing that takes place between profit centres inside a decentralised company.

In the context of managerial interactions, internal marketing needs to be based on negotiation and so depends upon joint or consensus planning and agreement; a focus on continuous value creation for all parties; and reciprocal rather than sequential interdependence (Joshi, 1995; Varey, 1995). It also needs to be based on the involvement of a number of individuals across functions and levels in the firm, including both general and functional managers and encompassing all marketing and marketing-related activities. Such involvement needs to have a long-term perspective in that interactions should be seen as continuous, ongoing, mutually active and adoptive; formal and informal. Interactions encompass relationships between individuals and external marketing assets (such as establishing relationships with other individuals) and involve management from all functions and levels in the firm. For such interactions to exist or develop, empowerment should be inherent in the organisation; that is, some degree of 'experienced responsibility for work outcomes' (Hackman and Oldham, 1980) which encourages all employees (including managers) to be accountable and responsible for their results.

Organisational context of internal marketing

It is well recognised that the nature of the organisational structure will impact upon the degree of management responsibility (for example, Mintzberg, 1973).

Organisational structures gradually change as a result of both internally (local) and externally occurring circumstances. As an organisation develops, grows and reorganises, management decision-making evolves, managers move and the structures change. Similarly, as the organisation adapts to a changing external environment this will have an impact on the structure.

Typically, as organisations grow they develop more structure. Traditionally, structure is built around the functional activities of an organisation. This can create distinct departments, each being developed with individual emphasis and priorities. Often as organisations become larger, they can become unwieldy and the overall goal or purpose of an organisation can become outmoded, over-looked, or vague. Different types of decisions will be required at different levels within a functional structure in an organisation. For example, some levels of management will be involved in planning, different levels of managers will be responsible for making operational decisions, and different levels of staff will be involved in carrying out the required operational activities.

Often, organisational structures become inappropriate for the nature and type of management decisions needed in order to remain competitive. When this occurs, it reflects a failure of management to understand the arising organisa-tional development problems. This, in turn, can result in an organisation becoming frozen in its present stage of evolution regardless of potential marketing opportunities. Traditionally, the purpose of an organisational struc-ture was to create and support a system of management hierarchy, authority, power and control. Where there are many levels in the hierarchy from top management to frontline staff there are likely to be more standardised and formalised role definitions and demarcations of responsibilities. In this situation, decision-making occurs at many levels away from the frontline. Often managers and staff in different levels tend to deal with their immediate areas of responsi-bility only, with little appreciation of the activities of the organisation as a whole. In addition, decision-making in organisations occurs against the background of 'political' power struggles and, therefore, is influenced by managerial manipula-tion, keeping control, attempting to repress social interactions, and informal negotiation (often manipulated by 'behind closed doors' communication). Such weaknesses are inherent in traditional hierarchical structures where managerial power and control are held as paramount by the management group. In this way, hierarchical, formal structures restrict both individual and functional creativity and flexibility and limit any quick responses to environmental changes.

Because such structures have been criticised for stifling individual role respon-sibility and managerial accountability, many organisations have attempted to reduce the number of managerial levels, to devolve managerial responsibility and accountability, and to move decision makers closer to the (external) customer interface level.

Given that internal marketing occurs within an organisational environment, the nature of such organisational inter-relationships and interactions need to be recognised. Organisations are networks of interacting groups where power depen-dencies and relationships occur between internal departments (Mastenbroek,

1993). Some of the more common barriers to developing and sustaining effective internal marketing in an organisation are now discussed.

Barrier One: resistance to change

Many organisations suffer from an organisational 'resistance to change' at various stages in their lives. A 'built-in' natural resistance of management to change can cause many problems (Kotler, 1990; Piercy and Morgan, 1990). In many cases, this is caused by a reluctance of management and employees to consider new ideas, where key managers (and gatekeepers) may feel their power could be eroded, and an overall fear of the unknown and concern about job security or future promotion. In association with this, many managers' resistance to change is based on the protection of vested interests where managers have built departments and teams around them and they want to keep this power and control. Thus, in a large organisation there may be a number of managers who feel this way and will do everything they can to maintain the established orthodox organisational structure.

Given that an organisation's daily life can be designed around the implementation of past plans, any new plans will require different company patterns and habits and these are often resisted. Additionally, new plans will depend upon managers becoming proactively involved in making action happen. Often, this can be very different from past activities and habits. Kotler (1990) writes that the more different the new strategy from the old, the greater the resistance to implementing it. This can create a circumstance of managerial uncertainty, particularly in relation to individual managers' changing roles where the levels of responsibility for decision-making may be relatively unfamiliar.

Furthermore, resistance to change is often exacerbated if frontline and supervisory staff in an organisation perceive that the organisation is being led by 'ivory tower' planners; where management are too far removed from the actual functional activity and operational delivery to understand the 'real' issues requiring attention.

Another barrier to change can exist where one level of management tries to control the degree of power and responsibility taken by another level of management. For example, even within organisations where there may be an implicit need for managers to make timely decisions related to external issues, there is often pressure from within the organisation to limit individual proactive behaviour because of high-level decisions and exigencies of hierarchy.

Barrier Two: inter-functional conflict

Senior managers often have misguided assumptions about their organisation's culture (Hofstede, 1991), in that they may be unaware of the problems and issues which impede the productive accomplishment of co-operation and integration. Inter-functional conflicts may be one such area. In many organisations, functional conflicts exist where one function fails to recognise that other functions' perspectives may have different priorities and emphasis and will often see things differently. For example, marketing's view of personnel, production and finance departments within an organisation will be different from each department's respective view of themselves.

Equally, these different departments will have varying views of the marketing function (Weinrauch and Anderson, 1982; Ruekert and Walker, 1987). For example, the marketing managers' emphasis may be on increasing sales, offering a range of products, frequently changing products, using pricing incentives, offering good value for money, and so on. These often require staff to accept flexible work patterns. However, production, finance and HRM managers may consider managers implementing these practices to be either under-selling or over-selling, to not be cost-conscious, to be flexible to a fault, and to be ultra-optimistic and uncontrollable. So, functionally organised companies may in fact be working against themselves; the consequence of which will be inefficient performance.

Barrier Three: intra-functional conflict

Intra-functional conflict occurs where organisational and departmental goals may be very different from individual and personal goals. It occurs because individuals have different goals, desires and ambitions, and will be submerged in different social spheres of interaction that will impact upon their overall attitude and behaviour.

Such conflict often occurs where there are a small number of internal promotions available for a large number of people. Therefore, colleagues can become very competitive in their work-related activities. Such conflict often leads to secretive practices, for example avoiding interaction so as not to share ideas, work plans or initiatives with colleagues; and to restrict flows of information. Work-related 'possessiveness' entails poor communication in not letting others know the whole perspective in any work context such as a new development or initiative. These practices lead to an incidence of 'one-upmanship', where individuals try to be seen as the initiator of good ideas, in the context of playing down others' contributions. Indeed, this often leads to a 'blame' culture where individuals are 'accused' of or linked to inefficiencies and mistakes; and 'personality clashes' interfere with best working practices.

Barrier Four: lack of individual responsibility

Lack of individual responsibility in an organisation manifests itself where action is required but managers are unable or unwilling to take decisive action or make new decisions. In this vein, Piercy and Morgan (1990) describe the 'problem of incrementalisation' where managers fail to review and to take new decisions but instead merely adapt the previous year's plans.

The problem of finding individuals to actively implement plans is also addressed in the management literature by Belbin (1981), who writes about the importance of finding individuals within organisations who will be 'planning champions'; and the 'finishers' of tasks. Individuals need to: know why and how to communicate at all levels, with peers, supervisors, and subordinates; have a clear understanding about where to fit in; and understand their duties and responsibilities. Indeed, managers who will be involved with the implementation of new activities need to be contributors to the design of action plans which state explicitly the specific allocation of activities needed at each stage of implementation.

Given that change is a real and continual element in a manager's career, managers need to see their jobs as an ongoing process of learning in which they acquire new knowledge and skills. The further up the organisation hierarchy a manager ascends, the greater the need to develop accordingly. A competent decision-making manager will have the appropriate mix of attitudes and/or skills relevant to his/her position. If he/she is promoted to a higher or different managerial level and does not acquire the necessary competencies, then he/she will be inefficient. The mix of skills required by a manager is dependent on a number of factors, including the size of organisation, position and degree of responsibility. From his experience with British Petroleum, Donegan (1990) recognised the constant change that organisations face and recommends that people must be trained and facilitated in helping companies to adapt to change. Competencies for each managerial situation will be defined according to the work situation's requirements and will be related to the performance of specific functional tasks.

The possession of appropriate competencies also applies to the effectiveness of the entire management team, particularly where managers are proactive in initiating changes in response to pressures from the business environment. Specific managerial competencies are required at all levels in an organisation if internal marketing is to help integrate the organisational goals. Implicit in this requirement is the existence of employee empowerment, which is generally considered to be at the opposite end of a continuum with the 'production line' approach. Empowerment entails giving employees the discretion to make day to day decisions about their job-related activities.

Summary of barriers to internal marketing

Clearly there are a number of organisational barriers to the acceptance of internal marketing. Often, these are created and manifested through the structure itself, particularly through a managerial resistance to change. Inter-functional and intra-functional conflict will impede any attempts to introduce or develop the benefits of internal marketing. Receptiveness to change is an important attribute for an organisation to successfully apply internal marketing, especially if it is to be an adaptive or learning organisation (Garratt, 1987). Therefore, the implementation of internal marketing cannot rely on organisational structure alone. The current relationships, interactions and interdependencies within an organisation have an impact on the organisational decision-making process, and these will depend on the structure and nature of interrelationships within the organisation at any given time. Naturally, changes in organisational direction and purpose will have an impact on the nature of decision-making. The use and recognition of informal networks are important if internal marketing is to be effective.

Managing interactions and relationships for internal marketing

Following on from the discussion above, the thinking and behaviour of the key managers are particularly important in organisations (Brass, 1984; Goffee and Scase, 1984; Williams and Huber, 1986; Heller *et al.*, 1988; Sahlman and Stevenson, 1991). The willingness and ability of individual managers to adapt and change is a prerequisite for successful use of internal marketing in the improvement of managerial interactions and development.

Weinshall (1975) argues that any change in the nature of management decision-making necessitates a change in managerial structure and in the individual competencies and roles of managers. This will occur as an organisation evolves through its life-cycle and/or adapts to a dramatically changing environment. Thus, the 'fit' between the organisational structure, management decision-making and the development of managers is of vital importance. The effectiveness and suitability of this 'fit' varies throughout the life-cycle of an organisation, particularly in a situation of rapid organisational change in relation to internal or external circumstances (Gilmore, 1997). An example of this, which illustrates how organisational structures, management decision-making and individual managers' competencies changed over a three-year period in a large company is summarised below.

In the first year of a three-year period, the company under study operated a centralised structure with four divisions in different geographical areas and a UK headquarters. The major managerial decisions relating to marketing and operations were made at headquarters. The divisional structure was built around control rather than responsibility and allowed for directives from headquarters management in relation to each specific operational activity. Managers at divisional level focused upon operational activities and were generally reactive to any changing circumstances.

In Year Two of this period the organisation was decentralised. During Years Two and Three, decentralisation gradually led to increased management responsibility and accountability, with some management groups becoming more proactive than others. Over time, the managerial decision makers developed a level of knowledge and experience in terms of specific role responsibilities, and gradually gained some expertise in decision-making related to specific areas of marketing activity. In this way, over time, they became more competent managers in the context of the company's specific situation within a changing external environment.

The overall effect of the changing organisational structure was that marketing decisions specific to the local division were made at divisional level rather than headquarters level. There was a gradual move from head-quarters control to divisional level managerial responsibility and accountability. Over time, the key decision-making managers at local level progressed and adapted to meet new challenges. This compared favourably with some of the original marketing managers from headquarters who did not take full responsibility for planning or decision-making and preferred to be directed by higher management.

(for a full description of the study see Gilmore, 1998)

As an organisational structure evolves around the interrelationships and inter-dependencies among positions there are times when it may offer a better 'fit' for decision-making activity and management responsibility than others. Weinshall (1975) proposes that the solution to the lack of 'fit' between the required responsibilities and tasks of managers and their current capabilities is to bring in new managers with suitable capabilities in order to transform the existing managerial structure back to being a balanced one. In many organisations, a more realistic solution is to initiate and encourage appropriate development of existing managers and employees as occurred in the company example introduced above.

How can managers and staff be developed in order to improve their internal marketing interactions and performance in the context of their organisational role? The criteria for internal marketing interactions will depend upon the development of competencies for the key managers in each functional area, with particular emphasis on those that will impact upon the management of internal marketing.

Recent developments in the management literature focus on the importance of management competencies for the specific roles and tasks of individual managers in order to improve overall performance. Although much has been written about management competencies (for example, Wrapp, 1967; Mintzberg, 1973; Katz, 1974; Boyatzis, 1982; Rugman, 1984), consideration of which competencies are most suitable for marketing has only recently been given attention (see for example, Carson, 1993; Gilmore and Carson, 1996). However, the specific roles of the organisation's managers, and the areas of decision-making which most concern them, need to be taken into account before the most suitable management competencies can be explicitly recognised. Furthermore, the notion of competence development recognises and promotes the existence of 'learning' managers who are continually improving their competence in relation to their specific role, rather than assuming that training programmes should 'teach' managers how to think and behave. Instead, effort is focused on identifying how each manager's competencies can be developed and, thus, building on his/her experiential knowledge.

Requirements for internal marketing management interactions

Managing interactions within an organisation involves establishing, developing and facilitating co-operative relationships for mutual benefit. Within the services marketing literature (Berry, 1983; Grönroos and Gummesson, 1985), and the Industrial Marketing and Purchasing (IMP) group's literature (Häkansson, 1982; Ford, 1990), and more recently in the relationship literature (Gummesson, 1995), 'interaction' in a marketing context implies face-to-face interaction between managers and managerial networks. Thus, this type of interaction occurs at an individual level where personal contacts are made, bargaining and information exchange carried out, and individual relationships established (Cunningham and Turnbull, 1982). Much of the relationship literature advocates that 'the focus shifts from products and firms as units, to people, organisations, and the social processes that bind actors together in ongoing relationships' (Webster, 1992). Managing interactions involves handling complex, personal interactions; the recruitment of internal marketing techniques can be used as a vehicle or mechanism for this. Interactions are based on social exchange, involving mutual orientation, dependence, satisfaction, commitment, and adaptation. Success or otherwise of managing interactions through internal marketing depends on getting people involved in two-way, interactive relationships; and developing interactions between people and various technologies and systems. All of these should occur in the context of, and within the priorities and purpose of, the organisation. Thus, the management of interactions should be guided by having a mutual orientation, and be developed through dialogue and social exchange processes.

The development of core competencies will be crucial to the cross-functional dimensions of internal marketing management interactions. Some competencies will be more fundamental than others for each specific functional area. Core competencies which contribute to the roles and responsibilities in each manager's own functional area will be required in order to provide a basis for building and developing further refined and specific competencies for more cross-functional and integrative activities within an organisation.

Requirements for internal relationship building

Managing business relationships involves integrated thinking about relationships, networks and interactions. Relationships require at least two parties who are in contact or interact with each other (for example, a provider and a customer). Although Gummesson (1995) advocates that networks emerge when the number of relationships increase and, therefore, become more complex; in many business circumstances, networking occurs first out of a particular business need and relationships develop over time after this. Business networks occur implicitly in the context of current and potential internal relationships involved in management and marketing within a company, its profit centres, owners and investors (i.e. the total stakeholder network). Organisations are dynamic networks; the interactions within and between these networks involve the establishment and development of relationships on an ongoing basis. Indeed, organisations can be comprised of 'imposed' relationships at varying levels. Therefore, in order to manage the interactions of internal marketing effectively, the aim should be to improve relationships by exploiting networks. It is contended here that relationship networks can be improved and sustained through the explicit development and refinement of competencies for managing purposive social interactions within an internal management network. This idea is developed in the remainder of this discussion.

Competency development for internal marketing networks and relationships

How can competencies for internal marketing and structured interaction network management be developed? Firstly, through the proactive use and integration of networking and building relationships. A simplistic representation of this is given in Figure 5.1. The implication is that management and staff must have, or develop, appropriate competencies for networking and building relationships in order to successfully implement and sustain internal marketing. Such competencies will consist of a range of attributes, each of which is given relevance in a task environment as appropriate for the particular activities of managers. These include both core competencies and those which are very specific to managerial responsibilities.

From the descriptions in the literature of 'general' management competencies, the most frequently mentioned include competencies for dealing with peers, decision-making under conditions of ambiguity, conflict resolution, information-processing, resource-allocation, leadership, entrepreneurship, and introspection

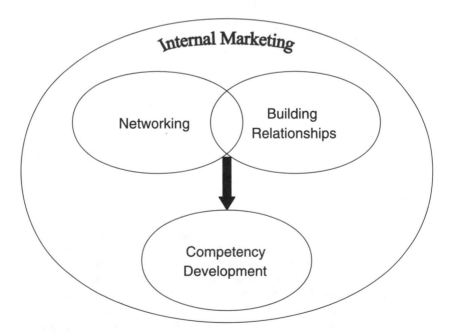

Figure 5.1   Components of internal marketing

(reflexivity). Which of these, if any, are appropriate for internal marketing and management? The answer is that all are appropriate in some combination. Some internal managerial and marketing competencies will be more fundamental than others; core (or 'building block') competencies may be required in order to provide a basis for building and developing further refined and specific competencies.

These core competencies will include the inherent or basic competencies of knowledge creation and deployment, learning from experience, communication and judgement, and therefore they form the bedrock of any manager's 'level of expertise'. However, these competencies may then be used as a basis for building more specific competencies as dictated by the manager's role responsibilities. For example, competencies for people management, such as networking and relationship building, will have particular importance in an internal management situation. This is illustrated in Figure 5.2. Furthermore, some of these competencies may require particular emphasis for different interactions and with certain levels of management.

The key to this is the willingness and ability to develop a specific competence for networking and relationship building based on experiential knowledge in the context of managers' roles and responsibilities. Management competencies will become more refined and specific depending on the particular managerial situation and context.

For internal marketing management to work in practice, individual managers need to possess competencies which relate to both planning and long-term

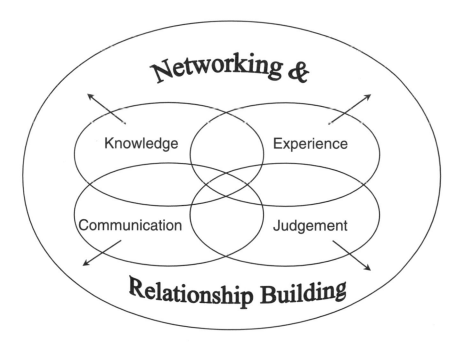

Figure 5..2   Core and specific competencies

activity as well as the ability to actually implement, that is, the ability to 'get things done' within the working environment. Competencies relating to the participation and co-operation of others such as networking and the building and maintaining of relationships are most relevant. The core competencies of knowledge, experience, communication and judgement can be used as the basis for building and refining more specific competencies dictated by each manager's role responsibilities. At any point in time, each manager will possess some competency in relation to knowledge, experience, expertise and judgement in the context of their managerial roles. The core competencies of knowledge, experience, communication and judgement are described below; followed by some discussion on how these can be built upon and refined for managing internal networks and purposive co-operative relationships.

Core competencies

Gilmore and Carson (1996) argue that in any successful organisation managers will quickly develop experiential knowledge. Experiential knowledge (EK) is built upon the existing knowledge, experience, communication and judgement (K+E+C+J), and the 'common sense knowing' of managers. A manager's common sense in relation to the work environment at any given time can be described in terms of his/her level of the current organisational situation. Such knowledge, experience, communication and judgement is often based on some years of working in the same environment, building a general familiarity with the industry and executing planning decisions and operational and tactical activities. Common sense *knowledge* entails a clear understanding of the specific details and requirements of the job, the company's markets, competitors and different customers (Gilmore, 1998). Managers have some level of knowledge about their job through gathering information about their business activities and knowledge of the industry in which they operate. In particular, managers will have a knowledgeable understanding of the processes and activities required for the successful integration of their business responsibilities, how each process impacts on the other, specific details of their planning requirements, action-oriented implementation and the issues which may affect it. Knowledge of the interdependencies and conflicts between staff will also be important as they will have an impact on how 'things get done' within the organisation. Knowledge in managing internal marketing is, therefore, not only about the market in which the firm exists and knowledge of competitors and the threats they represent, but also about the key informants and networks within the organisation, and how to facilitate cross-functional participation in serving the external market.

Managerial *experience* is more difficult to describe and access. Although managers' experience can be counted in terms of years, in effect their experience could sometimes be described as 'one year repeated several times' (Kolb, 1984). Experience can be described in terms of both 'width' and 'depth'. The depth of experience relates to the circumstance of working in the same area over a period of time and allowing detailed, concentrated, involvement and understanding of specific managerial tasks and responsibilities. From the internal marketing viewpoint, this will include experience of building and sustaining relationships with the key informants and the internal networks within the organisation; experience of using the interpersonal attributes which work best; and lessons gleaned from past mistakes and successes. All of this will contribute to the manager's depth of experience. The width of experience is also important in relation to allowing managers to translate their experience to other situations, contributing to the building and development of their overall performance. This could be stimulated by taking the opportunity to experiment, try out new ideas, learn from experience. In this way managers could develop the ability to expand their experience for future challenges. The variety of experience is also important in order to develop openness, confidence, vision, and flexibility, in the context of seeing and understanding other possibilities within their own company situation.

A *communication* competence is about knowing which communication approaches work best; what emphasis to give, when and to which audience; and how to glean and give information from and to key actors. In particular, it is the ability to recognise what and when specific knowledge, meaning, and identity should be co-produced by peers, subordinates and superiors; and how to be consistent in the provision of balanced communication process with and for all three. A *judgement* competence is determined by the ability to bring all the features of knowledge, experience and communication together and 'judge' how best to take a decision and to 'appreciate' which decision is best in a specific circumstance.

While earlier studies contend that managers' common sense knowledge can be developed through the transformation of experience, it is argued here that the development of *Experiential Knowledge as applied to Knowledge + Experience + Communication + Judgement* is a more comprehensive and meaningful competency framework for marketing management decision-making. This is based on Dewey's (1938) argument that what an individual has learned in one situation becomes an instrument of understanding and dealing effectively with the situations which follow; thus, relating to the more comprehensive picture outlined above. An adaptation of Dewey's model to illustrate the core concept of experiential knowledge (Dewey, 1938; Kolb, 1984; Lewin, 1951; Piaget, 1970) is shown in Figure 5.3. This illustrates a progressional development of experiential knowledge over time (Gilmore and Carson, 1996). This model highlights that an internal manager's involvement in current decisions and activities aids the development of 'Experiential Knowledge' (K+E+C+J) to achieve managerial expertise at time period 1. This level of 'Experiential Knowledge' is then applied to current managerial decisions and activities at time period 2, and so aids the further development of K+E+C+J to further 'EK' at this time. This can then be applied to the manager's required decisions and activities at time period 3, and so on.

Experiential knowledge will take account of both internal and external changes in circumstances, and of the growth and development of management responsibility, as managers progress within the organisation or through different positions with specific roles and responsibilities provided these are clearly recognised. Thus, managers in each functional area need to develop core compe-

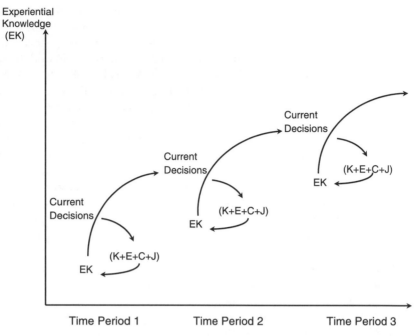

Figure 5.3   Experiential knowledge
Source: adapted from Dewey 1938

tencies of experiential knowledge in relation to their specific functional purpose, and roles, to suit or match their job requirement. Therefore, managers in the finance department will require experiential knowledge in aspects of financial management such as financial control, forecasting, budgeting, costing, estimating, employment of capital. Personnel managers will require experiential knowledge in areas such as manpower planning, recruitment and selection, job evaluation, remuneration, and labour relations. Production managers will require experiential knowledge in areas such as costing methods, production scheduling, quality control and production systems. Marketing managers will require experiential knowledge in areas such as researching markets, pricing planning, advertising, selling and, indeed, relationship marketing (i.e. social interaction, negotiation, etc.) Experiential knowledge competency requirements will change with every promotion or change in job roles and responsibilities. However, these competencies will be the building blocks for the development of more specific competencies as required by the managerial situation; such as developing a networking competency for managing internal marketing interactions.

Development of a networking competency for internal marketing

Organisations can be conceptualised as networks of interrelated structural positions, with individual employees occupying these relational positions, within the context of a more formalised structure (Brass, 1984). In an internal marketing management context, the core competencies contributing to experiential knowledge can be developed to include a networking and relationship building competence.

Networking in this context is defined as: the interactive activities of a collection of individuals, who may or may not be known to each other; and who contribute in some way to the organisation, either reactively or proactively; whether specifically elicited or not (adapted from Gilmore and Carson, 1998). In bringing together the deliberations on internal marketing and definitions of networks and networking, this debate focuses on the notion of 'managing interactions through networking competence'. Managing by networking is a naturally inherent aspect of management decision-making, where managers exchange and seek ideas, knowledge and market-related information through all their business activities and contacts. Internal managing by networking is based around people-orientated activities: it is informal, often discreet; interactive; interchangeable; integrated; habitual; reactive; individualistic and highly focused around the individual manager. The way in which managing by networking is carried out is often pre-determined by organisation and industry behaviours and norms, through regular or irregular meeting occasions and industry activities or in just conducting routine business. The frequency and focus of networking activity may vary depending on the nature of the organisation, the industry, and the nature of the markets in which the organisation operates. For example, international networks may be more focused than domestic networks because of the need to plan ahead, whereas contact with domestic markets may be more frequent than with international markets because of convenience.

Managing by networking is used by managers to develop, progress and support all aspects of their management responsibility both with customers and potential customers, and industry and business networks. A natural extension of this is to use such competencies for internal marketing activities especially in relation to word-of-mouth communication, idea promotion and information-generating activities. This clearly contributes to the integrative/holistic way in which managers can integrate their activities with the rest of the organisation. The creation and existence of a network and networking will intuitively be concerned with maximising management opportunities and directing all internal activities towards survival and development. Networking represents the intangible 'glue' holding people, functions and management activities together; matching different management functions, goals and operational activities with the more intangible interactive, communicative, and personal characteristics inherent in the internal environment.

An internal network manager can move in any way between and amongst the various network groups represented in the organisation, depending on his/her requirements at any time. An observer may not see such a framework except by constructing such a frame and attaching 'events' to it. Initial observations might create an impression of chaos where activities are apparently haphazard, sponta-neous, informal, and so on.

It is important to recognise that managing by networking will be enhanced and improved with the advent of experiential knowledge. This is often mani-fested where managers use their networking abilities and what they know to be their strengths to overcome their inherent weaknesses. For example, managers may learn from mistakes by assessing what went wrong in a given situation and how to avoid such mistakes (both internal and external) in the future. Such expe-riential learning has very strong links with the learning of the organisation as a whole, given that such learning is derived from the capability of an organisation to draw valid and useful inferences from experience and observation and to convert such inferences to effective action (Argyris and Schon, 1978). Thus, the internal manager has the power to create and sustain a 'learning organisation'.

As a manager develops more organisational and business contacts, managing by networking may become more strategic; and his/her management of internal and external communication will become integrated. Much of this networking development can be attributed to increased *experiential knowledge*. That is, having made certain decisions before in the past, the manager will have learnt from previous mistakes and will approach the task in a more prepared and structured way and, hence, develop a more refined networking competency for internal marketing.

Conclusion

Competencies for managing internal marketing management interactions can be developed through building on the core marketing managerial competencies of knowledge, experience, communication and judgement. A networking compe-tency for managing internal marketing interactions can be developed and improved by a consciously proactive approach. Such an approach simply requires a manager to address an issue or problem of managing interactions around a two-part construct: first by tentatively defining the managerial issue or problem, then making a list of people who might offer an opinion on the issue. These people are likely to be regular contacts of the manager, although some more distant contacts, possibly from other organisational functions, may emerge. The manager is now in a position to trawl his/her newly defined network. Nothing much is different from normal activity except that the trawling process may be accelerated because it has been consciously defined, and the trawl is now proactive and organised, and not merely routine. The manager will know, intu-itively, what information is relevant and make a *judgemental* assessment of the issue and a decision on how to address it. In addition, the manager needs to communicate with all individuals involved at various stages of this process to keep them participant and open to the potential suggestions for change.

Internally, it is important to recognise the significance of participating in formal and informal networks. Competency development for managing internal customers should build upon the core building blocks of knowledge, experience, communication and judgement already in existence, by focusing on how to develop networks of internal customers. Over time, such competency development will lead to effective networking, positive productive relationships, and to internal marketing managerial interactions. This will create and sustain a suitable environment for staff responsibility, participation, and contribution.

References

Argyris, C. and Schon, D. (1978) *Organisational Learning: A Theory of Action Perspective*, Reading, MA: Addison-Wesley.

Belbin, R.M. (1981) *Management Teams*, London: Heinemann.

Berry, L.L. (1983) 'Relationship Marketing', in Berry, L.L., Shostack, G.L. and Upah, G.D. (eds), *Emerging Perspectives on Services Marketing*, Chicago: American Marketing Association, 25–8.

Boyatzis, R.E. (1982) *The Competent Manager: A Model for Effective Performance*, New York: John Wiley & Sons.

Brass, D.J. (1984) 'Being in the Right Place: A Structural Analysis of Individual Influence on an Organisation', *Administrative Science Quarterly* 29(4): 518–39.

Carson, D. (1993) 'A Philosophy for Marketing Education in Small Firms', *Journal of Marketing Management* 9(2): 189–204.

Cunningham, M.T. and Turnbull, P.W. (1982) 'Inter-organisational Personal Contact Patterns', in Häkansson, H. (ed.), *International Marketing and Purchasing of Industrial Goods: An Interaction Approach*, Chichester: John Wiley & Sons, Section 5.2, 304–16.

Dewey, J. (1938) *Experience and Education*, New York: Kappa Delta Pi.

Donegan, J. (1990) 'The Learning Organisation: Lessons from British Petroleum', *European Marketing Journal* 8(3): 302–12.

Ford, D. (1990) *Understanding Business Markets: Interaction, Relationships and Networks*, London: Academic Press.

Garratt, R. (1987) *The Learning Organisation*, London: Fontana.

Gilmore, A. (1997) 'Understanding Marketing Management Competencies within a Services Context', *Irish Marketing Review* 10(1): 36–46.

—— (1998) 'Services Marketing Management Competencies: A Ferry Company Example', *International Journal of Service Industry Management* 9(1): 74–92.

Gilmore, A. and Carson, D. (1996) 'Management Competencies for Services Marketing', *Journal of Services Marketing* 10(3): 39–57.

—— (1999) 'SME Marketing by Networking', *New England Journal of Entrepreneurship* 2,2,Fall, pp 31–38.

Goffee, R. and Scase, R. (1984) 'Proprietorial Control in Family Firms: Some Functions of "Quasi-Organic" Management', *Journal of Management Studies* 22(1): 53–68.

Grönroos, C., (1990) 'Relationship Approach to the Marketing Function in Service Contexts: The Marketing and Organisation Behaviour Interface', *Journal of Business Research* 20(1): 3–12.

Grönroos, C. and Gummesson, E. (1985) *Service Marketing: Nordic School Perspectives*, Stockholm: Stockholm University.

Gummesson, E. (1991) 'Marketing-orientation Revisited: The Crucial Role of the Part-time Marketer', *European Journal of Marketing* 25(2): 60–75.

—— (1995) 'Relationship Marketing: Its Role in the Service Economy', in Glynn, W. and Barnes, J. (eds), *Understanding Services Management: Integrating Organisational Behaviour, Operations and Human Resource Management*, Dublin: Oak Free Press, ch. 9, 244–68.

Hackman, J.R. and Oldham, G.R. (1980) *Work Redesign*, Reading, MA: Addison-Wesley.

Häkansson, H. (ed) (1982) *International Marketing and Purchasing of Industrial Goods: An Interaction Approach*, Chichester: John Wiley & Sons.

Heller, F., Drenth, P., Koopman, P. and Rus, V. (1988) *Decisions in Organisations: A Three-Country Comparative Study*, London: Sage Publications.

Hofstede, G. (1991) *Cultures and Organisations: Software of the Mind*, New York: McGraw-Hill.

Joshi, A.W. (1995) 'Long-term Relationships, Partnerships and Strategic Alliances: A Contingency Theory of Relationship Marketing', *Journal of Marketing Channels* 4(3): 75–94.

Katz, R.L. (1974 [1955]) 'Skills of an Effective Administrator', *Harvard Business Review*, September–October: 90–102.

Kolb, D.A. (1984) *Experiential Learning:. Experience as the Source of Learning and Development*, Englewood Cliffs, NJ: Prentice-Hall.

Kotler, P. (1990) *Principles of Marketing*, Englewood Cliffs, NJ: Prentice-Hall.

Lewin, K. (1951) *Field Theory in Social Sciences*, New York: Harper & Row.

Mastenbroek, W.S. (1993) *Conflict Management and Organisational Development*, New York: John Wiley & Sons.

Mintzberg, H. (1973) *The Nature of Managerial Work*, New York: Harper & Row.

Piaget, J. (1970) *Genetic Epistemology*, New York: Columbia University Press.

Piercy, N. and Morgan, N. (1990) 'Organisational Context and Behavioural Problems as Determinants of the Effectiveness of the Strategic Marketing Planning Process', *Journal of Marketing Management* 6(2): 127–43.

Ruekert, R.W. and Walker, O.C. (1987) 'Marketing's Interaction with Other Functional Units: A Conceptual Framework and Empirical Evidence', *Journal of Marketing* 51(1): 1–19.

Rugman, N. (1984) 'What is a Marketer?', *Marketing* 6(7): 37.

Sahlman, W.A. and Stevenson, H.H. (1991) *The Entrepreneurial Venture*, Boston: Harvard Business School Publications.

Varey, R.J. (1995) 'Internal Marketing: A Review and Some Interdisciplinary Research Challenges', *International Journal of Service Industry Management* 6(1): 40–63.

Webster, F.E. (1992) 'The Changing Role of Marketing in the Corporation', *Journal of Marketing* 56(October): 1–17.

Weinrauch, J.D. and Anderson, R. (1982) 'Conflicts between Engineering and Marketing Units', *Industrial Marketing Management* 11(4): 291–301.

Weinshall, T.D. (1975) 'Multinational Corporations: Their Study and Measurement', *Management International Review* 15(4/5): 67–76.

Williams, J.C. and Huber, G.P. (1986) *Human Behaviour in Organisations*, 3rd edn, Cincinnati, OH: South West Publishing Co.

Wrapp, H.E. (1967) 'Good Managers Don't Make Policy Decisions', *Harvard Business Review*, September–October: 35–40.

6 Internal marketing in small manufacturing firms

Extending the concept to encompass organisational learning

Ian Chaston

Introduction

Over the last twenty years, both academics and marketing practitioners have sought to develop systems and processes that can be used by organisations to improve service quality (Lewis, 1995). The concept of internal marketing has arisen as part of these efforts (Band, 1988; Berry, 1981; Gummesson, 1987). It is usually portrayed in the literature as being concerned with how groups within an organisation, who together constitute an 'internal market', co-operate with each other to ensure intra-organisational customer wants and needs are fulfilled. Management of process is typically based on the premise that individuals, groups and/or entire departments need to comprehend their role as internal suppliers servicing the product/service requirements of others who are their internal customers, and vice versa.

Research on internal marketing has tended to focus on the issue of ensuring the effective co-ordination of internal activities in order that the organisation achieves the business goal of fulfilling the service quality expectations of external customers. Only occasionally have writers sought to expand beyond the boundaries of service quality theory and extend the concept to encompass other intra-organisational activities. One exception is provided by Piercy (1995), who proposed that internal marketing could also be used to promote acceptance of a new strategy or plan. In this case, the internal marketer is the person and/or department wishing to have the plan implemented and who uses various marketing techniques to gain acceptance for the activity by relevant employees and/or departments.

There is clearly a rich vein of additional knowledge to be gained from further studies on the role of internal marketing in the delivery of quality (for example, on how programmes are implemented and their impact is measured (Richardson and Robinson, 1986)). However, the tendency to focus on this issue creates the risk that both marketing and management academics and practitioners may ignore the important role that internal marketing can have in guiding other areas of intra-organisational activities. The purpose of this discussion is, therefore, to posit internal marketing as a concept that can be utilised to manage the accomplishment of other organisational goals. This broader perspective will be achieved by examining the issue of the organisational competences of small manufacturing firms in supply chain scenarios, and illustrating how the principles of internal marketing might be applied to fulfil the aim of matching organisational competences with those necessary to meet customer needs.

The role of competences

Possibly the earliest mention of how competences might influence the market performance of firms is contained within the pioneering work of Penrose (1959). Interest in his approach of portraying the firm as a bundle of resources and competences has seen a resurgence in the academic literature following articles by authors such as Prahalad and Hamel (1990) and Wernerfelt (1989). Specific attribution of the concept within the small firms sector in relation to the management of growth can be found in the paper by Chaston and Mangles (1997). This study drew on a variety of sources in the building and validation of a model involving competences across the areas of strategic planning, new product management, human resource management, employee productivity, quality and information systems. In a subsequent study, focusing upon the specific issue of small firm innovation, Clarysse and Dierdoneck (1998) concluded that competences such as control over employee activity and flexibility in production are essential in the successful development and launch of new products.

Possibly one of the most important catalysts for the increased interest in organisational competences in recent years has been the move by both large manufacturing firms and retailers to create highly integrated supply chains in which members focus upon fulfilment of those aspects of value-added processes where they have acquired specialist expertise. They also share the common philosophy of applying just-in-time management principles to minimise operating costs. Two frequently occurring events which accompany the creation of these integrated supply chains are (1) large firms significantly reducing the number of 'approved' suppliers from whom they are willing to purchase goods and (2) the outsourcing of services which had previously been carried out in-house (for example, some retailers appoint specialist logistics firms to manage distribution and warehousing; some direct marketing firms contract out their data management operations to a computer services company such as EDS).

Although during the 1980s, the creation of integrated supply chains was primarily a large firm sector activity, in the last few years small firms, especially those involved in highly competitive industries such as car parts and electronics, have increasingly been compelled to learn how to participate in relational forms of exchange in order to sell products to larger Original Equipment Manufacturers (OEMs) (Barringer, 1997). It is pointed out, however, that there is as yet little empirical data available on the nature of competences which small manufacturing firms need to acquire in order to fulfil their role as preferred suppliers to OEMs and/or national retail chains.

A possible model for meeting market expectations for competence

The academic literature suggests that where firms seek to work in close partnership with customers they are expected to exhibit higher levels of competences than competitors. On the basis of this conclusion, it seems reasonable to theorise that the ongoing success of small manufacturing firms within supply chain scenarios is critically dependent upon being able to fulfil customer expectations over the competences which they require of their suppliers. Furthermore, by drawing upon Parasuraman *et al.*'s (1985) service gap model, it is possible to evolve a similar model concerning the management of competences.

As illustrated in Figure 6.1, this management model posits that there are five possible gaps which can influence whether or not small manufacturing firms are able to fulfil the competence expectations of downstream customers in a highly integrated supply chain; namely:

Gap 1: a failure of management to be aware of the key competences expected of the organisation by customers.
Gap 2: a failure of management to translate customer requirements into standards of internal competence that can be used to guide the behaviour of staff within the firm.
Gap 3: a failure to ensure that all internal operations are achieving the standard of competences required by customers.
Gap 4: a failure to ensure that all promotional communication with customers only specifies claims of competence that match the level of achievement that the firm can actually fulfil.
Gap 5: representing the combined influence of Gaps 1–4.

Gap 2 is equivalent to the situation in service market environments where the firm sets standards that employees are expected to achieve in the fulfilment of their job role. In supply chain situations, these will probably include competences such as those necessary to supply the correct product, meet just-in-time delivery dates, and generate the appropriate accounting information required by the customer. Gap 4 can be assumed to be concerned with ensuring that any promises concerning the activities of the firm which may be communicated to the customer are achievable, feasible, claims. However, where there would appear to be the need to further validate the conceptual model shown in Figure 6.1 is in the areas of (a) Gap 1, in terms of whether or not small firms are aware of the customers' competence requirements, and (b) Gap 3, in relation to how firms ensure employees are provided with the knowledge required to evolve appropriate standards of competence.

Supplier awareness of relational competences

In view of Barringer's (1997) observation that there is, as yet, little empirical data

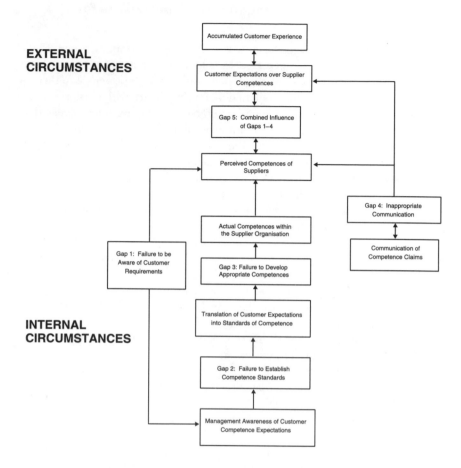

Figure 6.1 A gap model for use in identifying actions for applying internal marketing to enhance supplier performance

available on the nature of competences which small manufacturing firms need to acquire in order to fulfil their role as preferred suppliers to OEMs and/or national retail chains, it was concluded that there is need for further research on this issue. This was achieved by mailing a survey to the managing directors of 500 small UK manufacturing firms selected at random from the 3400–3600 SIC code section of a Dun and Bradstreet data base. For inclusion in the sample, firms were required to (a) have 10–50 employees, and (b) be autonomous trading entities (i.e. not branch plants of national or multi-national organisations).

A literature review revealed that few validated tools exist for measuring all aspects of the competences required of small firms. Consequently, it was decided to use possibly the most exhaustive list available in the UK; namely that contained within a computer-based planning tool known as 'The Way Ahead'

(Modbury, 1995). The attraction of this source as a possible research tool is that the definition of management practices has been achieved through an extensive validation involving a large number of UK small firms and staff from a UK support agency. The thirty-five areas of competence extracted from The Way Ahead materials are summarised in Table 6.1. Respondents in this study were asked in relation to each activity, using a seven-point scale ranging from 'very strongly agree' to 'very strongly disagree', whether this is an area of organisational practice where they believe that it is important to their customers that they have a higher level of competence than many of their competitors who operate in the same market sector.

In order to identify which respondent firms are operating as members of an integrated supply chain, the survey included a scale developed by Chaston (1998). This marketing orientation scale is designed to distinguish transactionally-orientated firms which operate at 'arms' length' from their customers, usually offering standard components at a competitive price, from those firms who have built close, long-term, working relationships with their customers. The scale is based upon requesting respondents to comment on the applicability to their organisation, using a seven-point scale ranging from 'Very strongly disagree' to 'Very strongly agree', of each of the following six statements:

1   Revenue is primarily generated from repeat sales to customers with whom the firm has developed long-term, close, personal relationships.
2   In-depth understanding of customer need is achieved through building close working relationships over a number of years.
3   New and improved products are developed by working in close partnership with customers.
4   The firm's quality standards are specifically tailored to meet the needs of individual customers.
5   Staff are strongly committed to meeting the needs of others both inside and outside the organisation.
6   Staff at all levels within the firm interact with customers in seeking solutions to identified problems.

Usable survey responses were received from 116 firms representing a final overall response rate of 23.2 per cent. Classification of firms in relation to whether they operate in close partnership with their customers or have adopted a transactional philosophy is achieved by calculating the overall mean score for responses to the six questions which comprise the marketing orientation scale. In this study, the overall mean score was 4.74 (SD 1.09). Firms working in close partnership with customers were selected on the basis that their mean score is greater than the overall sample mean. Transactional firms are presumed to be those with a mean score equal to or less than the overall sample mean. In this study, seventy-six firms were classified as exhibiting a customer partnership (supply chain) marketing style, and the other forty firms were classified as operating a transactional style of operation.

To determine the degree to which respondents considered that their customers expect them to be more competent than many of their competitors, a t-test comparing each area of management practice for firms participating in supply chains and transactionally orientated firms was undertaken. The results are summarised in Table 6.1. No statistically significant differences were found for 21 out of the 35 areas of organisational competence. Nevertheless, for five aspects of the marketing process – three areas of personnel management and four areas of financial systems management – firms involved in forming close relationships with customers in a supply chain, when compared with transactional firms, reported significantly higher scores for their management practices relative to those of their competitors.

By drawing upon the original sample frame, twenty-three firms orientated towards working in close partnership with their customers within supply chains, and willing to participate in a telephone interview were identified. Virtually all of these managing directors believe that many of their competitors are involved in offering standard products to a relatively wide and diverse customer base with individual contracts being won or lost on the basis of competitive price. Furthermore, because these competitors only manufacture standard products, this usually requires them to expend significant efforts on promotion, using techniques such as attendance at trade shows, trade advertising, and direct marketing. Most respondents also believe that the importance placed on price by most buyers in the market environments in which many of their competitors operate means that these latter organisations have fewer direct customers. Hence, to maximise market coverage they are forced to appoint a large number of distributors to represent them in the market place.

This is in contrast to the respondents who tend to operate on a strategy of seeking to establish close business links with a relatively small number of very loyal customers. They focus their promotional efforts towards building close working relationships with their customers. Typically, this is achieved by concentrating on having employees establishing and maintaining close, personal, '1:1' links between themselves and their respective counterparts in the customer organisations. When probed on the issue of HRM practices, most respondents reported that managing effectively the establishment of closer links between themselves and key customers requires an intra-organisational environment in which employees are flexible, prepared to take decisions without referring back to management, self-responsible, and can communicate effectively with their counterparts in the customer organisations. Similar findings have been noted by other authors (for example, Kalwani and Narayandas, 1995; Moller and Wilson, 1995); namely that in order to optimise the management of supplier–customer relations, such firms have usually found it necessary to upgrade their competence in recruitment, appraisal and employee development.

A number of authors (for example, Ford *et al.*, 1997; Buzzell and Ortmeyer, 1996) have reported that the move to form closer supplier–customer relationships is typically accompanied by the creation of sophisticated information systems for the rapid and detailed interchange of data between organisations.

Table 6.1 Assessment of perceived competence by relationship-orientated firms versus transactionally-orientated firms

Competence	Mean Supply Chain Firms	Mean Trans. Firms	t-value
Ability to define marketing strategy	4.02	3.38	3.54*
Ability to target marketing effort	4.17	3.40	4.82*
Ability to offer a superior product	4.35	4.25	0.79
Ability to offer superior value to customers	3.93	3.50	2.28*
Ability to deliver customer satisfaction	4.01	3.30	4.49*
Effective promotional programme	3.93	3.50	2.28*
Utilisation of appropriate distribution channels	4.05	3.32	4.49*
Management of customer relations	4.29	3.22	6.69*
Adequately resourced marketing operation	3.55	3.22	1.58
Employee skills to fulfil job roles	3.90	3.68	1.45
Employee skills to respond to changing future market conditions	3.55	3.30	1.77
Adequacy of current workforce size	3.59	3.20	1.83
Effectiveness of HRM practices	3.60	2.64	4.62*
Effectiveness of employee appraisal systems	3.69	3.15	5.74*
Effectiveness of recruitment systems	3.52	3.13	2.28*
Provision of employee development	3.51	3.32	1.06
Employees' abilities to use new technologies	3.46	3.15	1.95
Adequacy of organisational structure	3.88	3.64	0.96
Optimise employee productivity	3.54	3.68	1.86
Production system effectiveness	3.46	3.78	1.95
Management of product/service quality	3.54	3.85	1.96
Management of procurement activities	4.12	4.32	1.16
Supplier relationship management	4.08	4.20	1.08
Current cash flow management	4.31	4.15	1.04
Manage future cash flows	4.25	4.05	1.15
Current profitability management	4.26	4.08	1.05
Manage future profitability	3.87	3.85	0.71
Current management of assets	4.35	4.18	1.08
Manage asset position in the future	4.14	4.15	0.03
Ability to fund future plans	4.00	3.93	0.39
Diagnose developing financial performance problems	4.23	3.73	2.75*
Rapidly respond to developing financial performance problems	4.21	3.47	4.22*
Systems for acquiring information on internal operations	4.19	3.73	2.30*
Design and operation of internal control systems	3.81	3.10	3.27*
Utilise IT systems to acquire information	3.86	3.40	1.82

Note: *Difference significant at p<0.05.

Information technology in the form of electronic data interchange (EDI), for example, has permitted the development of more flexible manufacturing systems which permit faster response to customer demand through the adoption of a just-in-time operating philosophy. The comments of the respondents in the telephone survey very much mirrored these views. Over time they have found it necessary to upgrade their information and control systems in order to meet their customers' requirements for both higher service levels and the provision of a rapid, flexible, response to changing market circumstances.

Table 6.1 apparently indicates that firms working closely with their customers are more able to identify and respond to potential financial problems. On probing, some telephone interview respondents indicated that this is a side-effect resulting from their investment in improved information systems. Other respondents, however, felt that it was more of a reflection of their close relationship with customers, who if noting a change in downstream market demand, would rapidly inform their suppliers in order to ensure appropriate revisions are made to manufacturing schedules. This latter group of respondents appears to base this perspective on either their earlier experiences in more transactional markets and/or their observation of competitors in such markets. They view these latter types of market, where standard products are purchased on a bid-type pricing basis, as comprising customers who are much less concerned about keeping suppliers informed about possible impending changes in procurement patterns. Hence, under such circumstances, suppliers may encounter difficulties in assessing accurately the impact on financial performance of emerging, adverse, trends in market demand.

Competence acquisition and organisational learning theory

On the issue of competence acquisition, a number of researchers have undertaken studies concerned with factors that can influence optimising of performance within integrated supply chains. One contributory stream has been the issue of developing effective channel relationships (for example, Buzzell and Ortmeyer, 1996). Research on the role of relationships in supply chains has provided a second stream (for example, Norman and Ramirez, 1993), and, finally, a third emerging stream is concerned with the impact of information technology on relationships within and between organisations. A common thread linking these various streams of research is the view that managing relationships within integrated supply chains represents a much more complex organisational philosophy than equivalent management processes in transactionally-orientated organisations and markets. In their assessment of the importance for suppliers to optimise internal processes, Christopher *et al.* (1991) have proposed that this will require a broader range of competences than those required of employees in transactional marketing organisations. In discussing the activities associated with the management of customer–supplier relationship marketing strategies, some scholars (see Christopher *et al.*, 1991) have drawn upon the increasingly popular area of academic theory known as 'organisational learning' as an appropriate process through which to develop higher employee competences across the areas of delivering customer satisfaction, orchestrating organisational processes and the management of quality.

The origins and theoretical foundations of organisational learning can be traced back to the work of Cyert and March (1963), Bateson (1972), March and Olsen (1976) and Argyris and Schon (1978). Over the last few years, the literature on this topic has grown very rapidly, attracting interest from a diverse variety of academic perspectives. Easterby-Smith (1997), in his review of the theoretical roots from which the subject has evolved, suggests that contributions have been made from the subject areas of psychology, organisational development, management science, strategic management, production management, sociology and cultural anthropology.

Given the increasing academic interest in organisational learning, perhaps not unsurprisingly, numerous definitions have been presented in the literature. Schein (1996) has concluded that, as a result, there is considerable confusion about what is really meant by the term. Possibly, one of the reasons to explain this situation is the problem about the degree to which various authors have endeavoured to present inclusive definitions covering all of the issues surrounding knowledge acquisition, organisational structures, and systems for processing new information. A not unusual outcome of the desire of some authors to proffer a totally inclusive definition, is that one encounters statements which treat the subject with almost a religious, inspirational, fervour. Such a perspective is, for example, present in the definition offered by Senge (1990, p.7) who describes the learning enterprise as 'organisations where people continually strive to expand their capacity to create the results they truly desire, where new and expansive patterns of thinking are nurtured, where collective aspiration is set free, and where people are continually learning how to learn together'. In the context of this discussion, however, the author feels that it is more appropriate to follow Schein's guidance that in discussing organisational learning, one should primarily focus on how 'companies utilise, change and develop corporate knowledge' (Schein, 1996, p.11).

Bell (1993) commented upon the importance of exploiting new knowledge. He proposes that the information and knowledge acquired by employees is now more important than the more traditional orientation of assuming that the machine technology of the firm's fixed capital assets can provide the primary means for delivering products superior to competitors. Similar views have been expressed by Slater and Narver (1995), who believe that the skills learned by employees which are difficult to imitate provide the source of competitive advantage that can permit the organisation to offer superior value by building closer relationships with customers. Woodruff (1997) also concluded that learning about the market place is an activity central to offering greater customer-based value.

In those market situations where small firms desire to differentiate themselves from competition, through the adoption of a strategy of forming close relationships with customers in an integrated supply chain, then it will be necessary for these organisations to adopt a more adaptive learning style (Nevis *et al.*, 1995). For this type of organisation Senge (1990) feels that a more appropriate learning style would be to adopt a 'double-loop learning' orientation involving the exploitation of new knowledge to evolve new practices, perspectives and operational frameworks. Thus, if one accepts a definition of internal marketing which extends beyond the narrow confines of service quality, it seems reasonable to propose, in the context of organisational learning, an important purpose of internal marketing is that of providing the systems whereby areas of competence enhancement are identified and by implementing actions to link those who require new knowledge with knowledge providers, to achieve the goal of closing any competence gaps that might be an obstacle to meeting customer expectations concerning supplier performance.

One of the few published studies on the incidence of single-loop versus double-loop learning in the small firms sector (Matlay, 1998), would appear to support this perspective. Matlay undertook a series of face-to-face interviews with owner/managers of firms that had recently encountered significant operational problems. He concluded that, in the majority of cases, the correction of mistakes was based upon continuing to operate 'within the guidelines of existing organisational norms'. In a small proportion of cases, however, the learning process involved a degree of reflective analysis that led the organisations to evolve new behaviours more appropriate for coping with changing market circumstances. This conclusion is compatible with the view of Nevis *et al.* (1995) that, in those market situations where small firms face periods of significant discontinuous change and/or there is a desire to differentiate firms from competition through the adoption of a relationship marketing style, then possibly an incremental, more adaptive, learning style may be more appropriate.

Although instruments to differentiate between single-loop and double-loop (or higher order) learning can be found in many of the texts on the subject, in virtually every case it would appear that, although recommended as appropriate by the respective author, no real attempt is ever made to validate their application as an effective research tool. An exception to this situation was found in the case of a scale developed by Badger *et al.* (1998). This scale was evolved from a detailed review of the literature, and subsequently extensively tested in both the large and small firm sectors.

The original scale was created to measure expectation gaps by assessing differences between employees' desired learning environment and the organisation's current approach to learning (Sadler-Smith and Badger, 1998). This is achieved by comparing rating scores of what respondents 'wished the situation was' versus those for 'the current situation within the organisation'. As the purpose of this present study is merely to examine the actual learning approach within small firms, only that section of the scale has been adopted which asks respondents to comment, using a five-point scale ranging from 'never like this' through to 'always like this', on nine statements (see Table 6.2) concerned with various aspects of the current learning environment within their organisation.

The originators of the scale suggest that organisational learning should be perceived as a continuum, with at one end of the scale the reliance on building upon existing knowledge and at the other, exploiting new sources of knowledge

Table 6.2 A comparison of learning styles

	Company Behaviour	Mean Supply Chain Firms	Mean Trans. Firms	t-value
1	Constructive feedback is given to all employees on how they are doing	3.95	2.83	6.21*
2	Employees encouraged to undertake training and development activities	3.84	3.48	1.88
3	Employees share training/development learning lessons with others	4.28	3.40	5.77*
4	Employees share knowledge and resources	4.25	3.90	2.39*
5	Company goals made clear to all employees	3.75	2.50	5.36*
6	Employees, suppliers, customers all encouraged to let firm know if anything is going wrong	3.89	3.01	3.92*
7	Employees not afraid to voice differing opinions	3.86	2.93	4.89*
8	Company always willing to change working practices	4.33	3.38	5.43*
9	Company on lookout for new ideas from any source	4.22	3.43	4.18*

Note: * Difference significant at $p<0.05$.

as the basis for becoming ever more versatile, flexible and adaptive. In relation to the nine statements in Table 6.2, the higher the respondent firm rates the statements as 'in our company it is always like this', then the greater is the probability that the firm is exhibiting what Glyn (1996) has described as a higher order style of organisational learning.

To evaluate the organisational learning style of firms operating within supply chains versus their transactionally-orientated counterparts, respondents to the competency survey mentioned above were also asked to comment on various aspects of learning behaviour. T-tests were undertaken to compare the responses of relationship versus transactionally-orientated firms to the nine questions concerning their organisational learning styles. The results of this analysis are presented in Table 6.2. It can be seen that for eight out of the nine company behaviour variables, firms participating in supply chains reported significantly higher scores than their transactional counterparts.

Conclusions and implications

It is apparent from Table 6.1 that, in the case of twenty-one out of a total of thirty-five areas of management practice, there are no significant differences between the mean scores reported by firms involved in supply chains versus those exhibiting a transactional marketing style. In presenting this conclusion, however, it is important to register that in the case of fourteen aspects of management practice covering the areas of marketing, HRM, and information/control systems, small firms involved in supply chains, when compared with their transactional counterparts, reported a significantly higher level of competences than that which they believe to be exhibited by many of their competitors. Furthermore, the data generated from the telephone interviews support the conclusion that across these areas of company operations, respondents from firms participating in supply chains are aware that these variables are critical components in sustaining strong customer relations. Hence, if supplier firms ignore these factors they may run the risk of creating a Gap 1-type situation, which can lead to customer expectations being damaged.

The implication which can be drawn from this conclusion is that the marketer in firms involved in supply chains will need to ensure that, through application of internal marketing principles, the entire organisation is made aware of the importance of exhibiting competences in the areas such as defining strategy, targeting effort, offering superior value, and delivering customer satisfaction. Similar aims for building awareness through internal marketing are necessary for certain HRM and information management competences.

As can be seen from Table 6.2, in the case of eight out of the nine company behaviour variables describing various aspects of organisational learning style, the scale of difference between firms involved in supply chains versus transactional firms was found to be statistically significant at the $p<0.05$ level. Hence, it would appear that these results support the conclusions that in firms participating in supply chains, another critical role of internal marketing is to orchestrate the processes associated with the exploitation of a higher order level of learning as a path through which to acquire the competences that customers expect of the organisation. The implication of this conclusion is that, in utilising internal marketing to create and implement an effective organisational learning system, the small firm should establish the aim of seeking to exploit the benefits of double-loop learning to create an internal environment in which:

1   Constructive feedback is given to all employees on how they are doing their jobs.
2   Employees who have experienced learning, training or development are encouraged to share learning with colleagues.
3   Employees actively share their knowledge and/or resources with others.
4   Information systems are created which ensure that the organisation's goals and strategies are clearly communicated to all employees.
5   Systems are in place which encourage and ensure that employees, customers and suppliers are all motivated to immediately let the organisation know about failings across any area of its operations.

6   Employees are not afraid to voice differing opinions on company matters and to ensure that any conflicts are worked through constructively.

7   The company is able to continually evaluate current working practices and be willing to modify these if such actions would further enhance the delivery of internal and external customer value.

8   The company must establish systems that permit the rapid identification of new ideas, from any source both within and outside the organisation, that offer potential to improve on current operational practices.

Need for further research

In finalising the list of competences to be covered by this research study, in order to optimise response rates by not mailing an excessively lengthy questionnaire, a less than a totally inclusive list of issues was addressed. Clearly, therefore, further research is needed so that many of the generic competences are probed in greater depth (for example, the use of IT systems in relation to different activities such as customer segmentation, electronic data interchange, production management, etc., and the nature of processes and policies associated with management of product and service quality). It is also necessary to acknowledge that further research is required with small non-manufacturing firms and also larger firms to determine whether or not the conclusions reached about the need to be aware of specific customer demands over competence, and appropriate learning style to be supported by the internal marketer, are applicable in the context of other sectors of the UK economy.

The other critical research issue is that concerned with the actual mechanics of implementing an internal marketing programme designed to manage effectively the potential performance gaps described in Figure 6.1. It is believed that most texts and articles focus mainly on describing what a learning organisation is and/or the characteristics associated with higher versus lower order learning. If, however, internal marketers wish to acquire a detailed understanding of the actual processes of implementing a specific facet of learning (for example, using knowledge gained from customers as the basis for improving HRM competences), then availability of such guidance appears to be severely limited. Hence, there does appear to be a need for further research on the nature of the managerial processes associated with the application of internal marketing theory to guide the organisational learning process in 'real world' organisations.

Such research will probably need to focus on the process variables identified by DiBella *et al.* (1996); namely knowledge source, product-process focus, documentation mode, dissemination mode, learning focus, value-chain focus and skills development. The issue of knowledge source is concerned with the extent to which the internal marketer should draw upon new knowledge from elsewhere within the organisation, versus the extent to which they should seek inputs from external sources. Product-process focus refers to the preference for accumulating knowledge on products or services versus investing in new knowledge to improve internal organisational operating processes. Documentation mode is concerned with where knowledge is stored. At one extreme, it may be vested within the specific experiences of individual employees. This contrasts with the organisation which seeks to create documentation centres that act as repositories for all aspects of 'organisational memory'. Related to the documentation variable is dissemination mode. This can be under the control of centrally directed, highly structured, internal marketing systems, and/or be undertaken through the internal marketer encouraging informal exchanges of information between employees concerned with fulfilling assigned task roles.

Learning focus pertains to the style of learning. As demonstrated in the research reported in this chapter, the tendency of small firms involved in supply chains is towards the adoption of a double-loop learning style. Value-chain focus indicates which areas of core competence are considered critical to the execution of a firm's chosen strategy. Again, data from the reported research appear to indicate that small firms who are members of a supply chain will need to focus on meeting customer expectations for certain of their marketing, HRM and information systems competences because these are critical to building a base of highly loyal customers. Skills development is concerned with how learning among employees is achieved. Some skills are developed best through learning programmes for specific individuals, whereas other skills may be learned more effectively through involvement in team or group learning environments.

Clearly, the issue of how firms use internal marketing to embed new knowledge in order to support more effectively the delivery of a chosen marketing strategy represents a topic that, as yet, has received little attention in the academic literature. Researchers attracted to this topic area will need to recognise, however, that adoption of a 'classic' traditional, positivist, survey-based, approach will probably not generate the richness of data required to gain a detailed understanding of this aspect of internal marketing. Instead, it will probably be necessary to apply the methodological approach recommended by Nevis *et al.* (1995). This is based upon the use of extensive in-depth interviews of employees across all levels of a firm, field observations of actual managerial practices, and analysis of corporate documents to comprehend how internal marketing is being used to ensure that no gaps exist between customer expectations and the actual competences exhibited by the supplier organisation.

References

Argyris, C. and Schon, D.A. (1978) *Organisational Learning: A Theory of Action Perspective*, Reading, MA: Addison-Wesley.

Badger, B., Chaston, I. and Sadler-Smith, E. (1998) 'Developing small firms through managerial competence and organisational learning', *Proceedings of the British Academy of Management Annual Conference*, University of Nottingham, 25–7.

Band, W. (1988) 'Customer satisfaction studies, changing marketing strategies', *Marketing News* 22: 23–31.

Barringer, B.R. (1997) 'The effects of relational channel exchange on the small firm: a conceptual framework', *Journal of Small Business Management* 35(2): 65–79.

Bateson, G. (1972) *Steps to an Ecology of Mind*, New York: Ballantine Books.

Bell, D. (1993) *The Coming of Post Industrial Society*, New York: Basic Books.

Berry, L.L. (1981) 'The employee as customer', *Journal of Retail Banking* 2: 25–8.

Buzzell, R. and Ortmeyer, G. (1996) 'Channel partnerships streamline distribution', *Sloan Management Review*, Spring: 85–96.

Chaston, I. (1998) 'Evolving "new marketing philosophies" by merging existing concepts: application of process within small high-technology firms', *Journal of Marketing Management* 14(1): 45–51.

Chaston, I. and Mangles, T. (1997) 'Competences for growth in SME sector manufacturing firms', *Journal of Small Business* 35(1): 17–29.

Christopher, M., Payne, A. and Ballantyne, D. (1991) *Relationship Marketing: Bringing Quality, Customer Service and Marketing Together*, Oxford: Butterworth-Heinemann.

Clarysse, B. and Dierdonck, R.V. (1998) 'Inside the black box of innovation: strategic differences between SMEs', Working Paper No. 98/44, Universitiet Ghent, Ghent.

Cyert, R.M. and March, J.G. (1963) *A Behavioural Theory of the Firm*, Englewood Cliffs, NJ: Prentice-Hall.

DiBella, A.J., Nevis, E.C. and Gould, J.M. (1996) 'Understanding organisational learning capability', *Journal of Management Studies* 33(3): 361–79.

Easterby-Smith, M. (1997) 'Disciplines of organisational learning: contributions and critiques', *Human Relations* 50(9): 1085–113.

Ford, D. *et al.* (1997) *Managing Business Relationships,* Chichester: John Wiley & Sons.

Glyn, M.A. (1996) 'Innovation genius: a framework for relating individual and organisational intelligence', *Academy of Management Review* 21: 1072–85.

Gummesson, E. (1987) 'The new marketing: developing long-term interactive relationships', *Long Range Planning* 20(4): 10–20.

Kalwani, M.U. and Narayandas, N. (1995) 'Long-term supplier relationships: do they pay off for supplier firms', *Journal of Marketing* 50(1): 1–16.

Lewis, B.R. (1995) 'Customer care in services', in Glynn, W.J. and Barnes, J.G. (eds), *Understanding Services Management: Integrating Marketing, Organisation Behaviour, Operations and Human Resource Management*, London: John Wiley & Sons, 57–88.

March, J.G. and Olson, J.P. (1976) *Ambiguity and Choice in Organisations*, Bergen: Universitetsforglaget, Bergen.

Matlay, H. (1998) 'The learning small business: myth or reality?', in *Celebrating the Small Business, Proceedings of the Institute of Small Business Affairs 21st National Small Firms Policy and Research Conference*, University of Durham, 984–1005.

Modbury Marketing Computer Services (1995) *The Way Ahead*, Modbury, Devon (commercial software product).

Moller, K. and Wilson, D. (1995) *Business Marketing: An Interaction and Network Perspective*, Norwell, MA: Kluwer.

Nevis, E.C., DiBella, A.J. and Gould, J.M. (1995) 'Understanding organisational learning as learning systems', *Sloan Management Review*, Winter: 61–74.

Norman, R. and Ramirez, R. (1993) 'From value chain to value constellation: designing interactive strategy', *Harvard Business Review*, July–August: 65–77.

Parasuraman, A., Berry, L.L. and Zeithaml, V. (1985) 'A conceptual model of service quality and the implications for future research', *Journal of Marketing* 49(2): 41–51.

Penrose, E. (1959) *The Theory of the Growth of the Firm*, London: Blackwell.

Piercy, N. (1995) 'Customer satisfaction and the internal marketing: marketing our customers to employees', *Journal of Marketing Practice and Applied Marketing Science* 1(1): 22–44.

Prahalad, C.K and Hamel, G. (1990) 'The core competences of the corporation', *Harvard Business Review*, May–June: 79–91.

Richardson, B.A. and Robinson, C.G. (1986) 'The impact of internal marketing on customer service in a retail bank', *Journal of Bank Marketing* 4(5): 3–30.

Sadler-Smith, E. and Badger, B. (1998) 'Developing small firms through management competency and organisational learning', *Proceedings of the British Academy of Management Annual Conference*, University of Nottingham, 237–48.

Schein, E.H. (1996) 'Three cultures of management: the key to organisational learning', *Sloan Management Review* 37(Fall): 9–20.

Senge, P. (1990) *The Fifth Discipline: The Art and Practice of the Learning Organisation*, New York: Doubleday.

Slater, S.F. and Narver, J.C. (1995) 'Marketing orientation and the learning organisation', *Journal of Marketing* 59(July): 63–74.

Wernerfelt, B. (1989) 'From critical resources to corporate strategy', *Journal of General Management* 5(1).

Woodruff, R.B. (1997) 'Customer value: the next source of competitive advantage', *Journal of the Academy of Marketing Science* 25(2): 139–53.

7 Employee attitudes and responses to internal marketing

Gillian Hogg
Sara Carter

Introduction

Internal marketing, or the use of marketing techniques within the organisation to create and communicate corporate values, is an essential part of a marketing orientation. Kohli and Jaworski (1990) define a marketing orientation as an emphasis on the generation of marketing intelligence, and its dissemination across departments, together with an organisation-wide response to it. Empirical evidence suggests that the strength of a firm's marketing orientation has a positive effect on business performance and impacts on employee commitment and '*esprit de corps*' (Jaworski and Kohli, 1993). This approach acknowledges that marketing is an organisational not a departmental function, and that it requires a certain organisational culture for such an approach to be adopted (Deshpande and Webster, 1989; Deshpande *et al.*, 1993; Varey, 1995). The application of internal marketing provides organisations with the potential to achieve a marketing orientation and resulting corporate culture. There is, however, little agreement as to the appropriate marketing tools for use internally.

The essence of internal marketing is those activities that improve internal communications and customer-consciousness among employees, and the link between these activities and external market place performance (Ballantyne, 1997). The components are many and varied. Berry (1981), for example, views employees' jobs as internal products and the workforce as internal customers, an adaptation of the Japanese quality management techniques. Piercy and Morgan (1991) suggest the application of the external 4Ps marketing management approach to internal markets; however, this would appear to present some difficulties in practice. Grönroos (1990) draws a distinction between tactical and strategic approaches. At the tactical level, internal marketing may include ongoing training, encouragement of formal and informal communication, and internal market segmentation. At the strategic level, internal marketing extends to the adoption of supportive management styles and personnel policies, customer service training and marketing planning procedures. However, as Tansuhaj *et al.* (1991) point out, the demarcation between tactical and strategic is blurred and any internal marketing programmes must include a holistic approach to human resource management and marketing. What is lacking in this literature is, as

Ballantyne (1997) points out, any empirical evidence as to how internal marketing develops or influences customer-consciousness among employees. With the exception of Ballantyne's work, and Gummesson's (1987) case study of a programme of culture change, little has been written about how internal marketing techniques actually affect and influence employees. The purpose of this study is to examine the success of an internal marketing initiative, based on the UK government's Investors in People (IIP) programme, in influencing employee attitudes to their organisation and work. Although primarily viewed as a training initiative, IIP carries with it a number of communication imperatives which suggest that it can be a useful framework for internal marketing and a catalyst for changing the culture of an organisation towards achieving and sustaining a marketing orientation. Indeed, internal marketing may be a strategy for implementing the IIP programme.

Investors in People and internal marketing

Traditionally, the field of 'people management' has proved a particularly fertile breeding ground for ostensibly innovative policies and practices. Recent decades have witnessed the emergence, and demise, of TQM, JIT, BS 5750/ISO 9000 and many other apparently novel approaches to managing employee relationships. The latest manifestation of this trend in the UK is the Investors in People (IIP) initiative. IIP was introduced to British industry and commerce by the Conservative government in 1990 with the aim of establishing a benchmark that would enable organisations to improve the quality and effectiveness of their training and development practices (Down and Smith, 1998). Although primarily a training initiative, IIP's emphasis on the employees' role in the organisation and its explicit customer focus place it within the domain of the market orientation literature.

Rooted in the TQM (total quality management) principles of Deming (1982), IIP is a threshold standard built around the principles of commitment, planning, action and evaluation. Primarily a human resource initiative focusing on the training and development of the workforce, with its explicit customer focus, IIP forces a link between business strategy and human resources by linking the development of people (i.e. the producer employees) to the goals and targets of the organisation. In essence, it aims to deliver strategic objectives by harnessing the power of every employee within a structured framework, underpinned by effective evaluation. By placing the employee at the centre of organisational strategy, the dual benefits of improved employee motivation and customer service – the cornerstones of a marketing orientation – are assumed to ensue. IIP is effectively a 'national standard' that progressive employers are exhorted to pursue in order to create an organisational culture based on effective communication, feedback, and recognition of customer values. It is significant for three reasons. Firstly, there is its comparative longevity. Successive governments, both Conservative and Labour, have promoted the initiative since its introduction in 1990. Secondly, IIP appears to be growing in popularity, particularly in large firms. By late 1996 some 4,160 companies had been recognised by IIP and 20,638 had made a 'commitment' to work towards the standard, representing 28 per cent of the working population (Alberga *et al.*, 1997). Thirdly, and perhaps most significantly, IIP constitutes a deliberate intention to influence the conduct of management within the firm towards the creation of a customer-focused market orientation amongst employees.

The value of IIP as internal marketing

IIP offers organisations a framework with which to implement changes in organisational culture and can be used to transmit new, as well as reinforcing existing, organisational messages. Importantly, however, IIP is only a medium and not the message. If the core values of an organisation remain incompatible with their stated strategic objectives, programmes which aim to instigate changes in culture cannot succeed.

According to Alberga *et al.* (1997), IIP is predicated upon three assumptions that are largely untested. First, there are definable standards of 'best practice'. Such standards were drawn from a review of the employment practices of 'best' employers; these were 'successful' organisations from a wide range of sectors. Second, a direct link is assumed to exist between human resource practices and organisational performance. Although there is evidence on, for instance, the influence that training can have on the performance of the firm (Legge, 1988; Hendry and Pettigrew, 1992), establishing causality is particularly difficult. This is mirrored in the small firms literature, where there has been an intense discussion on the extent to which a connection exists between human resource practices and the performance of small enterprises. Storey and Westhead (1997), for example, maintain that the link between management training and small firm performance is extremely weak. Gibb (1997) argues for a more holistic approach to the issue, with an emphasis on the dynamics of organisational learning rather than mechanistic linkages. The third assumption is that all kinds of organisations, irrespective of size, sector or stage of development, should adopt so-called 'best practices'.

This last assumption can be challenged on two fronts. Firstly, there is an implicit association of best practice with progressive approaches to managing the employment relationship. Studies of avowedly 'enlightened' employers (Geary, 1995; Scott, 1994) have pointed to the persistence of low levels of trust between managers and workers and inefficient working practices. Interestingly, employees interviewed in Rix *et al.*'s (1994) qualitative study of IIP found that many workers were suspicious of training, believing, for instance, that multi-skilling would lead to redundancies. Furthermore, critical investigation of the related discourse of Total Quality Management has highlighted practices at variance with the unitarist image (Wilkinson and Wilmott, 1995). For example, 'empowerment', an oft-cited necessity of quality, may be more a mask for work intensification than a genuine attempt to facilitate more autonomous decision-making (McArdle *et al.*, 1995). Relatedly, the drive for quality can lead to the individuation (even isolation) of workers and their assuming greater responsibility without a commensurate increase in rewards (Roberts and Corcoran-Nantes, 1995). Indeed, quality initiatives often lack coherence with other organisational change programmes and people management initiatives (Kerfoot and Knights, 1995).

Secondly, the view that 'best practices' are applicable to organisations of all sizes and operating in any sector is also highly contentious. Many would support Welsh and White's (1981) view that the small business is not a 'little' large business (Hendry *et al.*, 1995; Curran, 1991; Curran *et al.*, 1997). Indeed, Ghobadian and Gallear (1996: 86) argue that 'Differences exist in structure, policy making, procedures, and utilization of resources to the extent that the application of large business concepts directly to small businesses may border on the ridiculous'. Moreover, the dangers of assuming homogeneity within small firms themselves have been known to researchers in this field for some time (Scott, 1986). For example, on the particular subject of employment relations in small firms, there is reputed to be considerable difference between the 'low-skill' manufacturing sector that has been the predominant focus of empirical research, and the 'high-skill' firms engaged in activities such as new technologies or business services (Scase, 1995). Generalisations across different sectors are, therefore, likely to be problematic (Curran, 1991; Scase, 1995).

Despite these limitations, there remain a number of advantages in using IIP as an internal marketing tool. Firstly, training and development are important features of internal marketing. Indeed, it has been suggested that training is the single most important activity (Grönroos, 1981; Varey, 1995). Secondly, IIP carries with it a number of communication imperatives which place it clearly within the boundaries of internal marketing and employee involvement programmes. The aim of IIP is to adapt the beliefs, attitudes and behaviours of the workforce with the resulting effects on the culture of the organisation (Alberga *et al.*, 1997; Ram, 2000). Thus, IIP can be seen as a conduit for the management of change, a process that facilitates cultural change and greater participation in decision-making within an iterative learning process. The IIP process depends on four key elements: communication via regular briefings with staff about the organisation's aims, goals and achievements; staff training in company values, policies and so on; staff appraisal and feedback systems; and finally, customer-consciousness through customer visits to ensure that employees have some awareness of the end users' perceptions of the organisation and the quality of the product they produce.

A key element of any successful internal marketing programme is the two-way process: the views of the management group are communicated to the workforce, and the views of the workforce are fed back to the management group. As Hatch and Schultz (1997) point out, managers are participants in, controllers of, and symbols of, their culture. The reflexivity of managers to employee concerns is both a product of the prevailing culture and a necessary pre-condition. IIP's focus on feedback and communication is, therefore, vital in achieving a marketing orientation.

Culture and organisations

Before discussing the reactions of employees to IIP as a particular internal marketing initiative, it is worth considering the notion of corporate culture and the employees' role within the organisation. Harris (1998) points to a recent resurgence of interest in the concept of organisational culture, linked to a recognition of the pivotal importance of organisations adopting a marketing orientation and the role of internal marketing in that culture. Definitions of culture in the literature vary and include ideology, a coherent set of beliefs, shared core values, important understandings, or 'the collective programming of the human mind' (Hofstede, 1980: 25). An organisation's strategic values are, as Osborne (1996) points out, the rationale for the viability of a business and link the organisation to its environment. These values are reflected in, and are a reflection of, the prevailing culture within the organisation. As organisations are collections of people, the climate or culture of an organisation is dependent on how the employees view that organisation and its goals. Through the medium of work people co-operate so that their personal goals can be incorporated into organisational goals. A market orientation is the culture which most effectively and efficiently creates the behaviours that lead to the provision of superior customer value (Narver and Slater, 1990).

The concept of organisational culture has developed primarily from the field of anthropology where it has been defined in a variety of different ways (see, for example, Kroeber and Kluckholm, 1952; Smircich, 1983). The literature in this area concentrates on cognitive components such as assumptions, beliefs and values, which are all individual characteristics (Sathe, 1983; Sapienza, 1985). Given that organisations are contrived and purposive, a consideration of how members regard the expressed ideas and actual practices is an important manifestation of the prevailing culture (Deshpande and Webster, 1989; Deshpande *et al.*, 1993).

Academic authors tend, as Sackman (1992) points out, to adopt an interpretive point of view, with culture being viewed as something an organisation 'has', as compared with something an organisation 'is', or as Dowling (1993) suggests, the 'glue' that holds the organisation together. In the tradition of the interpretative perspective, individuals use their cognitive structuring devices to perceive situations and interpret their perceptions (Seiler, 1973). What differentiates a collective sense from an individual sense, is that the former is held by a group of people in a given organisation, even though members of the group may not be aware of what they hold in common. The process of 'enculturation' results in these cognitions becoming rooted in the group and ultimately existing independently of the individual group members, who become carriers of the culture (Sackman, 1992).

Organisational identity and culture

Linked to this idea of corporate culture are concepts of organisational identity and image. Organisational identity refers to how members perceive, think, and feel about their organisation (Hatch, 1993). Whilst the marketing literature has tended to focus on the notion of corporate identity, which is a function of both leadership and visual representation, the organisational behaviour literature has been more concerned with the relationship between employees and their organisation. It is assumed within this literature that an organisation's identity is a commonly shared understanding of the values of the firm held by the employees and, similarly, that an image is the way that a particular stakeholder views their organisation (Hatch and Schultz, 1997). Thus, the way employees perceive the organisation influences the projection of an image of that firm to external audiences, including customers. Within this tradition, the views of top management are of less importance than those of the workforce, at all hierarchical levels, in determining the interdependent culture, identity and image. As the boundaries between internal and external aspects of organisations are eroded, then the employees' view of the organisation becomes paramount. As Hatch and Schultz (1997) point out, it is less and less possible for organisations to separate their internal and external functionings. The days when a limited number of departments, or even individuals, handled external affairs have been replaced with a realisation that in order to deliver customer service all employees need to understand their customers and become 'customer-conscious'. In this scenario, internal marketing, with its focus on employees' awareness of their role and how that role fits into the overall functioning of the organisation, becomes crucial.

The importance of internal marketing can be most easily recognised in times of organisational change. As culture is dependent on the attitudes, values, and beliefs of individuals within the organisation then if people do not change their view, there is no organisational change (Schneider *et al.*, 1996). Although culture is deeply rooted and not directly manipulable, by changing the attitudes and assumptions of the workforce, cultural change will ensue. The question addressed by internal marketing scholars is how to bring about this change. Many organisations do at least pay lip service to customer and employee care programmes, yet suitable tactical tools to deliver results are less well defined. One such set of tools is provided by the Investors in People (IIP) initiative which brings together both of these objectives and provides a framework for implementation.

Employees and IIP

The study reported here is specifically aimed at establishing employees' perceptions of, and responses to, IIP as an internal marketing initiative. The research reported concentrates on one organisation, considering employee perceptions of the organisation at the outset of the IIP initiative (Year 1) and after the first year of implementation (Year 2). The remainder of this discussion has four aims: firstly, to establish employee attitudes towards the organisation at the inception of the IIP programme and twelve months later; secondly, to consider how employee awareness of the business goals and targets of their organisation has changed over this time period; thirdly, to consider changes in employee views of the organisation in which they work and the subsequent effect of these changes on organisational culture; and finally, to draw some conclusions regarding the benefits of IIP as an internal marketing approach and implications for developing a marketing orientation.

The case study firm

The organisation participating in this study was a medium-sized, family owned, manufacturing firm operating in a declining smokestack industry. Originally started as an iron foundry, the business has grown over three successive genera- tions and currently employs 300 people. Diversification into related industries has brought restructuring and the firm now operates as three distinctive sections within the overall company framework. It has been noted that growth-oriented firms of this size are likely to be more amenable to 'formal' labour practices in the sphere of training and communication (Atkinson and Meager, 1994). Moreover, the management team appeared to express a genuine interest in 'progressive' approaches to people-management and achieving a market orienta- tion; hence, the interest in IIP. All employees in the organisation were surveyed in two successive years, once soon after the start of the scheme and again after the IIP programme had been running for a year.

In the first year of this study (1997) the employee profile suggested a mature, stable workforce: 48 per cent had served with the company for longer than five years and 26 per cent had been employed for longer than ten years. Nearly a third of employees (30 per cent) were aged over 50, compared with 15 per cent between the ages of 16–25. By the second year (1998) this profile had altered slightly. The number of long-serving employees had been reduced by retirement while new, younger, recruits to the firm reduced the employee age profile. As a result, by Year 2, 30 per cent of employees were in the 16–25 age range and only 25 per cent were in the over-50 bracket. Overall, however, it remained a predominantly stable workforce, with 46 per cent having been employed by the organisation for over five years.

Given the subjective and exploratory nature of the topic, at the outset a series of exploratory focus groups and interviews with manual and managerial employees were held to attempt to establish how the various members of the organisation viewed the important features that influence the prevailing culture. Focusing on these issues enabled the development of a questionnaire which was administered to all company employees including the management team. In the following sections, the results of both qualitative and quantitative phases of the research are presented together, giving an overview of the success of IIP in creating a marketing-orientated organisation.

Employee views on company values

Based on the qualitative phase of the research, eight statements were formulated each illustrating one of the principles espoused in the 'guiding principles' of the organisation, a document which summarised the management's view of the prevailing culture. These included employee-centred statements such as 'The company values and trusts its employees', 'My contribution makes a difference to the company's success' and 'The company encourages employees to make their own decisions', and customer-focused statements such as 'The company always seeks to improve customer service'. Using Likert scales (where 5 = definitely agree and 1= definitely not agree), employees were asked to indicate the extent to which they agreed with the statements (Table 7.1). All of the principles achieved a mean score of 3 and above in both years, indicating broad endorsement of the guiding principles of the organisation by employees. The statements that gained the strongest endorsement were those in which the employee was asked to express a personal opinion. Lower mean scores were received for statements in which employees merely affirmed a company commitment. After the introduction of IIP, although the mean scores were largely similar, employees were more convinced of the importance of customer-focused statements and importance of the firm's consumer orientation, but rather less convinced that their own contribution made a difference to the company's success.

The importance of action in the communication of the prevailing company values was demonstrated by comparing the perceptions of those employees who had been through the process of training and appraisal and those who had yet to undergo this process (Table 7.2). Respondents who had received training in the previous year were significantly more likely to agree with the principles of training, appraisal, improving customer service, individual responsibility and recognising employee worth.

Table 7.1 Employee perceptions of company principles: mean scores

Statement of Company Principles *1=strongly disagree, 5=strongly agree*	*Year 1* *N=236* *Mean score*	*Year 2* *N=225* *Mean score*
Team working improves efficiency and effectiveness	4.6	4.5
My contribution makes a difference to the company's success	4.4	4.2
It is important that each employee is appraised every year	4.3	4.4
The company always seeks to improve customer service	4.2	4.1
It is important that each employee visits at least one customer every year	3.7	4.2
The company is committed to training	3.3	3.4
The company values and trusts its employees	3.1	3.1
The company encourages employees to make their own decisions	3.0	3.4

Table 7.2 Employee perceptions of company principles, year 1 (trained vs untrained employees): Mann-Whitney U Test results

Statements of Company Principles	n =	Mean of n	St.D	Mann-Whitney	Sig.
My contribution makes a difference to the company's success	233	4.44	0.89	5779.5	.178
It is important that each employee is appraised every year	236	4.29	1.04	4450.0	.000
The company always seeks to improve customer service	236	4.17	0.97	4910.0	.001
It is important that each employee visits at least one customer every year	234	3.67	1.31	5973.5	.380
The company is committed to training	235	3.31	1.28	3371.5	.000
The company values and trusts its employees	235	3.14	1.20	3946.5	.000
The company encourages employees to make their own decisions	233	3.04	1.27	5291.0	.025

Employee awareness of business goals and company performance

The prevailing management view suggested a strong belief that the organisation is committed to engaging in dialogue with employees on the vision of where the organisation is going and the contribution employees will make to its success. To achieve this, weekly meetings are held at which employees are briefed on the performance of their own business unit. Progress is communicated using five different criteria: profitability; order book; rework; absenteeism; and delivery. Knowledge of how their section was performing on these criteria was tested using dichotomous (yes/no) measures. There were very high levels of self-reported knowledge in both of the research years, ranging from 94 per cent of employees who stated that they were aware of the profitability of their particular section, to 84 per cent stating that they were aware of the order book position. No attempt was made to determine the veracity of this knowledge as the aim was to determine the employees' perception rather than fact. It is clear, however, that even before the implementation of IIP, employees believed themselves to be well informed about the working of the organisation and the profitability of the company for which they worked. Although this reported knowledge did increase after the implementation of IIP, this was not statistically significant. On this criterion, therefore, it was not possible to establish whether or not the internal marketing programme had the desired effect of increasing employee awareness and commitment.

It was believed by the company's managers that employee awareness of business progress across the five different criteria would be transferred into an understanding of the organisation's overall performance. When probed about this, however, responses varied greatly revealing a surprising disparity of understanding. At the outset, 12 per cent of the workforce stated that they did not know how the organisation's overall performance compared to the previous year, 54 per cent believed it had either deteriorated or stayed the same, and only 34 per cent believed it had improved. By Year 2, the percentage of employees who did not know how the organisation was performing overall was similar at 13 per cent, but the portion of employees believing it had improved were in a majority of 53 per cent with a consequent decrease in those who thought it had either deteriorated or stayed the same. This suggests that some of the workforce were more optimistic about the company's performance than previously. There remained, however, a surprising disparity of views suggesting that the message was either not reaching large sections of the workforce or was not believed by them.

Knowledge of factors which determine company success

Management defined the company's broad mission as providing 'outstanding customer service through a commitment to total quality'. They believed that effective communication of the business plan should convince employees that key factors in determining the company's future success are 'outstanding customer service' and 'commitment to total quality'. Presented with a range of six different factors, of which they were asked to select the three most important, not all employees selected these two critical factors in year 1. Although 60 per cent selected 'outstanding customer service', only 42 per cent selected the total quality factor. After the introduction of IIP this increased to almost 70 per cent agreeing that customer service was vital, and 64 per cent selected commitment to quality. However, 'investment in plant and machinery' was viewed by employees as more important than 'total quality' in determining success. At the start of the IIP programme, 'better quotation pricing' was chosen as a key factor by more than half of the employees but this fell to only 18 per cent in Year 2. This suggests an increased confidence in the management of the company and a shift in emphasis to customer service, rather than pricing, as the basis of competition.

These results appear to indicate a strengthening confidence in the company's management and an acceptance of the principles of the IIP programme as beneficial to the running of the organisation. The results demonstrate that the aims of the IIP initiative and its connection to organisational success had been effectively communicated to employees. Taken on its own, however, this does not necessarily indicate that the IIP initiative had influenced the prevailing corporate culture.

Employee views on the organisational culture

Twenty descriptors were generated during the qualitative phase of the study and from the organisation's own statements about itself. These included employee-focused descriptors such as 'caring', 'appreciative', 'fun' and organisation-focused descriptors such as 'customer-focused', 'cost-conscious', 'traditional' and 'cautious'.

From this list, employees were asked to select the five that, in their opinion, best described the predominant culture of the organisation. At the start of the IIP programme, the two most frequently cited descriptors were 'quality-conscious' (73 per cent) and 'cost-conscious' (70 per cent). As the programme progressed, however, 'ambitious' and 'customer-focused' had overtaken 'cost-conscious' as key descriptors, indicating an interesting change of perception of organisational culture (Table 7.3). Similarly, at the start nearly 27 per cent thought the company was 'secretive' and 22 per cent 'traditional'. This fell to only 19 per cent believing it to be 'secretive' and 14 per cent 'traditional'. At the same time, whereas only 10 per cent of employees viewed the company as 'employee-focused' at the outset, this rose to 17 per cent. This marks a clear shift away from the view of the company as old-fashioned, cost-driven and uncommunicative, to a more open, employee-focused, operation. However, it still indicates that a majority of the workforce are not convinced that the company is employee-focused, despite the internal marketing efforts of IIP. The five most frequently cited descriptors could be interpreted as factors deemed important to the company's growth ambitions. Conversely, the five least cited descriptors could be interpreted as factors that relate to the employees' sense of enjoyment within, and loyalty to, the firm. This is an interesting finding in the light of the IIP objectives that place emphasis on the role of the individual and their worth in the organisation. Taken with the result in the previous section that found that employees were less likely to rate their own contribution to the company's success in Year 2, compared with the outset, this suggests that although the culture is improving, employees still do not find that the prevailing culture values their own contribution or provides an enjoyable working environment.

The final part of the analysis was to examine differences in opinion between management, who are responsible for the IIP initiative and are attempting to drive corporate change, and the majority of the workforce who are manual shop-floor workers. Overall, there was a strong convergence in the descriptors selected by management and those selected by employees. Across the two groups, the only statistically significant difference to emerge across all of the descriptors was that management were less likely than manual workers to believe that the company was cost-conscious. This is an interesting finding as it was assumed that management would be more likely than manual workers to find, for example, that the organisation is open or trusting. In the event, 56 per cent of manual workers felt the organisation was open compared to 34 per cent of the managers, and 4 per cent of workers said it was trusting compared to 2 per cent of managers, but neither of these differences were significant at the 95 per cent level.

Conclusion

An assessment has been made of the impact of a particular internal marketing initiative on the employees of one organisation as a means of examining participating employee responses.

Despite the exploratory nature of this research, several valuable conclusions

Table 7.3 Company descriptors selected by employees

Company Descriptor	Year 1 n=236	%	Year 2 n=224	%
Quality-conscious	172	72.9	154	68.8
Cost-conscious	166	70.3	119	53.1
Ambitious	131	55.5	147	65.6
Customer-focused	120	50.8	133	59.4
Improving	93	39.4	94	42.0
Cautious	70	29.7	37	16.5
Secretive	63	26.9	42	18.8
Traditional	51	21.6	31	13.8
Successful	48	20.3	79	35.3
Responsible	44	18.6	32	14.3
Short termist	42	17.8	21	9.4
Flexible	41	17.4	49	21.9
Open	31	13.1	31	13.9
Employee-focused	23	9.7	39	17.4
Innovative	15	6.4	15	6.7
Appreciative	12	5.1	13	5.8
Caring	12	5.1	7	3.1
Creative	9	3.8	12	5.4
Trusting	9	3.8	9	4.0
Fun	3	1.3	7	3.1

can be drawn in relation not only to the operation of IIP as an internal marketing initiative within one particular organisation but, by extension, internal marketing's role in influencing employee perceptions of their organisation.

Within this particular organisation, the results of the survey demonstrate that IIP can be used to some effect in creating new, as well as reinforcing existing, organisational messages. This was demonstrated by the relatively high numbers of employees, especially in manual positions, who were confident in their knowledge of the organisation's performance criteria, values and critical success factors. It is clear, however, that despite the strong organisational emphasis on training and personal appraisal, both of which are fundamental to IIP, certain messages appear to be best shared by organisational action, rather than rhetoric. A strong linkage was found to exist between employees who, in Year 1, recognised 'outstanding customer service' as a factor critical to the company's success and those who had actually undertaken a recent customer visit. Similarly, the increased recognition of customer service as a factor critical to the company's success between Year 1 and Year 2, could be attributed to the intensive programme of customer visits by all employees which is linked to the IIP initiative.

Nevertheless, evidence of the limitations of communication effectiveness within this organisation could be seen in the employees' inability to convert individual measures of performance criteria into a composite whole. While IIP demands the dissemination of organisational performance and progress to all employees, few were able to extend the individual components of performance into a coherent and correct overall appraisal.

The role of internal marketing in communicating messages among employees was apparent in employee perceptions of company values. Between the baseline survey in Year 1, immediately prior to the implementation of the IIP programme, and the follow up survey in Year 2, significant changes were apparent in the values employees associated with the company. Employees believed the company to be more open and less cautious and secretive, but this did not translate into a belief in an employee-focused organisation. In fact, although the percentages believing that the organisation was employee-focused rose, a substantial majority of employees still did not believe that the organisation was indeed employee-focused, trusted its employees, or was appreciative of their efforts. Employees did, however, perceive an improvement in the customer-focus of the organisation, a key element in achieving a marketing orientation. The evidence that employees still gave low rankings to descriptors which related to their role within the organisation and their sense of loyalty and worth, even following the successful implementation of IIP, suggests that organisational culture is resistant to short-term measures and can only be changed by a long-term commitment from the organisation itself.

Overall, this research demonstrates that internal marketing affects both how the individual interprets their role within the organisation and how these roles relate to the wider operation of the organisation with its environment. This is important given the paucity of empirical work in this area (Ballantyne, 1997, is a notable contribution) and the emphasis in the marketing orientation literature of organisations adopting a customer focus. In terms of Grönroos's (1981) distinction between strategic and tactical approaches, IIP not only provides a strategic framework for the application of internal marketing techniques, but also offers organisations the tactics for implementation. However, like any initiative designed to alter the culture of an organisation, it cannot succeed in isolation. Successful implementation of change in organisational culture requires a portfolio of linked communication activities. Culture, as Osborne (1996) notes, is a reflection of the organisation's strategic values. By communicating key success factors among employees, internal marketing offers a forum for purposive interactions as a catalyst for change within the organisation's culture, but it is the medium not the message. If the core values of the organisation remain incompatible with a marketing orientation then internal marketing programmes will fail.

References

Alberga, T., Tyson, S. and Parsons, D. (1997) 'An Evaluation of the Investors in People Standard', *Human Resource Management Journal* 7(2): 47–60.

Atkinson, J. and Meager, N. (1994) 'Running to Stand Still: the Small Firm in the Labour Market', in Atkinson, J. and Storey, D. (eds), *Employment, the Small Firm and the Labour Market*, London: Routledge.

Ballantyne, D. (1997) 'Internal Networks for Internal Marketing', *Journal of Marketing Management* 13: 343–66.

Curran, J. (1991) 'Employment and Employment Relations in the Small Enterprise', in Stanworth, J. and Gray, C. (eds), *Bolton 20 Years On: The Small Firm in the 1990s*, London: Paul Chapman Publishing.

Curran, J., Blackburn, R., Kitching, J. and North, J. (1997) 'Small Firms and Workforce Training: Some Results, Analysis and Policy Implications from a National Survey', in Ram, M., Deakins, D. and Smallbone, D. (eds), *Small Firms: Enterprising Futures*, London: Paul Chapman Publishing.

Deming, W. (1982) *Quality, Productivity and Competitive Position*, Boston: MIT Press.

Deshpande, R. and Webster, F.E. (1989) 'Organizational culture and marketing: defining the research agenda', *Journal of Marketing* 53(1): 3–16.

Deshpande, R., Farley, J.U. and Webster, F.E. (1993) 'Corporate Culture, Customer Orientation, and Innovativeness in Japanese Firms: A Quadrad Analysis', *Journal of Marketing* 57(1): 23–38.

Down, S. and Smith, D. (1998) 'It Pays to be Nice to People – Investors in People: The Search For Measurable Benefits', *Personnel Review* 27(2): 143–55.

Geary, J.F. (1995) 'Work Practices: The Structure of Work', in Edwards, P. (ed.), *Industrial Relations in Britain*, Oxford: Blackwell.

Ghobadian, A. and Gallear, D.N. (1996) 'Total Quality Management in SMEs', *Omega* 24(1): 83–106.

Gibb, A. (1997) 'Policy Research and Small Business: From Know What to Know How?' in Ram, M., Deakins, D. and Smallbone, D. (eds), *Small Firms: Enterprising Futures*, London: Paul Chapman Publishing.

Grönroos, C. (1981) 'Internal Marketing: Theory and Practice', *AMA Services Marketing Conference Proceedings*, Chicago: AMA, 236–8.

——— (1990) *Services Marketing and Management: Managing the Moments of Truth in Service Competition*, Lexington, MA: Macmillan.

Gummesson, E. (1987) 'Using Internal Marketing to Develop a New Culture: The Case of Ericsson Quality', *Journal of Business and Industrial Marketing* 2(3): 23–8.

Harris, L. (1998) 'Cultural Domination: The Key to Market-orientated Culture?', *European Journal of Marketing* 32(3–4): 354–73.

Hatch, M.J. and Schultz, M. (1997) 'Relations Between Organisational Culture, Identity and Image, *European Journal of Marketing* 31(5–6): 356–65.

Hendry, C. and Pettigrew, A. (1992) 'Patterns of Strategic Change in the Development of Human Resource Management', *British Journal of Management* 24(5): 137–56.

Hendry, C., Arthur, M.B. and Jones, A.M. (1995) *Strategy Through People: Adaptation and Learning in the Small–Medium Enterprise*, London: Routledge.

Hofstede, G. (1980) *Culture's Consequences: International Differences in Work Related Values*, Beverley Hills, CA: Sage Publications.

Jaworski, B. and Kohli, A. (1993) 'Market Orientation: Antecedents and Consequences', *Journal of Marketing* 57(July): 53–70.

Kerfoot, D. and Knights, D. (1995) 'Empowering the "Quality Worker"?: The Seduction and Contradiction of The Total Quality Phenomenon', in Wilkinson, A. and Willmott, H. (eds), *Making Quality Critical: New Perspectives on Organisational Change*, London: Routledge.

Kohli, A. and Jaworski, B. (1990) 'Marketing Orientation: The Construct, Research Propositions and Managerial Implications', *Journal of Marketing* 54(April): 1–18.

Kroeber, A.L. and Kluckholm, C.K. (1952) *Culture: A Critical Review of Concepts and Definitions*, Harvard University Peabody Papers, No. 47, Cambridge, MA: Harvard University.

Legge, K. (1988) 'Personnel Management in Recession and Recovery: A Comparative Analysis of What the Surveys Say', *Personnel Review* 17(2) (monograph issue).

McArdle, L., Rowlinson, M., Proctor, S., Hassard, J. and Forrester, P. (1995) 'Total Quality Management and Participation', in Wilkinson, A. and Willmott, H. (eds), *Making Quality Critical: New Perspectives on Organisational Change*, London: Routledge.

Narver, J. and Slater, S. (1990) 'The Effect of a Market Orientation on Business Profitability', *Journal of Marketing* 54(October): 20–35.

Osborne, R. (1996) 'Strategic Values: The Corporate Performance Engine', *Business Horizons* 39(September–October): 41–8.

Piercy, N. and Morgan, N. (1991) 'Internal Marketing: The Missing Half of the Marketing Programme', *Long Range Planning* 24(2): 82–93.

Ram, M. (2000) 'Investors in People in Small Firms: Case Study Evidence from the Business Services Sector', *Personnel Review*, forthcoming.

Rix, A., Parkinson, R. and Gaunt, R. (1994) *Investors in People: A Qualitative Study of Employers*, No. 21, Research Series, London: Department of Employment.

Roberts, K. and Corcoran-Nantes, Y. (1995) 'TQM, The New Training and Industrial Relations', in Wilkinson, A. and Willmott, H. (eds), *Making Quality Critical: New Perspectives on Organisational Change*, London: Routledge.

Sackman, S. (1992) 'Culture and Subcultures: An Analysis of Organisational Knowledge', *Administrative Science Quarterly* 37: 140–62.

Sapienza, A. (1985) 'Believing is Seeing: How Organisational Culture Influences the Decisions Top Managers Make', in Kilmann, R., Saxon, M. and Serpa, R. (eds), *Gaining Control of Corporate Culture*, San Francisco, CA: Jossey-Bass.

Sathe, V. (1983) 'Some Action Implications of Corporate Culture', *Organizational Dynamics*, Autumn: 5–23.

Scase, R. (1995) 'Employment Relations in Small Firms', in Edwards, P. (ed.), *Industrial Relations in Britain*, Oxford: Blackwell.

Schneider, B., Brief, A.P. and Guzzo, R.A. (1996) 'Creating a Climate for Sustainable Organisational Change', *Organizational Dynamics* 24(4): 6–20.

Scott, A. (1994) *Willing Slaves? Workers under Human Resource Management*, Cambridge: Cambridge University Press.

Scott, M. (1986) 'The Dangers of Assuming Homogeneity in Small Business Research', in Rosa, P. (ed.), *The Role and Contribution of Small Business Research*, Aldershot: Avebury Press.

Seiler, T.B. (1973) *Cognitive Structuring Theories, Analysis and Results*, Stuttgart, Germany: Kohlhammer.

Smircich, L. (1983) 'Concepts of Culture and Organisational Analysis', *Administrative Science Quarterly* 28: 339–58.

Storey, D. and Westhead, P. (1997) 'Management Training in Small Firms: A Case of Market Failure?', *Human Resource Management Journal* 7(2): 47–60.

Tansuhaj, P., Randall, D. and McCullough, J. (1991) 'Applying the Internal Marketing Concept Within Large Organisations: As Applied to a Credit Union', *Journal of Professional Services Marketing* 6(2): 193–202.

Varey, R.J. (1995) 'A Model of Internal Marketing for Building and Sustaining a Competitive Service Advantage', *Journal of Marketing Management* 11: 41–54.

Welsh, J. and White, J. (1981) 'A Small Business is Not a Little Big Business', *Harvard Business Review*, July–August: 18–32.

Wilkinson, A. and Willmott, H. (eds) (1995) *Making Quality Critical: New Perspectives on Organisational Change*, London: Routledge.

8 Get close to the internal customer or keep your distance?

Susan K. Foreman

Introduction

Internal marketing has been the subject of much discussion and debate for a number of years. From one perspective it seems quite straightforward and relatively simple to implement and many practical internal marketing plans and campaigns have been developed. Yet there seem to be a number of unanswered questions. This work, which takes a transaction cost perspective, tries to reach the fundamental issues that underpin internal marketing, and explores a number of issues that require further explanation. This means getting to grips with the appropriate economic framework for investigating internal marketing, for understanding the organisation as a marketplace, and for investigating the characteristics of the employer–employee interface. Accordingly, there is one fundamental question: 'is internal marketing relevant in all employer–employee exchanges and in all organisations?'

While there are many different perspectives on internal marketing, this work concentrates on internal marketing in the whole organisation. This chapter begins by examining the foundations of marketing and develops an understanding of the organisation as a market with its own buyers and suppliers. Is it necessary to understand the firm as a market in the same way that marketers consider their traditional external markets? This discussion is based on a transaction cost economics perspective and has been influenced to a great extent by the work of Bowen and Jones (1986), and Jones (1987) who used this approach to examine client relations in the service sector.

A transaction cost economics perspective is concerned with the identification of the sources of transaction costs in the exchange relationship between the employer and the employee. Two sources of transaction costs are identified: performance ambiguity and goal congruence. From this, a model to help understand the nature of the organisation–employee exchange has been developed to describe the way in which employee-related transaction costs become apparent. This can give insight into the nature of the employer–employee interface, to show whether or not internal marketing is necessary and in identifying when internal marketing may be most effective. From this understanding, suggestions for developing and implementing internal marketing can be developed.

The firm as an internal market

Understanding the concept of the firm as a market is a precursor to developing an understanding of marketing inside an organisation (Foreman and Money, 1995). The foundations for considering the firm as a market have not always been laid clearly by many who discuss internal marketing. Many writers work on the basis that microeconomics is an appropriate foundation for their research. More recently, alternative approaches have been considered which include transaction cost approaches.

Kotler and Levy (1969) produced one of the most influential pieces of work on the scope of marketing. They showed that marketing could be expanded to include products, services, people, organisations, ideas and consumers. While their work does not deal directly with internal marketing, it does consider the value of marketing inside the firm, as they place the boundaries of marketing on the 'publics' and note that 'members of the organization recognise that they are all in marketing, whatever else they do' (Kotler and Levy, p.13). An important component of a market is the existence of exchange that goes some way to meeting the criteria established by Kotler (1991). In addition, Flipo (1986, p.8) states that 'the more numerous the people to be persuaded inside the company, the more relevant the term "market" will be'.

Much of the work on internal marketing presupposes that the firm is a marketplace consisting of a heterogeneous group of suppliers, and considers employees as internal customers or employees. Indeed, much of the literature on internal marketing has tended to follow the conventional approach and considers internal marketing from a microeconomic standpoint. Yet, the notion that the science of marketing is based on the microeconomic paradigm in which transactions occur in perfect markets in order to maximise profitability has been questioned, as the appropriate background for marketing theory in general. (Foreman and Money, 1995; Anderson, 1982; Carman, 1980; Day and Wensley, 1983) Indeed, when considering the firm as a market it is necessary to consider whether discrete transactions, rationality, lowest price and profit maximisation reflect the nature of exchanges inside or indeed between firms (Foreman and Money, 1995).

In microeconomics, transactions are discrete, and based upon the lowest price available in a competitive market. These transactions, according to Coase (1937), cannot be isolated and have additional costs, 'the costs of using the price mechanism'. These comprise the price, negotiation, managing contracts and supplier. Microeconomics does not recognise the transaction costs associated with using the system yet microeconomics is the foundation that underpins marketing and, in particular, the management of the marketing mix (McCarthy, 1960) and extended in the services literature by Booms and Bitner (1981). According to Arndt (1983), this is an inappropriate foundation/paradigm in understanding marketing as an exchange. For example 'Pure transactions are rare' and whilst the micro economic approach may be appropriate for discrete transactions, most transactions 'take place in the context of ongoing relationships between marketers and customers' (Webster, 1992. p.5). In response to this debate, Arndt (1983) suggests that the organisational political economy paradigm is the appropriate paradigm to understand exchange. Nevertheless, the organisation of exchanges lays a foundation that goes beyond the micro perspective and includes the management of conflicts within and between organisations.

One of the most important developments in marketing theory has been the concept of marketing as an exchange '…the essence of marketing relates to the structuring and organising of the exchanges between (and within) marketing institutions'. Day and Wensley (1983, p.81) highlight '…the notion of exchange, and the related concepts of exchange rules, transaction costs, information alternatives and power as a general paradigm'. However, the boundaries between the firm and the market are fluid, according to Lusch *et al.* (1992) with internal exchanges competing with exchanges in the external marketplace. They state that it is inappropriate to consider that internal and external exchanges are mutually exclusive; rather they are at opposite ends of a spectrum or continuum: 'there exists an infinite number of points between the two end points, each representing a unique configuration of exchanges or value creation behaviours'.

The employee as customer in the internal market

There is considerable support for the notion that, where transactions and exchanges take place between employees and the organisation, the employees can be considered to be customers of the organisation (Lehtinen and Lehtinen, 1982; Riddle, 1988). Indeed, the concept of the internal customer is well established in the marketing and the organisational behaviour literature. Fisk, Brown and Bitner (1993) identify two main threads of internal marketing: firstly, the idea of the employee as the internal customer and secondly, the organisational need to satisfy the internal customer or employee so that he or she is best prepared to serve the external customer.

The relevance of internal marketing may be influenced by the nature of the particular firm's relationship with its employees, or specific groups of them. There are some fundamental issues facing managers and it is necessary to ask:

- is internal marketing relevant in all organisations?
- are all exchanges with internal customers the same, or do they have different characteristics?
- when and under what conditions should the organisation encourage employee participation in as many activities as possible, treat them as customers and market to them?
- what characteristics of the exchange would support the inclusion and participation of employees in organisational strategy?
- what conditions exist that would discourage managers from involving employees as customers closely in the organisations?
- what would make internal marketing more relevant, useful and effective?

It seems that many organisations (especially in the service sector) interact with employees in a way similar to that in which they transact with external customers. The nature of the interaction rests on a degree of participation by these employees in the management, operations, and delivery of the firm's activities and offerings. However, managers are faced with the dilemma of just how far to allow participation by employees and, indeed, customers (Pitt and Foreman, 1999; Connor, 1992; Cotton *et al.*, 1993; Bruning and Liverpool, 1993; Shetzer, 1993; Stanton, 1993; Sagie and Koslowsky, 1994).

Employee exchanges and participation

The degree of participation between the organisation and the employee is interesting, because both parties can adopt different strategies to influence the nature and the level of involvement. The employees can adopt a number of strategies. They can support the firm by co-operating with it in the implementation of its strategies. Alternatively, employees can be troublesome if they fail to act in accordance with the organisation's policies and procedures. Sometimes, employees identify more with the customers' view (Aldrich and Herker, 1977) and in doing so can neutralise or frustrate the organisation's efforts in meeting goals.

If the employees are a cause of uncertainty in the organisation as they attempt to pursue their own objectives, the organisation can, if it chooses, adopt strategies to manage the level of employee participation it would like to achieve. On one hand the employee can be kept 'at arm's length', by restricting employees' involvement and participation. Here, employees are encouraged to focus on the 'technical core of their jobs' (Pitt and Foreman, 1999; Bowen and Jones, 1986) and are discouraged from 'taking part in organisational decision making, as a means of maximising strategic efficiency' (Pitt and Foreman, 1999). Thus, employees will concentrate on their work because of the financial rewards and, according to Chase and Tansik (1982), management will be more efficient. On the other hand, the organisation could support the employee and encourage participation in its activities. In this way, like the customers of some service organisations, they will be more motivated and understanding of the nature of the firm's business and its problems (Pitt and Foreman, 1999).

Using transaction cost analysis in internal markets

Given this emphasis on transactions and exchanges, it seems appropriate to look at some of the features of transaction cost analysis in order to establish whether or not it could be used to understand the different transactions that exist in the organisation with employees; to ask whether or not it can help to assess the appropriateness of managing relationships with employees as customers; and to decide whether or not to use and implement internal marketing strategies.

Coase (1937) in his seminal work on transaction cost analysis considered the boundary between the firm and the market. He argued that 'firms arise voluntarily because they represent a more efficient method of organising production than the market'. The essential components of his work were focused on 'the composition of the costs of co-ordinating the activities of factors of production within the firm with the costs of bringing about the same result by market transactions or by means of operations undertaken within some other firm' (Coase 1988). These ideas had little influence until the 1970s when Williamson (1975), in particular, used them to explain how firms develop. He suggested that the boundaries of firms are influenced not just by economic factors but also by the nature and efficiency of the structure of the firm. He was interested in all activities that a firm carries out including the costs of managing and controlling the transaction.

While market transactions are carried out under contracts that tend to be formal and explicit, many transactions carried out within an organisation are not subject to the same rigorous contractual arrangement. Inside organisations, some employees have formal contracts but others have vague contracts that do not specify in any detail what they should do and how they should work. Employees operate within accepted rules, patterns and procedures and as custom and practice and the culture dictate. Inevitably, there are costs incurred in implementing and controlling transactions within an organisation and exchanges with and between employees although these costs are often hidden (Pitt and Foreman, 1999).

Some key questions arise when considering exchanges with employees. Would it be appropriate to work closely with the employees and include them within the boundary of the organisation (or hierarchy in the language of transaction cost economics) as much as possible? Or should it attempt to resist employee involvement and rely on a more distant exchange, which has more in common with the market based approach? Within the firm, there may be a number of different relationships and the organisation must decide how to manage various employee groups. It may be necessary to adopt different approaches with different groups. Thus, in transaction cost terms it is necessary to consider the most efficient 'boundary' between the organisation and its employee. Should the organisation involve the employee and integrate them closely into the organisation or should it keep a distance? This depends on the nature and the level of transaction costs present in the exchange environment and, it is, therefore, necessary to outline the possible sources of these costs.

Goal incongruence and performance ambiguity

Jones (1983), and Williamson (1975) have highlighted several sources of transaction costs in the employee–organisation exchange, where 'exchange' includes wage or financial reward in exchange for work effort, and other interactions between employer and employee. The work of Bowen and Jones (1986) and Jones (1987) is particularly important in this area. They condense these transaction costs into two key areas: the nature of the relationship between the parties, and the characteristics of the object of the exchange itself:

Goal incongruence.   Here the employee or the employer has self-interest and is motivated to advance their own interests at the expense of the other because the benefits are greater than co-operation.

Performance ambiguity.   This occurs when any part of the exchange makes it difficult for the employee or the employer to appraise the performance of the other (Alchian and Demsetz, 1972; Ouchi, 1980).

Where these conditions exist there can be an increase in transaction costs, either by making it harder for the parties to agree, or by making agreement very costly (Pitt and Foreman, 1999).

Goal incongruence

The *raisons d'être* for employees and organisations are frequently different and even, incongruous. Klein (1989), in drawing attention to transaction costs or 'controlled losses' inside organisations, stated that these can be incurred when people in organisations act in an opportunistic manner, what Williamson (1975) describes as 'self interest seeking with guile'. This necessitates additional effort when they have to be monitored and controlled and, thus, can be a significant source of transaction costs. In this case, the employer and the employee may have conflicting or just different goals which can only be achieved at the other's expense.

There are a number of conditions in the employer–employee transaction which lead to goal incongruence and opportunistic behaviour. For example, when either the employer or employee possesses more information than the other, and thinks that their own conduct can be beyond reproach, there may be a temptation to deceive the other party.

The level of asset specificity (Kay, 1992; Nooteboom, 1993), that exists in employment exchanges is a key source of transaction costs that can affect the level of goal incongruence. If the employees' skills are available in the market in abundance, the control lies with the employer. Thus, when the power lies disproportionately with the firm, opportunism is likely and goal incongruence may be high. Where the employees' skills are in short supply and in demand, they possess power and may command an employment situation to suit their own specific requirements (Pitt and Foreman, 1999).

When the relationship between the employer and employee is a long-term one there will be a tendency to act honourably to reduce goal incongruence. If employment transactions are infrequent – for example, vacation and holiday jobs, or in a one-off contract – the organisation might be more likely to behave in an opportunistic fashion. Firms that give attention to the development of long-term relationships will enjoy the benefits of employee commitment, while employees gain rewards from staying with one organisation, as this reduces their information search costs and increases their long-term security (MacNeil, 1974). Goal congruence will occur where employers and employees work towards the same objectives, and where these parties perceive there to be greater advantages to be gained from co-operation.

Performance ambiguity

If performance ambiguity is often caused by an inability to measure the performance of employees, or even if performance can be measured, it may be difficult to accurately gauge its value. Where it exists in the employer–employee exchange, costs are incurred in negotiating, managing, and enforcing agreements between the organisation and its employees. Employment arrangements are complex, intangible, and 'perishable' exchanges and this means that valuation by either party is only possible over the long term.

There are a number of sources of ambiguity in the employment exchange: (1) in many employment relationships, the employee is embarking essentially on employment under a promise that present and future conditions of employment will be provided satisfactorily; (2) there is greater perceived risk in an employment transaction than in the case of most product or service purchases as failure has serious repercussions; and (3) the employing organisation and the employee will often have different information about the inputs (time or resources) necessary to produce the employment exchange, or different abilities to evaluate these inputs (Pitt and Foreman, 1999).

One option for employees is to develop long-term relationships with a trusted employer in order to reduce these costs. Nevertheless, performance ambiguity is a principal source of transaction costs. As the employment, role, or job becomes more complex, performance ambiguity increases.

Governance mechanisms and employer–employee transactions

A transaction cost approach can be used to help understand the form and nature of the approach or, in transaction cost terms, 'the governance mechanism' that will maximise the efficiency of exchange between organisation and employee. Specifically, the level and nature of goal congruency and performance ambiguity influence how organisations can manage marketing to employees as customers. Using these dimensions, which are based on the typology of service organisation exchanges developed by Bowen and Jones (1986) and Jones (1987, 1990), organisations can identify which internal customers can participate closely alongside the organisation and which internal customers must be kept at a distance. The model outlined below helps to identify these groups in the organisation and indicates whether or not internal marketing is relevant. In other cases it is clear that, given the nature of incongruence and performance ambiguity, internal marketing is necessary, for some it is nice to have but in some cases internal marketing may not be relevant and in extreme cases it could be illegitimate. What is clear is that internal marketing strategies can and should be targeted to different customer groups.

The two dimensions of performance ambiguity and goal incongruence are used to highlight four levels of transactions costs and following Bowen and Jones (1986) and Jones (1990) reveals four governance mechanisms, within each quadrant, which are based on either the market or the firm (see Figure 8.1).

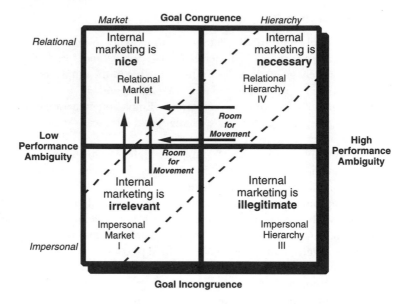

Figure 8.1 Performance ambiguity and goal congruence and internal marketing

Sources: Foreman (1995); Pitt and Foreman (1999)

Performance ambiguity, goal congruence and internal marketing

Where internal marketing is irrelevant

In the impersonal market (I) (Figure 8.1), there is low performance ambiguity and goal incongruence: internal marketing is irrelevant. The nature of employment in this quadrant is routine. There are job specifications, published pay scales and standardised job advertisements, which are widely available and comparable with other similar companies. Therefore, the employees have little difficulty in understanding and evaluating the quality, merit and value of their job. These circumstances exist for the employers and employees and any assessment of the potential of the employment situation is relatively easy for both parties. The goal incongruence in this situation means that employers and employees will tend to act in their own interests, or opportunistically (Williamson, 1975).

In these circumstances, the organisation will tend to concentrate on reducing employee involvement in order to minimise the transaction costs involved in employee participation. This is also in the employees' interests, as they can shop around easily for alternative employment because job information would be readily available at low cost. Here, loyalty only exists because of the financial reward and not because of goal congruence. Typical examples of this type of employment situation would be certain routine full-time and casual appointments in supermarkets, such as cashiers and shelf stackers; pickers and packers in mail order warehouses; or standardised, piecework sewing in mass produced garment manufacture (Pitt and Foreman, 1999). There would be little need for any advanced type of internal marketing because both parties tend to be familiar with the employment market and have a good and clear understanding of rates of pay and conditions entailed. Thus, in the impersonal market organisations would practise very little internal marketing.

Where internal marketing is nice

In the case of the relational market (II), there is also low performance ambiguity but in this case there is goal congruence, which means that this quadrant has the lowest level of transaction costs. Here, the organisation can rely to a large extent on personal relationships and procedures when working with employees. These relationships are useful because goal congruence means that employers and employees will both gain from the trust in the transactions. Employees feel empathy for the organisation's goals and, thus, their rewards come from job satisfaction, higher wages, and additional, sometimes intangible, benefits.

The organisation can also benefit from the goal congruence and low performance ambiguity because the employees are less likely to search for other employment if they perceive that their current role and organisational ties are valuable. Here, both parties sacrifice a degree of independence in order to obtain longer-term security (Pitt and Foreman, 1999). In this quadrant, internal marketing is 'nice', as it enhances the feeling of well-being the employee experiences in his/her employment situation. However, it should be seen that it is not imperative, as the employee already exhibits a high level of commitment to the organisation and the work it does. Common examples of this situation would be people who are employed by charities, certain types of hospitals, hospices and in the teaching profession.

Where internal marketing is illegitimate

Transaction costs are highest in the impersonal hierarchy (III), with both goal incongruence and high performance ambiguity. Employee participation is inappropriate as goal congruence and its benefits do not exist. Employment of this kind is rare as employers cannot normally coerce employees into accepting hierarchical arrangements. It will only happen when the employer can exact compliance in some way, for example military service and conscription.

Negotiation with employees merely increases transaction costs, and is unnecessary as the employer could use their power to force compliance on the employee. Rules are prevalent as they minimise transaction costs. There is limited if no real occurrence of these types of employment phenomena in various parts of the world. In most Western and developed economies today, this kind of employment would be regarded as 'illegitimate' (Pitt and Foreman, 1999). Obviously, internal marketing would not be necessary as the organisation has found a coercive way in which to make employees transact.

Where internal marketing is necessary

The nature of the employer–employee exchange in the relational hierarchy (IV) is complex. Performance ambiguity and goal congruence are high and both employer and employee may share mutual goals.

Initially, the firm can encourage involvement in its activities. Employees will be proactive and the organisation will benefit from their participation. Here, the organisation can cultivate long-term relationships where both employer and employee can manage the performance ambiguity which exists in the job. Employees at all levels may be invited to participate in the formulation of strategy, and to engage in policy formulation at the very highest levels (Pitt and Foreman, 1999).

Participation provides the employee with the opportunity to assess whether or not the quality of their work and the employer matches their expectations. This may help to moderate or reduce performance ambiguity. The employee can also assess over time whether or not the organisation intends to act in their best interests and establish whether goal congruence exists. In this situation, internal marketing is more than nice; it is necessary. It is a mechanism for assessing the attitudes, opinions and feelings of employees; a tool for communicating with employees on aspects of strategy formulation and implementation; and a device for providing feedback to them on the progress reached by the firm and its members towards their mutual (congruent) goals. Examples of this kind of employment situation would include hospitality industries, financial and professional services, and consulting firms (Pitt and Foreman, 1999).

As ever, there is often an alternate viewpoint to consider and Rafiq and Ahmed (1992) ask whether or not internal marketing is appropriate when there could be an element of coercion in the exchange. The internal 'product' may be unwanted, yet employees may feel compelled as a customer by the contractual nature of the employment. This has had some support over the years as Kotler and Levy (1969) stated that marketing exchanges should consist of 'non-coercive' activities.

Assessing internal marketing, levels of performance ambiguity and goal incongruence

When considering internal marketing from a transaction cost perspective, it highlights a number of alternative approaches. It suggests that the nature of the employment situation in terms of transaction costs will determine whether or not internal marketing is irrelevant, illegitimate, nice or necessary. It is, therefore, now worth considering how to develop internal marketing strategies. One way to begin is to consider the employees by finding out about levels of goal incongruence, performance ambiguity and their perceptions of the nature of internal marketing inside their organisation.

Internal marketing

The extent and nature of internal marketing practice, where internal marketing is focused on the whole of the organisation rather than a departmental approach, could be established by asking the employees' agreement with the following statements:

- Our organisation offers employees a vision that they can believe in.
- We communicate our organisation's vision well to employees.
- We prepare our employees to perform well.
- Our organisation views the development of knowledge and skills in employees as an investment rather than a cost.
- Skill and knowledge development of employees happens as an ongoing process in our organisation.
- We teach our employees 'why they should do things' and not just 'how they should do things'.
- In our organisation we go beyond training and educate employees as well.
- Our performance measurement and reward systems encourage employees to work together.
- We measure and reward employee performance that contributes most to our organisation's vision.
- We use the data that we gather from employees to improve their jobs, and to develop the strategy of the organisation.
- Our organisation communicates to employees the importance of their service roles.
- In our organisation, those employees who provide excellent service are rewarded for their efforts.
- In this organisation, the employees are properly trained to perform their service roles.
- This organisation has the flexibility to accommodate the differing needs of employees.
- We place considerable emphasis in this organisation on communicating with our employees.

(Foreman and Money, 1995).

Goal incongruence

The degree of goal incongruence present in the employment relationship can be established by asking whether or not:

- The performance goals of our employees are concise and are not ambiguous.
- It would be inexpensive for this organisation to monitor whether or not employees are pursuing their own goals at the expense of the organisation's goals.
- The goals of this organisation and the personal goals of its employees overlap to a considerable extent.

- Our employees fully understand the goals of this organisation.
- Our employees fully support the goals of this organisation.

(Foreman, 1995)

Performance ambiguity

Similarly, the extent of performance ambiguity faced in the employment transaction may be assessed by asking whether or not:

- Our organisation has a good understanding of what the performance of employees is worth.
- Most of the jobs done by employees in this organisation are relatively straightforward.
- It is easy for employees such as those who work in this organisation to know what the job they do is worth in financial terms.
- This organisation routinely monitors the availability of potential employees.

(Foreman, 1995).

There are practical steps that managers can take and include in the internal marketing strategies. In managing goal incongruence, a supermarket might gain competitive points by emphasising that contact level jobs are not routine or menial, but important ways of enhancing the service delivery to external customers. Performance ambiguity could be decreased by applying many of the tools commonly used by services marketers. The employment exchange, like services, tends to be intangible, and the firm could reduce performance ambiguity by attempts to make the employment situation simpler. They could introduce clear contracts; lucid job descriptions in order to cover as many eventualities as possible; comprehensible performance measures and targets; and reward systems which are equitable and easily understood. Indeed, as situations change and turbulent environments raise or reduce the level of transaction costs, some organisations might see advantages in shifting between quadrants as a means of managing cost but also maximising the employees' potential and in enhancing the service of the external customer. This model does not need to be static, and in Figure 8.1 the dashed lines indicate that given the position of employees in the quadrant there may be 'room for movement' and internal marketing may be used to manage the level and nature of performance ambiguity. Indeed, it may be important, strategically, to consider movement between the quadrants.

Conclusion

It is evident that application of a transaction costs approach offers a different way of thinking not only about the external customer exchange, but also about the employer–employee relationship. A 'macro' approach to internal marketing is not necessarily the best approach; the levels of performance ambiguity and goal congruence may influence the organisation's understanding of the employee as a customer and impact on the internal marketing approach. Furthermore, if the costs which are incurred in developing and implementing internal marketing strategies and programmes can be adequately recovered during the external customer exchange, then internal marketing would be more likely to become integrated in overall marketing and corporate strategy.

Note

This work is a synthesis of research undertaken by Susan K. Foreman with Arthur H. Money and Leyland Pitt at Henley Management College and published in Foreman (1995), Foreman and Money (1995), and Pitt and Foreman (1999).

References

Alchian, A.A. and Demsetz, H. (1972) 'Production, Information Costs, and Economic Organization, *American Economic Review* 62: 777–95.

Aldrich, H. and Herker, D. (1977) 'Boundary Spanning Roles and Organizational Structure', *Academy of Management Review* 2: 217–30.

Anderson, P.F. (1982) 'Marketing, Strategic Planning and the Theory of the Firm', *Journal of Marketing* 46(Spring): 16–26.

Arndt, J. (1983) 'The Political Economy Paradigm: Foundation for Theory Building in Marketing', *Journal of Marketing* 47(Fall): 44–54.

Booms, B.H. and Bitner, M.J. (1981) 'Marketing Strategies and Organisation Structures for Service Firms', in Donnelly, J. and George, W.R. (eds), *Marketing of Services*, Chicago: American Marketing Association.

Bowen, D.E. and Jones, G.R. (1986) 'Transaction Cost Analysis of Service Organization–Customer Exchange', *Academy of Management Review* 11(2): 428–41.

Bruning, N.S. and Liverpool, P.R. (1993) 'Membership in Quality Circles and Participation in Decision Making', *Journal of Applied Behavioral Science* 29(1): 76–95.

Carman, J.M. (1980) 'Paradigms for Marketing: The Theory', in Sheth, J.M. (ed.), *Research in Marketing*, vol. 3, Greenwich, CT: JAI Press, 1–36.

Chase, R.B. and Tansik, D.A. (1982) 'The Customer Contact Model for Organization Design', *Management Science* 29(9): 1037–50.

Coase, R.H. (1937) 'The Nature of the Firm', *Economica* 4: 386–405.

—— (1988) 'The Nature of the Firm: Origin, Meaning, Influence', *Journal of Law Economics and Organisation* 4: 3–47.

Connor, P.E. (1992) 'Decision-Making Participation Patterns: The Role of Organizational Context', *Academy of Management Journal* 35(1): 218–31.

Cotton, J.L., McFarlin, D.B. and Sweeney, P.D. (1993) 'A Cross-National Comparison of Employee Participation', *Journal of Managerial Psychology* 8(1): 10–19.

Day, G.S. and Wensley, R. (1983) 'Marketing Theory: A Strategic Orientation', *Journal of Marketing* 47(Fall): 79–89.

Fisk, R.P., Brown, S.W. and Bitner, M.J. (1993) 'Tracking the Evolution of the Services Marketing Literature', *Journal of Retailing* 69(1): 61–103.

Foreman, S.K. (1995) 'Internal Marketing: A Transaction Cost Perspective', unpublished Ph.D. thesis, Henley Management College/Brunel University.

Foreman, S.K. and Money, A.H. (1995) 'Internal Marketing Concepts, Measurement and Application', *Journal of Marketing Management* 11: 755–68.

Flipo, J.-P. (1986) 'Service Firms: Interdependence of External and Internal Marketing Strategies', *European Journal of Marketing* 20(8): 5–14.

Jones, G.R. (1983) 'Transaction Costs, Property Rights, and Organizational Culture: An Exchange Perspective', *Administrative Science Quarterly* 28: 454–67.

—— (1987) 'Organization–Client Transactions and Organizational Governance Structures', *Academy of Management Journal* 30(2): 197–218.

—— (1990) 'Governing Customer-Service Organization Exchange', *Journal of Business Research* 20(1): 23–9.

Kay, N.M. (1992) 'Markets, False Hierarchies and the Evolution of the Modern Corporation', *Journal of Economic Behavior and Organization* 17(3): 315–33.

Klein, S. (1989) 'A Transaction Cost Explanation of Vertical Control in International Markets', *Journal of the Academy of Marketing Science* 17(3): 253–60.

Kotler, P. (1991) *Marketing Management: Analysis, Planning, Implementation and Control*, 7th edn, Englewood Cliffs, NJ: Prentice-Hall.

Kotler, P. and Levy, S.J. (1969) 'Broadening the Concept of Marketing', *Journal of Marketing* 33: 10–15.

Lehtinen, U. and Lehtinen, J.R. (1982) *Service Quality: A Study of Quality Dimensions*, Helsinki: Service Management Institute.

Lusch, R.F., Brown, S.W. and Brunswick, G.J. (1992) 'A General Framework for Explaining Internal vs. External Exchange', *Journal of the Academy of Marketing Science* 20(2): 119–34.

McCarthy, E.J. (1960) *Basic Marketing: A Managerial Approach*, Homewood, IL: Irwin.

MacNeil, I.R. (1974) 'The Many Futures of Contract', *Southern California Law Review* 47: 691–748.

Nooteboom, B. (1993) 'Research Note: An Analysis of Specificity in Transaction Cost Economics', *Organization Studies* 14(3): 443–51.

Ouchi, W.G. (1980) 'Markets, Bureaucracies and Clans', *Administrative Science Quarterly* 25: 129–41.

Pitt, L. and Foreman, S.K. (1999) 'Internal Marketing's Role in Organisations: A Transaction Cost Perspective', *Journal of Business Research* 44(1): 15–36.

Rafiq, M. and Ahmed, P.K. (1992) 'The Limits of Internal Marketing', Proceedings of the 2nd Workshop on Quality Management in Services, European Institute for Advanced Studies in Management, May, 184–98.

Riddle, D.I. (1988) 'Culturally Determined Aspects of Service Quality', paper presented at the Quality in Services Symposium, University of Karlsbad, Sweden, August, 14–17.

Sagie, A. and Koslowsky, M. (1994) 'Organizational Attitudes and Behaviors as a Function of Participation in Strategic and Tactical Change Decisions: An Application of Path–Goal Theory', *Journal of Organizational Behavior* 15(1): 37–47.

Shetzer, L. (1993) 'A Social Information Processing Model of Employee Participation', *Organization Science* 4(2): 252–68.

Stanton, E.S. (1993) 'Employee Participation: A Critical Evaluation and Suggestions for Management Practice', *SAM Advanced Management Journal* 58(4): 18–23.

Webster, F.E. (1992) 'The Changing Role of Marketing in the Corporation', *Journal of Marketing* 56(October): 1–17.

Williamson, O.E. (1975) *Markets and Hierarchies: Analysis and Anti-Trust Implications*, New York: The Free Press.

Part IV

Communication and service delivery

9 Minimizing internal communication gaps by using Business Television

Bernd Stauss
Frank Hoffmann

Introduction

With increasing competition, customer orientation becomes the central business maxim. In order to provide the internal prerequisites necessary for customer orientation, the traditional marketing thought must be expanded from the external to the internal target group. Internal marketing, therefore, becomes a crucial success factor needed in winning customer-oriented and motivated employees, to develop them and to promote their commitment to the firm.

In this context, employee communication plays a pivotal role, as its function lies in mediating the required skills and the necessary customer-related information within the company. Unfortunately, traditional methods of employee communication do not meet the rising requirements towards quality, quantity, speed, and targeting precision of information mediation. Given these difficulties, much attention is being focused on so-called new media, which encompass Business Television.

Proven evidence, however, with respect to the suitability and efficiency of Business TV for the communication purposes of internal marketing, is yet to be found. Theoretical-conceptual and empirical research regarding the communication effects of Business TV, its operating conditions, and cost–benefit analyses are all still pending. Therefore, it is the goal of this discussion to clarify the potential suitability of Business TV as an instrument of employee communication and to illustrate this through practical examples.

Furthermore, we will discuss the position of employee communication within the framework of internal marketing, and its goals and instruments will be described in more detail. In addition, traditional methods will be evaluated with regard to their suitability to achieve core goals of employee communication. The gaps in internal communication, identified thereby, are the starting point for the question: how can Business TV contribute to better goal achievement?

Following this, the new medium, Business TV, its mode of operation, and its applications will be presented. On this basis, we will give differentiated answers to if and how Business TV offers companies a way to reduce or close the identified communication gaps. Finally, we summarize the results, identify substantial consequences for internal marketing, and point out further open questions.

Employee communication in internal marketing

The relevance of employee communication in internal marketing

The development of internal marketing – as a mode of customer orientation directed towards target groups within the company – began when it became clear that marketing strategies and concepts which focused exclusively on the external clientele were no longer sufficient to achieve economic goals such as sales and profits. Marketing concepts directed exclusively at external customers are in danger of failing if internal subsystems and processes are not properly focused onto the customer-related objectives, and if employees lack the necessary customer-oriented attitudes and behaviours. In this situation, the basic conviction, that the marketing perspective directed towards the external market needs to be completed through internal marketing (George, 1990; Piercy and Morgan, 1990; Bruhn, 1995; Varey, 1995; Boshoff and Tait, 1996; Stauss, 1997), is gaining in importance.

Applying the marketing concept internally, several target groups and various marketing instruments can be taken into consideration. Of these, the target group of employees and the instrument of communication policy are of highest relevance.

The marketing variant directed toward the target group of employees, also known as personnel-oriented internal marketing (Stauss, 1995a, 1995b), covers the well-planned arrangement of the exchange relations between management and employees on different hierarchical levels. The necessity of this arrangement task was acknowledged first in services marketing because many services are produced in direct interaction of customer and personnel, with employee behaviour substantially influencing the service quality as perceived by the customer. As a result, assuring customer-focused employee behaviour becomes a goal of (internal) marketing (Berry, 1981; Grönroos, 1985; Varey, 1995). To that end, contact personnel who are to behave in a customer-oriented fashion, need appropriate internal operating conditions and incentive structures, and must be furnished adequately by their 'internal suppliers'. So, it becomes clear that personnel-oriented internal marketing is required not only for customer contact personnel and not only in service companies.

Among the instruments of internal marketing, internal communication policy is particularly important (George, 1986; Tansuhaj *et al.*, 1988; George and Grönroos, 1991). While the other instruments of internal marketing are frequently rather well-known business matters, renamed with marketing terms, internal communication policy covers a new extensive area. It comprises all measures with an impact on knowledge, attitudes, and behaviours of internal customers (for example, current, former, potential employees, departments, and affiliates) on different hierarchical levels (George, 1990). The part of the internal communication policy which in personnel-oriented internal marketing is targeted towards employees, is called employee communication.

This communication policy with respect to employees is gaining relevance. One result of an ever-faster change in competitive fields and customer requirements, a shortening of product life cycles, technological innovations, and rapid changes in marketing concepts is obvious. The need to provide – and difficulty of providing – employees with information in a manner that is targeted, fast and tailored to their needs, while at the same time making better use of the personnel as an information source, is rising.

Therefore, we agree with Broßmann's appraisal that internal information and communication will become key factors in business success (1997).

Goals of employee communication

Employee communication denotes the planned use of communication actions to systematically influence the knowledge, attitudes and behaviours of current employees. This definition comprises several substantial components:

- Employee communication goes along with a planned application of communication measures. Therefore, not all internal information processes are enclosed in the underlying definition, but rather those measures that are used intentionally.
- This does in no way imply that employee communication must always be one-sided top-down communication. Included are also measures of planned bottom-up (or feedback) communication and lateral communication between employees on the same hierarchical level.
- Employee communication is directed potentially towards all current employees, which means that no target group should be excluded in principle, while it may still be reasonable to differentiate between internal target groups (for example, high-level personnel, office personnel, customer service representatives, and so on).
- Employee communication is systematically aligned to influence employees, thus serving to attain business goals.

The goals that can be achieved through managed employee communication are numerous. For systematization, and for external communication policy, one can differentiate between economic and communication goals (Bruhn, 1997). Economic goals, such as improving profits by reducing costs and/or increased revenues, can be achieved by employee communication only indirectly, for example, by improved work performance. In contrast, communication can be concerned to directly affect the knowledge, attitude, and behavioural level of the addressees. Because the latter effects can be measured directly, communication goals are remarkably more useful here for controlling the company than are economic goals. This is why the further discussion here will focus on this specific set of goals. This can also be justified by the reason that communication goals and economic goals are in a means–end relation.

The communication goals of employee communication can be differentiated according to the levels of influence specified in the definition regarding knowledge, attitudes, and behaviour. On the knowledge level, employees must be informed about customer requirements, products and services, marketing concepts and strategies, as well as about substantial aspects of business matters (Lobscheid, 1988; Stauss and Schulze, 1990; Dotzler, 1995; Kurz and Altgeld, 1995; Bühler, 1997). Regarding the attitude level, a primary concern is the creation of customer-oriented and service-oriented attitudes. Furthermore, this level is concerned with winning understanding for (and contribution to) management decisions, identification with the company, and establishing a cohesive attitude with respect to economic and social issues.

Knowledge and attitudes become evident then on the behaviour level, proven when employees act responsibly and independently to find customer-oriented solutions, to actively gather and pass on information, and to contribute to the company internal dialogue (see Figure 9.1).

Traditional instruments of employee communication

In view of the relevance of these goals, it is astonishing that enterprises place such little emphasis on this area of work. Employee communication is far from receiving the same emphasis or professional treatment as external communication. This can also be said for the type and scope of the media applied. Bruhn (1997) speaks of 'medium poverty' and interprets this as an expression of management's low esteem of its employees.

The instruments used in enterprises (Klöfer, 1996; Gruninger-Herrmann and Willems, 1997) can be divided by the direction of their effects into media of top-down, bottom-up, and horizontal communication, whereby some instruments can be assigned to more than one category (see Figure 9.2).

Knowledge	Attitudes	Behaviour
▪ Customer requirements	▪ Customer-orientated thinking	▪ Customer-orientated behaviour
▪ Products, product innovations and variations	▪ Understanding for management decisions	▪ Self-sufficiency
		▪ Responsibility
▪ Marketing concepts and strategies	▪ Identification with the company	▪ Commitment
▪ Changes within the company	▪ Attitude towards overall economic questions	▪ Active informative feedback

Figure 9.1 Examples of goals of employee communication

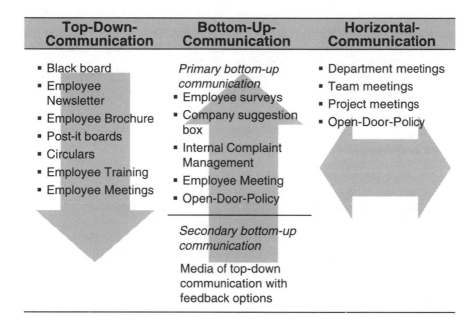

Figure 9.2 Traditional instruments of employee communication
Source: Klöfer (1996); Bruhn (1998)

As empirical studies on media usage in employee communication show, instruments of top-down communication such as blackboards, employee newsletters, employee brochures, notices or circulars are undoubtedly dominant (Thom and Cantin, 1994; Klöfer, 1996). They serve to transmit the information judged as relevant by higher hierarchy levels to employees on lower levels. The media of bottom-up communication can be differentiated further. The instruments of the primary bottom-up communication serve exclusively for information exchange with higher hierarchy levels. Employee surveys, suggestion boxes, or internal complaint management fit into this category. Conversely, secondary bottom-up communication instruments are those of top-down communication, which offer an option for the lower hierarchical levels to give feedback to their superiors, for example, in an employee magazine with a letter column (Bruhn, 1997). For horizontal communication, a number of communication types (for example, department meetings, project meetings, team meetings and so on) take place, in which an information exchange occurs on a horizontal level.

This discussion is concerned only with the instruments of top-down communication and secondary bottom-up communication. This is for three reasons:

•   Horizontal communication serves to a high degree for the internal coordination and alignment of procedures and not primarily for the goals of employee communication specified above.

- A large majority of the goals of employee communication refer to the influence on knowledge, attitudes, and behaviours of employees by the management, and thus to top-down communication. Enabling a feedback mechanism is the intention of secondary bottom-up communication.
- Top-down communication is attached to the usage of a specific medium; and it is here that the question of the possible relevance of Business TV as an alternative medium arises.

Gaps in the application of employee communication

Recent developments call for an ever-increasing ability of internal communication media to perform. The increasingly dynamic development of competition, business, and technology requires companies to undergo adjustments and modifications. This situation not only brings about employees' constantly growing need for more information (Bühler, 1997; Bullinger and Schäfer, 1997; Herold, 1997), but also promotes rising requirements with regard to the quality of the information provided, the efficiency of information dissemination, and possibilities of direct interaction. If one considers this development, then traditional applications of employee communication are no longer sufficient for the new demands of the system (Schick, 1995; Bühler, 1997).

As major deficits in the application of media, eight internal communication gaps can be identified. Figure 9.3 shows an overview.

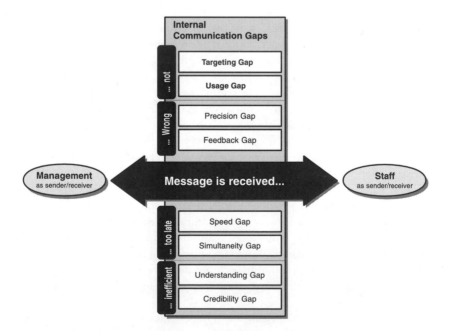

Figure 9.3 Overview of potential internal communication gaps

Messages do not reach the recipient: targeting gap and usage gap

This category encompasses one serious failing: the message is not even perceived by the intended recipient. This may be caused on the one hand by a lack in the precision of targeting (targeting gap) or, on the other hand, by media-specific usage barriers (usage gap).

The targeting gap

A possible reason for missing the intended recipients is that there is a targeting gap. This gap occurs if the media applied do not, or only insufficiently, allow for target-group-specific addressing.

This problem has both a personal and geographical dimension. With regard to *persons*, this problem will occur whenever media are used which can disseminate information but cannot assure that a message arrives at the relevant group of recipients. Typical examples of this are media used for a heterogeneous set of addressees, such as bulletin boards or employee newsletters. A *geographical* targeting gap exists when a message is transmitted to places where the intended recipients are not located at that moment, so it does not reach them. For example, when an important circular is sent to the assumed location of the receiver, who has actually been absent for some time, for example due to a business trip, and so the addressee misses out on the information without the sender ever knowing.

To avoid the occurrence of such a targeting gap, it is important to complete the traditional mix of instruments through media which provide an option of exact addressability of information and which ensure a successful delivery independent of the geographic location of the addressee.

The usage gap

A further cause for management information not reaching employees can be that the employees do not use the media (usage gap). Reasons for this are that they may feel it is too time-consuming, arduous, and not stimulating to use the medium or media. Active media use takes time and cognitive effort. If media lack attractiveness and user-friendliness, employees are unwilling to put forth this effort, so that in these cases they do not receive the information correctly targeted to reach them. An example from traditional media is the circular letter, which is rarely read with concentration (Burgmaier and Hornig, 1997).

Instead of media that are unattractive or not easy to use, employees have come to expect media that are similar in form and design to the kind that they use away from work, which transmit information in an entertaining manner.

Messages reach recipients falsely: precision gap and feedback gap

Further communication problems occur whenever the contents of communication are passed on falsely or selectively. This can result from distortion effects through the media applied (precision gap) or because the media offer no way to ensure full understanding through recipients' follow-up questions (feedback gap).

The precision gap

Traditionally in enterprises, information is passed on along hierarchy levels in a cascading manner. This method leads to an information distortion by filtering and selection. Studies show that messages lose about 25 per cent of their contents per step of forwarding (Schüller, 1997). If a message must be transmitted throughout a large enterprise with multiple hierarchy levels, then traditional, indirect, and hierarchy-bound media prove severely deficient. Therefore, the traditional methods must be supplemented by media that offer sufficient possibilities of direct, i.e. hierarchy-spreading, communication.

The feedback gap

Even if information is correct and it passes through the transmission process with no distortions, it is possible that the recipients do not, or at least not properly, understand the message. If the medium does not provide a feedback option, such misunderstandings can neither be articulated instantly by the recipient, nor can they be detected immediately by the sender. When reviewing traditional media mixes of internal communication, it becomes evident that these different applications offer only a very restricted range of feedback options. Sometimes, reader letter columns in employee newsletters are mentioned as an example, but these are quantitatively insignificant and usually have come to be irrelevant at the time of publication. First, barriers exist for the use of these (apparent) two-way communication media. Second, operational inefficiencies result from inappropriate message interpretation, due to a lack of inquiry options. Then, absence of communication feedback leads to lack of motivation and commitment for employees in lower hierarchy levels, who have little chance of coming into contact with actual decision makers (Bruhn, 1998).

To reduce these problems, media are required which offer employees a possibility of substantial feedback. Given this, it is desirable that feedback can be addressed directly to the sender. Only then can the occurrence of new targeting gaps and precision gaps be avoided in the subsequent communication loops. Ideally, the communicating parties can enter into a synchronous dialogue because problems of understanding can be eliminated most directly this way.

Messages reach the recipient too late: speed gap and simultaneity gap

Much information is, to a considerable degree, time sensitive. For example, employees must be informed about the relevant features of a product before launch, or, if the company was publicly criticized in the media, they must be informed about a management statement on this issue. Therefore, the media of internal communication must fulfil high requirements of mediation speed. However, traditional information infrastructures and media are often not able to meet the demands that are placed on them. Potential causes are to be found in their low transmission speed and their inflexibility in application (speed gap), as well as their insufficient ability to address various and dispersed groups of employees at the same time (simultaneity gap).

The speed gap

The speed gap denotes the inability of media to inform employees at short notice about acute events or changes. The necessity to do so is a result of the dynamic aspect of the marketplace, for example, when a competitor's move calls for prompt reaction in order to defend the current market position. On the other hand, the ability to transport information is also crucial in a situation of a general company crisis, for instance when employees feel insecure about public criticism of the company, so that management must address employees very flexibly by means of 'crisis communication' (Bruhn, 1998).

Many traditional instruments of employee communication do not allow for this flexibility. For example, due to the long intervals between releases, employee newsletters or brochures are inappropriate to make recent information accessible to the addressees (Seibold and Turowsky, 1997). Therefore, supplementary media must be sought, which can be applied flexibly and within a short time. Furthermore, the possibility of synchronous dialogue should be available because this helps to clear up misunderstandings in general and also ensures that the necessary corrections are made in a timely manner.

The simultaneity gap

A specific cause for information reaching employees too late is that many media used have only a limited capability of reaching all the employees at the same time. Many enterprises have several, geographically scattered, locations on a national or international scale. Furthermore, different internal information paths exist in the different organizational units so that a message will often reach the members of the internal target group with considerable delay and most frequently at different times. In certain situations, where the immediate dispersion of information is necessary, this can lead to problems. Thus, a medium is needed, which is able to address employees at the same time, independent of their geographical location.

Messages reach recipient inefficiently: understanding gap and credibility gap

Another problem with traditional forms of employee communication is that, although the intended message may reach the recipient undistorted and within an appropriate time frame, it may be in an inefficient manner. This is the case when the message is difficult to decode (understanding gap), or when the message is not taken seriously due to doubts about the credibility of the sender or the medium (credibility gap).

The understanding gap

The assigned media must be able to fulfil the respective communication goals efficiently. This implies that they create the optimal conditions for fast and correct message reception by the employee. This is even more necessary when the media offer possibilities of presentation in a real-life manner and multi-sensory communication. The predominantly used classical traditional internal communication media – for instance, circulars – are text-oriented and require the receiver to engage in concentrated, time-intensive reading. This clearly limits their suitability for the fast dispersal of extensive or more complex information. For example, if employees need to be informed how repairs are to be performed on a machine – which has been newly added to the product range – or how to react correctly to customer complaints, then those media are not fully capable of achieving the desired degree of understanding. Therefore, they should be supplemented by media that enable efficient information processing and, consequently, aid in the understanding of the message through additional options of message design and an appeal to several senses.

The credibility gap

The efficiency of communication also concerns the extent to which a message is seen as true, reliable, and trustworthy. The assumed credibility, however, does not depend solely on the content of the message but also on the medium used and the source. On the one hand, there are medium-specific credibility differences from the user perspective. On the other hand, the medium selected in each case influences the credibility attributed to the sender of the message. A circular, which carries the signature of the CEO, may be viewed as less authentic and credible than a live transmission of his/her speech with exactly the same content. As a result, internal communication must make sure that the right medium is used to increase message credibility and, at the same time, the efficiency of information reception and storage.

In summary, it can be shown that traditional media of internal communication prove to be insufficient to achieve the goals mentioned. As a result, hopes are focused on the application of new communication instruments. In this respect, especially the Internet, intranet, and electronic mail (e-mail) are of growing importance. Another instrument of communication gaining considerable attention is company-internal television, or Business Television, which will be analysed in more detail after a brief definition and explanation of its mode of operation.

Business Television: term and mode of operation

The term Business Television originated in the mid-1980s and was developed from the areas of 'tele-conferencing' and 'video-conferencing' (Broßmann, 1997). Choosing a broad definition, Business Television consists of any enterprise communication by means of audiovisual media (BTI, 1997). A narrower definition of the term is offered by Kienel *et al.* (1998). They describe Business Television as an on-line information medium for a closed user group, by means of which information can be provided and distributed from one place to any number of recipients, at short notice, fast, and with identical appearance. Figure 9.4 shows an overview of the mode of operation of Business Television.

The technical infrastructure of a Business TV network can be divided into the following components:

- television studio
- transmission of the programme
- receipt
- feedback channels
- encoding and addressing

The Business TV programme is produced in a studio (alternatively by mobile transmission units at every other scene) and transmitted live. At present, the transmission takes place almost exclusively by satellite. The cause for the selection of this medium is the lack of alternatives with comparable quality of data

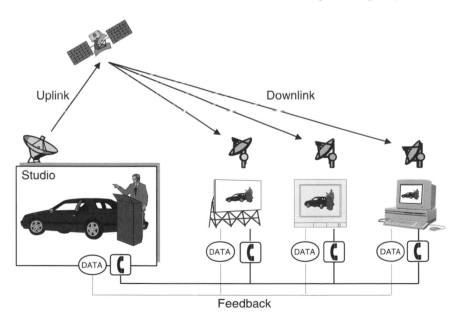

Figure 9.4 Mode of operation of Business Television

transmission. Another advantage of satellite communication is that any number of recipients can be reached, without influencing the transmission costs; this is a restriction for terrestrial transmissions. For the transmission radius alone, the illuminating area of the satellite, the so-called 'footprint', is crucial (Seibold and Siebert, 1997). Within this footprint, signals can be received with a commercial parabolic antenna and then transferred to a large-screen television set, or workstation PC (Seibold, 1997). Disadvantages of satellite transmission are the high transmission costs and the necessity for accurate advance planning and reservation of satellite capacity (Szyperski *et al.*, 1998).

In order to protect confidential company information against unauthorized access, transmission signals are sent in encoded form and translated back into a visible picture at the various reception points through a decoder (Jäger and Geiger, 1997). This allows for addressing data to individually specified groups of users.

One goal of Business TV is to provide an alternative to the customary one-way communication methods (Nörder, 1997). Thus, interactive Business TV always provides feedback channels, through which the employees can actively contact the transmission studio (Broßmann, 1997). Participation can be implemented by telephone and fax as well as by means of data transfer (such as e-mail, Internet or keypad). In special cases, such as at virtual congresses, a live video return line is also possible (Ernst, 1997).

Suitability of Business Television for reducing internal communication gaps

Basically, Business TV can be used in the context of internal communication for the purpose of achieving all communication goals. However, it must be asked, whether or not the diagnosed communication gaps can be eliminated this way?

Reducing targeting gap and usage gap

A target gap occurs if media do not enable target-group-specific addressing. This gap can be reduced substantially through the application of Business TV.

On the personal level, exact target addressing is possible, since with Business Television the message is digitally encoded, and only special decoders can translate the signal into a picture and sound. By listing the codes of specific receiving stations, the internal television programme can be focused and restricted to a desired group of recipients. Furthermore, the technology of satellite transmission warrants the independence of reception from geographical location, as a programme can be received throughout the whole footprint of the satellite.

These advantages are used frequently in company practice; for instance the FordStar network transmits, among other things, information exclusively to the 6,000 North American Ford dealers (Careless, 1996). In Germany, K-TV, operated by Kaufhof department stores, is a Business TV pioneer in the field of retail sales. Here, addressability is used to transmit product-related training courses only to the employees in the shop departments affected. For example, if news about kitchen equipment is to be presented, it is possible that only the personnel of the houseware departments see this information (DeMetri, 1998).

The usage gap, when media do not receive the attention intended by the sender, often stems from the low attractiveness of the communication medium. There are good reasons to assume that Business TV does not show this deficiency, or at least to a lesser extent. First, television usage fits a behaviour pattern which employees know from their social life. Second, the medium has characteristics that increase its attractiveness, for example, it allows for a broad variety of content design, live presentations, and the possibility of direct feedback.

This assessment is widely shared among companies that use Business TV (Meunzel, 1996; Fresenborg and Pflüger, 1997; Hasebrook and Wolf, 1997). An evaluation of the pilot programme of *Wision*, the Business TV of the Wüstenrot building society, reveals a broad acceptance and readiness to use among the recipients. In a user survey, the statement 'Business TV should be used permanently as an internal communication medium in the future', scored the impressive average of 1.09 on a six-item scale from 1='totally agree' to 6= 'totally disagree' (Hoffmann, 1999).

A general verdict, however, on how far the usage gap can be closed by Business TV cannot be stated here. The attractiveness, and hence the readiness to use, do not only depend on the medium alone, but also on a number of other factors. Among them are aspects such as the selection of programme contents appropriate for the target group, the choice of a moderating host, the duration of the programme, the type of feedback options, the quality of accompanying information materials, or the incorporation of Business TV in company organization processes (Fresenborg and Pflüger, 1997; Babiel, 1998).

Reducing precision gap and feedback gap

The falsification and distortion of information contents by step-wise information transfer (precision gap) can be avoided, to a large extent, with the application by Business TV. One of the chief advantages of Business TV is that it enables the integration of top management and allows direct addressing of employees on various hierarchy levels. A CEO can turn to all employees directly and be assured that his/her message reaches everyone without distortion effects. In order to exploit this advantage, many enterprises have developed and implemented specific programme concepts. An example of this is Deutsche Bank, which offers a programme with the title *What to do, Mr. Breuer?* Here, employees can enter into a hierarchy-spanning dialogue with the speaker of the executive committee (Schneider, 1998). In other companies, there are no special programmes for members of the board, but they are given a firm space in the programme structure (Burgmaier and Hornig, 1997).

By means of such dialogue programmes, the feedback gap can also be closed. Business TV is basically an interactive medium, whereby feedback can be organized in various ways. One German study reports that the majority of the companies (67%) fall back on the conventional telephone channel: however, an increasing number of businesses are turning to more innovative concepts. Currently, already, 40 per cent of all Business TV users indicate that they use video conferencing technology (Jungbeck *et al.*, 1998). An alternative to this is the interaction technology provided by the supplier OneTouch, which permits feedback by means of a hand-held terminal. Each viewer is able to intervene directly in a running programme through the use of a keyboard. In Germany, until recently, this variant was implemented in the programme *GISS*, from Gerling Insurance (Oden, 1998).

Independent of the technological variant being used, users stress that the feedback mechanism of Business TV is a substantial advantage for the purposes of internal communication. Employee questions are attributed high importance, in order to prevent internal false perceptions and misinterpretations, and to project credibly that top management takes employees' information needs seriously. Thus, the speaker of the executive committee of Kaufhof, Lovro Mandac, promised before the pilot programme of K-TV that 'Every question will be answered' (Kulling, 1997).

Reducing speed gap and simultaneity gap

The problem that information does not arrive fast enough from the sender to the recipient – the speed gap – can be closed by Business TV primarily because of two characteristics that it offers. First, Business TV makes direct and synchronous communication possible. Second, on a technical level, the satellite transmission technique offers an unbeatably high data transmission capacity (Diebold, 1997). Therefore, even large quantities of information will not jam lines and, hence, will not cause the transmission to slow down (Herold, 1997; Seibold and Turowsky, 1997), as is often the case with the World-Wide Web.

In practice, this superior performance characteristic has led to Business TV being appreciated increasingly, as the primary medium for crisis communication, by which the employee community can be reassured quickly and, therefore, threatening developments can be prevented (Trilling and Maurer, 1998). An example is the crisis of Daimler-Benz, when reports that the A-class Mercedes had toppled over in a Swedish driving test ('moose test') raised unwanted attention internationally. Internally, the company immediately offered special Business TV programmes, informing employees about the facts and the company's standpoint, and providing aid in how to argue in customer talks (Paterak, 1998). Deutsche Bank reacted in a similar manner to a sensationalized fraud charge (Schneider, 1998).

Here, also, the advantage pays off that employees on all hierarchical levels and locations can be addressed at the same time, closing the simultaneity gap (Rafiq and Ahmed, 1992). This offers not only substantial advantages for crisis communication, but it also helps to shorten the time-to-market. For example, with the introduction of FordStar Network, Ford was able to launch twenty instead of four new products per year (Burgmaier and Hornig, 1997). Daimler-Benz also uses its training channel, Akubis, to help overcome barriers from national and language borders. Thus, the programme for the introduction of the new A-class was simultaneously transmitted in Germany and France and translated synchronously (Paterek, 1998).

However, the short-term and flexible application of Business TV does have its limitations. For instance, Daimler–Chrysler take some precautions: the corporation has its own studio capacity and transmits programmes on three channels around the clock, ensuring that satellite capacities are permanently available (Herold, 1999). For other enterprises, without a studio of their own and who rely on renting the facilities from other firms – in Germany, this represents a considerable 41 per cent of the companies using Business TV (Jungbeck *et al.*, 1998) – the short-term need for a Business TV programme can turn into a problem. Another bottleneck is the availability of satellite transmission time, which must be booked in advance by the minute. A short-term change to an alternative satellite is only possible within limits, due to the adjustment of the receiving antennas. Furthermore, all of the current applications of Business TV use the satellites Astra (33 per cent), Intelsat (8 per cent), Eutelsat (33 per cent) and Kopernikus (25 per cent). This limits the choice of alternatives (Jungbeck *et al.*, 1998).

Reducing understanding gap and credibility gap

Internal communication is inefficient, if the recipient cannot easily decode the message (understanding gap). Indeed, there is no unanimous consent over whether or not different media generally make it easier or harder to decode messages (Trilling and Maurer, 1998), but Fischer speaks in favour of the thesis from communication sciences, namely that human receptiveness rises with the number of senses used (Fischer, 1987). Furthermore, this thesis corresponds with the media richness theory of Daft and Lengel (1984), according to which audio-visual communication proves to be superior for the transmission of complex information (Trevino *et al.*, 1990). It can be expected then, that the application of Business TV will lead to an improved reception and storage of the transmitted information and, hence, an increased communication efficiency.

This applies also because Business TV increases the credibility of communication. On the one hand, one can use results from mass communication research in Germany, which consistently show that media users attribute the highest credibility to television (Institut für Demoskopie, 1997). These results, which originate from the area of private media usage, cannot be fully transferred to internal business applications without further testing. Still, they permit at least the assumption that Business TV belongs to the company-internal media with the highest credibility. In terms of content design, the credibility effect is increased because Business TV offers employees a way to first-hand information, for example from top management, and allows them to get a clearer picture by responding.

Altogether, the available experiences with the application of Business TV in employee communication show that enterprises have an extraordinarily promising medium at their disposal. Not only conceptual considerations on the applicability of Business TV, but also empirical evidence show that Business TV possesses the potential to close many of the gaps that remain from the application of the classical instruments of employee communication.

Conclusions for internal marketing and open questions

A central range of activities of internal marketing is employee-related internal communication. The ever-growing dynamics in the marketplace and social environment demand that enterprises constantly and flexibly learn and adapt (Varey and Gilligan, 1996), which at the same time increases the requirements for internal communication. When considering the traditional media mix of internal communication, it is felt that these media are not capable of meeting these requirements. Conventional media, which permit only limited feedback, cannot be sufficiently targeted, and are too slow and not flexible enough. They are barely capable of reaching non-centrally located employees simultaneously, are unattractive, have little credibility, are hard to use, and their indirect use entails the danger of information distortion. On the basis of these difficulties, internal communication gaps were identified here, and it is suggested that companies strive for a reduction of these gaps by using new media.

A reflection of the basic capabilities of Business TV, and the analysis of practical experiences, shows that this medium possesses an extraordinarily high potential to lift internal communication to a new performance level. However, the possible benefits of this new medium will only be realized if the challenges for the management of internal communication connected with the application of Business TV are detected and mastered. Business TV is not just one medium among others that can be integrated into the media mix without greater modification. The introduction of Business TV is a fundamental strategic decision. This decision not only requires a substantial investment, but also implies lasting consequences for the internal organization, co-ordination and human resources management.

Programme production and usage need differentiation in respect of content, technology, and personnel. For many enterprises, feedback, that may cross several hierarchy levels and is publicized (within the company), is a newly adopted form of 'bottom-up' communication that implies a change in company culture. It is also important to remember that Business TV and the other media of internal communication must be adjusted with respect to formal aspects, release time and content. Furthermore, being broadcast on Business TV brings to light new requirements for top management in terms of appearance and rhetorical skills.

In comparison to its high importance for management, knowledge of science and practice about the attainable effects of Business TV with respect to various goals of internal communication is extraordinarily small. Therefore, there is not only a challenge for practical internal marketing, but also one for research. One aim is to analyse, in comparative empirical studies, the effects of Business TV on information acquisition and storage for different areas of application (for example, product information and behaviour training). Hereby, the determinants of the effects and the strength of their impact may be identified (Stauss and Hoffmann, 1997). Furthermore, the specific suitability of different Business TV formats, such as tele-training, tele-information, tele-events, tele-data services and telecommunication, must be examined. Only after a substantially higher base of empirical knowledge is provided can the opportunities and cost efficiency of Business TV in the context of employee communication be realistically assessed.

References

Babiel, D. (1998) 'Business Television bei Würth', in Broßmann, M. and Fieger, U. (eds), *Business Multimedia*, Wiesbaden: Gabler, 267–80.

Berry, L.L. (1981) 'The Employee as Customer', *Journal of Retail Banking* 3(1): 33–40.

Boshoff, C. and Tait, M. (1996) 'Quality Perceptions in the Financial Services Sector', *International Journal of Service Industry Management* 7(5): 5–31.

Broßmann, M. (1997) 'Interaktives Business Television – Module, Applikationen und Strategie', unpublished working paper of the Daimler Benz Corporation, Stuttgart, Germany.

Bruhn, M. (1995) 'Internes Marketing als Forschungsgebiet der Marketingwissenschaft', in Bruhn, M. (ed.), *Internes Marketing*, 1st edn, Wiesbaden: Gabler, 13–61.

—— (1997) *Kommunikationspolitik: Bedeutung-Strategien-Instrumente*, München: Vahlen.

—— (1998) 'Interne Kommunikation', in Meyer, A. (ed.), *Handbuch Dienstleistungs-Marketing*, Stuttgart: Schäffer-Poeschel, 1045–62.

BTI (1997) 'BTI-Präsentation: Business TV', working paper of the BTI Corp., Hamburg, Germany.

Bühler, A. (1997) 'Business TV: Kanal zum Außendienst', *Die Bank* 1: 8–9.

Bullinger, H.-J. and Schäfer, M. (1997) 'Entwicklungstrends und Herausforderungen im Informationszeitalter', in Bullinger, H.-J. and Broßmann, M. (eds), *Business TV – Beginn einer neuen Informationskultur in den Unternehmen*, Stuttgart: Schäffer-Poeschel, 3–15.

Burgmaier, S. and Hornig, F. (1997) 'Zur Belohnung', *Wirtschaftswoche* 51(34): 84–5.

Careless, J. (1996) 'Business TV: Applications Via Satellite', *Via Satellite* 11(11): 24–9.

Daft, R. and Lengel, R.H. (1984) 'Information Richness: A New Approach to Managerial Behaviour and Organizational Design', *Research in Organizational Behaviour* 6: 191–233.

DeMitri, A. (1998) 'Mehr als tausend Worte', *Management Berater* 1: 52–3.

Diebold, J. (1997): 'Die Daten kommen über viele Wege', *Handelsblatt* 12 October, 56.

Dotzler, H.-J. (1995) 'Gestaltung der internen Kommunikation als Grundlage marktorientierter Veränderungsprozesse-am Beispiel der Hypo-Bank, in Bruhn, M. (ed.), *Internes Marketing*, 1st edn, Wiesbaden: Gabler, 221–35.

Ernst, G. (1997) 'Der virtuelle Kongreß', in Bullinger, H.-J. and Broßmann, M. (eds), *Business TV – Beginn einer neuen Informationskultur in den Unternehmen*, Stuttgart: Schäffer-Poeschel, 61–72.

Fischer, K. (1987) *Bildkommunikation – Bedeutung, Technik und Nutzung*, Berlin: Springer.

Fresenborg, C. and Pflüger, F. (1997) 'Nutzungsmöglichkeiten von Business-TV im Bildungsbereich', working paper of the Deutsche Post Consult, Berlin.

George, W.R. (1986) 'Internal Communications Programs as a Mechanism for Doing Internal Marketing', in Venkatesan, M., Schmalensee, D.M. and Marshall, C. (eds),

Creativity in Services Marketing: What's New, What Works, What's Developing, Chicago: AMA, 83–4.

—— (1990) 'Internal Marketing and Organizational Behaviour: A Partnership in Developing Customer-Conscious Employees at Every Level', *Journal of Business Research* 20(1): 63–70.

George, W.R. and Grönroos, C. (1991) 'Developing Customer-Conscious Employees at Every Level: Internal Marketing', in Congram, C.A. and Friedman, M. (eds), *Handbook of Marketing for the Services Industries*, New York: Amacom, 85–100.

Grönroos, C. (1985) 'Internal Marketing: Theory and Practice', in Bloch, T.M., Upah, G.D. and Zeithaml, V.A. (eds), *Services Marketing in a Changing Environment*, Chicago: AMA, 41–7.

Gruninger-Hermann, C. and Willems, A. (1997) 'Der Einsatz von Unternehmensfernsehen (Business TV) bei Verbundgruppen', *Der Verbund* 3: 18–22.

Hasebrook, J. and Wolf, A. (1997) 'Digital-TV in der Bankausbildung, Bericht über die Pilotsendung der Bankakademie', working paper of the Bankakademie, Frankfurt.

Herold, B. (1997) 'Effiziente Unternehmenskommunikation mit Business-TV', *Technologie & Management* 41(3): 27–9.

—— (1999) 'Business TV via Satellit-Anwendungen deutscher Unternehmen im Überblick', unpublished working paper, Friedrichsdorf.

Hoffmann, F. (1999) 'Ergebnisse der Pilotsendung zu Wision', unpublished working paper, Ingolstadt.

Institut für Demoskopie (1997) *Jahrbuch für Demoskopie*, München:Verlag für Demoskopie.

Jäger, W. and Geiger, T.F. (1997) 'Business-TV als Kommunikationsinstrument der Zukunft', *IT Management* 4(10): 36–42.

Jungbeck, K., Ritter, S. and Goedhart, J.P. (1998) *Business-TV in Deutschland*, Starnberg: R.S. Schulz.

Kienel, H., Zerbe, S. and Krcmar, H. (1998) 'Business Television im Marketing und Vetrieb', in Hippner, H., Meyer, M. and Wilde K.D. (eds), *Computer Based Marketing – Das Handbuch zur Marketinginformatik*, Wiesbaden: Vieweg, 117–24.

Klöfer, F. (1996) *Mitarbeiterkommunikation*, Mainz: F.H. Mainz.

Kulling, L. (1997) 'Interne Kommunikation – Zoff im TV', *Handelsjournal* 10: 46–8.

Kurz, E. and Altgeld, J. (1995) 'Informations- und Kommunikationstechnologien – treibender Faktor für innovative Dienstleistungen, in Bullinger, H.-J. (ed.), *Dienstleistung der Zukunft*, Wiesbaden: Gabler, 455–70.

Lobscheid, H.G. (1988) 'Internes Marketing für Beschäftigte', *Der Betriebswirt* 29(4): 21–3.

Meunzel, R.M. (1996) 'Mehr als nur Fernsehen – Informationsvermittlung per Business-TV', *Autohaus* 16: 42–4.

Nörder, G. (1997) 'Good Morning, News!', *pr magazin* 11: 44–5.

Oden, P. (1998) 'Schlung mit GISS', *Office Management* 7: S16–17.

Paterak, J. (1998) 'Fernsehen aus der Chefetage', VDI-Nachrichten, Vol. 7, 23-4

Piercy, N. and Morgan, N. (1990) 'Internal Marketing: Making Marketing Happen', *Marketing Intelligence and Planning* 8(1): 4–6.

Rafiq, M. and Ahmed, P.K. (1992) 'The Limits of Internal Marketing', in Lemmink, J. and Kunst, P. (eds), *Quality Management in Services*, Assen: Van Gorcum, 184–98.

Schick, S. (1995) 'Strukturierung und Gestaltung der Mitarbeiterkommunikation als Personalaufgabe', in Bruhn, M. (ed.), *Internes Marketing*, 1st edn, Wiesbaden: Gabler, 453–70.

Schneider, G. (1998) 'Krisen mit internem Auftritt gemanagt', *Horizont* 15: 31–4.

Schüller, S. (1997) 'Corporate TV – eine neue Strategie in der internen Kommunikation', *bank und markt* 9: 28–31.

Seibold, B. and Siebert, P. (1997) 'Management by Television – Technische Herausforderungen von Business Television', in Bullinger, H.-J. and Broßmann, M. (eds), *Business TV – Beginn einer neuen Informationskultur in den Unternehmen*, Stuttgart: Schäffer-Poeschel, 155–68.

Seibold, B. and Turowsky, H.-J. (1997) 'Management by Television', working paper of the BTI Corporation, Hamburg.

Stauss, B. (1995a) 'Internes Marketing als personalorientierte Qualitätspolitik', in Bruhn, M. and Stauss, B. (eds), *Dienstleistungsqualität*, 2nd edn, Wiesbaden: Gabler, 257–76.

—— (1995b) 'Internes Marketing', in Tietz, B., Köhler, R. and Zentes, J. (eds), *Handwörterbuch des Marketing*, 2nd edn, Stuttgart: Schäffer-Poeschel, 1045–56.

—— (1997) 'Internes Marketing', *Die Betriebswirtschaft* 57(5): 717–20.

Stauss, B. and Hoffmann, F. (1997) 'Business Television in Aus- und Weiterbildung', unpublished working paper, Ingolstadt.

Stauss, B. and Schulze, H.S. (1990) 'Internes Marketing', *Marketing ZFP* 12(3): 149–58.

Szypersky, N., Gasch, S., Korschinsky, C. and Trilling, S. (1998) 'Business Television – Einordnung, Wertschöpfungsprozesse, Entwicklungstrends', working paper, Cologne.

Tansushaj, P., Randall, D. and McCullough, J. (1988) 'A Services Marketing Management Model: Integrating Internal and External Marketing Functions', *Journal of Services Marketing* 2(1): 31–8.

Thom, N. and Cantin, F. (1994) 'Verständigungsgrad verbessern', *Gabler's Magazin* 8(3): 26–30.

Trevino, L.K., Daft, R.L. and Lengel, R.H. (1990) 'Understanding Managers' Media Choices: A Symbolic Interactionist Perspective', in Fulk, J. and Steinfield, C. (eds), *Organizations and Communication Technology*, Newbury Park, CA: Sage Publications, 71–94.

Trilling, S. and Maurer, M. (1998) 'Potentiale des Business Television als Instrument der Mitarbeiterkommunikation in Krisensituationen', working paper, Cologne.

Varey, R. J. (1995) 'Internal Marketing: A Review and Some Interdisciplinary Research Challenges', *International Journal of Service Industry Management* 6(1): 40–63.

Varey, R.J. and Gilligan, C.T. (1996) 'Internal Marketing: Interfacing the Internal and External Environments', in Kunst, P. and Lemmink, J. (eds), *Managing Service Quality*, vol. 2, London: Paul Chapman Publishing, 59–77.

10 The business value of buy-in

How staff understanding and commitment impact on brand and business performance

Kevin Thomson
Lorrie A. Hecker

Introduction

An internal marketing strategy is becoming an essential management tool due to a combination of market forces. First, intense competition is not limited to the external marketplace. Today's buoyant economy has produced strong growth in jobs and a shortage of professional staff. At the same time, flatter management structures and tougher business decisions mean that you cannot 'sell' people, employees or recruits, the promise of a big promotion or a job for life.

When people have choices, the law of supply and demand comes into play. Now more than ever before, organisations have to satisfy their internal customers if they are to operate effectively. At the same time, organisations across the board are going through dramatic and fundamental changes in order to survive in an increasingly competitive, fast-moving global environment. Organisations are flatter and more streamlined. Reporting lines are less clear. Roles and job titles have been blurred. Decisions are made much more quickly. As a result, the lines of communication are far more complex and business messages more difficult, and often worrying, for staff.

In this environment, the future of the relationship between organisations and their people depends on the way they communicate with each other, not as employees but as internal customers. Like external customers, staff have 'buying' decisions to make: whether to buy-in to a business objective or initiative, whether to take ownership of a company vision, whether to aspire to achieve organisational goals and to make a valuable contribution, or to live up to its collective values.

The term 'buy-in' has found its way into the management vernacular, yet it is often misunderstood. This chapter will explore the meaning and business value of buy-in using a combination of theory, anecdotal evidence, market research and short case studies.

Intellectual and emotional buy-in

Buy-in is, in fact, a two-sided coin. One side is about intellectual buy-in, which means that people are aware of and aligned with key business issues and understand how they can positively affect them. The other, equally valuable, side of the coin is the need to build commitment and engage people in the achievement of goals. Emotion in an organisation is like petrol to a car. You cannot go very far without it.

The mistake many managers make is to concentrate solely on understanding or on winning minds without also striving to build commitment or winning hearts. Looking after people's minds is the principle behind intellectual capital and knowledge management, management concepts that have become popular recently. Yet, knowledge is only half the battle. Even more importantly, the hidden resources of feelings, beliefs, perceptions and values determine whether or not people apply their knowledge constructively in support of organisational goals. These beliefs, feelings and motivations are the foundation of emotional capital.

Think of the emotions that have been very common for employees to feel in recent years, such as anxiety, stress, anger, fear and suspicion. Then think of the workplace and marketplace challenges described earlier. Common sense tells us that an organisation cannot possibly meet these challenges with such negative emotions at work. Over time, these emotions may manifest themselves as overt industrial action or as more subtle, individual, behaviours such as poor attitudes, increased absenteeism and low productivity. Either way, a business' reputation and personality will suffer.

On the other hand, positive emotions are an energy source that can drive a company forward. When organisations win hearts and minds and build a strong base of emotional capital, their people become engaged. They feel a sense of ownership for business goals and strive to build strong and profitable relationships with external stakeholders.

To understand the components and value of buy-in, the Marketing and Communication Agency (MCA) commissioned Market & Opinion Research International (MORI) in August 1998 to conduct a nationally representative quota sample of 350 managers and staff from British organisations employing 1,000 or more people within a cross-section of industry sectors. About 60 per cent of those interviewed worked in organisations with 5,000-plus employees, and 41 per cent were managers (see Arganbright and Thomson, 1998).

The survey was undertaken to gauge the levels of staff understanding of, and commitment to, their organisations' business objectives and goals, both on an emotional and intellectual scale. Interviews were carried out in respondents' homes using CAPI (Computer Assisted Personal Interviewing). Data have been weighted to reflect the national population profile. Where responses do not add up to 100 per cent, the balance is accounted for by those who neither agreed nor disagreed or those who do not know, or is due to rounding of figures.

To compare the levels of intellectual and emotional buy-in and to understand the areas for improvement, respondents were asked about their level of agreement with key benchmarking statements based on MCA's work with many of *The Times*'s top 100 companies. The critical success factors were then identified for cultivating 'champions': people who both understand business goals and brand values and are strongly committed to delivering them.

The benchmark findings are outlined in Table 10.1, showing the extent of strong agreement with particular statements. The Emotional Benchmarks are written in plain text while the Intellectual Benchmarks are italicised.

Organisations depend on their people having a strong understanding of the business direction. Yet, surprisingly, only 39 per cent of respondents agreed strongly that they understand what they need to do as individuals to support business goals (see Table 10.1).

Even worse, just 27 per cent of respondents strongly agreed that they have a clear sense of their organisation's vision and direction for the future, and only 14 per cent strongly agreed with all five intellectual benchmarking statements. When asked about their overall awareness and understanding of key business goals, less than half (48 per cent) of respondents rated this as high.

Emotional buy-in fared no better in the survey. The research shows that 51 per cent of respondents rated their overall level of commitment as high. Nonetheless, the responses to the emotional benchmarking statements show a noticeable drop in levels of agreement overall. For example, only 9 per cent of those interviewed felt strongly that their views and participation were valued by their organisation (see Table 10.1). This should send a clear signal to business leaders seeking employee loyalty and buy-in.

There is also a noticeable lack of confidence in leaders, with a mere 15 per cent strongly agreeing that they had confidence in their organisation's leadership. This

Table 10.1 Findings of the 1998 MCA/MORI survey

Benchmarks at a glance	Strongly agree
I understand what I need to do in my own job to support organisational aims and goals	39%
I feel I play an important part in meeting our customers' needs	38%
I have the knowledge/skills to do my job in a way that supports organisational goals	37%
I can see how my job performance affects my organisation's success	34%
The people in my team/work area know how we contribute to organisational goals	28%
I have a clear sense of my organisation's vision and direction for the future	27%
I am committed to giving my best to help my organisation succeed	27%
My organisation's culture encourages me to work in innovative ways	17%
I believe in my organisation's vision for the future	16%
I have confidence in my organisation's leadership	15%
My views and participation are valued by my organisation	9%

may explain why only 27 per cent of respondents strongly agreed that they were committed to giving their best to help their organisation succeed. In fact, only 5 per cent of the respondents strongly agreed with all six emotional benchmarks.

Buy-in and business performance

For those respondents who do buy-in both intellectually and emotionally to business goals, they consistently say it improves their job performance and makes them up to twice as likely to recommend their organisation to others, such as customers, potential recruits and other stakeholders.

Other research confirms the value of the emotional capital of internal customers. When *Fortune* magazine (Grant, 1998) announced the 100 best companies to work for in America in 1997, as voted for by more than 20,000 employees, there was a powerful demonstration of the emotional contract between these people and their organisations and the impact on business performance. Of the sixty-one companies in the group that had been publicly traded for at least five years, forty-five had consistently yielded higher returns to shareholders than industry averages. These sixty-one companies averaged annual returns of 27.5 per cent, compared with the typical 17.3 per cent (see Grant, 1998).

Another study by the Institute of Work Psychology at the University of Sheffield (Patterson *et al.*, 1997) correlated a direct link between employee attitudes such as organisational commitment and job satisfaction and company performance in terms of profitability and productivity. According to the researchers, '12% of the variation between companies in their profitability can be explained by variations in the job satisfaction of their employees. Moreover, 13%...can be explained by the differences between companies in organisational commitment.'

In the MCA/MORI study, the combination of understanding plus commitment is shown to create what we have called 'champions'. These are people who are both willing and able to give their best to help the organisation to achieve its vision and goals, and who will act as ambassadors for their brand and/or organisation (see Arganbright and Thomson, 1999).

These champions are vital to overcoming the neutral or negative responses likely from others in their organisation. The MORI normative database (called 'Perspectives') has determined that in Britain today around one in five employees are 'saboteurs'. This means that in an organisation with 1,000 employees, there are some 200 people who would bad-mouth their organisation.

The research suggests that understanding and commitment lead to greater advocacy and, therefore, provide organisations with a much-needed way to counteract saboteurs by creating champions. Yet the research shows that 63 per cent of staff are not champions (see Table 10.2), and unfortunately fall into one of three other camps. These are:

- 'bystanders', who clearly understand organisational goals but do not have the emotional drive to support them;

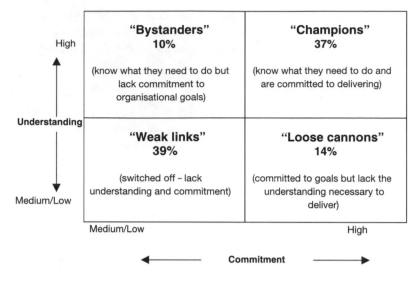

Table 10.2 Buy-in among the British workforce

- 'loose cannons', who are highly motivated to support business goals but do not understand what they are or how to achieve them;
- 'weak links', who are not aware or concerned about business goals.

Communication as a tool to increase buy-in

The survey shows a direct link between good communication and strong buy-in. People with high levels of buy-in rate their company's communication highly, and those with low levels generally rate communication as average or poor.

Fortunately, effective communication can strengthen both intellectual and emotional buy-in. As shown in Table 10.3, those who score their communication satisfaction higher also show higher levels of buy-in. In fact, increasing the effectiveness of communication from a 6 to 8 out of 10 can potentially double levels of buy-in.

Unfortunately, the respondents in our survey gave the effectiveness of communication a mean score of 6 out of 10. This is consistent with MORI's 1997 Omnibus Communications Survey, which shows that the effectiveness of internal business communication in Britain is weak and in fact has not improved in the past twenty-seven years. It also is consistent with a 1996 study conducted by MCA and the Corporate Communication Research Unit at the University of Salford (Arganbright *et al.*, 1996), which explored the effectiveness of traditional top-down employee communication compared with a more involving, two-way, approach.

Impact of change on buy-in

Managers are being hit more heavily by change, which may explain their disap-

Table 10.3 How employees rate the effectiveness of communication

Communication Mean Score	% with high intellectual buy-in or understanding	% with high emotional buy-in or commitment
1–3	36%	34%
4–6	25%	32%
7	44%	50%
8	64%	67%
9	68%	71%
10	85%	79%

pointing levels of understanding and commitment. About 40 per cent say a restructuring or merger/acquisition has directly affected them in the last twelve months, compared with 29 per cent of non-managers (Arganbright and Thomson, 1998).

Levels of communication and internal marketing during periods of dramatic organisational change can have profound effects on the overall effectiveness of staff. Schweiger and Denisi (1991) reported on research that compared the impact of communication within two merging Fortune 500 companies. One plant had no formal communication until the formal announcement; the other had early and frequent communication throughout the planning process. The plant without communication saw a 20 per cent decrease in performance, a 24 per cent increase in uncertainty, a 21 per cent decrease in job satisfaction and an 11 per cent decrease in commitment. By comparison, the plant with early and frequent communication saw no change in performance or commitment and only a 2 per cent decrease in job satisfaction.

Supporting this finding is a survey of more than 5,000 managers in the UK. The report, 'The Quality of Working Life' (Worrall and Cooper, 1997) found that the majority of those surveyed had been affected by organisational change during the preceding twelve months, yet had failed to see the business benefits. When asked about possible improvements, the largest single category of suggestions was about communication, such as greater involvement, the need for more listening by senior managers, and more honest and two-way communication.

Case study: buy-in during a period of change

When Abbey National acquired First National Bank in 1995, the published objective was 'to provide 10 per cent of Abbey National's profits'. This was a laudable aim – but not terribly inspiring. Without a stronger mission for First National, staff were losing their sense of belonging. In a survey, the staff were more likely to see themselves as part of Abbey National or their own specialist division than as part of First National. Nevertheless, the organisation did expand to achieve the Abbey National objective through organic growth and a series of acquisitions. Although this all added up to good news for the business, it only added to the lack of identity and unity internally.

Initially, First National, which is a subsidiary of Abbey National specialising in business, consumer and motor financing, was seen as a conglomerate of disparate businesses, and staff within the new businesses did not feel integrated. As one member of staff commented, there were 'so many different companies and cultures, it's hard to know where everything fits in'. Another said, 'People need to be aware that we all work for the same organisation.' The finance industry is notoriously competitive, and it became clear that the lack of cohesion and direction was holding First National back. The only way forward was to secure staff buy-in to a challenging yet commonly shared goal.

Many organisations have not yet realised the value of having their people share a common goal or vision for the future. Those that do often fail to secure the very support they seek from their people. Why? Because the vision is issued as a top-down edict that does not address people's interests, questions and concerns.

To avoid this common pitfall, First National asked the MCA to carry out a strategic review of First National's communication activities that included extensive research to help shape their business strategy. This research involved a combination of one-to-one interviews to isolate key issues among staff and key messages from top managers; MCA's Issues Groups to explore these issues and identify solutions; and benchmarking research to enable First National to compare itself to industry norms and track its progress.

The research revealed a gap between the aims of the Board and what staff actually understood, and highlighted a number of actions that needed to be taken:

*   Develop a strong brand
*   Align effort around a motivating objective
*   Reengineer the organisation to integrate newly acquired businesses into the whole
*   Introduce a communication strategy to unify the restructured business

First National has already developed a compelling new brand that graphically represents the link between the customer, the intermediary and First National. The new branding has proved very popular: 90 per cent of First National's managers agreed (41 per cent of them strongly) that the new branding is 'a positive move forward'.

A second action point was to focus effort on a motivating goal. One person interviewed expressed a commonly held view that the original Abbey National objective was constraining: 'Why limit our achievement? Why not go for the lot?' Accordingly, First National's Executive Chairman, Tim Ingram, forged a straightforward yet challenging new objective: 'To become the UK's leading finance house'. A bulletin, *Achieving Our Vision Together*, clearly sets out the implications of this objective, together with what it means both corporately and individually. Each bulletin contains information on the staff feedback and what managers are doing about it.

To meet the third action point, the organisation is currently undergoing a major restructuring and reengineering project. The acquired businesses are being integrated into a clearer structure, delineated by product: motor, consumer, business, and retail finance. MCA is working with First National's Project Team to integrate a marketing-driven communication strategy with the changes.

The internal–external link

After a decade of cost cutting, downsizing, reengineering and the like, greater understanding and commitment offer another avenue for enhancing business performance. Every organisation has the ability to unlock the full potential of its business and its brand through its people. Yet most organisations fail to do so.

Today's service-driven economy has moved the marketing discipline from a mass approach to one focused on investment in targeted relationships. As such, it is essential that marketers consider the question 'who are customers really having relationships with these days?' They are certainly not having them with those inanimate products or services that are offered for sale or with the logos or two-dimensional branded images.

Relationships are about people and personalities. This means that customers are building relationships with the people they encounter within organisations – the employees – and the personality that these people give to their organisations. This simple truth is at the heart of internal marketing, which is, in essence, marketing from the inside, out.

This relationship between internal and external customers is not well understood. For this reason MCA commissioned a second survey with MORI in April 1999 (Arganbright and Thomson, 1999) to provide a national benchmark for the effectiveness of staff interactions with customers today, and the commercial benefits that can be gained when people represent their organisations and brands well. This research shows the damage that negative encounters with staff are having on customer loyalty. Fortunately, it also shows the power of staff in building profitable and long-term relationships with customers, and offers vital insights for companies aiming to help their people become a 'living brand'.

For this survey, MORI conducted face-to-face interviews with a nationally representative quota sample of 925 people in the British general public. Interviews were carried out in respondents' homes, using CAPI (Computer Assisted Personal Interviewing). Data have been weighted to reflect the national population profile.

Respondents were asked to think about the companies that make products/services rather than the retailer distributing them. The interviewers were also able to give further instruction at their discretion, asking the respondents to focus on occasions when they have bought or considered buying a company's product or service and also had dealings with that company's staff.

Staff impact on customer relationships

Staff attitudes and behaviours have a significant impact on customer loyalty, more so than many traditional marketing tools. The top three factors that determine whether customers will make a repeat purchase or recommend a company to others are quality, price, and how the staff treats them. In terms of advocacy, 41 per cent of customers say that they are most likely to decide whether to buy or not buy a company's products or services again because of the way staff treat them, ahead of advertising, branding and promotions.

Unfortunately, consumers say that staff currently are not up to the challenge and in many cases are actually damaging relationships with them. The primary reason consumers give for feeling put off from purchasing a company's product or service is how they were treated by staff; ahead of price or quality. In the previous three months alone, one in six consumers have been put off from a purchase because of the way they were treated by staff.

Younger and more affluent consumers – a group sought after by most companies – appear even more dissatisfied with their treatment from staff. Nearly a quarter of those aged between 15 and 34 (22 per cent) and those with a household income of £30,000 and above (23 per cent) were put off from making a purchase because of the treatment received from staff.

'Brand ambassador benchmarks'

To understand what customers experience, we asked them to consider the effectiveness of staff against twelve 'brand ambassador' benchmarks (see Table 10.4). These explore how well the staff are representing their organisation or brand in dealings with customers. They reveal that what customers experience is a far cry from the brand and corporate values most companies espouse:

- Less than half of customers feel staff showed a genuine interest in helping.
- Only one in five say staff showed appreciation for their interest or purchase.
- Less than a third say that staff appeared committed to doing their best, and only one in ten were seen to show pride in their products and services.

The link to competitiveness

The well-known marketing mix of product, price, place and promotion certainly does require a fifth 'P' – people. Only price and quality – which can be replicated by competitors – are on occasions more important to customers than their dealings with staff. When customers feel that staff show a genuine interest in helping (the characteristic that most influences their decision to buy), they are more than twice as likely to purchase a company's products and services again and more than three times as likely to recommend the company to others.

What happens when customers experience more of these brand ambassador benchmark behaviours? As staff deliver against more of these, customers'

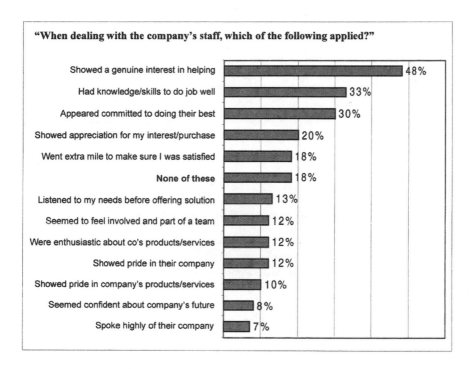

Table 10.4 The effectiveness of staff against twelve 'brand ambassador' benchmarks

intention to repeat purchase and recommend the company increase significantly. In Table 10.5, each star represents the number of benchmarks that customers say applied to their last purchase. One star means only one benchmark was mentioned; four stars indicates that four or more benchmarks were mentioned.

According to our survey, 22 per cent of customers today experience 'no-star' interactions and only 21 per cent have 'four-star' experiences. The benefit for companies is that moving from a no-star experience to a four-star experience makes a customer five times as likely to recommend their company and more than doubles their plans to definitely purchase again.

Companies can boost profits by almost 100 per cent by retaining just 5 per cent more of their customers, according to Reichheld in *The Loyalty Effect* (1994). Our survey shows this link between brand ambassadors and customer loyalty. The question for many organisations is how to turn their people into brand ambassadors?

We at MCA believe that low levels of staff buy-in, as revealed in the research conducted by MCA and MORI in 1998, are causing the staff attitudes and behaviours found in this latest survey (Arganbright and Thomson, 1998). In our opinion, and our experience with numerous clients, it is internal marketing that holds the key to building buy-in and ultimately better relationships with internal and external customers.

	No stars	★	★★	★★★	★★★★ or more
I'd definitely buy their product or service again	31%	61%	62%	71%	76%
I'd recommend to others without being asked	10%	28%	31%	39%	51%

Base: All GB general public (925 people)

Table 10.5 The customer-value index

Note: Based on number of brand ambassador benchmarks that applied

Case study: preparing for competition in the Royal Mail

The direct mail/delivery market in the UK will open to competition in the year 2000, making business clients easy prey for any provider that is better able to service their needs. The Royal Mail's goal is to protect and grow their share of this key market by ensuring they are seen as the Number One quality provider.

Despite the importance of business clients and the threats posed by future competitors, many people working in the Royal Mail did not understand the significance of the business market. In fact, many front-line sorters and mail deliverers had a negative conception of direct mail; they saw it as becoming an obstacle to good service and market growth. As a result, the delivery times for direct mail were often longer than those for first-class and second-class post sent by private consumers. With two-thirds of turnover coming from business clients and direct mail, this trend could have serious consequences for the Royal Mail.

The organisation recognised that an internal marketing approach was needed to shift the attitudes of more than one million staff and prepare for new competition. The first step was a research programme to clarify the strategic messages that senior management wanted to communicate, specifically on direct mail and also more generally on the future of the organisation and its business. Once the key messages were defined, MCA and the Royal Mail worked to uncover the cause of the negative views and to agree the means to reverse them. Jane Tebbey, MCA's senior consultant on the project, explains: 'We needed to find out what would make a difference to people. In a series of focus groups we discovered that many of their views were coloured by their own experiences with direct mail as a consumer and by the views of the domestic customers to whom they delivered mail.'

In addition to their notion of direct mail as 'junk mail', delivery staff understandably felt a strong sense of identity with the doorstep customer, and much less affiliation with the business clients. There was also confusion between direct and unaddressed mail that was fuelling the negative perceptions even more.

Previous internal communication had not helped matters either, according to Jane: 'We discovered that some people didn't believe what they'd been told or hadn't made the link between the importance of direct mail and the future threat of competition.' For example, one focus group participant commented,

'We don't see the results from all this extra mail.' Another remarked, 'They say competition will be a threat, but I just don't believe it.'

The results of the research have formed the basis for an internal marketing plan in which messages are rigorously and consistently delivered using every available media channel. The plan also addresses a need to introduce mechanisms for listening, regular focus groups, and collecting and acting on feedback.

Conclusion

Marketing-based internal communication is the key to forging strong emotional contracts between individuals and the organisation (Thomson, 1998). Emotional and intellectual capital are created through this emotional contract, because there is an honest attempt to balance and satisfy the needs of the organisation and those of internal customers. The critical part of this contract is that internal customers know what is going on, where they fit and what they need to do. Feeling valued and engaged, and knowing that individual contributions count, will increase employees' stock of emotional capital in the business. Indeed, the single most important force affecting internal and external marketing is the what's in it for me? (WIIFM) interest of people involved. Unless they experience relationship marketing themselves, internal customers are never likely to understand, or be motivated enough to use, the approach to drive all their dealings with external customers or with other vital stakeholders within and around the organisation.

In short, if 'inside in' (the organisation talking to itself) is not working, 'inside out' and 'outside in' (the organisation talking to customers and others) is even less likely to work. The business may achieve some of its goals, but it will fail to achieve its full potential for lifetime relationships and profitable business dealings.

Why then are all organisations not practising internal marketing as a management discipline? The answer may rest in the statement of accounts. Goodwill is the accepted accounting principle that reconciles a larger-than-normal return on tangible assets and highlights brand value on a company's financial statements. By and large, the only other intangible assets that are taken into account are patents, trademarks, copyrights and the like: the most overt representations of 'intellectual assets'.

The fact that knowledge is beginning to be treated as an asset is no small achievement. But knowledge held in people's heads is only valuable when they *want* to apply it constructively. Emotional capital, the other side of 'buy-in', also merits a place in financial valuation. Without hard financial measures, internal marketing will not receive the attention it deserves from the business community. Relationships must also be valued as central to the business.

While the value of internal marketing may be a new idea for business leaders, customer retention is not. The number of businesses citing 'customer retention' as a critically important measure in the next five years has jumped to nearly 60 per cent, according to a 1998 survey of 200 senior executives in North America, Europe and Asia by Anderson Consulting and the Economist Intelligence Unit (Graham and Goodman, 1998).

A comprehensive survey by The Conference Board and Heidrick & Struggles confirms that CEOs share this view (Berman, 1999). This survey of more than 650 CEOs worldwide reports that the top management challenges are to find ways to build customer loyalty, reduce costs, engage their employees, and manage mergers, acquisitions or strategic alliances.

The evidence of the research and case studies explored in this chapter suggests that an internal marketing approach can lead to more satisfied internal customers who have the understanding and commitment needed to build more profitable relationships with external customers and more than fulfil the organisation's brand promise. In a world where virtually everything is replicable and building relationships with external customers is invaluable, internal customers are the greatest – and perhaps only – sustainable competitive advantage. Can any organisation or marketer afford to overlook them?

References

Arganbright, L. and Thomson, K. (1998) *The Buy-in Benchmark*, Marlow and London: The Marketing & Communication Agency Ltd (MCA) and Market & Opinion Research International (MORI).

—— (1999) *The Brand Ambassador Benchmark*, Marlow and London: The Marketing & Communication Agency Ltd (MCA) and Market & Opinion Research International (MORI).

Arganbright, L., Thomson, K. and Varey, R.J. (1996) *Breaking out of the Employee Communication Time Warp*, London and Salford: The Marketing & Communication Agency Ltd (MCA) and the Corporate Communication Research Unit, University of Salford.

Berman, M.A. (1999) *The CEO Challenge*, New York: The Conference Board and Heidrick & Struggles.

Graham, A. and Goodman, A. (1998) *Managing Customer Relationships: Lessons from the Leaders*, New York: Anderson Consulting and the Economist Intelligence Unit.

Grant, L. (1998) 'Happy Workers, High Returns', *Fortune*, 12 January.

Patterson, M.G., West, M.A., Lawthom, R. and Nickell, S. (1997) *People Management, Organisational Culture and Company Performance*, Institute of Work Psychology, University of Sheffield, and the Centre for Economic Performance, London School of Economics.

Reichheld, F.F. (1994) *The Loyalty Effect*, Boston, MA: Harvard Business School Press.

Schweiger, D. and Denisi, A. (1991) 'Communication with Employees Following a Merger: A Longitudinal Field Experiment', *Academy of Management Journal* 34(March): 110–35.

Thomson, K. (1998) *Emotional Capital*, London: Capstone Publishing.

Watson Wyatt (1997) 'Work Studies' (annual survey of more than 9,000 employees), London: Watson Wyatt.

Worrall, L. and Cooper, C.L. (1997) 'The Quality of Working Life: 1997 Survey of Managers' Changing Experiences', London: The Institute of Management.

11 Services marketing starts from within

Commentary by *Leonard L. Berry* and
A. Parasuraman

We wrote "Services Marketing Starts From Within" (Berry and Parasuraman, 1992) nearly a decade ago. Much has transpired in the fields of services marketing and management since our article was published. We are pleased our article holds up to the test of time.

The article's basic premise that a company selling performances can only be as good as its performers is as sound today as when originally proposed. Service companies cannot compete effectively without effective service which to one degree or another is performed by people. To create value for customers, service companies must invest in attracting, developing, motivating, and retaining quality people to perform the service. Stated differently, to excel in external marketing, service companies must first excel in internal marketing.

A critical message

If anything, the internal marketing message is even more critical today than in 1992. The labor shortfall we predicted for the service sector in America is now in full swing and competing for talent has never been more important. From hotel housekeepers to restaurant workers to long-distance truck drivers to registered nurses to information technology specialists, service sector employees are in short supply and an alarming number of jobs in these and other fields are going unfilled today.

Moreover, intense price competition reigns in virtually every service industry making excellent service increasingly important. Quality service becomes more important in industries dominated by price competition because without the differentiating force of superior service, a company has little choice but to match competitors' price cuts. Excellent service gives customers non-price reasons to select a company. Can anyone really doubt the importance of strong internal marketing in today's marketplace?

Values and vision

The internal marketing model that we proposed in the 1992 article is sound. Eight years later, we would not de-emphasize any of the model's content but we would offer several refinements based on our most recent studies (for example, Berry, 1995; Berry, 1999; Berry and Parasuraman, 1997). First, we would stress attracting new employees to the firm whose personal values match the firm's values. Humane organizational values that reinforce and celebrate the potential of human beings to develop, achieve and contribute are central to realizing sustainable services success. In our original paper we discussed offering employees a vision that would enrich their work with meaning and purpose. With insights from our newer research, we would make a clearer distinction between *values* (the ideals, philosophy, and principles at the center of the enterprise) and vision (the strategic purpose of the business). Sustaining human excellence in organizations requires both values and vision. They are related but separate constructs that we blended together in the original article.

We would make the values and vision distinction by amending the "compete for talent" component of the model. Replacing "compete for talent" would be "compete for the *right* talent" to stress the hiring not only of talented people, but ones whose values fit the company. Values compatibility between company and employee is powerful. The stronger the fit between the values of senior executives and those of service providers, the stronger the guiding and motivating influence of those values (Berry, 1999). Hiring people who share the company's values and then promoting managers from within the organization generates the values consistency, emotional energy, and decision-making guidance that characterize all great service companies.

Ownership attitudes

A second refinement of our model concerns "leveraging the freedom factor". We would go further today and subsume service freedom – an important issue in service improvement – under "create ownership attitudes", a broader, more powerful concept. The freedom to act on behalf of the customer, to be creative in solving problems, to be a "thinking server", comes from an emotional connection to the company. This is what we mean by ownership attitude. Ownership in its truest form is a state of mind, a sense of attachment, personal responsibility, and pride. Financial ownership can contribute to this state of mind, but does not guarantee it. Other conditions also must be present to bring ownership attitudes to full flower, including openly and honestly sharing company information with employees and offering wide solution spaces within which providers can perform their service.

Inclusion is a central factor in nurturing ownership attitudes in the organization. Being part of an important journey. Being informed, accountable, and in control. Being expected to think on the job, to be resourceful. As one of us recently wrote: "Employees who feel like part-owners of a company are more likely to do what is necessary to sustain the company's success. Owners not only have more to gain if a company succeeds, they have more to lose if it fails" (Berry, 1999: 174).

Teams and teamwork

Finally, if we were to rewrite the article today, we would make a clearer distinction between teams and teamwork in the section "stress team play". Teamwork clearly is essential to any company aspiring to truly excellent service. However, companies do not need to organize with formal teams to have teamwork. Service delivery teams like the AAL and Aetna Life examples in our article are a formal structural approach to service delivery that will not be appropriate for every company's strategy. Teams are not for every company. Teamwork, however, is for every company. Teams require teamwork, but teamwork does not require teams. In rereading our original article we should have made this distinction more clearly. The model label, "stress team play" is correct but the content of the section evolves from teamwork to teams without the necessary distinction being made between them.

Marketing to the marketers

Everything we know about marketing can be applied to employees. After all, employees actually are "customers" of the company in the sense that they enter into an exchange of resources with their employer. Employees "buy" and may choose to leave their jobs. Internal marketing helps a company attract the right kind of job-buyers and minimize employee turnover. Internal marketing also helps a company realize maximum effort from employees. After all, a principal difference between excellent and average service companies is the discretionary effort of service providers. Discretionary effort is the difference between the maximum amount of energy employees can bring to a job and the minimum amount required to avoid penalty. Internal marketing properly executed inspires high levels of discretionary effort.

In a service company, the service providers are the principal marketers because their actions strengthen or weaken the company's reputation with customers and prospects. This is why we need internal marketing. When the product is a performance, the company must market to the marketers, so they in turn will market effectively to the external customer.

August 1999

References

Berry, L. (1995) *On Great Service: A Framework for Action*, New York City: The Free Press.
—— (1999) *Discovering the Soul of Service: The Nine Drivers of Sustainable Business Success*, New York City: The Free Press.
Berry, L. and Parasuraman, A. (1992) "Services Marketing Starts from Within," *Marketing Management*, Winter: 25–34.
—— (1997) "Listening to the Customer – The Concept of a Service Quality Information System," *Sloan Management Review*, Spring: 65–76.

Services marketing starts from within*

A service company can be only as good as its people.

If they aren't sold, customers won't be either.

Leonard L. Berry
A. Parasuraman

Internal marketing, essential to services marketing success, attracts, develops, motivates and retains the qualified employees' excellent service delivery demands.

The best internal marketers share a common approach, no matter what their industries. They compete aggressively for "talent market share," offering a vision that brings purpose and meaning to the workplace.

They equip their people with the skills and knowledge to perform excellently, then give them the freedom to excel. They encourage team play, yet they motivate individual achievement through measurement and rewards. And they base their job design decisions on research.

Because they share a core belief in human potential, they build achievement cultures, knowing that the service product they sell is a stellar performance that satisfies their external and internal customers alike.

For most services, the server cannot be separated from the service. The accountant is a significant part of the accounting service, the agent a significant part of the real estate service, the teacher a significant part of the educational service. In reality, customers "buy" the people when they buy a service.

Service, after all, is a performance and the performance is often labor-intensive. To practice services marketing successfully, firms must practice internal marketing successfully. They must compete imaginatively and aggressively for new employees so that the right people are serving customers. And they must service existing employees well so that these servers will be willing and able to serve their customers well.

Internal marketing is *attracting, developing, motivating, and retaining qualified employees through job products that satisfy their needs.* Internal marketing is the philosophy

* This article is reprinted from *Marketing Management*, Winter 1992, 25–34.

of treating employees as internal customers and it is the strategy of shaping job-products to fit human needs.

The idea of jobs as products may seem far-fetched at first. Yet, a job must satisfy employees' needs to attract and sustain their investment of time, energy, and ego – just as any other product must fulfill customers' requirements to be successful. Not only are jobs products, they are among the most important products that people will ever buy. The best way to attract, develop, motivate, and retain first-rate employees is to market jobs worth buying.

Our purpose in this article is to give definition and direction to the *practice* of internal marketing. Although internal marketing is not a new idea, it is an idea that is often discussed without the specifics needed for implementation. In this article we attempt to get specific by discussing seven essentials for internal marketing as shown in Exhibit 11.1. Weakness in even one of these areas severely limits a firm's internal marketing effectiveness.

Compete for talent

Hiring the best possible people to perform the service is a key factor in services marketing. Yet, many service companies have ill-defined or woefully low standards for the personnel they hire.

They involve few employees in the recruiting, interviewing, and selection process, sometimes delegating these tasks entirely to the personnel department. They tolerate incredibly high employee turnover rates, assuming this is a fact of life they cannot change.

One of the principal causes of poor service quality is hiring the wrong people to perform the service. In a large, empirical study of customer-contact employees from five major service firms, we found that employees who felt their units were not meeting service standards also felt their company was not hiring people qualified to do their jobs.

Why do so many executives permit the wrong people to carry the company flag in front of customers? Part of the answer is the failure to think and act like a marketer when it comes to human resource issues. Read the look-alike employment ads in the fine print of the local newspaper. Is this an effective way to compete for talent? The same firms that compete intensely and imaginatively for customers compete meekly and mundanely for employees.

If ever there was a time for service firms to compete more effectively for talent, that time is now. The service sector is experiencing a labor-force shortfall that will intensify in the years immediately ahead. An expansion of service-sector jobs and an elevation of the skills required for these jobs are occurring just as the labor pool of young adults to assume these positions is shrinking. Moreover, many of the young adults who are available do not possess the required educational background and skills.

Competing for talent market share requires that firms aim high, use multiple recruiting methods, cast a wide net, and segment the market. It is tempting of course to lower hiring standards given the intense competition for capable

Exhibit 11.1 Essentials of internal marketing

employees for certain types of positions. Smart internal marketers ignore this temptation and instead work harder than competitors to find the right people.

They develop ideal candidate profiles for each type of position based on customer service expectations, and they use these profiles in recruiting candidates. They interview multiple candidates for one position, involve multiple employees in the interviewing process, and interview the more promising candidates on multiple occasions. They are tenacious in their pursuit of talent. As Cadillac dealer Carl Sewell writes in his book, *Customers for Life*: "If you haven't talked to 25 people, you haven't looked hard enough" (Sewell and Brown, 1990).

Smart internal marketers also pay more for the best talent and then earn back the higher pay (and more) with greater productivity, improved service quality, lower employee turnover, and additional business. Fidelity Bank of Philadelphia increased customer service representatives' wages by 58% over a two-year period. Customer satisfaction, as measured by customers' willingness to recommend the bank to a friend, climbed from 65% to 90%. Au Bon Pain, a chain of quick-service French bakery cafés, offers a Partner-Manager program under which restaurant managers earn twice the industry average. The program has contributed to double-digit sales and profit gains for individual units, reduced employee turnover, and improved service quality (Schlesinger and Heskett, 1991).

Using a variety of methods to reach prospective employees is also important. Firms seeking new employees need not use only classified advertisements in newspapers, need not use only newspapers when advertising, and need not use only advertising when recruiting. Company-sponsored career fairs, tuition assistance for students who work while attending college, and employee-recruit-an-employee programs with finder fees or other incentives are just a few of the possibilities. In 1991 Wal-Mart Stores employed 20 students from our University as summer interns with the objective of attracting at least half of them into full-time employment upon graduation. Wal-Mart has similar programs at other universities.

Creative internal marketers also capitalize on the opportunities that demographic diversity brings, recruiting more women, minorities, seniors, disabled people, and immigrants. Pizza Hut is hiring hundreds of disabled people each year, tapping into a large pool of disabled Americans who wish to join the labor force.

Wal-Mart employs more than 10,000 people aged 65 or older.

The greater the heterogeneity of the labor pool, the greater the need to accommodate it with job-products tailored to different market segments. Research in the fast-food industry identifies several employee market segments, including people who work mostly for the money, people whose priority is a consistent work schedule, and people who want to advance and make a career in the industry. Fast-food operators offering one employment package for all are clearly missing the mark.

The growth in the 1980s of such human resource concepts as flexible benefits and flexible work hours ("flextime") is indicative of the growing heterogeneity of the labor force and the need to be responsive. Rigid thinking is *passé*. Flexibility is in.

Connecticut's Union Trust Bank has been able to hire more mothers of young children as tellers by accommodating their desire not to work when their children are home from school. Dayton-Hudson, the Minneapolis-based retailer, is training thousands of home care providers so its employees can hire qualified babysitters (Dreyfuss, 1990).

Original Research II, a Chicago telephone research company, successfully employs full-time college students to work part-time as interviewers. One factor in its success is allowing the students to redesign their work schedules every two weeks. The company pays bonuses to meet staffing requirements at unpopular times like Saturday (Posner, 1989).

Toys R Us captures employees' locational preferences in its on-line human resources information system. Jeffrey Wells, Vice President of Human Resources for Toys R Us, reports that when the company decided to open stores in Germany, his department immediately provided a list of 42 employees who wanted to work in Germany.

Offer a vision

The attraction, development, motivation, and retention of quality employees require a clear vision worth pursuing. A paycheck may keep a person on the job physically, but it alone will not keep a person on the job emotionally. People delivering service need to know how their work fits in the broader scheme of business operations. They need to understand and believe in the goal to which they contribute: they need to have a *cause* because serving others is just too demanding and frustrating to be done well each day without one.

Successful internal marketing companies stand for something worthwhile and they communicate this vision to employees with passion. Passion is a strange word to use in a marketing article, yet it is a word that captures the fervent commitment to goal-oriented values that characterizes the best internal marketing companies.

ServiceMaster's vision is to add dignity to work. Managing janitorial, laundry and other unglamorous support services for hospitals, schools, and companies, ServiceMaster lives by the principle of "before asking someone to do something you have to help them be something" (Heskett, 1987). The Downers Grove, Ill., company invests in a variety of basic skills training and educational programs to help employees improve their self-image and future prospects. ServiceMaster also emphasizes the contribution each server makes to the end customer. For example, a physician might be asked to address hospital janitorial staff on how a sanitary and neat room improves patients' recovery chances. Chairman and CEO C. William Pollard states: "We have housekeepers relating to their task and saying, 'Hey, I've got something to do with that person being well'…[our people] work better when they understand the value of their contribution" (Ferguson, 1990).

Visions should be simple, communicated at every opportunity, and communicated personally by top management. Seattle restaurant owner Timothy Firnstahl illustrates the virtues of a simple vision:

> I spent considerable time writing Ten Tenets of Excellence for our organization. We included them in our training manuals and posted them in the restaurants and the offices. One day about a year later, someone asked me what the sixth tenet was, and I couldn't tell her. It came to me that if I couldn't remember the Ten Tenets of Excellence, surely no one else could either. That meant the company had no strategy known to its employees.
>
> (Firnstahl, 1989)

At Stew Leonard's, renowned for its excellent service, the vision is conveyed by the word STEW where S stands for satisfy, T for teamwork, E for excellence and W for wow. At Deluxe Corporation (formerly Deluxe Check Printers) the vision is error-free printing of bank checks and next-day order shipment. At South West Airlines the vision is productivity, fun and working together as a family.

Smart internal marketers use every opportunity to convey the vision. Delta Airlines considers employees a critical second audience for its advertising and runs campaigns with the dual objectives of reaching the flying public and communicating its vision to employees. Delta frequently uses its own employees in its advertising. Before opening its new headquarters building in Dallas, Southwest Airlines put 11,000 employee photographs on the walls. Russell Vernon, the owner of West Point Market, an award-winning specialty food store in Akron, Ohio, uses an Associates Handbook to help define what the company believes in for all employees.

Senior management's personal involvement in communicating the vision to employees is a must. When British Airways presented more than 400 two-day seminars between 1983 and 1985 to focus employee attention on service improvement, the new CEO, Sir Colin Marshall, was personally involved. "Sir Colin personally opened or closed 70% of those classes around the world", says Anthony

Lane, a human resources consultant. "That is extraordinary commitment. But it sends a message that isn't soon forgotten" (quoted in Zielinski, 1990).

Prepare people to perform

Preparing people to perform and market the service enhances every sub-goal of internal marketing: attracting, developing, motivating and retaining superior employees. Unfortunately, servers are often ill-prepared for the service role. They receive training, but it is too little, or too late, or not the kind of training they need. Or they may receive adequate technical skills training, but they do not receive enough *knowledge*: they learn *how* but not *why*.

A common mistake that companies make is to view employee skill and knowledge development as events (a three-day course, an annual seminar) rather than an ongoing process. The inclination to put employees through a specific training programme and then to consider them "trained" is both strong and wrong. Servers need to learn continuously as learning is a confidence builder, a motivating force, and a source of self-esteem. What managers perceive as unmotivated employee behavior is often unconfident employee behavior. Employees are unlikely to be motivated to perform services they do not feel competent and confident to perform.

Middle Managers as Teachers. One of the most positive actions firms can take to improve employee learning is to promote better teachers into middle management. Most employees in large and medium-size organizations are exposed daily to the middle managers to whom they report. The opportunity for teaching is great – and often wasted because the wrong people are in charge. Individuals are frequently promoted to management positions because of their success in non-management positions: their service philosophy, their commitment to helping others improve their performance, and their communication skills may not have been considered. The capacity for teaching is one of the principal criteria that should be used when selecting people for middle management positions.

Companies need to help existing middle managers become better teachers in addition to improving the selection criteria for new managers. Indeed, managers should take the courses designed for frontline servers before the frontline servers take them. It is demoralizing for an employee to return from training and education experiences enthusiastic about applying new skills or knowledge only to confront an insecure supervisor threatened by something new. It is also wasteful because new learning requires repetition and reinforcement to take hold. Just as learning boosts the confidence of frontline servers, so does it boost the confidence (and openness) of the managers for whom they work. As Berry, Bennett, and Brown write: "Training and education for managers is truly pivotal – for the example it sets, for the understanding it builds, and for the leadership and coaching skills it nurtures" (Berry *et al.*, 1989).

Investing in Learning. A company that makes a strategic commitment to the skill and knowledge development of its employees develops a reputation for investing in people and benefits accordingly.

Original Research II offers its employees numerous short workshops or reading packages, many on subjects requested by the employees, such as using a calculator and memo writing. GTE Mobile Communications unconditionally guarantees employees at least 40 hours of formal classroom education and training annually. Here are some guidelines for making the training and education investment:

1 **Be guided by data.** Use employee and customer research data to determine what skills and knowledge to teach. For example, companies can learn more about employees' perceived skill and knowledge deficiencies, as well as their interests, by offering employees some "tuition credits" to spend on in-house courses of their own choosing. Companies can also use employee surveys and focus group interviews to identify learning priorities. Two critical, open-ended questions to ask employees who complete a course are: "Did you learn what you need to perform your job well?" and "What topics were not covered that you wish had been covered?" Customer service expectations and perceptions data are also important in revealing subject and skill areas requiring greater attention. Customer surveys that indicate important service dimensions on which the company is perceived to be deficient clarify the learning priorities.

2 **Use a mix of learning approaches.** Use multiple learning approaches, such as classroom instruction, role playing and self-instructional programming: no single approach fits all needs and people. Be bold and creative. Meridian Banking Group has had employees prepare deposit slips with Vaseline smeared on their glasses and count money with three fingers taped together to help them understand the problems that elderly customers with poor eyesight or arthritis might face in the bank.

3 **Use role models.** Invite the most credible executives to be instructors on company courses. Put them in the position to share their expertise and model their values and style. Also invite successful peers to be instructors and session leaders.

4 **Institutionalize learning.** Devote part of regular staff meetings to skill and knowledge development. Distribute selected articles, videos, or other educational materials systematically. Take employees on field trips to visit other companies and then ask them to share with each other the best and worst of what they saw.

5 **Evaluate and fine-tune.** Administer multistage evaluations of skill and knowledge development efforts. Find out from employees and their managers what on-the-job changes have resulted from participation in a learning program. Evaluate at several different times after the program has ended, for example, after one and three months.

Stress team play

Service work is demanding, frequently frustrating, and sometimes demoralizing. The sheer number of customers to serve, such as on a full airline flight, can be psychologically and physically overwhelming. Some customers are rude. Control over the service is often dispersed among different organizational units that function without cohesion or a unified spirit, limiting contact employees' ability to effectively serve their customers.

It is common for service providers to be so stressed by the service role that they become less caring, less sensitive, less eager to please. What customers perceive as impersonal or bureaucratic behavior is often the coping behavior of weary servers who have endured too many punches in the real world of service delivery.

One important dynamic in sustaining servers' motivation to serve is the presence of service "teammates." An interactive community of coworkers who help each other and achieve together is a powerful antidote to service burnout. Team involvement can be rejuvenating, inspirational, and fun. It also raises the stakes for individual performance. Letting down the team may be worse than letting down the boss (Berry *et al.*, 1990).

CRST Inc., an Iowa-based trucking company, now uses teams of two drivers on long-haul runs. The program was started to bolster service reliability, but it has also improved driver morale in what tends to be a stressful, lonely, high-turnover occupation.

Specifically trained personnel at CRST coordinate the teams and their schedules. The company helps each driver assess his or her preferences, habits and personality type and then attempts to pair up drivers who will be compatible (Ponzani, 1991).

One way teamwork supports the willingness to serve is by enhancing the ability to service. For servers to come through for their customers, others within the organization must come through for them. Teamwork enhances internal service. Our research shows convincingly that teamwork is central to delivering excellent service. Contact employees in five major service firms who indicate that their organizational units are *not* meeting service standards *disagree* with the following statements:

- I feel that I am part of a team in my unit.
- Everyone in my unit contributes to a team effort in serving customers.
- I feel a sense of responsibility to help my fellow employees do their jobs well.
- My fellow employees and I cooperate more than we compete.
- I feel that I am an important member of this company.

The more people and functions involved in the chain of services leading to the end service, the greater the need for service teams. As University of Southern California's Edward Lawler says: "You have to ask. 'How complex is the work?' The more complex, the more suited it is for teams" (quoted in Dumaine, 1990).

The richest form of service teamwork requires long-lasting team membership; regular team contact; team leadership; shared goals; and team performance measurement and rewards (in addition to individual employee measurement and rewards). Traditional functional organization structures impede the development of these teamwork characteristics and more and more companies can be expected to shift to market-team structures in the 1990s.

Aid Association for Lutherans (AAL) totally reorganized its $50 billion insurance business from a functional structure to a market-team structure in 1987. Before reorganizing, AAL field agents contacted various internal departments for support services, a cumbersome and impersonal process. Field agents now contact an assigned home office team to receive the internal service they need. These all-purpose teams perform more than 150 internal services previously spread throughout the organization. Management gives the restructuring credit for reducing case-processing time by as much as 75% (*Business Week*, 1988).

Aetna Life has reorganized its operations staff into cross-functional teams and has even installed "team" furniture to support the groups. The furniture provides a central work area for team meetings and nearby desks that offer privacy for individual work. *Fortune* quotes Aetna executive William Watson, "You don't need to run around the building to get something done."

Leverage the freedom factor

Human beings were not meant to be robots. Yet, when managers use thick policy and procedure manuals to severely limit employees' freedom of action with customers they robotize the service role.

Rule book management undermines employees' confidence in managers, stifles employees' personal growth and creativity, and chases the most able employees out the door in search of more interesting work.

Rule book management usually does not benefit end-customers either. Unempowered employees deliver regimented, "by-the-book" service when a creatively tailored "by-the-customer" service is really needed. While managers rein in servers, customers wish they could be served by "thinking servers".

Two stories demonstrate the virtues of leveraging the freedom factor in service. One concerns a banking office manager who kept shivering customers outside on a cold day while he stood inside the door in full view, watch in hand, waiting for opening time to let customers in. When asked why he didn't open early to accommodate the waiting customers, the banker claimed that banking law prevented him from doing so. In fact, it was the bank's policy: law had nothing to do with it.

The second story concerns a distressed bank customer whose ATM card was swallowed by the machine just as she was leaving on a trip. Needing cash for the trip and not near the bank, the customer telephoned a bank officer who sent her the needed $200 in a taxicab.

The two stories illustrate the difference between unthinking and thinking service behaviors. The manager in the first story is an enforcer of rules; and the officer in the second story, it turns out, ignored bank policy in sending the money by cab. Although his actions were inexpensive and helped a desperate customer (who now raves about the bank's fantastic service), the banker probably would have been turned down had he asked his superior, according to the bank's executive vice president. Nonetheless, thinking behavior prevailed and the customer, banker, and bank benefited.

Frequently, the opposite occurs. Unthinking behavior prevails and customer, server, and company all lose out.

Service companies do need rules, of course. Airline travelers certainly want pilots to follow the rules of flight safety. We are not advocating the elimination of policies and procedures to advance internal marketing: what we are advocating is thinning the service rule book to its bare essentials. Good internal marketing involves giving servers the opportunity to create for their customers and achieve for themselves.

Practicing the other facets of internal marketing discussed in this article encourages empowerment. Executives have more confidence to award authority and responsibility when they truly compete for talent. A strong company vision guides employee behavior and fewer rules are needed. Skill and knowledge development gives employees the confidence to innovate for customers. And the inter-dependencies and shared goals of team play stimulate individual initiative.

Empowering employees is not easy. Managers will not necessarily welcome more authority for their direct reports – and less control for themselves. Some servers would prefer everything spelled out to avoid the additional pressure of creating problem-solving and the risk of making mistakes. It is, after all, less work and less risky to tell a customer that nothing can be done than to send the customer $200 in a taxi.

For most servers, however, the freedom to create for customers, to be innovative and smart, to do the right thing, adds richness and dignity to their work. Coming through for customers is simply more fun than impersonating a robot.

Pushing authority and responsibility downward into the organization, close to the customer, requires conscious efforts to thin the rule book, determination and patience. Most service companies would benefit from task forces that review existing policies and procedures with the mandate to modify or discard those that unnecessarily restrict service freedom. Companies would also benefit from education programs that teach frontline servers values, not just rules. And performance measurement and reward systems need to encourage creativity and initiative on behalf of customers.

Moreover, firms need to directly address the issue of empowerment in educating and training managers. Managers must be taught the dangers of over-management: they must learn about the good that can come from widening the solution boundaries for their people.

Measure and reward

The goals of internal marketing are thwarted if employee performance is not measured and rewarded. People at work need to know that they will be measured by how well they do and that it is worthwhile to do well. Job-products that offer the opportunity for achievement are most likely to fit the needs of human beings, yet achievement remains unidentified and uncelebrated without measurement and rewards.

Unfortunately, many service companies do a poor job of building an achievement culture. Performance measurement systems often focus exclusively on *output measures*, such as size or accuracy of transactions, and ignore *behavioral measures*, such as customer perception of the responsiveness or empathy of the service.

Moreover, performance feedback to employees may be infrequent or not presented constructively. Sometimes measurement leads to no apparent consequence: the employees who perform well fare no better than others in compensation, advancement, or recognition.

Firms intent on rewarding the best performers often focus too narrowly on financial incentives and do not reap the benefits of multiple forms of recognition. Studying the relative importance of different rewards to commercial and corporate account managers in a large North American bank, Dallas consultant George Rieder found that they considered responsibility and authority, a personalized development plan, and sales skills training to be among the most important. Dollars were important but not all-important.

A Few Guidelines on Measurement. The key to an effective reward system is an effective performance measurement system that identifies who deserves the rewards. An effective system measures performance that most contributes to the company's vision and strategy, and it does so in a clear, timely, and fair manner. Convoluted or complicated systems fail to focus employee attention – one of the principal objectives of performance measurement. Infrequent feedback does not provide the regular reinforcement that the objectives of teaching and continual improvement require. Unfair systems undermine the credibility of the measurement feedback they produce and the reward decisions they influence. Characteristics of a fair performance measurement system are enumerated in Exhibit 11.2.

Exhibit 11.2

Characteristics of a fair performance measurement system

- The measures relate directly to service standards. There is consistency between the priorities of a service role and the manner in which role performance is measured.
- Service providers are prepared to perform the service role. They have been given the opportunity to learn the skills and knowledge they need to do well in the measurement system.
- Service providers have provided input on the appropriateness and fairness of the measures that are used.
- The measurement approaches have been explained to those whose performance is being measured.
- The measures are administered on an ongoing basis to minimize the impact of a single measurement encounter.

> • The measures are as uniform as possible among work groups so that everyone plays by the same rules.
> • Multiple measures are used to overcome the disadvantages of any one approach and to provide different-angled views of service performance.
> (Adapted from Leonard L. Berry, David R. Bennett and Carter W. Brown, *Service Quality – A Profit Strategy for Financial Institutions*, Homewood, Illinois: Dow Jones-Irwin, 1989, p.176)

Performance measurement and reward systems powerfully symbolize a company's culture.

Employees know that management measures and rewards what is important. Thus, it is beneficial to disseminate performance measurement data to the appropriate senior executives.

People in the trenches of service organizations performing work that at least some of the time is intrinsically unrewarding need to know that significant others in the organization will be aware of their performance.

A Few Guidelines on Rewards. Here are several reward-system guidelines developed from our studies of service organizations and interviews with service employees:

- Link rewards to the firm's vision and strategy. Reward performance that moves the firm in the intended direction.
- Distinguish between competence pay (compensation for doing one's job) and performance pay (extra rewards for outstanding performance).
- Use multiple methods to reward outstanding performers, including financial rewards, nonfinancial recognition, and career advancement. Consider the possibilities of rewarding employees with stock and making them owners.
- Remember the power of a pat on the back. Rewards need not always be elaborate or expensive; the sincerity of the recognition is most important.
- Compete for the sustained commitment of employees. Develop enduring reward systems and use short-term programs such as sales contests sparingly or not at all.
- Stress the positive. Use reward systems to celebrate achievement rather than to punish.
- Give everyone a chance. Avoid the trap of rewarding people in some positions (for example, field salespeople) but not in other positions (for example, secretaries).
- Reward teams and not just individuals. Reinforce team play with team rewards, while also rewarding superior individual performers.

Know thy customer

Marketing's oldest axiom is to know the customer. Designing job-products that attract, develop, motivate, and retain employee-customers demands sensitivity to their aspirations, attitudes, and concerns. Marketing research is as important in internal marketing as in external marketing.

Linda Cooper, Vice President of Consumer Affairs at First Chicago, describes a situation in her bank where mystery shopping scores for tellers were consistently low on the item "willingness to help." This was a real problem because the bank's analysis of what factor most influences customers to recommend the bank to a friend showed it was "willingness to help." Another bank executive believed the remedy was more training. Cooper was not so sure and held several discussions with groups of tellers. What she learned was that the tellers were upset at their supervisors and the bank.

One significant issue was that tellers were closely instructed about which transactions were acceptable and which were not: for example, exceeding check-cashing limits. However, if customers complained, supervisors sometimes overrode the tellers – with tellers losing face in front of customers. Cooper had the tellers and supervisors jointly agree on a written guideline for overrides. (In this case, adding to the rulebook made sense.)

This story illustrates the need to listen to service performers in service businesses. The bank used research with end-customers to learn that it had a problem. Had it relied on the assumption about the cause of the problem and not made the effort to listen to the tellers, time and money would have been wasted on the wrong solution.

First Chicago is an ardent practitioner of employee research. In addition to holding monthly focus group interviews with employees, the bank has installed an employee telephone hotline called "2-Talk." Answered in the Consumer Affairs Department's Action Center, employees are encouraged to call 2-Talk whenever they receive poor service themselves, witness service problems, or have service-improvement ideas.

Each quarter, retail bank employees receive a questionnaire to which they respond anonymously. The questionnaire is accompanied by a letter from the banking group head summarizing the findings from the previous survey and the actions taken. In a recent year the first quarter's survey included questions such as: "Do you have what you need to do your job?" and "Does the equipment work?"

The second quarter survey concerned employees' attitudes toward the bank's services, prices, and communications. The third quarter survey focused on employees' perceptions of internal service quality. The fourth quarter survey covered employees' satisfaction with their immediate supervisor and senior management. Employees rated managers on issues such as whether they discussed work priorities, appreciated extra effort, and were visible. The following questions also were asked:

• Would you refer a friend to work here?

Does your company	YES	NO
View attracting the best employees as important as competing for end-customers?		
Use creative approaches to compete for talent?		
Assign the right people to represent and recruit for the company?		
Offer a strong vision in which employees can believe?		
Have a succinct statement of its vision?		
Communicate its vision frequently?		
View employee skill and knowledge development as an investment rather than an expense?		
View employee education as an ongoing process?		
Help employees understand the "why" and not just the "how" of their jobs?		
Encourage and facilitate teamwork among employees?		
Help employees appreciate how they contribute to the company's overall goals?		
Strive to eliminate policies and rules that unnecessarily restrict employees?		
Celebrate and reward "thinking" behavior from employees?		
Teach managers the power of empowerment?		
Measure and reward employee performance that contributes most to the company's vision?		
Use multiple methods for measuring and rewarding performance?		
Provide all employees with the opportunity to be recognized for their excellence?		
Think of employees as customers with needs to be fulfilled by the company?		
Use formal and informal means to ascertain employees' attitudes, concerns, and needs?		
Act on employee research findings to improve the quality of worklife?		

SCORING PROCEDURE:
Give your company one point for each YES answer (assign zero points to NO answers). Interpret your company's total score as follows:

19 – 20 points	Excellent internal marketer
17 – 18 points	Good internal marketer
15 - 16 points	Fair internal marketer
Less than 15 points	Poor internal marketer

Exhibit 11.3 Rate your company's internal marketing effectiveness

- Would you bank here if you weren't an employee?
- If you were president of the bank, what changes would you make to improve service quality and morale?

(Cooper and Summers, 1990)

Internal marketing research backfires unless management is prepared to take action on significant findings. First Pennsylvania Bank vice chairman Les Butler states: "Don't ask if you really don't want to hear. Don't ask if you only seek your preconceived answer. Value the input, value the participation, explain why their ideas are being sought and how they will be used."

In summary

A service company can be only as good as its people. A service is a performance, and it is usually difficult to separate the performance from the people. If the people don't meet customers' expectations, then neither does the service.

To realize its potential in services marketing, a firm must realize its potential in internal marketing – the attraction, development, motivation, and retention of qualified employee-customers through need-meeting job-products. With services, internal marketing paves the way for external marketing.

The companies that practice internal marketing most effectively will: (1) compete aggressively for talent market share; (2) offer a vision that brings purpose and meaning to the workplace; (3) equip people with the skills and knowledge to perform their service roles excellently; (4) bring people together to benefit from the fruits of team play; (5) leverage the freedom factor; (6) nurture achievement through measurement and rewards; and (7) base job-product design decisions on research. Exhibit 11.3 presents a rating sheet that readers can use to evaluate internal marketing effectiveness in their organizations.

The best managed service companies are strong internal marketers. A theme that connects the companies mentioned in this article – Wal-Mart, Southwest Airlines, Stew Leonard's, ServiceMaster, First Chicago and many others – is a fundamental core belief in the potential of human beings to achieve. The managements of these companies invest in building achievement cultures which is the best way to meet the wants and needs of internal *and* external customers when the product is a performance.

Authors' note

This article is adapted from Chapter 9 of Leonard L. Berry and A. Parasuraman's *Marketing Services: Competing Through Quality* (New York: The Free Press, 1991). Professors Berry and Parasuraman have collaborated on another book in this area, *Delivering Quality Service: Balancing Customer Perceptions and Expectations* (New York: The Free Press, 1990).

Further reading

Berry, L.L., Bennett, D.R. and Brown, C.W. (1989) *Service Quality: A Profit Strategy for Financial Institutions*, Homewood, IL.: Dow Jones-Irwin, p. 160.

Berry, L.L., Zeithaml, V.A. and Parasuraman, A. (1990) "Five Imperatives for Improving Service Quality," *Sloan Management Review*, Summer, p. 33.

Business Week (1988) "Work Teams Can Rev Up Paper-Pushers, Too," *Business Week*, November 28, pp. 64–72.

Cooper, L. and Summers, B. (1990) *Getting Started in Quality*, Chicago, IL.: The First National Bank of Chicago, p. 14.

Dreyfuss, J. (1990) "Get Ready for the New Work Force," *Fortune*, April 23, pp. 172, 176.

Dumaine, B. (1990) "Who Needs a Boss," *Fortune*, May 7, p. 53.

Ferguson, T.W. (1990) "Inspired From Above, ServiceMaster Dignifies Those Bel
  Wall Street Journal, May 8, p. A21.
Firnstahl, T.W. (1989) "My Employees Are My Service Guarantee", *Harvard
  Review,* July–August, pp. 28–9.
Heskett, J.L. (1987) "Lessons in the Service Sector," *Harvard Business Review,* March–April,
  p. 121.
Ponzani, L. (1991) "Keeping Drivers Is Not Impossible. Just Difficult", *Transport Topics,*
  March 11, p. 13.
Posner, B.G. (1989) "Taming the Labor Shortage," *Inc.,* November, p. 168.
Schlesinger, L.A. and Heskett, J.L. (1991) "Breaking the Cycle of Failure in Services",
  Sloan Management Review, Spring, p. 20.
Sewell, C. and Brown, P.B. (1990) *Consumers for Life,* New York: Doubleday Currency, p.
  68.
Zielinski, D. (1990) "Effective Services Messages Are Sent Often – and at All Job Levels,"
  The Service Edge, May, p. 3.

12 Internal Marketing

A relationships and value-creation view

Peter A. Dunne
James G. Barnes

Introduction

More than ever before, marketing planners must pay careful attention to the design of an integrated *internal* marketing programme. Increased attention toward the internal market (i.e. employees) is warranted owing to the challenge facing organisations in today's increasingly competitive global climate. The nature of business has evolved such that both manufacturing and service industries are realising the importance of efficient and tailored customer service as a source of competitive advantage in a service economy (Grönroos, 1990a).

Upon close analysis it would be difficult to argue that any sector exists within the marketplace that does not contain, or rely upon, a service component. Under such circumstances, employees become a critical resource with a vital role in long-term success. As the global economy moves toward reliance upon innovation-based organisations and knowledge-based workers, firms will have to look internally for sources of competitive advantage. Amidst the current environment of change, the only competitive weapon remaining is organisation (Ulrich, 1998). In an environment of great flux where profound changes occur, it is perhaps only this resource that the firm can depend upon as possessing ongoing potential for sustainable competitive advantage. The employees represent the most constant and fundamental component of the organisation as they, in fact, *are* the organisation and are the basis upon which to begin the development of sustainable firm competencies.

The development of a 'human resource as customer' initiative would best be served through the contributions of both the marketing and human resources functions as it reflects the common roots of each discipline within psychological theory. The theoretical underpinnings explored herein have traditionally fallen under the marketing rubric and have been developed as internal marketing (IM). It is suggested that a convergence has emerged between what has come to be called IM and the direction that human resources must take to remain effective in the changing economy and workplace.

The role of human resources

It is necessary to discuss internal marketing independently from the historic human resources (HR) function of an organisation to connote the perceived similarities, differences, complementary and disparate elements, and to elucidate the common intentions and interests of each function. Whether such a function ultimately becomes the domain of marketing or HR, it is argued that an IM initiative must be formulated in familiar marketing terms in order to develop the appropriate focus and an effectual perspective. This is not to infer a failure on the part of the HR function, but to enunciate broad changes that have occurred in the relevant environments. A shifting emphasis is required in most industries in order to remain competitive in the face of advancing competition and new technologies. A marketing approach allows a more relevant focus and possible reorganisation of the marketing and HR functions in light of these changes.

As the functional unit within an organisation responsible for the recruitment, selection and retention of employees, it must be seen that this implicitly proposes a marketing role be established within the HR department, particularly in service organisations. In this sense, HR is an integral component of the promotional mix in the broadest sense. Its function is to prepare employees for life in the firm, to become a part of the culture, to be productive and contributing members, to positively evaluate the firm, and to recruit desirable candidates. An internal marketing programme would be based upon explicit marketing principles and models and *could* be integrated into the HR function, or with ongoing integration or co-management between departments. Such a perspective allows greater appreciation of what is required for success and provides frameworks from which to build a suitable response and initiative.

The HR function has, perhaps, never been more necessary than it is in today's turbulent environment. Unfortunately, this is at a time when some believe HR to be often ineffective, incompetent and costly (Ulrich, 1998). The HR function has not evolved to meet the changes in the firm and the marketplace. Many who write about business or operate businesses have debated the utility of the administrative function and have expressed doubts about its contribution to organisational performance under its current constitution (for example, Ulrich, 1998). Today's organisation requires more innovative and creative HR processes through shifting from traditional activities such as staffing, compensation, policy policing and the role of regulatory watchdog towards more outcome-based activities. HR should be defined not by what it does but what it delivers. These 'deliverables' should be results that enrich the organisation's value to customers, investors, and employees. In envisioning the future of HR, Ulrich (1998) believes organisational excellence can be pursued in the following four ways, by HR becoming (1) a partner in strategy execution, helping to move planning into the marketplace; (2) an expert in how work is organised; (3) a champion for employees, representing their concerns while working to increase employee contribution and commitment; and (4) an agent of continuous transformation, shaping processes and a culture that improves the organisation's capacity for change.

The process of change itself requires assistance. This is of particular relevance in regard to the last two applications suggested by Ulrich. But success in the new marketplace requires resources beyond that of the marketing function alone. It requires the integrative efforts of the organisation as a whole, and in particular the individual employees that form the firm. As such, the integration of these two units may be beneficial to the overall success of the firm. In its current role, HR activities appear to be, and often are, disconnected from the real work of an organisation (Ulrich, 1998). To be of value in today's environment, HR must develop beyond its old niche and become more integrated with the rest of the organisation.

A cooperative programme is required to initiate change. Tasks such as shaping the vision, leading the change, creating and communicating a shared need, and mobilising commitment are all very strongly marketing-oriented tasks. At the least, they can be appreciated for the benefits achievable by undertaking a marketing perspective in their design and implementation. Change is often resisted and scares employees and management as recent capricious times have taught employees to be wary. The development of a marketing-oriented initiative that delivers a relevant value proposition will help reduce such apprehension and replace resistance with resolve, commitment, greater loyalty and understanding. This will ultimately help both the marketing and HR functions to provide greater utility and results to the organisation.

Background of internal marketing

Although the term 'internal marketing' has been employed in the marketing and human resources literature for over twenty years, there still remains an ambiguous cloud around how it is conceptualised, and the extent to which a shared definition exists among researchers and practitioners. As well, there would be issues between the disciplines as to the appropriateness of placing such an initiative under the umbrella of marketing. This is not meant to assert that this is correct or that the HR function should now fall under this umbrella. The discussion takes this form as the theoretical writings dealing with this issue have, for the most part, been written by marketers, in marketing terms, and have been labelled as such.

As the term was conceived before the service 'revolution', it may be assumed that some 'evolution' in application and perception has led to this blurred conception. Sasser and Arbeit (1976) initially proposed internal marketing as an approach to service management whereby efforts were directed at the recruitment, training, motivation, communication and retention of suitable service-oriented employees. This, perhaps, indicates that early perceptions of the utility of such an initiative were seen for their value in contributing to the HR function although, clearly, marketing and promotional considerations weigh heavily in such considerations. Also, this recognised that the HR function held some direct relationship to the quality or efficiency of service delivery to the external customer.

Although much of the nature of 'work' has changed, as has the nature of many customer relationships, it can be argued that such a direct relationship between these functions still exists. The relationship is clearly demonstrated in the Service–Profit Chain (Heskett *et al.*, 1994). A stronger relationship, or a causal link, may also be argued to exist. The Sasser and Arbeit (1976) perspective remains today a valid view of internal marketing, as a decade after this definition was offered, MacStravic (1985) continued to define internal marketing as encompassing the efforts of an organisation to recruit, train, motivate and reward its members toward more satisfying marketing behaviour. It can be seen that these represent focal elements and still retain a balanced focus between the administrative and marketing perspectives. This focus is externally (market) driven; however, this requires an internal initiative to enhance the potential for success. What is suggested is a more implicit approach that focuses upon the employee as the internal customer, with internally focused goals that benefit and reward this stakeholder group. This involves greater inclusion of employees into the process. It is within this enlightened evolution that the two disciplines become blurred in their roles.

Grönroos (1990a) proposed that the purpose of IM is to motivate employees toward service-mindedness and customer-oriented performance by an active marketing-like approach, where a variety of activities are used internally in an active and coordinated way. While this effectively describes the goal of such initiatives, little is provided toward operationalisation. Compton *et al.* (1987) provided an expansive and concise definition that captured the nature of the task at hand. They state the objectives of IM initiatives are (1) to help employees understand and accept the importance of the interactions with the customer and their responsibility for the total quality and the interactive marketing performance of the firm; (2) to help employees understand and accept the mission, strategies, goals, services, systems and external campaigns of the firm; (3) to continually motivate the employees and inform them about new concepts, goods, services and external campaigns, as well as economic results; and (4) to attract and keep good employees.

Similar activities were described several years later, although in more operational (or tactical) terms. Gilmore and Carson (1995) describe the range of IM activities as including (1) the internal and external marketing interface; (2) the application of the marketing mix to internal customers; (3) the use of marketing training and internal communication methods to sell the staff on their role within the organisation; (4) the involvement and empowering of staff to allow them to make decisions in relation to dealing with customers; (5) the development of managers and employees' role responsibility and cross-functional participation; and (6) the functional responsibility of the organisation for internal marketing integration.

These objectives indicate the development of an integrated employee programme that inculcates employees into an environment that is focused upon the goals of the firm and their role in serving the external customer to achieve that end. It also supports an explicit marketing orientation in as much as the target of these efforts, the employees, should be viewed as a customer group.

They must receive the attention and consideration that is required to successfully 'market' these ideas. This allows for the tactical development and implementation of this programme. A marketing perspective provides familiar frameworks to develop a practical programme to achieve the buy-in of employees and prepares them to sell the company to others.

Clearly, there are common goals/purposes that represent a broad spectrum of influences that are relevant to the study of such a construct. A full appreciation of the concept extends far beyond consideration of the traditional external marketing model. The differences that exist are both quantitative and qualitative in nature. The traditional external model, however, provides a well-understood point of departure from which to investigate effective methods of internal implementation. From there, it is possible to apply and adapt well-recognised HR/personnel practices while evolving the IM model toward a 'relationships'-based approach.

The personality of a service firm is determined by the organisation of a complex set of interrelated interpersonal factors and, as such, it is critical to understand the importance of psychological integration with respect to various traits, feelings and attitudes regarding the relationships between employee satisfaction, customer satisfaction and profitability. Evidence suggests that success in the marketplace is predicated upon successful integration *within* the organisation (Congram *et al.*, 1987). The challenge lies with implementing these so that their positive benefits can be fully realised.

The literature portrays IM as having two primary focuses. It is designed to complement external strategic marketing efforts through the facilitation of personal interactions between staff and 'clients'. These interactions are seen to be instrumental in encouraging customer attraction and satisfaction. Secondly, and more fundamentally, it serves to develop and maintain a motivated and satisfied workforce that contributes to the organisation's external and strategic marketing objectives, as well as to quality, productivity and efficiency (MacStravic, 1985). As such, a successful IM initiative would serve both the organisation and the individual employee.

IM should, in principle, address two motives. It should address the issue of employee satisfaction through the creation of value within the employment relationship. It should also address service quality and efficiency for the internal customer. Through this internal service perspective, satisfaction and value for the employee should also be enhanced. In today's business environment, it is these issues that should be included among the mandates of both HR and marketing.

Reflections on internal marketing

The customer inside the organisation is represented by all those employees who rely on the roles and functioning of other employees to discharge their own duties. This demonstrates the importance and the impact of addressing such a market. It can also be seen how service provision *within* an organisation can greatly influence employees' ability to provide quality service or products to the end consumer. As such, there are two different perspectives from which internal marketing can be viewed: it can be conceptualised as the benefits (value) it delivers to the employee, or as the set of benefits it provides to the firm.

The traditional HR perspective focuses upon the employee and employee functioning primarily for the benefit of the firm. An IM perspective (within HR or not) also focuses upon the employee, but primarily for the benefit of the employee. But there is the belief that this will ultimately benefit the firm and clients. Although this distinction appears to be a subtle one, it is not. This places greater emphasis on the non-monetary value the employee receives through the employee relationship. This strategically creates a series of interrelated loops creating synergies that leverage benefits received by each group. Such an approach may be considered a part of a well-integrated marketing mix.

This demonstrates the consistency and complementary nature of such an approach with initiatives aimed toward the external market. This simply requires extension, and some modification, for the internal market where parallel functions and processes exist. The external market analogy provides a picture of the relationships that exist, providing appreciation for the roles of the players. What is required is the development of a parallel component to external marketing that recognises the special nature of this internal market. The link between the external and internal view is that, in service organisations, employees represent a critical success factor. The organisation must tailor a programme that will address the human resources issues that exist within such a marketplace and focus on the aforementioned motives.

The desired goal can be clearly recognised as a marketing function; particularly as one subscribes to the view that marketing is all about customer satisfaction. As such, the most qualified experience and skills in assessing the market needs and design of such an initiative, as well as the execution, are those of marketing. Like any marketing programme, development requires the involvement, input, and expertise of the 'market' experts. In this circumstance, this means the cooperation of the HR professionals of the firm as experts in the internal market.

Cultural initiative

An IM programme should be envisioned as a cultural initiative in that it transforms the orientation of the organisation to focus upon a service orientation and culture. Such a culture demonstrates an appreciation of *all* customers. The firm grows to value its employees through greater employee focus; employees treat their internal customers similarly, which is carried through to the external customer. A service and customer-oriented culture should come to dominate most of the functioning of the firm. Such a culture can be expected to create parallel streams of value for the two customer groups.

While it can be seen that traditional marketing has evolved to address changing environmental conditions, the school of (fragmented) thought surrounding IM has not progressed quite as far. The application of external market thinking in an intra-firm context has been too rigid and far too simplistic. It is, perhaps, not the marketing concept that is too rigid, but instead that it may be too narrowly interpreted and applied in the internal context. As the same focus and onus has not, over time, been placed on intra-firm marketing as on its external counterpart, this has resulted in the interpretation and application of a model which has long been outdated. Just as the external focus of marketing has progressed from marketing mix to relationship marketing, it would seem apparent that internal marketing should move toward more of a 'relationships' view of the world.

The marketing culture is part of the broader corporate culture of an organisation. The initiation of an IM programme may be seen to represent a cultural initiative geared towards reshaping the entire culture within a firm. Such an initiative should lead to much greater integration between functional departments. A customer-focused perspective would be developed in most areas of the firm to address the *moment of truth* in service encounters.

One recent successful implementation at cultural 'reshaping' has involved Sears Roebuck. This organisation developed a comprehensive programme that has revolutionised the logic and the culture of the business it operates. This has been achieved through the development of a model rigorous enough to serve as an integral piece of the management information system and as a tool that each individual in the company can use for self-assessment and self-improvement. Rucci *et al.*(1998) write that through the development of an employee–customer–profit model, Sears has come to understand the several layers of factors that affect employee retention, how employee retention affects the drivers of customer satisfaction, how customer satisfaction affects financials, and a great deal more. By focusing upon attitudes and behaviours, a cause-and-effect chain was developed.

The authors of Rucci *et al.*, all Sears executives, believe that it is important to engage the employees' creative power in the vital task of reshaping the company's future. This is essential to foster a sense of ownership and buy-in. This involves issues of both trust and business/economic literacy (information sharing). Further, establishing the mechanics of such a model is not enough, as it is difficult to create and the implementation is complex and integrated. They acknowledge it is important for employees to figure out what it is they should be doing as the process is developed. The experience of Sears reflects the full integration of internal marketing within the context of HR applications, and as a component of a full and comprehensive strategic marketing programme.

What should internal marketing mean?

IM has two primary focuses. It is designed to complement external and strategic marketing efforts through the facilitation of personal interactions between staff and clients that are conducive to attraction and satisfaction objectives. Secondly, and more fundamentally, it serves to develop and maintain a motivated and satisfied workforce that contributes to the organisation's external and strategic marketing objectives, as well as to quality, productivity and efficiency (MacStravic, 1985). It is proposed that these elementary motives have become increasingly critical pursuits and that they can be achieved through value-creation for the employee in the employment context. It can be seen that one motive supports the development of the other while fostering greater integration and consistency. It is these motives that represent the goals of internal marketing and provide a foundation upon which to develop and integrate external and strategic marketing initiatives.

IM should be a holistic management strategy that focuses on developing customer-conscious employees. The goods and services of the firm, as well as proposed external marketing campaigns, should initially be rolled-out to employees before they are marketed externally (Grönroos, 1990b). Not engaging in such a practice is to jeopardise marketing efforts, and thereby threaten the long-term performance of the firm. External advertising campaigns, for example, have been found to affect employees' ability to do their jobs as they affect judgement of the trustworthiness of their organisation, as well as their identification with and commitment to their company. Further, they can greatly influence the culture of an organisation in that they may become a source of organisational symbolism and be part of the cultural, ritual and interpretative organisational fabric that is the medium through which leadership creates a climate and, thus, organised action (Gilly and Wolfinbarger, 1998).

On a more practical level, exposing employees first to marketing campaigns ensures the education, understanding and preparedness of the employee. As such, it provides an opportunity to ensure that the firm can and will deliver what is indicated through the promotional messages. Further, this gauges the response and acceptance of the employee, indicating whether service consistent with the message will be offered. Can the firm live up to the promises it is making through the message? Are employees willing and able to do so? The answers to these questions greatly influence moments of truth for the firm's customers. An established IM plan ensures that management approaches a wide range of activities in a much more systematic and *strategic* manner.

Increasingly, it is important to stress marketing in roles that are traditionally considered non-marketing roles such as in areas of production, inventory management, technical support and so on. This represents an attempt to improve quality, performance and efficiency. The premise of IM is that the internal exchanges between employees must be operating effectively before the firm can successfully achieve superior performance in its external markets. If an organisation cannot conduct transactions satisfactorily within the firm, then this may be a reflection of its ability to do so in the external environment.

A narrow view of IM, as simply a marketing process to communicate external customer needs and requirements throughout the organisation, is a view that is based upon the assumption that knowledge will breed appropriate actions and responses. It denies appreciation of the firm as a social organisation and, as such, the key function of managing human resources within such a marketing initiative and a service environment. What is being discussed here is the process of transforming an organisation into a customer-focused entity. When communicating change to employees, the design and content of the communication are chosen to successfully 'sell' the change and the ideas behind it.

Executing a programme based fundamentally upon a customer focus throughout the internal and external market chain is difficult to implement. In fact, there are fundamental changes required of the firm as a whole. These are in three key areas: organisation, culture, and technology (McEachern, 1998). Change management is complicated for the most savvy of organisations, and execution of this nature requires sweeping changes and will affect almost every area of the organisation. As such, a focused, integrative, and evolutionary process is required to minimise disruption and enhance the potential for success.

Employees as internal customers

It is important to have the 'buy-in' of *all* within the firm. This includes management levels as their behaviour (attitudes) greatly influences the behaviour, and the resulting culture, of all other subordinates. All employees represent a market for those efforts that attempt to create the appropriate service-oriented and customer-focused culture within the organisation. All firms seek to produce a value proposition for the end consumer. In this pursuit, there exists a chain of customers. Such an orientation at each stage, or link, of the chain will increase the level of value that is generated through the chain. Such value feeds into two paths, one accumulating value for the customer and the other for employees through their experience of work. Ultimately, both generate benefit or value for the firm.

It is also important to stress the presence of customers and service encounters *within* the context of the firm, with employees interacting on a regular basis through their work functions. Employees provide services or information to other employees and units within the firm. As such, there is an exchange between an individual with a need and one whose role it is to meet that need. These transactions can be viewed as a chain of events that ultimately produces a service to a client at the end of the line.

It is important to develop customer focus within each level of the firm, as an initial step to enhancing employee satisfaction and external customer service. It is necessary that organisations appreciate the implications and the full breadth of the circumstance and the pervasive effect derived from such interactions throughout the service function. This opportunity is greatly enhanced if workers treat each other as customers or clients.

Internal customer value

Managers of enlightened service organisations recognise that, in the new economics of service, front-line workers and customers must be of central concern (Heskett *et al.*, 1994). It is understood that this requires investment in people, worker support, improved recruiting and training practices, and compensation systems linked to individual employee performance.

The service–profit chain establishes the relationships between profitability, customer loyalty, and employee satisfaction, loyalty and productivity. The ultimate goal of any marketing initiative is that of customer loyalty. Profit and growth are stimulated primarily by customer loyalty. Loyalty is derived from satisfaction, which is broadly influenced by the net 'value' of the services provided to the customer. The responsibility to realise, and deliver, the *full* value-potential to the customer is largely that of the employee(s). Satisfied, loyal and productive employees inherently create customer value. So, as important as it is to recognise that satisfaction and loyalty must be engendered in the customer, it is also seen from this perspective that the same applies at the employee level. It may be argued that greater focus should be placed on the initial links in the chain in that one satisfied customer group is largely contingent upon the other.

Traditional marketing has focused on the creation of external service value without an appreciation of providing service value within the context of the firm *and* within the employment relationship. Such efforts would support components of the service–profit chain such as employee satisfaction, retention, and productivity, thereby supplementing the creation of external service value.

Efforts to produce external customer value should include parallel development of inward functions aimed at creating value for the internal client as a means of leveraging all other marketing, promotional and service-quality initiatives. Such efforts would address variables such as internal communications, workplace design, job design, employee selection and development, employee reward/remuneration and recognition, as well as the tools and technology utilised. Both perspectives should be integral components of a prevailing service culture within any organisation. Such a culture would focus not only upon internal administration and functioning but also place great emphasis on the 'softer' components of the organisation and functioning on interpersonal levels. As such, great value and importance would be placed not only upon the customer, but also upon the employee as a valuable resource of the firm.

Successfully addressing both internal and external value issues will create a self-marketing environment that will perpetuate itself. As employees grow in their satisfaction and place more investment in their job performance, they develop into 'part-time marketers' for the organisation, creating greater customer satisfaction and attracting new customers and employment candidates. It must be remembered that it is quite often the service from employees that customers talk about when they praise or condemn their service encounters! This is the interface clients encounter in business transactions and which largely represents the company in their minds.

Internal marketing mix

The four components of the traditional marketing mix have, in recent times, come to include a fifth element. This additional element is *people*; an element that exists within both the internal and external marketing mix. It is the employees of the firm that represent these people in each marketing mix. *This is, in both instances, the domain of the HR/personnel function.* This mirrors two points of view that may be addressed when analysing the roles of employees in the firm. Internally, employees are customers to whom the firm must deliver value, while externally they are a value-added component of the product offering. The employee represents both a potentially valuable resource of the organisation as well as a valuable component of the external value proposition.

In the external context, this means going beyond the traditional mix and addressing the details of service provided to the customer and attending to the elements that affect how we make the customer feel. When this perspective is taken *within* the context of the organisation, this develops magnified importance. All marketing targets people, however this is different in that this perspective means to market toward a group for the express purpose of being better able to market a service and these employees to another, external, set of customers. There is a different relationship in operation between the firm and the internal customers. This requires enhancement in the service environment such that this group can be developed as a part of the product offering made to the external market. This emphasises the importance of employees as a means to gain a competitive advantage in today's market. A marketing mix, or value proposition, is required that attracts and retains good employees. This incorporates issues of benefits, incentives, work environment and skills. It should also create a satisfied customer who believes in, supports and enhances the organisation. It is proposed that the product of an internal marketing plan is the value proposition created for the employee in his/her position within the organisation. The development of an effective internal marketing programme requires an understanding of this target group (values and motives) in the same way that a marketing programme for the company's products and services requires an understanding of prospective customers (Barnes, 1989).

Any marketing plan requires a product that is acceptable to the proposed market. This is no different, in principle, for an IM plan. It is proposed that the *product* offered in this market be in the form of value for employees through their role in the organisation. This includes developing a variety of sources from which employees can derive personal value, and these in turn include financial, psychological and psychic variables. In some circumstances, the salary provided is largely sufficient but, in many situations and within some groups of employees, this alone is not enough to create satisfaction. Satisfaction is required in any market to create a loyal customer. What is required are working conditions and an environment that motivate the employees to respond favourably to management's need for customer focus by engaging as part-time marketers above and beyond their individual functional roles (Grönroos, 1990a). As well, this proposition should attract and retain suitable employees. By creating value for the employee, motivation and commitment are increased and the employee begins to internalise a set of values consistent with better customer service and cooperation. This commitment will be manifested toward both internal and external markets. The firm inculcates the employee with a long-term view that if customers are treated properly they will keep coming back (Barnes, 1989).

Glassman and McAfee (1992) recognise the need to integrate the marketing and HR/personnel functions to improve coordination between their respective goals. The creation of synergy may be achieved through a focus on the development of value-based relationships in both spheres. The framework of developing a value-based relationship with the external customer is a widely recognised and popular pursuit. The logic and value of such can be argued for the development of similar relationships within the firm. The creation of such an interface will develop synergies from the development of a double-looping service–profit chain; one process designed for the satisfaction of the external customer while the other addresses the special nature of the internal market as employees *and* customers. The second loop is based upon shared principles of relationship marketing, but operationalised differently. The double loop of satisfaction and loyalty creates improved service quality, decreased customer and employee churn, and enhanced fiscal performance. This enhances the value proposition for both customer groups.

The *distribution* component of the mix refers to the environmental conditions of the workplace. As discussed, the treatment expected to be provided to external customers is accorded to employees and becomes the expected standard of behaviour in all internal functioning. It is the responsibility of management to develop conditions that are so conducive. The development of an appropriate environment for a suitable culture to develop is required. The *price* to employees refers to the involvement of time and commitment and a range of associated psychic costs. The value offered to employees through their role in the organisation should be such that employees willingly maximise their investments. *Promotion* within the internal mix involves information sharing. Such information may take the form of, for example, newsletters or bulletins regarding the performance of the firm. This may also involve training sessions or informal coaching and recognition/encouragement. It can be seen that there is a great deal of functional overlap between these components as a part of an internal marketing mix.

The nature of value

Creating customer value is properly addressed and enhanced by organisations that are committed to a long-term perspective of creating genuine customer relationships (Barnes and Cumby, 1999). The same value-creation process must be engendered within the organisation toward employees. As value (and the relationship) exists in the customer's perception, so the same holds true for employees. As such, value must be understood from the employee viewpoint and not dictated through a unilateral top-down programme. Such forced programmes are broad, sweeping across the organisation, and do not address individual issues or incorporate the input of participants. Barnes and Cumby (1999) conclude that deeply rooted sources of value are those connected with interpersonal interactions between the customer and the firm's employees, and with the affective dimensions of those interactions. It is proposed that those sources of value to the external customer have, in large part, parallels within the employment relationship. It is suggested that sources of value within the employment context include: information-sharing, facilitation of job performance, autonomy, remuneration, internal service culture, association value of the firm, enabling positive self-regard and esteem, empowerment, and community ties or involvement. There also exists the potential within this relationship for deeply personal value-creation through what is referred to in external marketing as the 'wow factor', when the service or value delivered is surprising, or exceeds what would have been expected. This is seen when employees or external customers perceive that the company has noticed and genuinely cares about meeting their needs.

Value is more than a trade-off between quality and price as is seen through reports provided by consumers about their service encounters. These affective responses provide details and insight into the nature of these interpersonal inter-actions. It is readily acknowledged that customer satisfaction is critical to loyalty and there is implicit acceptance that value is a precursor to satisfaction (Zeithaml, 1988). Yet service firms have difficulty in determining the impor-tance/strength of value and its role in customer relationship-building. The impact of this role should not be as difficult to ascertain within the context of the employment relationship, as the status and quality of employee relations has often been the focus of attention within the firm. Although not explicitly concep-tualised in the present discussion, the idea of value has often been conceptualised within the employment relationship with regard to training, remuneration, fulfilment, purpose, appreciation and so on. However, this has been restricted to purely HR applications and has not been engaged in a more proactive process such as IM. This would focus upon the development of value for the employee through the employment experience.

The idea of a relationship existing between these parties is an accepted one. The employment relationship already has 'hard' structure regarding roles and obligations. It is the 'soft' components that need to be addressed and enhanced for a deep understanding of what value is to the *employee*. What is required is a modified approach to relationship marketing that recognises the needs and motives of the employee, and presents a value proposition that is conducive to operating and sharing the same vision of service-mindedness.

The term 'relationship' implies a dynamic of give-and-take with changes occurring over time, and so too it must be seen how this is magnified through time within the context of the firm. The importance of this must be recognised in the role of the employee (internal customer) in the creation, production and delivery of the 'product' in the service context. Value comes from the surren-dering of time, money, energy and psychological costs as is consistent with the theories of human motivation. This can be seen as applicable at the consumer and the employee level. An investment of time and energy is made in anticipa-tion of improved satisfaction. Lovelock (1996) views value as a dynamic measure of the balancing of perceived costs against perceived benefits and that this balancing act is often an unconscious act. The results are manifested through satisfaction, commitment and motivation. Changes in the level of concern/effort expended could signal that an employee is no longer satisfied or motivated by the existing employment relationship. This comes from a comparison of perceived performance/outcomes in relation to expectations. The impact, or the stakes, may be argued to have greater impact upon the employee because of the intensity of the bond with the organisation. In many cases, employees may have little choice but to continue their employment although they are dissatisfied: not unlike external customers who are locked into a relationship with a company because of the existence of barriers to exit.

Relationship marketing seeks to gain greater 'customer intimacy'. This is often difficult in a relationship that one side may not yet recognise exists. There already exists some measure of intimacy with the internal customer, and this is without actively seeking to have it. The social nature of the firm thrusts many employees into a context that, over time, becomes emotionally charged and comprises a significant component of the employee's life thereby constituting an element of self-esteem and meaning.

The nature of the internal market

It cannot be assumed that serving the internal market is the same as addressing the needs of the external market. Many changes have altered the nature and thrust of marketing in recent years. Further, the shift toward a service focus has also led to a re-evaluation of key success factors and core competencies. The increasing importance of comprehensive, integrated, marketing plans derives from the increasing level of competition that exists.

It is clear that the customer–supplier and the supply–demand relationships *within* the organisation are relatively fixed and, as such, do not impinge upon the actors in the same manner as the more variable external market environment. To address this internal market, in a manner consistent with a relationship marketing approach, is to recognise that these structures are not of great relevance. Instead, it is the value component of the exchange for the participants and the satisfaction that results that are important. Therefore, great attention must be paid to the psychological aspects of the interaction and the relationship. The value of affective responses is widely recognised in external marketing contexts, and should be seen to be equally relevant to the individual (internal customer) being served *within* the firm. The structure differs, but it is not the market structure that we address with initiatives aimed at adding value and developing relationships within the firm.

Adding value through internal relationships is to enhance the employment relationship such that the employee has the greatest potential to experience satisfying interactions, relationships and opportunities. Through increasing an employee's level of motivation and satisfaction, job performance should also increase. This means that the employee enjoys the greatest psychological benefit while minimising negative psychic costs. Employees perceive their high value within the firm and feel that they are regarded as valued and contributing members of the organisation and not as commodities of production. These elements must be nurtured within such a corporate culture, so that employees perceive their interests and those of the firm to be consistent.

It is important to remember that the customer being addressed in the internal market has an ongoing contractual and psychological relationship with the firm

(Argyle, 1983). This 'forced' relationship clearly distinguishes the two markets. Interaction with employees is occurring within an ongoing, socially complex environment. The workplace represents a person's livelihood and is where the employee will spend a large portion of time. It represents great personal and psychic involvement and investment. It is this psychological component that should be examined through an internal marketing initiative. These elements contribute greater weight, over time, to internal customer value. As such, it can be argued that the relevant internal circumstances, while not that different across the two markets, are potentially more important to the ultimate success of marketing initiatives.

Mudie (1987) argues that relationships between the firm and internal customers do not characterise authentic exchanges in the sense of the generic marketing concept, as the underlying dynamics of the relationship differ from that with the external customer. Perhaps it is not these differences that are of relevance, but instead the similarities; for example, how this relationship is authentic or mean-ingful, in the sense that it forms the framework of the employee's attitudes/perceptions that are the basis of satisfaction, value and loyalty.

Mudie (1987) also criticises the creation of *emotional labour* by management. The often conflicting interests and motives that exist between the firm and the employee will create worker resistance and cynicism. However, all employment conditions involve the inducement or suppression of personal feelings in order to perform tasks in the desired (or correct) manner. This is a prevalent character-istic of all social principles, whether or not participants are being remunerated. The impact of this has, perhaps, been overlooked in the context of interpersonal customer contact. Has such a burden upon the employee come to be taken for granted and thought impossible to lessen? This is often seen as a part of the cost of the job to the employee. Treating the employee as nothing more than a 'factor of production' fosters an environment that creates psychological resistance and costs, thereby creating less beneficial and productive employee relationships. Discretionary efforts by such employees will be minimal under such circum-stances. By improving internal customer service and creating a suitable working environment, there are social and psychic rewards to be gained by employees.

Internal marketing activities

A comprehensive IM strategy would include several components. These should each be designed to select and develop suitable employees, create intrinsic value for the employees, and contribute to enhanced service delivery to the internal customer. Such components should foster belief in the product and in the organisation, mental readiness to promote and deliver the product, and superior customer service. The strategy would stress value congruence, incentive prog-rammes, environment, working conditions and customer focus (Grönroos, 1990a).

As a social organisation, the workplace environment (particularly the service firm) cannot be overlooked with regard to the interpersonal relationships that are created for both internal and external customers. The impact, however, may be considered greater for those that are a *part* of the organisation. They are thrust daily into circumstances with groups of individuals that they have not chosen, and they may be required to remain as their employment is a means of financial support and investment that may not make leaving a practical alternative. As such, employees may feel compelled to stay despite the dissatisfaction and unhappiness experienced: they may have little choice. Further, many of these individuals are required, daily, to provide service to a stream of customers that demand their concern, time and effort. The situation is fraught with social complexities that require expending psychological resources and continued psychic investment. It should be determined how these circumstances can be engineered to derive the greatest benefit and value for both employees and customers.

Increased value for the external customer, through the provision of superior customer service, is recognised as a potential means to achieve profit and growth in today's economy. Such potential may also be captured within the firm. It may be interpreted that IM can be a source of sustainable competitive advantage. To be such, a component must be a valuable factor, rare among competitors, and costly or difficult to imitate (Barnes and Rowe, 1998). Creative and successful initiatives that are employee-focused fit such a description. They are valuable in that they are the required basis upon which successful service organisations provide their superior product, as well as providing savings through enhanced productivity, increased employee tenure and reduced turnover. They are rare and costly, if not impossible, to imitate because of the complexities inherent within a social organisation, possessing both complex public and private social dynamics. Research has shown clearly that these service transactions are, first and foremost, social encounters. The resultant culture within the successful organisation is costly to imitate and success is infrequent.

It is recognised that the quality of service can greatly influence customer satisfaction. If communal interaction can influence customer behaviour and responses, then it can be assumed that this will also elicit similar responses from employees involved in such exchanges. A customer's perception of actions and outcomes is different when a service employee is known or familiar than if an unfamiliar individual performs those actions. It is reasonable to expect that this effect holds for the employee serving familiar clients, but is also stronger for exchanges and relationships with colleagues, supervisors or employers. It can, therefore, be seen that positive and efficient transactions deliver benefit to both sides of such exchanges and enhance the relationship that each has with the firm.

The strength of the social component can be seen in behaviours that are demonstrated in circumstances not traditionally associated with communal behaviour (Goodwin and Gremler, 1996). Consumers often offer characterisations of social behaviour such as personalisation, friendliness, empathy and appreciation when describing positive service experiences. These behaviours are reported to have made them 'loyal' to particular providers. They describe loyalty through the use of social terms. Further, it is reported that increasing 'programmed' personalisation does not have the same desired effect. The design of service functions to include scripted exchanges and tag-lines is not largely effective. It must appear to be genuine and spontaneous, not planned and contrived, or it is thought to betray the professionalism of the organisation (Goodwin and Gremler, 1996). When not offered in authentic contexts, such behaviour may be perceived as demeaning or condescending.

Further support for the strong role played by employment socialisation is that derived through co-worker intimacy. This refers to workplace colleagues and clients who are treated with the same familiarity and closeness as co-workers. Although interactions between co-workers are often regarded as task-related or transactional, empirical data suggest that co-workers often offer one another a source of intimacy through discussion of personal matters, problem-solving or 'joking' behaviours. Goodwin and Gremler (1996) anticipate that fostering such intimacy will enhance satisfaction and loyalty.

The role of employees

Customer satisfaction, loyalty, efficient service provision, and the firm's image must become the joint responsibility of management, support and contact employees. This responsibility can only be successfully distributed if the cooperation of all involved is sought and nurtured. It is important that employees have a sense that their role is recognised and valued by management.

Employee involvement and commitment are obtained through the creation of 'ownership' of the responsibility for quality service delivery within and outside the firm. Such ownership cannot be dictated. In one respect, the employee can be seen as holding the power to control successful service delivery (Mills, 1986). Also, over time, employees increase in value to the firm as they develop an organisational memory. They have developed skills, contacts, associations and affiliations that enhance their organisational contribution. If such employees feel that the firm is not fulfilling its obligation as an employer to the internal market, and/or its role as a service provider to the external market, they may decrease the commitment they show to the firm, or even sabotage the process. Application of the law of reciprocity may demonstrate the dynamics operating here. Through a failure to develop such 'faith' in the employer, or in losing the respect of employees, the organisation will miss out on the full potential of employees through their conscious or unconscious reactions. Employees may behave in an undesirable fashion if they perceive that the firm is not fulfilling its role. Employee reaction may not be evident as it can manifest itself through a simple reduction in the expenditure of effort, their consideration for others in the firm or concern for outcomes of their job actions.

This has implications for the employee selection process. Selection must screen potential employees utilising an approach that will enable the identification of congruent values, cooperative nature and a service orientation. The emotional content of positions should be emphasised. Orientation should be meaningful, as it is the principal opportunity to inculcate the culture and orientation of the organisation (Henkoff, 1994).

Within the service organisation, human resources can be seen and utilised as a marketing resource. As such, HR can provide a potential competitive advantage through the development of integrated HR/personnel and marketing plans. Social complexity provides a formidable barrier to competition, thereby serving as a sustainable source of competitive advantage in a service economy. Social complexity is a function of the degree of integration and complexity of social and communicative functions within the firm. The greater the complexity, the lower the likelihood of successful imitation by competitors. Integration between functional units improves communication and understanding with regard to the desired goals. This can range from informal consultation and information to hierarchical, multi-point structures (Varey and Lewis, 1999). Integration between these units creates synergies that may not otherwise be achieved and further enhances potential competitive advantage.

Human resource innovation

There exist five critical business reasons why the HR function has increased in its relevance in recent years. The forces of globalisation impinge upon the firm as organisations are pressured to think globally and act locally. The profitability of the firm through growth, as the gains of downsizing, restructuring and consolidation have been realised, leaves only the age-old pursuit of increased market share and penetration. Technology abounds but the value achieved is not always obvious and, as such, management must figure out how to make it a productive part of the work setting. Intellectual capital has become an indirect competitive advantage for all companies that are trying to differentiate themselves by how they serve their customers. As such, successful companies will be those that are adept at attracting, developing, and retaining individuals for an organisation that is responsive to customers. Lastly, firms must be able to embrace non-stop change by learning rapidly and continuously, innovating ceaselessly and developing new strategic imperatives faster and with great comfort. This means a responsive and agile company that elevates the idea of the learning organisation to another plane.

Pressure such as this leaves the firm more dependent than ever before upon the contributions that can come out of the HR/personnel function. Many organisations have been slow to learn that the key undertaking to prepare for success in the new service economy is to take one step back from the customer and address fundamental HR issues that challenge traditional roles, relationships, and paradigms. These have changed within the firm; however, the HR function has not kept pace with these changes and often continues to operate on outdated business principles.

What is required, is the revitalisation of this function through the development of a new agenda incorporating cross-functional roles through the organisation. This new agenda would focus upon outcomes and not traditional administrative processes. Cross-functional roles enable organisations to achieve greater integration and better enable the delivery of quality service to all customer groups. Initiatives, as discussed, would serve as a tool for such a reinvention and evolution of the HR function. Concern may arise with regard to 'marketing' towards the employees and be perceived as a threat to the integrity of the HR function. The idea of 'selling' to the employees may be felt to portray the firm as less than forthright in its intention to inculcate employees into the organisation's culture. Thoughtless application would also risk increasing levels of employee cynicism toward the firm. As such, the positioning of such a programme must be carefully communicated and implemented.

Keltner and Finegold (1996) suggest that a new look for employment relationships would centre on two intuitively simple enterprises. The first is the construction of an employee contract based upon competence-based career ladders. This would emphasise internal promotion. Secondly, the forging of educational partnerships with local educational institutions to develop greater employee skill sets and competencies. This would support the ability to promote internally. Those authors believe that the key is to train and to empower employees, while placing some priority on minimising employee turnover. Turnover creates poor service provision while generating great expenditures that could otherwise be re-directed. Also, tenure gives an employee a better understanding of the firm, its processes and the needs of the clients. The experienced employee is better able to serve as an intermediary, with greater organisational memory, serving both employer and client. The value of this employee to both parties increases the longer the tenure.

Despite acknowledging the logic of responding to change, many organisations remain steadfast to a traditional industrial model of service delivery that focuses more on production and sales structures. Such an approach focuses on costs and not on the value of adapting to the changing environment. Continued adherence to such management practices will ensure the demise of many organisations in today's competitive marketplace. With minimal investment in employees and reliance upon revolving part-time workers, increasing belief in IT to supplant employees and historical antipathies of management/labour relations (Keltner and Finegold, 1996), such firms will be left wondering why their profits are dropping and market share eroding.

This perspective will produce improvements in the short term as costs and overhead appear to decrease, but will not allow the firm to achieve market growth or evolve with the changing economy. Such a market requires more long-term investment, yielding fewer immediate and tangible pay-offs.

Empowerment

A progressive movement in the reorganisation of the firm is the empowerment of employees. Today's service environment looks to the performer of tasks for the solutions to problems (Bowen and Lawler, 1992). What happens, however, if an employee is ill prepared or indifferent to providing solutions? In the functional role of customer service representative, employees are called upon to provide information and to resolve problems, real or *perceived* (an important concept). What are needed are the art of, and the authority for, improvisation. As such, employees are needed who are resourceful and resilient, empathetic and enterprising, competent and creative (Henkoff, 1994).

Empowerment is a concept that should be detailed in the role and responsibilities of each employee, causing it to pervade the culture of the organisation. Empowerment can be seen as a tool through which the responsibility of delivering efficient, quality, customer service is moved down through the ranks of the organisation. According to Bowen and Lawler (1992), there are four potential components that may comprise empowerment within a firm. These are the sharing of information on organisational performance, rewards based upon that performance, knowledge that enables workers to understand and contribute to improved performance, and the power to make decisions that influence organisational direction and performance. It can be seen that much of this view of empowerment involves very little delegation of authority or decision-making in the service context. Perhaps the greatest power of such a concept is the perception of involvement that it allows the employee. This allows the employee to gain a sense of responsibility and control.

Bowen and Lawler (1992), in their study of the benefits and costs of empowering employees, have determined that there are ranges of practices that empower employees to varying degrees. The choice of approach should be determined by key business characteristics, and it is important that there is a good fit between organisational needs and the approach to front-line employees. Three common options include suggestion involvement, job involvement and high involvement. This represents a continuum from a minor shift away from the control model through the solicitation of suggestions to the inclusion of employees in management decisions and employee ownership.

Bowen and Lawler (1992) have concluded that empowerment is not an all-or-nothing concept and have advocated a contingency approach that best meets the needs of both employees and customers. Ensuring success requires that such an approach be pursued. They delineate the contingencies of empowerment to be basic business strategy, degree of customer contact, utilisation of technology, prevailing business environment, and management type. Bowen and Lawler (1995) have also found that globalisation and resultant competition have increased pressure even on those in the manufacturing sector to maximise their human resource contribution through empowering employees.

Front-line personnel already possess a great deal of power in the delivery of the company 'product', largely through their discretionary decisions as they interact with the client. Each response and action, each subtle nuance that can influence the perception of the client, is at the choice and discretion of the employee.

The changing business landscape

Perhaps independent of the directional change toward a service orientation is the change resulting from various economic, political and globalising forces. Changes in structure and organisation have led to the confluence of downsizing, rightsizing, outsourcing, declining unionism and the increasing dependence on part-time, contractual and temporary workers. Many workers perceive these trends as threats. The impact of such trends has been tremendous in the United States; for example General Motors was displaced in the early 1990s as the largest employer by Manpower, Inc., a temporary employment agency (Higgins, 1996). It can be argued that, in the longer term, such a shift in human resource policy is not to the advantage of companies. Others argue that it is not societally ethical.

Ironically, this change is occurring in the lives of workers while companies are pressuring employees for greater participation, higher quality and productivity, and team-based work structures. Such broad dialectical change creates both societal and workplace anxieties that require practical and ethical attention. Such circumstances increase the difficulties involved with gaining employee buy-in to an initiative. Such challenges, however, emphasise the importance of making IM an integral component of the firm's culture. Of course, such efforts may take great time, planning and resources. There is, however, little choice.

Programmes utilised to pressure employees to make greater psychological and psychic investment (Lovelock, 1991) are intuitively simple. Direct the focus of every employee toward providing superior service and value that, in turn, increase external customer loyalty driving profits. However, in order to achieve such a self-reinforcing system, employees must be involved, empowered and participative (Higgins, 1996). This requires a strategic IM framework for building trust. What is required is an end to traditional adversarial employee–management relations. A spirit of cooperation, mutual trust and reciprocity is needed. This is not unlike the attempt to create customer commitment in the external market. This spirit is difficult to achieve, however, in the midst of the aforementioned dialectical change.

How can an organisation expect its remaining workforce to trust the firm, let alone *increase* their psychological investment? How can such employees maintain their belief in management, the firm or what it offers to the public? Such employees are likely to be cynical and detached, becoming disenfranchised and doubting that their participation and effort are appreciated or will be rewarded. The renewed call for involvement and increased productivity is viewed suspiciously as a means to recruit employees themselves to help eliminate yet more positions. The calls for teamwork develop a hollow echo as they reverberate through the workplace.

Perhaps, at the most basic level of human emotion, the issue is that of trust. Could the foundation to creating a solution to these problems, to developing successful internal and external marketing programmes, start with establishing trust? In the absence of trust, justification is provided for defensive, self-interested behaviour. Mutual trust has never been a strong trait within labour relationships, with its history of adversarial relations. As such, many of the new quality and team initiatives are viewed as propaganda rather than a legitimate means of corporate communication.

An integrated programme would coordinate the efforts of marketing and HR managers to identify and address the needs and concerns of employees. This would be aimed at improving the work environment and morale, thereby improving service (Lovelock, 1992). Most often, these 'involvement' programmes have been developed without any strategic thrust. They should be developed as an integral component of the basic business strategy (Higgins, 1996).

HR departments should develop a programme of internal relationship marketing aimed at developing the relationship between the employee and the company, thereby addressing both marketing and human resource issues.

The 'organisation' of organisations

Within the structure of today's organisations, which require greater employee participation, there is no longer room for the bureaucratic structures and hierarchies of the past. Such new structures resemble more of a participative democracy than the classical bureaucratic organisational style. The enlightened organisation places focus on human relations and resources, and on the input and involvement of individual employees. It is an orientation that recognises, particularly within the service sector, that the organisation is a reflection and composite of its members and that it is necessary to understand their behaviours before attempting to understand the behaviour of the organisation as a whole (Schneider, 1987). The 'classic organisation' approach lacked such a focus on intellect, emotion and motivational aspects of its members. Some suggest that the nature of the employees determines the character of the organisation; people make the firm what it is. This would not appear to be an unreasonable thesis within a service context, as the 'product' under consideration is largely the people that produce and deliver it upon demand.

Union environments

Although there is much talk of restructuring the service firm, there are practical considerations that may prevent willing management from undertaking such a project. This is the presence of unions that provide psychological and structural impediments. Do such programmes bear much relevance within such a regulated environment where workers possess greater bargaining power with regard to work activities, what they *owe* the firm, and where a much more prevalent adversarial position exists?

Union membership deals with many needs addressed by IM, through the increase of motivation and satisfaction within the workplace. These initiatives and the role of unions can be seen as sharing a similar goal, that is the satisfaction of needs as conceived by models such as that of Maslow. In both the industrial/organisational psychology and labour relations literature, such lower- and higher-order needs are discussed in explaining the role of unions. It is clear how union membership ensures provision for lower-order needs, but it is also believed that the security provided also fulfils needs with respect to status, belonging and esteem. Unfortunately for the firm and clients, loyalty may be felt more strongly toward the union than the employer. Also, the sense of empowerment felt through the union also emphasises the adversarial nature of the structure with the ultimate weapon, the strike threat.

There are, however, aspects of union involvement that threaten the intention of IM initiatives. Some facets of job satisfaction may be impeded through imposed supervision and promotion policies. While protected as a group, those employees who have a strong will to achieve and are highly motivated do not have the opportunity to be recognised.

The argument for a relationships approach

George and Jones (1996) have found a significant relationship between the interactive effects of value attainment, job satisfaction and mood in the experience of work. These appear to be prime contributors to the phenomenological experience of work. Further, these variables interact to influence individual and organisational outcomes. These researchers found that literature on the subjective experience of work has focused on values and their attainment, attitudes of job satisfaction, job involvement and organisational commitment, and work moods. Similarly, in the research literature on overall subjective well-being in life, three complementary entities have been focused upon. These are value attainment, life satisfaction and the extent to which a person experiences positive feelings or moods. This demonstrates clearly how the experience of work is deeply interwoven with overall well-being and happiness.

In addressing components such as these simultaneously, it is possible to yield a richer and more complete understanding of the relationship between an individual and his/her work. Further, it can be seen that issues such as motivation, job satisfaction, involvement and commitment, as well as organisational commitment, must be simultaneously addressed in the development of an internal marketing initiative to create the maximum effect by leveraging each of these components.

Ingredients in the internal marketing programme

In designing an IM programme there is the desire to create four ingredients: motivation, job satisfaction, job involvement and organisational commitment. Not surprisingly, these four variables are highly interrelated. In understanding motivation, or the values and needs, of employees it must be considered how changes in the economy and social fabric within post-industrial society have changed the forces that motivate employees.

Concern with pay level as a source of motivation ebbed and flowed through the 1970s and 1980s, with what would appear to be a declining interest in pay, beyond some level, as a source of intrinsic incentive. Pay level approaches motivation at a basic or lower common base of interest for the employee. Workers desire a more challenging work environment and a greater sense of participation in the organisation (Schultz and Schultz, 1990). There has been an increase in resistance to authority and a decline of the Protestant work ethic. Workers have become more self-oriented and emphasise job characteristics that lead to self-development and self-fulfilment. A spirit of expressivism can be seen through decreased levels of loyalty and commitment, the need for recognition of accomplishment, the desire to participate in decisions that affect their jobs, and opportunities for personal growth and the development of creativity.

Motivation involves needs and desires, some complementary and some conflicting. Further, this varies from one individual to another. But the question still remains: what is it that constitutes motivation and how can it be fostered across broad groups of employees? Several theories address the issue of increasing motivation. These emphasise and encourage the utilisation of variables such as empowerment, job enrichment and continuing feedback as potential sources for developing and maintaining high-achieving employees through fostering loyalty and greater employment satisfaction. The fulfilment of higher-order needs such as self-respect, esteem, prestige and feelings of personal success come through employee realisation of capabilities through workplace expression.

Job satisfaction refers to the attitudes that employees hold toward their employment position, their role within the organisation and the organisation as a whole. It is a collection of numerous attitudes and feelings. Like motivation, these may contain complementary and contradictory emotions. These facets of personality remain a challenge; however, through job re-engineering and enrichment, the ambivalence that may be created can be mitigated.

Job involvement refers to a person's psychological identification with his or her work, while organisational commitment refers to the attachment or identification with the organisation as a whole. The higher the identification and the involvement felt by the employee, the higher the job satisfaction. Satisfaction should lead to increased loyalty. In the external market, this loyalty results in increased patronage and commitment to the provider. Within the firm, this is believed to also result in greater commitment. This translates into enhanced job performance, which enables improved customer service at both levels. The high degree of relatedness indicates the strength of the effect these have upon individual and organisational performance.

Involvement and commitment involve three components: acceptance of the values and goals of the organisation, willingness to exert effort on behalf of the organisation, and a strong desire to remain within the organisation. Not surprisingly, these gain strength with employee tenure, and are created and fostered by the perception of how committed the organisation is to the employee.

Creating higher-order value

Cumby and Barnes (1997) have recognised the need for organisations to develop and genuinely appreciate the contribution of higher-order value-creators for their clients. This has also been demonstrated by Price *et al.* (1995), who have found that service satisfaction is influenced by emotional and affective content, temporal duration, and spatial proximity of service provider and client. These are the elements that aid in the creation of such value components as information, enabling and community value. It can be inferred that these same components can greatly influence the work experience of employees as they interact. That is, such experiences have greater meaning to those working in the firm daily (the internal customers) than to those patronising the firm. As such, any approach to address these higher-order needs of the external audience would be of considerable potential benefit if modified to the internal audience. It can be seen that these same types of value would create higher-order value for the internal market.

Cumby and Barnes (1995) further indicate that the following factors contribute to a customer's evaluation of satisfaction with a service encounter and can be used to predict or explain possible responses: the customer's level of involvement, risk, or investment; salience of the service; the influence of the customer's experience and expertise on expectations; the customer's locus of attribution concerning elements of the encounter; level of contact; whether the interaction is short- or long-term; perception of viable alternatives; the ability to differentiate the core offering from that of the competitor; and satisfaction with various aspects of the service encounter. It can be seen that these 'concerns' are paralleled by considerations of employees as they greatly impact upon many facets of their lives. A great deal of an employee's life is spent in the work environment, and its influence extends far beyond time spent on the job. Therefore, these variables have great potential impact upon the lives of employees.

Following the logic of Maslow's hierarchy of personal needs, and with consideration of Barnes's model of the drivers of customer satisfaction (Cumby and Barnes, 1997), a similar model of employee satisfaction can be developed. The difference between these models would be that different needs do not represent different levels within the model, but that different structures and relationships across firms differ in the level of 'satisfaction' that they achieve in the model. The lower levels of the model coincide with details regarding the core service needs, processes and technical performance components. In the employee model, this can likewise correspond to the core employment relationship (it's a job and I get paid!). Such a core element meets core needs and can satisfy higher-order psychological needs. The difference is in the design and nature of the element as it is executed by the firm. Also, process and technical performance deal with issues such as training and resources provided to carry out the assigned tasks. These are the tools of the job and the given ability to function. Value here may be only at a *core* level, and the risk exists that the employee may feel like a commodity of the firm; not unlike the firm that takes its customers for granted.

Higher levels of the model address issues of relationships with the firm, its employees and the affective dimensions of such relationships. With an internal model, the goal of an IM initiative would be to elevate the status of the employment relationship and the psychic benefits of the job, to the point of providing positive affective responses and meeting the higher-order needs of the employee. By enhancing the relationship, responding to employee needs and facilitating internal processes with appropriate training and resources, the levels of employee satisfaction, fulfilment, motivation, commitment and loyalty increase. This means that processes and technical performance are enhanced for the employee through empowerment, job details are enriched, and remuneration is outcome-based and modified through superior performance by the employee. The level of internal service is elevated through the hierarchy, as is the perception of the firm. As such, the core job emerges to fill a series of needs in the life of the employee. At a minimum, this improves service and satisfaction for the employee, firm and external customer by some measure over what would have been achieved otherwise.

The future of the workplace

The increasing utilisation of technology in the delivery of service to the external consumer has proven to be a continuing challenge in the maintenance of close, meaningful, customer relationships and in the implementation of relationship marketing initiatives. The increasing technologicalisation of the workplace has had parallel effects within the dynamics of internal employment relationships and attitudes.

Such effects also necessitate IM initiatives to protect further eroding of the 'social' variables previously discussed. The underlying component most greatly affected by technology is that of personal communication (Hallowell, 1999). The frequency of social contact, interaction and person-to-person communication is becoming irregular and fragmented. Voice mail and e-mail have become efficient, and sometimes essential, tools in everyday functioning. The processes introduced, and the technology placed on desktops, have reduced the need for interpersonal contact for the most ordinary and mundane tasks that in the past served to provide the basis for a large proportion of peer interaction. Just as alienation and disenfranchisement can occur with the customer held at arm's length, this can happen likewise among employees. This deficiency of human contact (Hallowell, 1999) can leave employees feeling lonely, isolated or confused.

As Hallowell (1999) has phrased it, we are losing the 'human moment'. These modern means of working and communicating lack the power of true human moments. The human moment is an authentic psychological encounter that occurs when people share the same physical space, and emotional and intellectual attention. Presence is not enough; energy is required to *participate* in that moment. In the increasingly hectic daily pace, this is becoming more difficult to do and such contact is diminishing. It is not that these encounters have to be emotionally wrenching or taxing, they can be professional and business-like, but those involved must feel, or acknowledge, that the exchange has been real.

Long-term reactions to such anomic environments can be pervasive. As this uncommunicative culture spreads throughout an organisation, the likelihood of dysfunction increases. As human moments become few and far between many things appear: over-sensitivity, self-doubt, boorishness, abrasive curtness and so on. Performance is affected as previously well-functioning employees underperform and, perhaps, look to leave the organisation. People become withdrawn and more self-interested, rather than focused on the overall organisation. The human moment becomes replaced by worry through the removal of those cues that mitigate worry: tone, facial expression and body language. Worry results with no basis in reality, leading to immobilisation that can contribute to indecision or destructive action. People begin to wonder if they can trust their organisations, and even question their own motives, performance and self-worth. The culture becomes unfriendly and unforgiving. Any sense of cohesiveness is lost and is, in fact, turned into a corrosive force. All this, paradoxically, is not from a lack of communication, but from communication of the wrong kind. These factors can be seen to have compounded effects within the context of a service industry where the employee would be expected to work amidst this culture, and yet be expected to behave differently, and communicate effectively, with the external customer. The example is not set, nor the skills exemplified, nor the employee in the mood for such interaction.

To have a meaningful counter-effect, such human moments must occur on a regular basis to impact upon the quality of internal and external customer service and greater overall employee satisfaction and motivation. This stresses the need for an internal initiative, and emphasises the importance of developing a communication component to facilitate employee interaction at some professional or personal level, as well as information distribution that allows the dissemination of information throughout the firm, allowing employees to feel 'plugged in'.

References

Argyle, M. (1983) *The Psychology of Interpersonal Behavior: A Functionalist Theory of Marketing*, Homewood, IL: Richard D. Irwin.

Barnes, J.G. (1989) 'The Role of Internal Marketing: If the Staff Won't Buy it, Why Should the Customer?', *Irish Marketing Review* 4(2): 11–21.

Barnes, J.G. and Cumby, J.A. (1999) 'Communicating Customer Value in Relationship-Focused Service Organizations', presented at the 1999 SERVSIG Services Research Conference of the American Marketing Association, 'Jazzing into the New Millennium', April 10–13, New Orleans.

Barnes, J.G. and Rowe, G. (1998) 'Relationship Marketing and Sustained Competitive Advantage', *Journal of Market Focused Management* 2: 281–97.

Bowen, D. and Lawler, E. (1992) 'The Empowerment of Service Workers: What, Why, How, and When', *Sloan Management Review* 34(1): 31–9.

—— (1995) 'Managing and Marketing to Internal Customers', in Glynn, W.J. and Barnes J.G. (eds), *Understanding Services Management*, Chichester: John Wiley & Sons, 269–94.

Compton, F., George, W., Grönroos, C. and Karvinen, M. (1987) 'Internal Marketing', in Czepiel, J., Congram, C. and Shanahan, J. (eds), *The Services Challenge: Integrating for Competitive Advantage*, Chicago: AMA Proceedings Series, 7–12.

Congram, C., Czepiel, J. and Shanahan, J. (1987) 'Achieving Internal Integration in Service Organizations: Five Propositions', in Czepiel, J., Congram, C. and Shanahan, J. (eds), *The Services Challenge: Integrating for Competitive Advantage*, Chicago: AMA Proceedings Series, 5–6.

Cumby, J.A. and Barnes, J.G. (1997) 'How We Make Them Feel: A Discussion of the Reactions of Customers to Affective Dimensions of the Service Encounter', presented at the New and Evolving Paradigms conferences of the American Marketing Association, Dublin, June 12–15, 140–52.

George, J. and Jones, G. (1996) 'The Experience of Work and Turnover Intentions: Interactive Effects of Value Attainment, Job Satisfaction, and Positive Mood', *Journal of Applied Psychology* 81(3): 318–25.

Gilly, M. and Wolfinbarger, M. (1998) 'Advertising's Internal Audience', *Journal of Marketing* 62(1): 69–88.

Gilmore, A. and Carson, D. (1995) 'Managing and Marketing to Internal Customers', in Glynn, W.J. and Barnes, J.G. (eds), *Understanding Services Management*, Chichester: John Wiley & Sons, 295–21.

Glassman, M. and McAfee, B. (1992) 'Integrating the Personnel and Marketing Functions: The Challenge of the 1990's', *Business Horizons* 35(3): 52–9.

Goodwin, C. and Gremler, D. (1996) 'Friendship Over The Counter: How Social Aspects of Service Encounters Influence Consumer Service Loyalty', in Swartz, T.A., Bowen, D.E. and Brown, S.W. (eds), *Advances in Service Marketing and Management*, vol. 5, Greenwich, CT: JAI Press, 247–82.

Grönroos, C. (1990a) *Service Management and Marketing: Managing the Moments of Truth in Service Competition*, Lexington, MA: Lexington Books.

—— (1990b) 'A Relationship Approach to Marketing in Service Contexts: The Marketing and Organizational Behavior Interface', *Journal of Business Research* 20(1): 3–11.

Hallowell, E. (1999) 'The Human Moment at Work', *Harvard Business Review* 77(1): 58–66.

Henkoff, R. (1994) 'Finding, Training, and Keeping the Best Service Workers', *Fortune*, 3 October, 110–22.

Heskett, J., Jones, T., Loveman, G., Sasser, W. and Schlesinger, L. (1994) 'Putting the Service–Profit Chain to Work', *Harvard Business Review* 72(2): 164–74.

Higgins, S. (1996) 'Towards Taming the Labor–Management Frontier', *Journal of Business Ethics* 15(4): 474–85.

Keltner, B. and Finegold, D. (1996) 'Adding Value in Banking: Human Resource Innovations for Service Firms', *Sloan Management Review* 38(1): 57–68.

Lovelock, C. (1991) *Services Marketing*, Englewood Cliffs, NJ: Prentice-Hall.

—— (1992) *Managing Services*, Englewood Cliffs, NJ: Prentice-Hall.

—— (1996) *Services Marketing*, Upper Saddle River, NJ: Prentice-Hall.

McEachern, C. (1998) 'Convergent Marketing: Executing on the Promise of 1:1', *Journal of Consumer Marketing* 15(5): 481–90.

MacStravic, R.S. (1985) 'Internal Marketing for Hospitals', *Health Marketing Quarterly* 3(2/3): 47–54.

Mills, P. (1986) *Managing Service Industries*, Cambridge, MA: Ballinger.

Mudie, P. (1987) 'Internal Marketing: Cause for Concern', *Quarterly Review of Marketing*, Spring/Summer: 21–4.

Price, L., Arnould, E. and Tierney, P. (1995) 'Going to Extremes: Managing Service Encounters and Assessing Provider Performance', *Journal of Marketing* 59(4): 83–97.

Rucci, A., Kirn, S. and Quinn, R. (1998) 'The Employee–Customer–Profit Chain at Sears', *Harvard Business Review* 76(1): 82–97.

Sasser, W. and Arbeit, S. (1976) 'Selling Jobs in the Service Sector', *Business Horizons* 19(3): 61–5.

Schneider, B. (1987) 'The People Make the Place', *Personnel Psychology* 40: 437–53.

Schultz, D.P. and Schultz, S.E. (1990) *Psychology and Industry Today*, New York: Macmillan.

Ulrich, D. (1998) 'A New Mandate for Human Resources', *Harvard Business Review* 76(1): 124–34.

Varey, R.J. and Lewis, B.R. (1999) 'Beyond the Popular Conception of Internal Marketing', presented at the 1999 SERVSIG Services Research Conference of the American Marketing Association, 'Jazzing into the New Millennium', April 10–13, New Orleans.

Zeithaml, V. (1988) 'Consumer Perceptions of Price, Quality, and Value: A Means–End Model and Synthesis of Evidence', *Journal of Marketing* 52(July): 2–22.

Part V

Developments

13 A meta-model of internal marketing

Mohammed Rafiq
Pervaiz K. Ahmed

Introduction

The literature on internal marketing (IM) is considerable and growing rapidly (see for example, Ahmed and Rafiq, 1995; Barnes, 1989; Berry, 1981; Collins and Payne, 1991; Flipo, 1986; George, 1977, 1990; Grönroos, 1981, 1985; MacStravic, 1985; Piercy and Morgan, 1991; Piercy, 1995; Rafiq and Ahmed, 1993, Sargent and Saadia, 1998; and Varey, 1995), yet there is little systematic work on how IM actually works in practice. One of the major reasons for this is the fact that as yet there is no agreed definition of IM. However, an examination of the literature shows that, essentially, there are two models of how IM works: one based on the work of Berry's concept of 'employees as customers' (Berry, 1981); and the other based on Grönroos's idea of 'customer mindedness' and interactive marketing (Grönroos, 1981).

The Berry and Grönroos models of internal marketing

In the existing literature, most authors do not distinguish clearly between Berry's and Grönroos's models of IM. The major reason for this is the fact that both Berry and Grönroos do not spell out the exact components of their models and how they are connected with each other. An examination of Berry's and Grönroos's work (as well as that of their collaborators) on IM shows that both these authors are concerned with improving service quality. However, they differ in their methods for achieving it. A problem in examining the work of the two authors in this area is that they do not present systematic models of IM. Hence, what is presented here are the implicit models underlying in the works of both Berry and Grönroos.

Beginning with Berry's model, the distinguishing features of this model are:

- The fundamental assertion that treating employees as customers will lead to changes in attitudes of employees, that is employees becoming service minded which leads to better service quality and competitive advantage in the marketplace.
- Treating employees as customers requires that jobs are treated as any other product of the company, that is, the needs and wants of the 'customer' are

taken into account and an effort is made to make the product attractive to the 'customers'.

- Treating jobs as products requires a new approach from human resource management and basically involves the application of marketing techniques internally both to attract and to retain customer oriented employees.

The full model is presented in Figure 13.1.

The original Grönroos model (Grönroos, 1981) is based on the premise that employees need to be customer conscious and sales minded so that they can take advantage of *interactive* marketing opportunities leading to better service quality and higher sales and, consequently, higher profits:

- The antecedents of customer conscious employees are supportive recruitment practices, requisite training and participative management style which give employees discretion in the service delivery process so that they can take advantage of resulting interactions between contact employees and customers. By giving employees discretion, that is by giving employees more control over their work, it is hoped that employee job satisfaction will increase and hence lead to more motivated and customer conscious employees.
- Additionally, employees need to be informed of any changes in marketing strategies and campaigns before they are launched on the external market. The idea behind this policy is that employees should thereby understand and realise the importance of their role in the service production and delivery process.
- All this requires a supportive senior management.

The full Grönroos model is presented in Figure 13.2.

While the objectives of the models are similar, it is clear that the mechanisms that they employ and their objectives are quite different. Moreover, the two models by themselves are incomplete in that the Berry model does not indicate the mechanisms that can be used to motivate employees other than a marketing approach. Similarly, the Grönroos (1981) model ignores a marketing-like approach. In fact, Grönroos amended his original definition of IM to the following:

> holding that an organisation's internal market of employees can be influenced most effectively and hence motivated to customer-consciousness, market orientation and sales-mindedness by a marketing-like internal approach and by applying marketing-like activities internally.
>
> (Grönroos, 1985: 42)

In order to provide a more comprehensive model of IM, both these approaches need to be combined. However, in order to produce a viable model it is necessary to re-examine the concept of 'employee as customer' as it is one of the major differences between the two models. This concept has a number of problems associated with it.

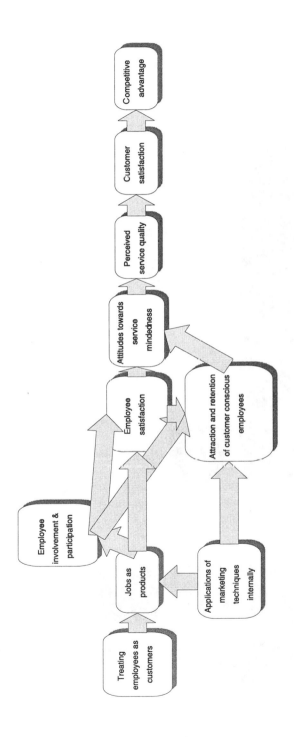

Figure 13.1 Berry's model of internal marketing

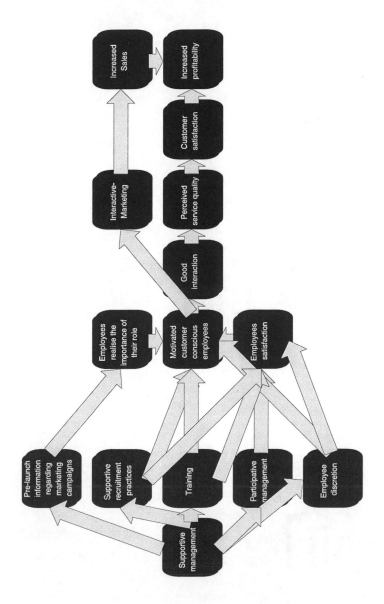

Figure 13.2 Grönroos's model of internal marketing

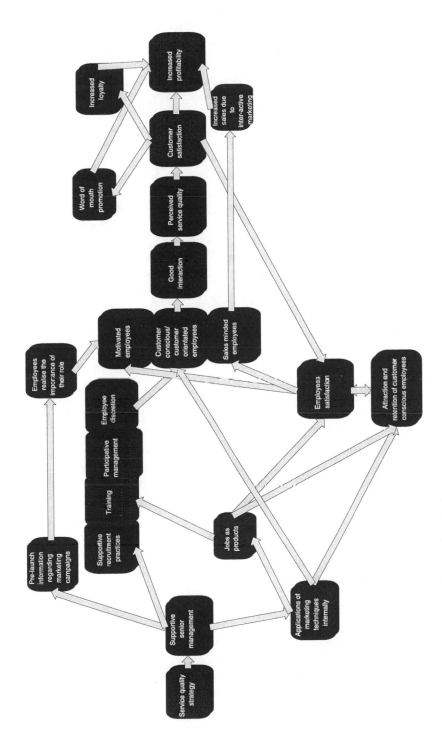

Figure 13.3 A meta model of internal marketing

Problems with the 'employee as customer' concept of internal marketing

In the 'employees as customers' approach to IM, underlying the notion of customer is the idea of exchanges, namely that customers receive products they desire in exchange for payment of some kind (that is, a price). In normal (marketing) exchange situations, products are bought in order to derive some form of utility. When the concept is applied to employees several problems are encountered.

One of the main problems with this approach is that the 'products' that employees are being sold may be unwanted or may in fact have negative utility for them; that is, they may not want them (such as new methods of working). In normal marketing situations, customers do not *have* to buy products that they do not wish to buy. This is not true for employees because of the nature of the employment contract. Employees must either accept the 'product' or (in the final analysis) they can be 'forced' into acceptance under the threat of disciplinary action or dismissal. In normal marketing situations, the consequences of non-purchase are not so severe. Additionally, in normal marketing situations customers have a range of (competing) products to choose from; this is unlikely to be the case in an IM situation where one particular policy will be on offer. According to Kotler, the marketing approach consists of *non-coercive* actions to induce a response in another social unit (Kotler, 1972: 50). That is, the use of force or formal authority is not considered to be a marketing solution to a problem.

Another problem with the notion of the employee as customer is the idea of customer sovereignty (that is the idea of customer is king, customer is always right and so forth). For if employees were to behave as if they were customers they would make impossible demands upon the organisation and its resources. It is for this reason that, in this approach, employees *do not know* they are customers even though they are treated as such. Moreover, the idea put forward by Sasser and Arbeit (1976) that 'personnel is the first market of a service company' appears to suggest that the employee market has primacy. This stands on its head the most fundamental axiom of marketing, namely, that the external customer has primacy; the external customer is the *raison d'être* of any company. For instance, many restaurant workers would prefer not to work late hours but nevertheless have to because that is when the customers prefer to dine out. Accommodating employee preferences in this case would lead to commercial suicide.

A meta-model of internal marketing in services

Given the aforementioned problems with the 'employees as customers' aspect of Berry's model it is, therefore, not included in the new model of IM derived from the combination of the Berry and Grönroos models. The resulting model is presented in Figure 13.3. A number of additional features in the model include the elaboration of the relationship between customer satisfaction and customer loyalty and increased profits. Profits are also increased by word-of-mouth promotion by satisfied customers.

The model also suggests that the antecedents of employee satisfaction are a function of adequate training, employee discretion and participative management. The job also needs to meet the needs of the employees. In addition, good communication between marketing and contact employee is also essential.

The proposed model has a number of advantages:

- The new model emphasises the fact that the Grönroos and Berry models are not competing models but highlight different aspects of IM and the new model uses these differences to build a more comprehensive conceptualisation.
- The model highlights a large number of implicit assumptions and relationships that need to be tested empirically.
- The model shows how IM works.
- Whilst the model is somewhat more complex than the original models it provides a more complete view of IM.

Basis of the meta-model in existing research

A closer examination of the model also shows that it links together a number of strands of research currently extant in the marketing field namely, customer orientation, customer satisfaction, customer loyalty, and the linkages between the three. In effect, the proposed model provides a meta-model for these strands of research. The major elements of the proposed model are now discussed in more detail.

Job satisfaction and its antecedents

A considerable amount of empirical research already exists on the antecedents of job satisfaction in the marketing area particularly relating to salespersons in industrial settings (for example, Churchill *et al.*, 1974, 1976; Walker *et al.*, 1975, 1977; Rogers *et al.*, 1994; Singh *et al.*, 1996). This literature is relevant to services marketing because the boundary spanning nature of salespeople is similar to that of contact employees in services in that they have to deal directly with customers and to resolve the conflicting demands of customers on the one hand, and the organisation on the other.

Much of this research is concentrated on the impact of role conflict and role ambiguity on job satisfaction. The results of these studies are fairly consistent in showing that role conflict, role ambiguity and role stress negatively affect job satisfaction (for example, Behrman and Perreault, 1994; Lysonski *et al.*, 1988; Teas, 1983; Siguaw *et al.*, 1994). In fact, after conducting a meta-analysis of fifty-nine studies, Brown and Peterson (1993) concluded that role conflict and role ambiguity were the key antecedents of job satisfaction. Jackson and Schuler (1985), in their meta-analysis of ninety-six reported organisational studies on role conflict and role ambiguity, found that the most frequent and significantly correlated organisational antecedents of role conflict and role ambiguity were autonomy, feedback from others, feedback from task, task identity, leader initiating structure, leader consideration, participation, formalisation and organisational level.

Employees experience role ambiguity when they do not have the necessary information to do their job properly (Walker *et al.*, 1977). Contact employees are more likely to experience role conflict because of the boundary spanning nature of their jobs as they attempt to reconcile the demands of the customers and the interests of the organisation. The frequency, quality and accuracy of downward communication moderates role ambiguity (Zeithaml *et al.*, 1988). Walker *et al.* (1975) suggest that role ambiguity can be reduced by training employees appropriately against the criteria used in the selection of employees.

Linking service quality and customer satisfaction

The basic thrust of the service quality literature is that service quality leads to increased customer satisfaction. This is supported by a considerable amount of empirical evidence for the proposition that service quality is the antecedent of customer satisfaction in services (for example, Anderson and Sullivan, 1993; Churchill and Suprenant 1982; Cronin and Taylor, 1992; Fornell, 1992; Oliver and Desarbo, 1988). The effects of loyalty include lower price sensitivity, reduced costs of attracting new customers as a result of word-of-mouth promotion, higher reputation of the firm and reduced impact of competitors' activities. For instance, Churchill and Suprenant, (1982) found that perceived service quality directly affected satisfaction for durables. Oliver and Desarbo (1988) also found that disconfirmation of expectations and perceived service quality had direct impact on satisfaction. Similar results were obtained by Anderson and Sullivan (1993).

Customer satisfaction, customer loyalty and profitability

In Berry's and Grönroos's models, there is little discussion of how customer satisfaction leads to profitability. However, the link between customer satisfaction and profitability is proposed by a number of authors (for example, Anderson and Fornell, 1994; Gummesson, 1993; Hallowell, 1996; Heskett *et al.*, 1990, 1994; Reicheld and Sasser, 1990; Rust *et al.*, 1995; Schneider and Bowen, 1995; Strobacka *et al.*, 1994; Zeithaml *et al.*, 1990). For Heskett *et al.* (1994), customer satisfaction operates via customer loyalty through to profitability. Other authors have simply proposed a direct link between satisfaction and profitability. Empirically, in the retail banking sector, Hallowell (1996) has shown that there were positive relationships between customer satisfaction and loyalty and between loyalty and profitability but did not find any conclusive evidence for the satisfaction–loyalty–profitability hypothesis.

The costs of implementing service quality are not usually discussed in the IM literature. In fact, the link between customer satisfaction and profitability is likely to display diminishing returns. That is, increasing investments in customer satisfaction will lead to decreasing returns after a point (Anderson *et al.*, 1994) which suggests that there exists an optimal level of satisfaction that the firm should be aiming for (Anderson and Sullivan, 1993).

Developing a researchable internal marketing model

While the model presented in Figure 13.3 shows how IM works, it is too complex for research purposes. Figure 13.4 restates the relationships in the model in a more tractable form. The relationships indicated in Figure 13.4 are derived directly from the IM literature. For instance, the motivation of employees via marketing-like activities is explicitly stated in the early literature on IM (Berry *et al.*, 1976, George, 1977; Berry, 1981). Grönroos (1981) and others also recommend the marketing-like approach to improve the inter-functional coordination and, hence, customer orientation. Inter-functional coordination and integration are central to more recent IM literature (for instance, Flipo, 1986; Tansuhaj *et al.*, 1987). Improving the customer orientation of the organisation has been a central concern of the IM concept from its inception. More recently, the central reason for interest in IM has been the potential contribution of IM to effective implementation of strategies via increased inter-functional coordination and employee motivation.

At the centre of this framework is customer orientation which is achieved through a marketing-like approach to the motivation of employees, and inter-functional coordination. The centrality of customer orientation reflects its importance in the marketing literature and its central role in achieving customer satisfaction and, hence, organisational goals. In fact, according to Narver and Slater (1990), inter-functional coordination is an essential facet of market orientation (see also Kohli and Jaworski, 1990; Jaworski and Kohli, 1993).

The inclusion of the empowerment variable is essential for the operationalisation of Grönroos's interactive marketing concept. In order for interactive marketing to occur, frontline employees need to be empowered; that is they require a degree of latitude over the service task performance in order to be responsive to

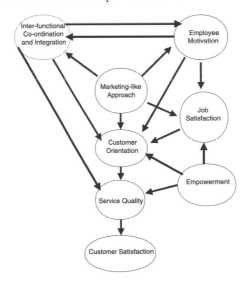

Figure 13.4 A research model for the internal marketing of services

customer needs and be able to perform service recovery. The degree of empowerment is contingent on the complexity/variability of customer needs and the degree of task complexity (see Rafiq and Ahmed, 1998). Empowerment in our model impacts on job satisfaction, customer orientation and service quality.

The empirical evidence on the relationships in the model is fairly limited and somewhat mixed. For instance, Hoffman and Ingram (1991) found that there was a weak correlation between job satisfaction and customer orientation ($r = 0.28$) and that role ambiguity, conflict and job satisfaction explained only 9 per cent of customer orientation. Kelley's (1990) study of bank employees also found a weak correlation of customer orientation with job satisfaction ($r = 0.18$) and with motivation ($r = 0.24$). However, when the effects of role clarity and motivation were held constant, job satisfaction was found not to be a significant predictor of customer orientation. Furthermore, although the study found that there was no significant difference in customer orientation among four groups of contact employees (managers, officers, customer service representatives and tellers), the tellers were significantly more dissatisfied with their jobs and significantly less motivated than the other groups of employees. What this suggests is that employees are quite capable of separating their feelings about their jobs (job satisfaction) from the actual performance of the job. Siguaw *et al.* (1994), found that customer orientation was not related to job satisfaction (this is the inverse of the relationship proposed in the IM model, where job satisfaction leads to increased customer orientation). Herrington and Lomax (1999), in their study of financial advisers in the UK, found no relationship between job satisfaction and customer perceptions of service quality. However, they did find a weak relationship between job satisfaction and customer intention to repurchase.

These studies seriously question the basic assumption underlying much of the IM literature that employee satisfaction is a key to having satisfied customers. Hence, instead of regarding employee satisfaction as a major precursor to performance, it can be regarded as one of a number of factors such as employee motivation, customer orientation and sales mindedness simultaneously determining productivity and the quality of the service. Hence, in our model the impact of job satisfaction on service quality occurs indirectly via customer orientation rather than directly between job satisfaction and service quality. This may explain, partially, the ambiguity in the empirical research noted above.

Empirical research on IM is limited mainly because of the lack of IM models. Money and Foreman (1996) attempt to operationalise the IM concept by developing a fifteen-item IM scale based on checklists suggested by Berry and Parasuraman (1991), and Berry *et al.* (1991). Their IM scale had three underlying factors which they term development (items relating to the development of employees), reward (items relating to rewarding of employees) and vision (items relating to goals and objectives of the organisation). Carruna and Calleya (1998) use this scale to assess its impact on organisational commitment, an important objective behind IM efforts to have satisfied employees. Carruna and Calleya found that, in their sample of managers from a retail bank, there was a significant but weak positive relationship between IM and organisational commitment ($R^2 = 0.185$).

However, their research showed that IM had significant effect only on the affective dimension of organisational commitment (that is, the strength of identification and involvement with an organisation) but not continuance and normative dimensions (see Allen and Meyer, 1990). Carruna and Calleya concluded that the IM construct requires further development and elaboration to distinguish it from similar human resource management constructs. These conclusions are not surprising given the underlying factors in the Foreman and Money IM scale.

Research directions

The model outlined includes constructs that are already well developed in the marketing and services literature and suggest ways of developing IM measures. For instance, the inter-functional coordination, customer orientation and marketing–like approach constructs could be measured by items adapted from the market orientation scales of Kohli *et al.* (1993). A number of scales are available for job satisfaction and employee motivation (for example, Wood *et al.*, 1986). Employee motivation, and the antecedents of job satisfaction, have been operationalised and researched using the role conflict and ambiguity constructs by a number of researchers (for example, Rizzo *et al.*, 1970; Chonko *et al.*, 1986). At present, there has been little research into the development of a scale to measure employee empowerment. However, Hartline and Ferrell (1996) present a usable scale which measures the degree to which managers encourage initiative, give employees freedom and trust employees to exercise their judgement.

Given that valid measures of the constructs in the model already exist, it should be possible to develop a reliable measure of the IM scale. This would be a considerable step forward in IM research. This measure could then be used to assess the claims made for IM, for instance regarding service quality, customer satisfaction, customer loyalty and profitability.

Conclusions and managerial implications

The model outlined in this chapter highlights the importance of employee attitudes in service quality via their impact on customer orientation, employee motivation and job satisfaction. Furthermore, effective service quality also requires high levels of inter-functional coordination and integration. Central to ensuring that employees have the requisite attitudes and high levels of inter-functional coordination is a marketing-like approach by management to these tasks. In addition, employees need to be supported by requisite levels of empowerment to deliver the required levels of service quality. Empowerment is also a key to service recovery, a key component in perceptions of service quality.

For managerial purposes, Figure 13.3 details how IM can be put into practice. Examination of Figure 13.3 shows:

- That supportive senior management is fundamental to the success of IM as it indicates to all employees the importance of IM initiatives, and thereby facilitates inter-functional coordination.
- The importance of communicating marketing strategies and objectives to employees so that they understand their role and importance in the implementation of the strategies and achievement of marketing and organisational objectives.
- That employee satisfaction can be increased by treating jobs as 'products', that is, designing jobs with features that prospective employees value.
- Ensuring that employees are highly motivated, customer oriented and sales minded requires recruitment practices that attract and select employees with the requisite attitudes, providing employees with the right type and level of training to perform their jobs, a participative management style, and a degree of discretion (contingent on the service strategy of the organisation) for frontline employees so that they can meet customer expectations and take advantage of interactive marketing opportunities.
- The importance of explicitly managing the interactions of employees and customers or 'the moments of truth' by training employees for customer orientation and 'sales mindedness'.
- The importance of using a marketing-like approach to the motivation of employees, and inter-functional coordination.

Delivering high levels of service has its costs. For instance, service quality may be improved by providing employees with additional or better training. However, this has a consequence of increasing costs. Unless these costs are recovered by attracting extra customers, an increase in repeat purchases or in fewer service delivery mistakes, there will be a negative impact on profitability. Hence, this suggests that there is an optimal level of service quality that management should be aiming for, not necessarily the highest. The level of service quality that an organisation offers is contingent on its positioning on service in the marketplace.

References

Ahmed, P.K. and Rafiq, M. (1995) 'The Role of Internal Marketing in the Implementation of Marketing Strategies', *Journal of Marketing Practice: Applied Marketing Science* 1(4): 32–51.
Allen, N.J. and Meyer, J.P. (1990) 'The Measurement and Antecedents of Affective, Continuance and Normative Commitment to the Organization', *Journal of Occupational Psychology* 63(1): 1–18.
Anderson, E.W. and Fornell, C. (1994) 'A Customer Satisfaction Research Prospectus', in Rust, R.T. and Oliver, R. (eds), *Service Quality: New Directions in Theory & Practice*, Thousand Oaks, CA: Sage Publications.
Anderson, E.W., Fornell, C. and Lehmann, D.R. (1994) 'Customer Satisfaction, Market Share and Profitability: Findings from Sweden', *Journal of Marketing* 58(3): 53–66.
Anderson, E.W. and Sullivan, M. (1993) 'The Antecedents and Consequences of Customer Satisfaction For Firms', *Marketing Science* 12(Spring): 125–43.

Barnes, J.G. (1989) 'The Role of Internal Marketing: If the staff Won't Buy it Why Should the Customer?', *Irish Marketing Review* 4(2): 11–21.

Behrman, D.N. and Perreault, W.D. (1984) 'A Role Stress Model of Performance and Satisfaction of Industrial Salespersons', *Journal of Marketing* 48(Fall): 9–21.

Berry, L.L. (1981) 'The Employee as Customer', *Journal of Retail Banking* 3(March): 25–8.

Berry, L.L., Conant, J. S. and Parasuraman, A. (1991) 'A Framework for Conducting a Service Marketing Audit', *Journal of the Academy of Marketing Science* 19(Summer): 255–68.

Berry, L.L., Hensel, J.S. and Burke, M.C. (1976) 'Improving Retailer Capability for Effective Consumerism Response', *Journal of Retailing* 52(3): 3–14.

Berry, L.L. and Parasuraman, A. (1991) *Marketing Services: Competing through Quality*, New York: The Free Press.

Brown, S.P. and Peterson, R.A. (1993) 'Antecedents and Consequences of Salesperson Job Satisfaction: Meta-Analysis and Causal Effects', *Journal of Marketing Research* 30(February): 63–77.

Carruna, A. and Calleya, P. (1998) 'The Effect of Internal Marketing on Organisational Commitment among Retail Bank Managers', *International Journal of Bank Marketing* 16(3): 108–16.

Chonko, L.B., Howell, R.B. and Bellenger, D. (1986) 'Congruence in Sales Force Evaluations: Relation to Sales Force Conflict and Ambiguity', *Journal of Personal Selling & Sales Management* 6(May): 35–48.

Churchill, G.A., Ford, N.M. and Walker, O.C. (1974) 'Measuring the Job Satisfaction of Industrial Salesmen', *Journal of Marketing Research* 11(August): 254–60.

—— (1976) 'Organizational Climate and Job Satisfaction in the Salesforce', *Journal of Marketing Research* 13(November): 323–32.

Churchill, G.A. and Suprenant, C.F. (1982) 'An Investigation into the Determinants of Customer Satisfaction', *Journal of Marketing Research* 19(November): 491–504.

Collins, B. and Payne, A. (1991) 'Internal Marketing: A New Perspective for HRM', *European Management Journal* 9(3): 261–70.

Cronin, J.J. and Taylor, S.A. (1992) 'Measuring Service Quality: A Re-examination and Extension', *Journal of Marketing* 52(3): 55–68.

Flipo, J.-P. (1986) 'Service Firms: Interdependence of External and Internal Marketing Strategies', *Journal of European Marketing* 20(8): 5–14.

Fornell, C. (1992) 'A National Customer Satisfaction Barometer: The Swedish Experience', *Journal of Marketing* 55(January): 1–21.

George, W.R. (1977) 'The Retailing of Services – A Challenging Future', *Journal of Retailing* 53(Fall): 85–98.

—— (1990) 'Internal Marketing and Organizational Behavior: A Partnership in Developing Customer-Conscious Employees at Every Level', *Journal of Business Research* 20(1): 63–70.

Grönroos, C. (1981) 'Internal Marketing: An Integral Part of Marketing Theory', in Donnelly, J.H. and George, W.E. (eds), *Marketing of Services*, Chicago: American Marketing Association Proceedings series, 236–8.

—— (1984) 'Internal Marketing: Theory and Practice', in Bloch, T.M., Upah, G.D. and Zeithaml, V.A. (eds), *Services Marketing in a Changing Environment*, Chicago: America Marketing Association, 41–7.

Gummesson, E. (1993) *Quality Management in Service Organizations: An Interpretation of the Service Quality Phenomenon and a Synthesis of International Research*, Karlstadt, Sweden: International Service Quality Association.

Hallowell, R. (1996) 'The Relationships of Customer Satisfaction, Customer Loyalty, and Profitability: An Empirical Study', *International Journal of Service Industry Management* 7(4): 27–42.

Hartline, M.D. and Ferrell, O.C. (1996) 'The Management of Customer-Contact Service Employees: An Empirical Investigation', *Journal of Marketing* 60(4): 52–69.

Herrington, G. and Lomax, W. (1999) 'Do Satisfied Employees Make Customers Satisfied?: An Investigation into the Relationship Between Service Employee Job Satisfaction and Customer Perceived Service Quality', in Hildebrandt, L., Annacker, D. and Klapper, D. (eds), *Marketing and Competition in the Information Age*, Proceedings of the 28th EMAC Conference, Humboldt University, Berlin, 11–14 May, 110.

Heskett, J.L., Jones, T.O., Loveman, G.W., Sasser, W.E. and Schlesinger, L.A. (1994) 'Putting the Service–Profit Chain to Work', *Harvard Business Review* 72(March–April): 164–74.

Heskett, J.L., Sasser, W.E. and Hart, C.W.L. (1990) *Breakthrough Service*, New York: The Free Press.

Hoffman, D.K. and Ingram, T.N. (1991) 'Creating Customer Orientated Employees: The Case in Home Health Care', *Journal of Health Care Marketing* 11(June): 24–32.

Jackson, S.E. and Shuler, R.S. (1985) 'A Meta-analysis and Conceptual Critique of Research on Role Ambiguity and Role Conflict in Work Settings', *Organizational Behavior and Human Decision Processes* 36(1): 16–78.

Jaworski, B.J. and Kohli, A.K. (1993) 'Market Orientation: Antecedents and Consequences', *Journal of Marketing* 57(3): 53–70.

Kelley, S.W. (1990) 'Customer Orientation of Bank Employees and Culture', *International Journal of Bank Marketing* 8(6): 25–9.

Kohli, A.K. and Jaworski, B.J. (1990) 'Market Orientation: The Construct, Research Propositions, and Managerial Implications', *Journal of Marketing* 54(2): 35–58.

Kohli, A.K., Jaworski, B.J. and Kumar, A. (1993) 'MARKOR: A Measure of Market Orientation', *Journal of Marketing Research* 30(4): 467–77.

Kotler, P. (1972) 'A Generic Concept of Marketing', *Journal of Marketing* 36(April): 346–54.

Lysonski, S., Singer, A. and Wilemon, D. (1988) 'Coping with Environmental Uncertainty and Boundary Spanning in the Product Manager's Role', *The Journal of Business and Industrial Marketing* 3(Winter): 5–16.

MacStravic, R.S. (1985) 'Internal Marketing for Hospitals', *Health Quarterly Marketing* 3(2–3): 47–54.

Money, A.H. and Foreman, S. (1996) 'The Measurement of Internal Marketing: A Confirmatory Case Study', *Journal of Marketing Management* 11(8): 755–66.

Narver, J.C. and Slater, S.F. (1990) 'The Effect of a Market Orientation on Business Profitability', *Journal of Marketing* 54(5): 20–35.

Oliver, R.L. and Desarbo, W.S. (1988) 'Response Determinants in Satisfaction Judgements', *Journal of Consumer Research* 14(March): 495–507.

Piercy, N. (1995) 'Customer Satisfaction and the Internal Market: Marketing our Customers to our Employees', *Journal of Marketing Practice: Applied Marketing Science* 1(1): 22–44.

Piercy, N. and Morgan, N. (1991) 'Internal Marketing: The Missing Half of the Marketing Programme', *Long Range Planning* 24(2): 82–93.

Rafiq, M. and Ahmed, P.K. (1993) 'The Scope of Internal Marketing: Defining the Boundary Between Marketing and Human Resource Management', *Journal of Marketing Management* 9(3): 219–32.

—— (1998) 'A Customer-Oriented Framework for Empowering Service Employees', *Journal of Services Marketing* 12(4–5): 379–94.

Reicheld, F.F. and Sasser, W.E. (1990) 'Zero Defections Comes to Services', *Harvard Business Review*, 68, September–October: 105–11.

Rizzo, J.R., House, R.J. and Lirtzman, S.I. (1970) 'Role Conflict and Ambiguity in Complex Organizations', *Administrative Science Quarterly* 15(June): 150–64.

Rogers, J.D., Clow, K.E. and Kash, T.J. (1994) 'Increasing Job Satisfaction of Service Personnel', *Journal of Services Marketing* 8(1): 14–26.

Rust, R.T., Zahorik, A.J. and Keiningham, T.L. (1995) 'Return on Quality (ROQ): Making Service Quality Financially Accountable', *Journal of Marketing* 59(2): 58–70.

Sargent, A. and Saadia, A. (1998) 'The Strategic Application of Internal Marketing: An Investigation of UK Banking', *International Journal of Bank Marketing* 16(2): 66–79.

Sasser, W.E. and Arbeit, S.F. (1976) 'Selling Jobs in the Service Sector', *Business Horizons* (June): 61–2.

Schneider, B. and Bowen, D.E. (1995) *Winning the Service Game*, Boston: Harvard Business School Press.

Siguaw, J.A., Brown, G. and Widing, R.E. (1994) 'The Influence of the Market Orientation of the Firm on Sales Force Behavior and Attitudes', *Journal of Marketing Research* 31(1): 106–16.

Singh, J., Verbeke, W. and Rhoads, G.K. (1996) 'Do Organizational Practices Matter in Role Stress Processes?: A Study of Direct and Moderating Effects for Marketing-Oriented Boundary Spanners', *Journal of Marketing* 60(3): 69–86.

Strobacka, K., Strandvik, T. and Grönroos, C. (1994) 'Managing Customer Relationships for Profit: The Dynamics of Relationship Quality', *International Journal of Service Industry Management* 5(5): 21–38.

Tansuhaj, P.S., Wong, J. and McCullough, J. (1987) 'Internal and External Marketing: Effects on Customer Satisfaction in Banks in Thailand', *International Journal of Bank Marketing* 5(3): 73–83.

Teas, R.K. (1983) 'Supervisory Behaviour, Role Stress, and the Job Satisfaction of Industrial Sales People', *Journal of Marketing Research* 20(February): 84–91.

Varey, R.J. (1995) 'Internal Marketing: A Review and Some Interdisciplinary Research Challenges', *International Journal of Service Industry Management* 6(1): 40–63.

Walker, O.C., Churchill, G.A. and Ford, N.M. (1975) 'Organisational Determinants of the Industrial Salesman's Role Conflict and Ambiguity', *Journal of Marketing* 39(January): 32–9.

Walker, O.C., Churchill, G.A. and Ford, N.M. (1977) 'Motivation and Performance in Industrial Selling: Present Knowledge and Needed Research', *Journal of Marketing Research* 14(May): 156–68.

Wood, V.R., Chonko, L.B. and Hunt, S. (1986) 'Social Responsibility and Personal Success: Are They Incompatible?', *Journal of Business Research* 14(3): 193–212.

Zeithaml, V.A., Berry, L.L. and Parasuraman, A. (1988) 'Communication and Control Processes in the Delivery of Service Quality', *Journal of Marketing* 52(April): 35–48.

Zeithaml, V.A., Parasuraman, A. and Berry, L.L. (1990) *Delivering Quality Service*, New York: The Free Press.

14 Internal relationship management

Broadening the scope of internal marketing

Paivi Voima

Introduction

This chapter focuses on analysing the present state of internal marketing. On the basis of a literature review, conclusions are drawn about the development and current state of internal marketing. Although internal marketing has been perceived traditionally as a homogenous concept, this chapter will show that internal marketing has undergone interesting changes since its inception some two decades ago. A model for conceptualising internal marketing comprising four perspectives is suggested. It is shown that the transactional research context of the 1980s has affected the internal marketing framework. It is argued that although the emphasis has gradually shifted to relationships, internally the internal marketing framework should be broadened further. A more relevant approach anchored to the ongoing discourse of relationship marketing is required, which is introduced in this chapter as the internal relationship management perspective.

Ever since the early 1970s, when Rathmell (1974) wrote the first book that discussed services marketing, the subject has fascinated researchers. During the past twenty years, services marketing has developed quickly and substantial progress has been made in research. One of the sub-categories that grew out of this research is the concept of internal marketing. Internal marketing first emerged in the services marketing literature and later in other literatures such as service management, total quality management, and relationship marketing (see, for example, Berry, 1981; Collins and Payne, 1991; George, 1984, 1990; Grönroos, 1981, 1982, 1997; Gummesson, 1984, 1987, 1994; Piercy, 1995; Piercy and Morgan, 1991; Rafiq and Ahmed, 1993, Thomas *et al.*, 1991; Varey, 1995, Voima and Grönroos, 1999).

An examination of the literature reveals that internal marketing as a concept engaged researchers especially in the 1980s, even though the term 'internal marketing' was introduced as early as the late 1970s. When trying to understand the evolution of internal marketing, it is essential to focus on the fact that the development was very context-based. When internal marketing as a concept emerged in the late 1970s and early 1980s, the research context was completely different from the relationship emphasis in research today. External marketing was more or less totally based on the marketing mix and its model of the 4Ps (product, price, place and promotion), which also had its effect on the development of internal marketing. The origins of internal marketing can, therefore, be found in the transaction-based approach to marketing, which can also be seen in the development of the theoretical framework of internal marketing.

The theoretical framework of internal marketing has not yet seen the same paradigm shift towards relational thinking as did external marketing in the late 1980s and in the 1990s. However, this is contradictory, because if relationship marketing is perceived as a management strategy, the strategy could be seen as incomplete if it does not take into consideration internal relationships. If the goal for the company is to achieve external relationships of high quality, it can be argued that this cannot be done without also implementing a relationship-based approach internally.

Internal marketing conceptualisation

In this discussion, a conceptualisation of internal marketing will be presented. The chapter analyses the contributions to internal marketing theory based on two dimensions: organisational objectives and focus (i.e. short-term v. long-term and internal v. external), and interaction orientation (i.e. the degree and type of interactions taking place between organisational members, transactional versus relational). Through these dimensions, presented in Figure 14.1, four perspectives on internal marketing emerge.

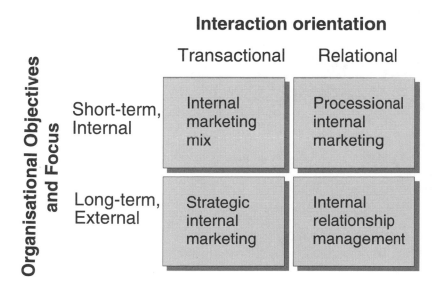

Figure 14.1 Internal marketing conceptualisation

Internal marketing mix

The internal marketing mix is characterised by a transactional interaction orientation and by short-term organisational objectives and an internal focus. The transactional view of the interaction orientation is highlighted in the degree and type of interactions taking place within the organisation. As the name of this perspective shows, weight is put on the internal marketing mix, and especially the 4Ps. This view of internal marketing has been stressed and developed by many researchers within the internal marketing context (Berry, 1981; Flipo, 1986; Grönroos, 1981, 1982; Trumbly and Arnold, 1989). The basic assumption within this perspective is that the same basic structures used for external marketing should be used also internally. Flipo (1986) argues for the importance of the 4P approach internally and explains what the internal features comparable to product, price, place and promotion are. The product is characterised internally by the attractive 'job' a firm must sell to the employees in order to attract the best people. Price refers to the unattractiveness of a job when an employee has to deal with, for example, aggressive and unpleasant customers. According to Flipo (1986), this represents a psychological cost, which is assimilated in the price to be paid, considered from a marketing point of view. In order for the best people to be able to 'buy' the most attractive jobs the branches must be located close to their living places, which is internally paralleled by Flipo with the external place dimension. Promotion refers to the communication taking place within organisations.

The attractiveness of the marketing mix approach internally is seen in a lot of definitions concerning internal marketing. Grönroos states (1992: 163) that 'The internal marketing concept – as a complement to the traditional marketing concept – holds that an organisation's internal market of employees can be influenced most effectively and hence motivated to customer-consciousness, market-orientation and sales-mindedness by a marketing-like internal approach and by using marketing-like activities internally'. Gummesson (1987: 24) again points out that 'the idea behind internal marketing is to apply the marketing concept, originally developed for the company's external marketing, to the internal market as well'. What these definitions show is that the transactional perspective that companies applied in external marketing in the 1980s should be applied also internally.

It is apparent with the internal marketing mix perspective, therefore, that the interaction orientation within the company is very transactional in its nature. Besides stressing the 4Ps, scholars within this perspective also argue for a very traditional approach to marketing. This is perceived in, for example, Berry's (1981) argument when he stated that applying marketing research, market segmentation and advertising to the internal markets illustrates the potential of thinking like a marketer when the task at hand is managing people. This same view has also been shared by Grönroos (1981) in what he has labelled tactical internal marketing. He has pointed out that internal marketing can be implemented on two levels in the organisation: strategic and tactical. The objective for the tactical level has, in line with Berry's view, been very transactional, stressing the importance of selling services, auxiliary services, campaigns and single marketing efforts to the employees. According to Grönroos (1982), in tactical internal marketing, traditional marketing activities such as personal selling and mass communication efforts may be used.

The organisational objectives of the internal marketing mix perspective are short-term and the focus is internal. The short-term objectives are characterised by the fact that the internal marketing mix stresses separate encounters and does not emphasise long-term relationships as the goal for the organisation. The organisational focus of this perspective is internal. The main focus for internal marketing is the internal market not the satisfaction of the final customer, so the weight is put on the well-being of employees. Employees, their motivation and satisfaction, are considered the main objective for internal marketing, which means that employees are seen as the primary market. However, Rafiq and Ahmed (1993) argue that this view of treating employees as primary customers has several problems. Firstly, it stands on its head one of the most fundamental axioms of marketing, that the external customer has primacy. Secondly, the employees are forced to 'buy' products (for example, new methods of working) that they do not want which in normal marketing situations is not the case, when the customer has the freedom to choose which products s/he buys or does not want to buy. Rafiq and Ahmed (1993) also point out that in normal marketing situations customers can choose from many competing products, which is not the case internally.

The marketing mix perspective is, therefore, characterised by a transactional approach both internally and externally. Although arguments have been put forth for stressing customer-consciousness and sales-mindedness (Grönroos, 1982) as the ultimate reason for motivational efforts of a firm, this approach can still be seen as transactional and short-term because the main goal externally has been on transactional selling not on building long-term relationships.

Strategic internal marketing

Strategic internal marketing is also characterised by a transactional interaction orientation. However, the organisational objectives are long-term and the focus is external. Compared to the internal marketing mix approach, the organisational objectives have shifted from short-term to long-term and the focus from internal to external. No longer are the employees seen as the primary market of the organisation; instead, weight is laid on the strategic goals of the organisation, the satisfaction of external customers. The emphasis is on the external customer and the external strategy determines what form internal marketing takes in the organisation. Contributors to this perspective include several scholars (Piercy, 1995; Piercy and Morgan, 1991; Rafiq and Ahmed, 1993). Piercy (1995) supports this perspective and views internal marketing as using marketing analysis and techniques aimed at the internal market of a company to make the changes necessary for the external strategy to be effective. It is stressed that the internal marketing programme should be built around external marketing strategies (Piercy and Morgan, 1991). It is also suggested that internal marketing involves a 'planned effort to overcome organisational resistance to change and to align, motivate and integrate employees towards the effective implementation of corporate and functional strategies' (Rafiq and Ahmed, 1993: 222).

In this perspective, the internal marketing programme is tied to the success of the external marketing programme. The internal marketing programme is, according to Piercy (1995), aimed at the critical people and groups inside the organisation without whose commitment, co-operation and support the organisation will not succeed in the implementation of the external marketing programme. What makes Rafiq and Ahmed's (1993) definition interesting are the long-term organisational objectives, which emphasise external customer satisfaction as part of a long-term relationship. Although external customers are perceived as most important, the central role of employees is recognised. However, in this perspective the other dimension, interaction orientation, is transactional. This view is supported also by Piercy (1995) and Piercy and Morgan (1991), who argue for an internal marketing programme consisting of product, price, communication and distribution in line with the 4Ps approach. The 4Ps approach holds in this context that the product is the strategy, the price is what people are asked to give up for the strategy to work, the communication is the channels of information and persuasion, and distribution refers to how the changes needed can be influenced and managed (Piercy, 1995). Rafiq and Ahmed (1993) also highlight the transactional interaction orientation, although the extended 7Ps (to include physical evidence, process and participants) are stressed instead of the traditional 4Ps. Piercy and Morgan (1991) also call for segmentation and targeting of the internal market, based on the goals the company has concerning the external marketing programme.

Processional internal marketing

Processional internal marketing is a perspective that supports relational interaction orientation in the organisation but is characterised by short-term organisational goals and an internal focus. A body of research stresses this perspective (Collins and Payne, 1991; Edvardsson *et al.*, 1994; George, 1990; Mohr-Jackson, 1991). Internal marketing is no longer seen as something the organisation markets to groups of employees, mainly front-line employees. Instead, the weight has shifted to horizontal relationships where employees make demands on each other rather than their organisation. This perspective supports the thought of internal customers and suppliers in line with the TQM approach, which differs from the service marketing view of internal marketing, and stresses the concept of employees being customers of the organisation.

This TQM related perspective is interesting in that it brings a totally new dimension to internal marketing, when relationships between internal customers and suppliers are put in focus. Instead of applying the same marketing structures used for the external market to internal groups of employees, all relationships between organisational members are put in focus. What makes the focus of this perspective internal is the fact that this view also supports inside-out thinking. What this means is what Rafiq and Ahmed (1993) stress, is that if the requirements of internal customers are met along the entire length of the production chain then the quality of the final product will be assured. If the organisational focus were external, the focus would be on the external relationships with the customers and the management of the internal customer–supplier relationships would take place through the goals set externally. Although processional internal marketing has a relational interaction orientation, it can be stated that the relationship orientation is still slightly transactional and, therefore, also short-term. Focus has been put on the technical dimension in the relationships, mainly the quality of information, or other 'products' supplied between the internal suppliers and customers. Social dimensions in the relationships have mostly been ignored, which is a weakness of the processional internal marketing perspective.

The processional perspective of internal marketing is perceived clearly in the following definition presented by Collins and Payne (1991: 264). 'Internal marketing is that form of marketing where both the customer and the supplier are inside the organisation'. Edvardsson *et al.* (1994) also argue for a TQM-oriented view of internal marketing, with the main aim being to improve communication between internal customers.

During the 1990s, more and more scholars have found an interest in the processional perspective to internal marketing. Several scholars have, when arguing for a market-oriented perspective, stressed the importance of broadening the market orientation concept so that an added focus is laid on internal customers from a TQM perspective (Mohr-Jackson, 1991; Lukas and Maignan, 1996). Mohr-Jackson (1991: 469) has argued that the internal customer focus implies that a customer orientation entails (a) understanding internal customers' requirements that affect external customer needs and preferences; (b) obtaining information about external customers' needs and preferences through internal customers; and (c) creating additional buyer value by increasing internal customer benefits.

The processional perspective stressing internal customer–supplier relationships has also encouraged researchers to focus on internal services and their quality. During the 1990s, internal service quality has, within the service quality discipline, been studied by Gremler *et al.* (1994), Lewis and Entwistle (1990), Neuhaus (1996), Reynoso and Moores (1995), Stauss (1995), and Vandermerwe and Gilbert (1991). It can be stated that these studies have deepened further the processional perspective to internal marketing although the focus has been put mainly on the technical dimension, that is how services or products are supplied internally and how the customer has perceived the quality of them.

Internal relationship management

The fourth perspective on internal marketing is called internal relationship management (Voima, 1998; Varey, 1996). The reason why the management aspect has been highlighted, instead of calling the perspective internal relationship marketing, is that this perspective supports the thought of managing internal relationships, not marketing internally to groups of employees. The internal relationship management perspective supports the dimensions of relational interaction orientation and long-term organisational objectives and an external focus. What this means is that the emphasis is no longer on some relational aspects as within processional internal marketing which focuses mainly on the technical; instead, the whole relationship and all its dimensions (economic, technical and social) are perceived to be important. This perspective also supports the external focus, which means that external relationships are perceived as the most central relationships. This view is in contrast with the internal marketing mix perspective, which stressed that employees are the first market of the company. The internal management perspective again stresses an outside-in view, which supports the notion of primacy of external customers. The organisational objectives are long-term and this perspective stresses the external relationships, and internal relationships are always managed in relation to the needs and expectations of external customers. External strategy, emphasising long-term relationships with customers, determines what form internal relationships and their management take in the organisation.

It can be stated that the scope of internal marketing is broadened through internal relationship management. Some scholars (Ballantyne, 1997; Gummesson, 1994; Lings, 1999; Lings and Brooks, 1998; Payne, 1993; Varey, 1995; Voima, 1998; Voima and Grönroos, 1999) have stressed this perspective during the 1990s, but further research needs to be carried out. An interesting definition, partly supporting this perspective, is presented by Payne (1993: 36–7) when he points out that one dimension in the internal marketing concept is that 'every employee and every department in an organisation is both an internal customer and an internal supplier'. Payne's view on internal marketing is nearly related to the internal relationship management perspective, and it falls somewhere between the processional internal marketing and internal relationship management. He argues for a view where 'internal marketing is concerned with the development of customer orientation: the alignment of internal and external marketing ensures coherent relationship marketing'. Payne also stresses that the internal market is only one of the six markets a company has (customer, referral, supplier, recruitment, influence and internal). All six markets should, according to Payne, have adopted a relationship philosophy as a key strategy, which also supports the internal relationship management perspective.

Ballantyne (1997: 354) presents another interesting view supporting internal relationship management. He stated that 'internal marketing is a relationship development process in which staff autonomy and know-how combine to create and circulate new organisational knowledge that will challenge internal activities which need to be challenged to enhance quality in marketplace relationships'. This definition is a modification of a definition presented by Ballantyne *et al.* (1995). Ballantyne sees internal marketing from a relationship perspective and the fundamental dimension of internal marketing as an employee satisfying philosophy is totally forgotten. What Ballantyne stresses are the internal activities, which are directly related to quality perception in external relationships. Gummesson (1994) has also taken a relationship emphasising view to internal marketing. He perceives internal marketing as one of a company's thirty relationships. One of these thirty relationships is labelled the 'relationship to the personnel market'. He argues that internal marketing is both the creating of relationships between management and employees and also between different functions. Gummesson combines two perspectives when he stresses both horizontal and vertical relationships. Although he argues for relationship construction between management and employees, and between different functions, his view is slightly transactional when he argues for using 'tools' such as mass marketing and segmentation internally.

Lings (1999) and Lings and Brooks (1998) have put forward interesting arguments, concerning internal relationships. Although their study focused on the measurement of internal and external service quality in a service company, their view is partly in line with the internal relationship management perspective. The focus of their study was on the external customer's perception of service quality. An innovative feature of their study was the use of service blueprinting to identify internal and external service quality exchanges. The internal and external service quality was measured at the start of the study and then again after six months. Over the period of the study, the quality of the service experienced by the external customers increased substantially. In Lings and Brooks's (1998) study, the notion of managing internal relationships was present although the focus was in line with processional internal marketing put only on the service quality dimension. Lings (1999) argued that 'the focus on internal factors, stressing the open transfer of information in the internal market, should also facilitate the formation of closer more co-operative relationships between departments, a prerequisite for successful relationships in the external markets'. Similar to most of the internal marketing researchers, Lings (1999) also focused on service organisations.

Varey (1995) presented an interesting model for internal marketing as a process for market-oriented management. The process he modelled is a highly iterative and interactive one, going beyond transactional exchanges and stressing internal relationships. Voima (1998) and Voima and Grönroos (1999) have also emphasised a relational view of internal marketing. It is emphasised that internal marketing from a relational perspective should not only be perceived between the management and the employees but also should be perceived as management of all the relationships that exist in the internal market, on all company levels.

Broadening the scope further

Differing views, related to internal relationship management, have been discussed. However, it is argued that an even broader scope should be taken. Instead of just focusing on service firms, it is stressed that internal marketing is needed in all organisations. When an internal relationship management perspective is taken, the focus has shifted from front-line personnel to all internal actors.

Internal relationship management stresses management of all internal relationships as an ongoing process. This perspective recognises the limitations of the transactional view of internal marketing and calls for a long-term perspective both internally as well as externally. The internal relationship management perspective focuses on relationships between actors in the internal market; seeing these relationships as processes which directly or indirectly affect both internal and external relationships. Instead of laying the focus on internal service quality and its effect on external service quality, internal relationship management supports the notion of focusing on relationships. Service quality should be perceived as just one quality dimension in an internal relationship, which consists of several dimensions. Different quality dimensions can be identified in different types of internal relationships, at different company levels. The weight put on separate quality dimensions in different internal relationships is completely dependent on the company level at which the relationships are positioned. The internal relationship management perspective also argues for a dyadic perspective where both parties' perceptions in (and of) the relationship are considered important.

This new perspective on internal marketing is, therefore, broadly defined as *the process of managing all internal relationships, affecting the external customers' perception of value, by identifying, maintaining, developing and when necessary terminating these internal relationships*.

However, it is argued that an even more specific definition is called for. Such a definition states that internal relationship management is *the process of managing all critical internal relationships, strongly affecting the critical external relationships, by identifying, maintaining, developing and when necessary terminating these internal relationships*.

The first part of this definition – the process of managing all critical internal relationships – stresses the importance of managing the most important relationships, the critical ones within the organisation. It is argued that it is impossible to manage all relationships effectively; therefore, the most critical have to be identified. This notion of internal criticality is related to the second part of the definition – strongly affecting the critical external relationships. An internal relationship is of high importance and critical if it strongly affects the external customer's perception of value in a positive or negative way. It is argued that all internal relationships do not affect the external customers' perceptions of value in an equal way, and, therefore, those internal relationships which are externally important should be the focus of relationship management.

The criticality of external relationships is again dependent on how important the relationships are for the company's success. In business relationships these critical external relationships are easier to identify than within service companies. The definition ends with '*by identifying, maintaining, developing and when necessary terminating these internal relationships*', which relates to definitions presented in the relationship marketing literature. It is argued that, by identifying the most critical internal relationships affecting the most critical external relationships and by maintaining, developing and, if required, even terminating these internal relationships, internal relationship management becomes reality.

Within the research on internal marketing, that which focused on the internal marketing mix and strategic internal marketing has put weight on the individual level. On the other hand, in the research on processional internal marketing, the internal suppliers and internal customers have most often been studied at a department level. Most internal service quality studies have also focused on the department level. However, it is argued that internal relationship management should not be restricted to one organisational level because critical internal relationships can be identified on all organisational levels: individual, team, department, unit. Relationships exist on all these levels and between all levels, within and across hierarchies. An organisation consists of business units, which consist of departments, which consist of teams, which consist of individuals.

Interaction levels in internal relationships

The different relationships within company levels can be analysed by dividing the relationships into smaller natural entities. Liljander and Strandvik (1995) have, within service marketing, divided relationships into episodes and acts, whereas Holmlund (1996, 1997) has included a sequence level in her study, one which focuses on business relationships. It is argued that internal relationships consist of natural entities through which the internal relationships can be managed better. In the same way, a relationship level comprises all sequences, which comprise all episodes, which again consist of all actions related to a relationship.

The lowest interaction level is the *action* level, which has been recognised by many researchers as a part of the external relationships (Holmlund, 1996; Liljander and Strandvik, 1995; Strandvik and Storbacka, 1996). *Actions* can also be seen internally as the lowest level of interaction. Internal actions can concern all kinds of exchange elements, and not only social contacts. Internal actions can be a telephone call or an e-mail message to another employee or to the management. On one of the higher levels, an interaction can be for example a report that is distributed to another department as a part of a larger project.

The next level of interaction is the *episode* level. Episodes are defined externally as several interconnected actions, which represent a small entity within the relationship (Holmlund, 1996: 49). Internally, these episodes can also be identified. An internal episode can for example be all telephone calls and meetings related to a specific problem, such as implementation of a new data system. All the telephone calls and meetings that are connected to solving the problem serve to build up the episode.

Internally, sequences can also be identified. An internal sequence consists of one or many episodes. Many problems can be related to the implementation of a data system and when all the telephone calls and meetings (actions) related to all the different problems (episodes) are summarised, a sequence can be identified. The implementation of a new data system can be considered a sequence because there are several actions and episodes related to this sequence. An internal sequence can also be at an individual level, for example, a change of work duties. An earlier sequence ends and a new one starts when changing job duties.

The final interaction level is the whole *relationship*. The final level of interaction refers to the level of analysis where the whole relationship is concerned and evaluated. This means that the focus lies in one particular relationship with one particular counterpart. Internally, this means that all relationships consist of sequences, which consist of episodes, which again consist of actions. It is emphasised that internal relationships at different company levels and between different actors can be divided into natural entities. The management and the employees should be aware of these natural entities and critical entities within the relationships to be able to manage more efficiently relationships in the internal market.

When recognising the different interaction levels in internal relationships, it becomes possible to start to analyse the internal customers' value creation process and how it is connected to the value creation process of the external customer. Externally, it has been recognised that it is important for management to understand the role of actions and episodes in the external customer's value creation process (Strandvik and Storbacka, 1996). However, it is argued that, internally, this is not enough. Internally, this view should be broadened so that not only does management try to understand the role of specific internal actions in the employees' value creation process, but also that all internal actors should try to understand what their and their actions' roles are in the value creation processes of other actors in the internal market, and of external customers. Pfau *et al.* (1991) also argue that communication is important in order to deepen the knowledge of what the needs and expectations of other internal customers are.

Internal relationship quality and value

Relationship quality has interested researchers during the past few years, but the focus has again been put on either business-to-business relationships (for example Holmlund, 1996, 1997) or on consumer relationships (Storbacka *et al.*, 1994; Liljander and Strandvik, 1994). Usually, it has been suggested that in consumer markets the customer is the one who evaluates the quality of the service. Liljander and Strandvik (1995) have argued that the buyer's evaluation of the quality is important also if the quality of the relationship is in focus. Holmlund (1997), when studying industrial markets, has pointed out that both parties, i.e. the buyer and the seller, are often equally active in the relationship. In the internal market, it is proposed that both the internal supplier as well as the internal customer should evaluate the relationship. Both perceptions can be perceived to be important, so the relationships in the internal market are in this sense more characterised by business-to-business relationships than relationships in consumer markets. In internal markets, both parties, and their perceptions of the relationship, are important although not necessarily equally important. The different perception configurations in an internal market are presented in Figure 14.2.

Figure 14.2 illustrates that there are four combinations of how the parties can perceive the relationship and its quality at different company levels. However, if the goal of the company is to create value for the external customer, the focus should be put on those critical internal relationships that affect the critical

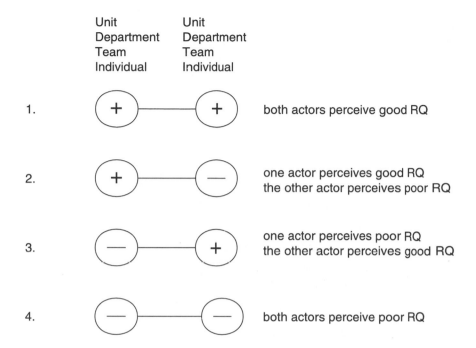

Unit   Unit
Department   Department
Team   Team
Individual   Individual

1.   (+)————(+)   both actors perceive good RQ

2.   (+)————(−)   one actor perceives good RQ
                   the other actor perceives poor RQ

3.   (−)————(+)   one actor perceives poor RQ
                   the other actor perceives good RQ

4.   (−)————(−)   both actors perceive poor RQ

Figure 14.2 Configurations of perceived relationship quality (RQ) in the internal market
Source: Modified from Holmlund 1997.

external relationship and the customer's perception of value the most. If the
internal relationship is strategically critical, when it is analysed from an external
relationship point of view, the goal should be put on achieving as high relationship quality as possible in this specific relationship. The quality perception is, for
example, related to how the internal actors in the relationship perceive different
dimensions in it but also on which comparison standards are used in evaluating
the quality of the relationship. Comparison standards are, for example, experience-based standards, predictive standards, ideal standards and minimum
tolerable standards. In the internal context, it is suggested that one of the most
important comparison standards would be the experience-based standard. The
experience-based standards are, according to Liljander (1995), standards that are
experiences from similar situations that a person uses as comparison. Halinen's
(1994) research also suggests that not only past experiences from the current relationship, but also past and current experiences from other parallel relationships,
are used as comparison standards.

Perceived relationship quality is not only dependent on how the separate
interactions are evaluated, and which comparison standards are used, but also on
how the relationship as a whole is evaluated. The relationships in the internal
market are characterised such that no relationship can be considered as isolated.
At all company levels, the relationships are influenced by other relationships that

also have a strong effect on the relationship quality. Even though the relationship quality could, in an isolated relationship, be considered very high, the network of other relationships can affect the relationship and its quality negatively.

Storbacka *et al.* (1994) have, in their relationship profitability model, identified perceived value as a comparison between perceived service quality and perceived sacrifice. When the value concept has been put in a relational context, perceived relationship value has been seen in the service marketing literature by Liljander and Strandvik (1994) as the result of a comparison between the perceived sacrifices and perceived relationship quality. Liljander and Strandvik (1994, 1995) have argued that the customer evaluates what he gets (relationship benefits) with what he gives (relationship sacrifice), and that this comparison leads to a perception of relationship value. Holmlund (1997) has developed further the perceived relationship value concept and presents perceived relationship value as a result of a dyadic view where both buyer-perceived value and seller-perceived value together form the perceived relationship value. Holmlund (1997) has, in her study, argued that in business-to-business relationships the concept 'relationship sacrifice' is misleading because in industrial markets both parties in a relationship invest in the relationship and these investments create bonds between them.

In internal relationships, the perceived relationship value concept can also be identified. How relationship value is perceived is totally dependent on what company level the relationship is positioned. In relationships at the individual level, the perceived sacrifice can consist of different types of sacrifices, for example money, effort in time spent and so on. When the higher company levels are in focus, the nature of the perceived relationship value changes because the relationships are characteristic more of business-to-business relationships. For example, at the unit level, perceived sacrifices could be seen more as investments because the investments in the relationships are often so relationship-specific and high that bonds are created between the units.

At the higher company levels, the relationships between different parts can be seen to be more isolated than on the lower levels. However, they are not completely isolated because all networks of relationships are dynamic. At the higher levels, the investments are also more relationship-specific and it is very difficult to transfer them to other relationships if, for example, the relationship between two units gets terminated. Generally, it can be said that the lower the relationship is positioned in the company levels, the more dynamic and replaceable the relationship is. The higher the relationship is positioned, the stronger the interdependence is between the parts and the more adaptations and investments have been made. This is also the reason why terminated relationships are more difficult to replace.

Summary and conclusions

Internal marketing as a concept emerged in the late 1970s and the early 1980s. In the 1980s, internal marketing fascinated a number of researchers and several definitions emerged. Research that emphasised the transaction context influenced the development of internal marketing in the 1980s: this can be seen in the definitions of internal marketing emerging during that time. Several of the definitions focus on 'marketing-like' activities or 'basic structures'. The message was that all the same elements that are used in external marketing should also be used for internal marketing. These elements were, in the 1980s, transaction-based and focus was put on the 4Ps. During the 1980s, internal marketing was characterised by a marketing mix approach, which in this chapter has been called the internal marketing mix perspective. This view on internal marketing stressed a transactional orientation both internally as well as externally, seeing employees as the primary market of the organisation. The focus was on separate encounters, which does not grasp the importance of entire relationships. Later on, this perspective has evolved into a more strategically oriented view that was characterised by a shift in focus towards external customers. However, although this strategic internal marketing perspective stressed external customers as the primary market, the interactions were characterised by a transactional orientation still based on the 4Ps. In the early 1990s, a processional perspective of internal marketing emerged. Instead of focusing on marketing to groups of employees, the focus shifted to relationships between organisational members. The notion of internal customers and suppliers was stressed and, especially, internal service quality within these internal relationships. The shortcoming of processional internal marketing became the emphasis put on transactional dimensions in internal relationships, not recognising the social dimensions in them.

During the 1990s, external marketing has developed towards a relational perspective, which has started to reflect gradually on internal marketing as well. Several scholars have presented relational views on internal marketing, but a pure relationship management-oriented perspective has been missing. This missing perspective has, in this chapter, been called internal relationship management, which further broadens the scope of internal marketing. The new perspective has, here, been defined as *the process of managing all critical internal relationships, strongly affecting the critical external relationships, by identifying, maintaining, developing and when necessary terminating these internal relationships.*

The new perspective views internal marketing as a process of managing critical internal relationships. The criticality is measured though the effect that the internal relationships have on critical external relationships. By identifying strategically important external relationships, which can be considered critical for the company's success, it becomes possible to specify which internal relationships have the strongest effect on these external relationships. After identifying the internally critical relationships, these relationships should be managed so that high relationship quality is achieved. The critical internal relationships should be analysed through the interaction levels and by focusing on the value creation process of the internal customer. Critical incident processes taking place within the critical internal relationships should be analysed and studied in relation to external relationships. When this is done, internal relationship management becomes reality.

References

Ballantyne, D. (1997) 'Internal Networks for Internal Marketing', *Journal of Marketing Management* 13(5): 343–66.

Ballantyne, D., Christopher, M. and Payne, A. (1995) 'Improving the Quality of Services Marketing: Service (Re)Design is the Critical Link', *Journal of Marketing Management* 2(2): 7–24.

Berry, L. (1981) 'The Employee as Customer', *Journal of Retail Banking* 3(1): 33–40.

Collins, B. and Payne A. (1991) 'Internal Marketing: A New Perspective for HRM', *European Management Journal* 9(3): 261–70.

Edvardsson, B., Thomasson, B. and Övretveit, J. (1994) *Quality of Service: Making It Really Work*, London: McGraw-Hill Book Company Europe.

Flipo, J.-P. (1986) 'Service Firms: Interdependence of External and Internal Marketing Strategies', *European Journal of Marketing* 20(8): 5–14.

George, W.R. (1984) 'Internal Marketing for Retailers. The Junior Executive Employee', in Venkatesan, M. *et al.* (eds), *Creativity in Services Marketing*, Chicago: American Marketing Association.

——(1990) 'Internal Marketing and Organizational Behavior: A Partnership in Developing Customer-Conscious Employees at Every Level', *Journal of Business Research* 20(1): 63–70.

Gremler, D.D., Bitner, M.J. and Evans, K.R. (1994) 'The Internal Service Encounter', *International Journal of Service Industry Management* 5(2): 34–56.

Grönroos, C. (1981) 'Internal Marketing: An Integral Part of Marketing Theory', in Donnelly, J.H. and George, W.E. (eds), *Marketing of Services*, Chicago: American Marketing Association, 236–8.

—— (1982) *Strategic Management and Marketing in the Service Sector*, Research Report No. 8, Swedish School of Economics and Business Administration, Helsinki.

—— (1997) *Relationship Marketing: Interaction, Dialogue and Value*, Research Report of the Swedish School of Economics and Business Administration, Helsinki.

Gummesson, E. (1994) *Relationsmarknadsföring: Från 4 P till 30 R*, Malmö: Liber-Hermods.

—— (1987) 'Using Internal Marketing to Develop a New Culture: The Case of Ericsson Quality', *Journal of Business and Industrial Marketing* 2(3): 23–8.

Halinen, A. (1994) 'Exchange Relationships in Professional Services. A Study of Relationship Development in the Advertising Sector', Doctoral Dissertation Series A-6, Turku: Turku School of Economics and Business Administration.

Holmlund, M. (1996) 'A Theoretical Framework of Perceived Quality in Business Relationships', Working Paper No. 347, Helsinki: Swedish School of Economics and Business Administration.

———— (1997) 'A Theoretical Framework of Perceived Quality in Business Relationships'. Doctoral Dissertation No. 66, Helsinki: Swedish School of Economics and Business Administration.

Lewis, B.R. and Entwistle, T.W. (1990) 'Managing the Service Encounter: A Focus on the Employee', *International Journal of Service Industry Management* 1(3): 41–52.

Liljander, V. (1995) 'Comparison Standards in Perceived Service Quality', Doctoral Dissertation No. 63, Helsinki: Swedish School of Economics and Business Administration.

Liljander, V. and Strandvik, T. (1994) 'The Nature of Relationship Quality', reprinted from Proceedings of Quality Management in Services IV, Paris, May.

Liljander, V. and Strandvik, T. (1995) 'The Nature of Customer Relationships in Services', in Schwartz, T., Bowen, D. and Brown, S. (eds), *Advances in Services Marketing and Management* 4: 141–67.

Lings, I. (1999) 'Balancing Internal and External Market Orientation', *Journal of Marketing Management* 15(4): 239–63.

Lings, I. and Brooks, R. (1998) 'Implementing and Measuring the Effectiveness of Internal Marketing', *Journal of Marketing Management* 14: 325–51.

Lukas, B.A. and Maignan, I. (1996) 'Striving for Quality: The Key Role of Internal and External Customers', *Journal of Market Focused Management* 1: 175–87.

Mohr-Jackson, I. (1991) 'Broadening the Market Orientation: An Added Focus on Internal Customers', *Human Resource Management* 30(4): 455–67.

Neuhaus, P. (1996) 'Critical Incidents in Internal Customer–Supplier Relationships: Results of an Empirical Study', in Swartz, T.A., Bowen, D.E. and Brown, S.W. (eds), *Advances in Services Marketing and Management* 5: 283–313.

Payne, A. (1993) *The Essence of Services Marketing*, London: Prentice-Hall International.

Pfau, B., Detzel, D. and Geller, A. (1991) 'Satisfy Your Internal Customers', *Journal of Business Strategy* 12(6): 9–13.

Piercy, N. (1995) 'Customer Satisfaction and the Internal Market: Marketing our Customers to our Employees', *Journal of Marketing Practice* 1(1): 22–44.

Piercy, N. and Morgan, N. (1991) 'Internal Marketing: The Missing Half of the Marketing Programme', *Long Range Planning* 24(2): 82–93.

Rafiq, M. and Ahmed, P. (1993) 'The Scope of Internal Marketing: Defining the Boundary Between Marketing and Human Resource Management', *Journal of Marketing Management* 9(3): 219–32.

Rathmell, J.R. (1974) *Marketing in the Service Sector*, Cambridge, MA: Winthrop.

Reynoso, J. and Moores, B. (1995) 'Towards the Measurement of Internal Service Quality', *International Journal of Service Industry Management* 6(3): 64–83.

Stauss, B. (1995) 'Internal Services: Classification and Quality Management', *International Journal of Service Industry Management* 6(2): 62–78.

Storbacka, K., Strandvik, T. and Grönroos, C. (1994) 'Managing Customer Relationships for Profit: The Dynamics of Relationship Quality', *International Journal of Service Industry Management* 5(5): 21–38.

Strandvik, T. and Storbacka, K. (1996) 'Managing Relationship Quality', paper presented at QUIS 5 Symposium, Karlstad, Sweden.

Thomas, R., Farmer, E. and Wallace, B. (1991) 'Health Care Marketing Minicase: The Importance of Internal Marketing: The Case of Geriatric Services', *Journal of Health Care Marketing* 11(1): 55–8.

Trumbly, J.E. and Arnold, D.R. (1989) 'Internal Marketing of a Management Information System', *Journal of Systems Management* 40(6): 26–30.

Varey, R.J. (1995), 'Internal Marketing: A Review and Some Interdisciplinary Research Challenges', *International Journal of Service Industry Management* 6(1): 40–63.

—— (1996) 'A Broadened Conception of Internal Marketing', unpublished PhD thesis, Manchester School of Management.

Voima, P. (1998) 'The Evolution of Internal Marketing', unpublished paper, Helsinki, Swedish School of Economics and Business Administration.

Voima, P. and Grönroos, C. (1999) 'Internal Marketing: A Relationship Perspective', in Baker, M.J. (ed.), *The IEBM Encyclopaedia of Marketing*, Cambridge: International Business Press, 747–51.

Vandermerwe, S. and Gilbert, D. (1991) 'Internal Services: Gaps in Needs/Performance and Prescriptions for Effectiveness', *International Journal of Service Industry Management* 2(1): 50–60.

15 Internal marketing

A step too far

Peter Mudie

Introduction

Ever since a debate in the late 1960s between professors Kotler, Levy and Luck
(Kotler and Levy, 1969; Luck, 1969) and the appearance of an article in 1972
entitled 'A Generic Concept of Marketing' (Kotler, 1972), argument has raged
over the legitimacy of applying marketing concepts and techniques in such fields
as education, religion, politics and employment. Marketing, in effect, had
become central to the analysis of human behaviour, exceptional in representing
itself as expert in the management of every conceivable kind of transaction
within organisations as well as between organisations and their stakeholders
(Willmott, 1999). Hitherto people were engaged as voters, students, passengers,
patients, churchgoers. Now they are to be seen as consumers. In the view of one
critic, 'the entire universe appears to have fallen within marketing's ambitious
orbit' (Brown, 1995: 37), and 'if the claims in introductory textbooks are taken at
face value, marketing is not only the secret of business success and personal
accomplishment, but it holds the key to socio-economic development, world
peace and human understanding' (Brown, 1995: 163).

Internal marketing cannot claim parity with the magnitude of world peace.
Nevertheless, it should raise questions of serious concern for academics, students,
and practitioners alike. It will be argued that marketing, as a discipline, is not
equipped in terms of concepts and techniques to confront the complexities of
organisational life and employee considerations. Work is a major part of
everyday life. It impinges on most aspects of our very existence. Many enjoy
great status; more feel despair and dehumanisation. Throughout its history
marketing has sought to foster and enjoy the company of the former. Now
internal marketing seeks to embrace the latter. Employees are to be cared for, not
to be understood. Confirmation of their role as consumers is the goal. In prob-
lematising the concept of internal marketing and its application the following
areas will be addressed:

- External marketing: a foretaste of what's on offer
- In search of an identity
- The language of internal marketing

- The realities of organisational life

External marketing: a foretaste of what's on offer

If the model of internal marketing is to be developed from the established principles of marketing for external consumers there needs to be, at the very least, a
confidence over the argument favouring transferability. Recent observations and
comment, in particular, do not offer much reassurance.

A major assumption that has dominated the marketing discipline is one of
consumer sovereignty. Consumers make up their own minds about what and
how they will consume, given their own needs and priorities. Organisations with
the right antennae feel the needs of the consumers in the market and provide the
products and services that will satisfy these needs. This, in essence, is the
marketing concept. However, the aims and practices of marketing in the capitalist
market economy have come under scrutiny (Thomas, 1999; Ungoed-Thomas,
1998; Gardner and Rigby, 1999). Social responsibility, ethics and consumer
welfare have found favour amongst those wishing to counter or temper the
perceived manipulative and exploitative conduct of marketing:

> We [the marketing profession] must recognise that, in addition to high stan-
> dards of objectivity, integrity and technical competence, we must, in
> responding to the changing environment, demonstrate that we can and will
> serve society in general. This requires a clear and articulate demonstration
> of our ability to be relevant in the political sense…if we remain tied to the
> forces of manipulation and hype, if we are seen merely to be servants of our
> capitalist masters, we will remain marginal and untrustworthy. If we can
> demonstrate that we have the keys to the knowledge base that will benefit
> society as a whole then we may prosper.
>
> (Thomas, 1996)

The future prospects for internal marketing may rest on a successful resolution of the above controversy. In particular:

- how much evidence is there of this enlightened view of marketing in practice?
- is internal marketing to be of the more enlightened or traditional variety?
- might internal marketing pursue a third way, clinical and rather sanitised?
- is internal marketing designed as just one more tool of management for
  control and socialisation of employees?

It does seem inappropriate for employees to be subject to the vast array of
techniques of persuasion so evident in today's marketplace. If the experience of
external consumers is anything to go by trust is the ingredient that is missing in
their dealings with business and marketers (Beckett, 1999). Exhortations to build
trust are not matched by appealing arguments of how this is to be achieved.
Marketing, it is argued, must address this issue not only because it is right but

also because 'massive new opportunities will emerge'! (Beckett, 1999). Trust is, of course, a key feature of organisational life. The challenge for marketing is thus both external and internal.

The discussion so far has characterised the concept of consumer as indivisible. However, the perception of marketing as 'an undemocratic, unfair business' means that some customers are more equal than others and should be recognised as such (Curtis, 1996). Pareto analysis reminds us that the majority of profits come from a minority of customers. The benefits from retaining these customers has been the driving force behind relationship marketing and loyalty-based programmes (Reichheld, 1996). The need to identify profitable customers is helping to drive the data mania that has taken hold of marketing (Curtis, 1996). However, one of the findings in a report from the Henley Centre was that consumers are becoming much more 'savvy' about what information is held on them and how it is used (Dataculture, 1995, The Henley Centre, London). If they realise these data are being used to exclude them, rather than offer them new benefits, then the trust that underpins relationship marketing and customer loyalty will be lost (Curtis, 1996). Although a vision of the dispossessed consumer is a touch 'apocalyptic', it nevertheless led one author of the Henley report to observe that:

> the trend toward 'differential marketing' risks polarising consumers in a way that raises profound social issues. As businesses use data to decide who gets the best offers and service, the gulf between the rich and poor will grow even wider. You have to question how this affects people's rights to participate in the consumer society. It's not in the spirit of stakeholding to share value only with your most profitable customers.
>
> (Curtis, 1996)

The trend towards 'differential marketing' has been detected in customer service. In one study (Ridley, 1999) of variation in response to customer complaints, the occupation, status and quality of the complainant's letter had largely determined the outcome. The speed and nature of response to the 'Right Honourable', doctor, lawyer and vicar was quite different to that of the single parent, student, unemployed and pensioner. The power of the complainer takes precedence over the legitimacy of the complaint. Legitimacy itself draws strength from the source of the complaint.

Parallels can be drawn between the disadvantaged, less profitable consumers of the external market and low level (including front-line) employees in service industries. They occupy the wrong end of the scale of marketing opportunities, albeit in a rather different capacity. On the other hand, there is seemingly no parallel to be drawn between the 'Right Honourable' as external customer and, for example, the human resource manager as an internal customer. Internal marketing finds no resonance in the realms of middle to senior management.

Whatever the observations and arguments so far, internal marketing, like its external counterpart, draws on the enduring philosophy, 'The Customer is

King'! However, evidence informs us otherwise. A survey of over 100 executives (Shaw, 1998) confirmed that customer satisfaction was considered to be critical by more managers than any other measure, yet the survey also showed that customer needs are not understood properly in most companies. Less than one-quarter of the respondents said they measured and analysed customer needs, and only half felt that it was critical to understand customer needs. Further evidence from a more substantive study (Coulson-Thomas, 1992) reveals the gap between rhetoric and reality. The following quotations are illustrative:

'We still regard the customers as targets. We bombard them with direct mail.'

'Our approach to customers is a question of what we can get away with, not what we can do for them.'

'Our short-term requirements for survival are taking priority over the long-term interests of customers.'

'Every contact revolves around selling or persuading. There is not much listening or sharing going on.'

'Ask people about themselves at a party and you are surrounded in no time. When we meet customers we talk about ourselves and wonder why they are not interested.'

'Most of our products and services revolve around the things we can do, rather than customer requirements.'

Do (or should) the above invoke surprise? Are they inconsistent with marketing as creator and manager of demand? Calls for making your customers feel understood are superfluous, and demands for a more empathetic, human-istic marketing are tautological for the pro-marketing lobby, and contradictory for the 'antis'.

Subscribers to the 'Customer is King' may be comforted by the forecast of 'a fundamental shift in the role and purpose of marketing from manipulation of the customer to genuine customer involvement; from telling and selling to communicating and sharing knowledge' (McKenna, 1991). However, 'genuine customer involvement', taken literally, is not without risk. Customer input may be deemed:

- unprofitable
- unrealistic
- impractical
- unreasonable

Therefore, the claim that 'The customer is always right' is nonsense (Iacobucci *et al.*, 1994). As for a detailed explanation of why the customer is wrong, expediency invariably triumphs over integrity.

Whatever the marketing concept proclaims there is a reality of consumers

- being manipulated

- being ignored
- being the subject of differential treatment

In search of an identity

Understanding how marketing manages its customers represents one half of the analysis. The other half needs to focus on the aims of marketing in respect of its customers. Both are vital for a critical assessment to be made of internal marketing. Overriding the commercial aims (for example, increased usage, profit and market share) is that of what marketers are marketing and consumers consuming. It can be summed up in one word, identity.

> Images of the consumer as identity seekers are compelling and account for the obsession with brands, the willingness to read stories into impersonal products, the fascination with difference, the preoccupation with signs, and above all the fetishism of images
>
> (Gabriel and Lang, 1997).

Consumers express themselves and communicate with each other through the consumption of goods and services. Respect and self-respect are the potential rewards of identity-seeking consumption behaviour. Advertising has moved from the 'rationality' of use value (for example, increasing convenience) to aggrandisement and fulfilment from symbolic value: 'there is little attempt to inform about the product – merely to associate it with some emotion, with sexuality, with power, with status – with whatever will prompt us to part with our money' (Hartley, 1997: 24).

Marketers, of course, see it rather differently. The market, indeed any market, is a place of 'freedom' where 'choice' and the 'sovereignty of the individual' consumer reign supreme. However, argument continues over identity as reproducer of the existing social structure, breeder of insecurity and anxiety, and inexorably ephemeral and fragile:

> We quite literally "buy" into ideas and experiences that are sold, for profit, as life styles. As illusions, or simulacra, these life-style "products" can enable us to "be" but only for a while, until we "need" a new set of illusions to help us to make sense of it all
>
> (Hartley, 1997: 23–4)

What then does the preceding account of identity imply for understanding the internal customer and his or her identity? Is the internal customer denied an identity or subjected to an enforced identity? In effect external marketing affords opportunities for 'liberating' the self, whereas internal marketing effects denial of the self. Both are controlling but the former portrays a more attractive proposition. As organisations grapple with problems over productivity, service quality and employee motivation, there is, coincidentally, interest in 'meaning' and 'quality of life' for people at work. 'Excellent organisations are those that "make meaning for people" by encouraging them to believe that they have control over their own destinies; that no matter what position they may hold in an organisation, their contribution is vital, not only to the success of the company for which they work, but also to the enterprise of their own lives' (du Gay, 1996:60). Employees are to achieve self-fulfilment and self-actualisation through and in work, and not at the expense of organisational goals.

> Employers and managers equipped with these new visions of work have thus claimed that there is no conflict between the pursuits of productivity, efficiency, and competitiveness on the one hand and the humanisation of work on the other. On the contrary, the path to business success lies in engaging the employee with the goals of the company at the level of his or her subjectivity, aligning the wishes, needs, and aspirations of each individual who works for the organisation with the successful pursuit of its objectives. Through striving to fulfil their own needs and wishes at work, each employee will thus work for the advance of the enterprise; the more the individual fulfils him or herself, the greater the benefit to the company.
>
> (Rose, 1991:56)

Excellent companies evidently seek to cultivate 'enterprising subjects' – autonomous, self-regulating, productive individuals who are enabled through work to construct and confirm their identity. Employees are no longer to be manipulated but empowered to release energy, encourage initiative and create self-reliance and personal responsibility (du Gay, 1996: 60–1). The employee, as internal consumer, parallels his external counterpart in search of meaning and fulfilment which through the enterprising self seeks to 'master, better and fulfil itself' (du Gay, 1996: 65). Where the parallel falters is over how consumer identity is mediated. Internally, mediation is through exchanges and relationships between employees. Externally, identity is achieved through the symbolism of goods and services. The essence of consumer culture is, nevertheless, deemed equipped to serve as a basis for understanding and promoting employee identity formation.

However, 'consumer sovereignty' is an inappropriate template for service organisation employees. Routinisation is the hallmark of much of service work together with managerial control over service employees' appearance, moods, demeanour and attitudes. Employees are invariably given very strict guidelines on what to say and how to say it. It is a management rationalisation that asserts that routinisation acts as a shield protecting employees from rude and inconsiderate customers. The employees' dignity and sense of self evidently remains intact. What employees are not afforded is 'opportunities to use and develop their capacities for solving problems and making decisions, preventing them from deriving self worth, meaning or deep satisfaction from work' (Leidner, 1993:4).

Addressing the 'needs and wishes' of employees seems profligate and superfluous. What needs to be done, and how, is the preserve of management, not employees. After all, service workers have been condemned for their 'stupidity, apathy, slowness, incompetence, and questionable moral character' (Harris, 1981: 39–59). Much of routinised interactive service work is however an affront to an individuality that is assumed 'not substantial or worthy enough of deference to interfere with the adoption of qualities designed for them (service employees) by others (service management)' (Leidner, 1993).

All this has given rise to what has been termed 'emotional labour' (Hochschild, 1983), the trained management of feeling, the commoditisation of feeling. For the front-line employee, what to say and how to behave and feel when interacting with customers is the prerogative of the organisation. Service interactions are renowned for bearing little resemblance to genuine interpersonal exchanges. Employees are encouraged to suppress or disguise feelings the organisation may deem ' unhelpful' in the course of service delivery. Authenticity falls victim to feigning. For service employees, there is an underlying tension between organisational imposed identities and self-identities. There is even evidence that workers whose emotions are managed by their employers 'become alienated from their true feelings and have difficulty experiencing themselves as authentic even off the job, as they lose track of which feelings are their own' (Hochschild, 1983). Employees inevitably develop strategies or mechanisms for coping and survival (Weatherly and Tansik, 1992; Ashforth and Lee, 1990). At times, from within the prison of subjugation and subordination, service employees are able to reclaim a sense of dignity and self-respect. The following examples are simply illustrative:

> The perfect way to deal with unpleasant 'Do you know who I am?' type of customers. An award should go to the United Airlines gate agent in Denver for being smart and funny, and making her point, when confronted with a passenger who probably deserved to fly as cargo. During the final days at Denver's old Stapleton airport, a crowded United flight was cancelled. A single agent was rebooking a long line of inconvenienced travellers. Suddenly an angry passenger pushed his way to the desk. He slapped his ticket down on the counter and said, 'I HAVE to be on this flight, it has to be FIRST CLASS'. The agent replied, 'I'm sorry sir. I'll be happy to try to help you, but I've got to help these folks first, and I'm sure we'll be able to work something out.' The passenger was unimpressed. He asked loudly, so that the passengers behind him could hear, 'Do you have any idea who I am?' Without hesitating, the gate agent smiled and grabbed her public address microphone. 'May I have your attention please?' she began, her voice bellowing throughout the terminal. 'We have a passenger here at the gate WHO DOES NOT KNOW WHO HE IS. If anyone can help him find his identity, please come to gate 17.' With the folks behind him in line laughing hysterically, the man glared at the United agent, gritted his teeth and swore '(Expletive) you.' Without flinching, she smiled and said, 'I'm sorry sir, but you'll have to stand in line for that, too.' The man retreated as the people in the terminal applauded loudly. Although the flight was cancelled and people were late, they were no longer angry at United.
> (Jill Colonna@OECD.org at internet-gateway)

Carmel Valley grocery cashier Sandi Lewtschuk was fired in October after 20 years at Safeway because, though she had no customer complaints, she was deemed deficient by management in executing the company's 'smile' policy. (Lewtschuk and other Safeway employees have criticised required smiling as phoney, and some female employees in San Francisco said the policy encouraged male customers to believe the women were flirting). And in January, flight attendants for Cathay Pacific Airways (Hong Kong), feuding with management over automatic pay hikes, threatened to violate that company's smile policy by frowning for one hour per flight.

(The *Guardian*, 27 March–2 April 1999, 'The Guide', 106)

Emotional labour is not confined to front-line service employees. Workers who are constrained to engage in false personalisation (regarded as equivalent to emotional labour) may lose the capacity to distinguish between coerced and genuine friendliness. The demand for false personalisation, with co-workers as well as consumers, is viewed as 'a principal barrier to autonomy in the sphere of work' (Riesman, 1953). Thus, the crisis of identity is felt 'further down the line'. From an internal marketing perspective, employees must endure the stress of a double identity, customer and supplier. For example, the front-line employee must serve the needs of the external customer whilst acting as customer of internal colleagues. Such dualism may reach far inside the organisation. This pressure chamber of controlled emotions is hardly in accordance with the 'freedom of choice' and 'sovereignty' of marketing's external customer. Although much of professional and managerial work entails emotional labour, it is largely self-regulated as distinct from the very specific directions afforded to many service employees. Emotional labour seems to service, somewhat ironically, 'the primacy of rationality and "manage-ability" in administrative thought'. However, this persistent and powerful rhetoric is 'at odds with recent perspectives on organisations as emotional arenas which are often far from manageable' (Fineman, 1997: 20). The reality of life at work is not the preserve of rationalised processes and systematic procedures. It is also a cauldron of emotions. Internal marketing needs to recognise that internal suppliers/consumers communicate, *inter alia*, passions and anxieties as well as error-free documents and timely responses.

The language of internal marketing

In 1977, Simon Majaro wrote an article entitled 'The Many Faces of Marketing' (Majaro, 1977). That title best sums up, unwittingly, the unabated rise in prefixes attached to marketing (Mudie, 1987). Internal marketing is one of the most recent. As for the motivation or rationale behind this development, one can only speculate:

- a natural progression in subject matter
- a response to a crisis of identity
- a colonisation of 'foreign territory' with the attendant reward, namely power
- an attempt to forestall terminal decline

Although not mentioning internal marketing by name, some have been forthcoming in their criticism of buzzwords, jargon and fashion statements.

First there was management jargon. Now there is management jargon to describe management jargon. 'Corporate graffiti', the latest addition to the language, is a derogatory term for a company's unthinking use of the lingo. It is (literally) the catch phrase to end all catch phrases. It is high time there was a backlash against this opaque, ugly and cliché-ridden language. Action-centred leadership, Benchmarking, Competences, Downsize, Empowerment, Globalisation. You can go through the alphabet many times without exhausting the vocabulary of management speak. Open any management book and you may find yourself suffering from what is known in the jargon as the 'mego' syndrome – my eyes glaze over.

(Kellaway, 1994)

Management gurus and business academics have come in for some quite explicit criticism:

The entire management guru industry is based around the belief that there is a Holy Grail of management, a solution, a cure, a potion, a quick fix that will work. Managerial effectiveness may or may not have improved but the managerial capacity for wishful thinking has certainly been enhanced in the business school era.

While they have not been to blame for creating many of them (the big ideas), business schools, as much as the people who attend their courses, have been victims of management fashions. Business schools have joined in the hullabaloo accompanying a series of cure-all business wonder drugs. In recent years, for example, these have included TQM, downsizing, empowerment, business process re-engineering and the learning organisation. They are managerial viagra.

These ideas were all supposed to make businesses more competitive, and were adopted wholesale by companies. Yet many of the initiatives they inspired failed to deliver the goods.

(Crainer and Dearlove, 1998)

As in all substantial changes in marketing practice and thought, new ideas pass through three stages in becoming accepted and established (Bartels, 1968). First, a stage of identification. When a new idea is perceived, even before its nature is fully recognised, it is often given a name to facilitate reference and communication concerning it. The designation may be a familiar term or one newly coined. It may have temporary or lasting usage. Second, a stage of conceptualisation, in which definition occurs as the idea gains distinctive form and meaning. Third, a stage of assimilation and integration into the established body of thought. This is the process of the enlargement of thought or theory and its enrichment with new ideas. While some might argue that internal marketing is well advanced in this process it should more thoughtfully be described as having stalled, even adrift, somewhere between identification and conceptualisation. There is, for example, evidence of difficulties with internal marketing's wider sphere, relationship marketing. It has been described as a concept 'in vogue where managers talk it up, companies profess to do it in new and better ways every day and academics extol its merits. Unfortunately, a close look suggests that relationships between companies and consumers are troubled at best' (Fournier *et al.*, 1998: 43). However, success for internal marketing will not rest solely on establishing well ordered relationships (between a supplier and a customer). Just as with social marketing, success or failure for internal marketing will depend on the relevance of its concepts and techniques (its language, if you like).

The process of identification is believed to have started with an article by Sasser and Arbeit entitled 'Selling Jobs in the Service Sector' way back in 1976 (Sasser and Arbeit, 1976). The authors argue that employees were of critical importance in the service delivery system and that competent, well-motivated employees became, in effect, the firm's product. To achieve this, employers had to identify the exchange values: what the employee seeks from the job (pay, prestige, excitement, security) and what he or she is willing to give up to get it. (The authors did not specify what this might be.) If that were to be autonomy, respect and a sense of self-worth, it would be 'understandable'. Jobs were to be positioned in a product space map of two attributes, wages (high versus low) and task diversity (routine versus variety). To heighten the desirability of the product it should be redesigned to be as close to the ideal as possible, in this case a high variety content and a moderate salary component. Notwithstanding the instability of 'high variety' and 'moderate salary', it is revealing that a quarter of a century later much of service industry is characterised by routinisation and relatively low wages. High variety in itself is ambiguous, as it could embrace task range and complexity. Given the mundane nature and general undesirability of many service jobs, it does seem strange for marketing to embrace such a proposition.

Nevertheless, 'It's the employees, stupid', has been the catalyst. Internal marketing is a prerequisite for success in the external market. Essentially, employees are pivotal to success. Such a proposition along with others needs to be researched and tested. In doing so, evidence will accumulate to question the underlying rhetoric. A sample from the literature will highlight some of the potential issues involved (italics are added).

Definition, aims and outcomes

Internal marketing focuses on achieving *effective internal exchanges* between the organisation and its employee groups as a *prerequisite* for successful exchanges with external markets (George, 1990: 63).

The premise of this philosophy is that if management wants its employees to do a great job with customers, then it must be prepared to do *a great job with its employees* (George, 1990: 64).

Internal marketing is directed at producing and maintaining a *motivated and satisfied group of employees* who will support the company's external marketing objectives and work towards ensuring quality, productivity and efficiency (Barnes, 1989: 14).

A strong focus on internal marketing will continue to pay *healthy dividends* in all areas of operations (Winter, 1985: 71).

We can think of internal marketing as viewing employees as internal customers, viewing jobs as internal products, and then endeavouring to offer internal products that satisfy *the needs of and wants of these internal customers* while addressing the objectives of the organisation (Berry, 1981: 34).

While internal campaigns may not enjoy the *glamour* of above-the-line advertising, marketers are beginning to understand that this can be a highly *effective* means of marketing…to some extent it has to be a *leap of faith*, since it can be *hard to isolate the impact* of internal marketing (Mazur, 1999: 22–3).

Indeed, one of the major attractions of talking about 'internal marketing' instead of cultural change, implementation, and so on, is that *we know how to do it* (Piercy, 1997: 593).

There is no doubt that the internal marketing concept has a *major role to play* in making employees customer conscious…However, as it stands in some of the current and earlier formulations of Internal Marketing, the concept of treating 'employees as customers' is *seriously flawed* (Rafiq and Ahmed, 1993: 230).

It is not appropriate, from this study, to attribute the increases in the quality of service delivered to the external customers to the increases in service quality experienced by the internal customers (Lings, 1998: 344).

What appears intriguing is the conviction as to internal marketing's indispensability and desirability matched by anxiety and insecurity over whether it works, and how. Moreover, as employees are deemed pivotal to success, they are both subjects of internal marketing and products of external marketing. Employees as consumers is an end in itself, whilst employees as products is a means to an end (the satisfaction of a final consumer). In effect, the process becomes one of marketing to employees (as customers) who in turn are marketed to external consumers (as products). Understanding how meeting the needs of internal customers transforms into products for meeting the needs of external customers is, without doubt, a tortuous process. Could it be that it is the needs of the organisation that are being met and to assuage any 'feelings of guilt' on the part of management, must be marketed to employees, as satisfiers of their needs. Organisation needs masquerading as employee needs is nothing new. Whatever the guise, an act of internal consumption is consummated.

Correspondence between external and internal marketing

External marketing is cited, not surprisingly, as a template for internal marketing:

> We suspect that *many of the principles that have been derived theoretically from a focus on the external customer may also provide insight for researchers who study the internal dynamics* of organisations.
>
> (Schneider and Bowen, 1985: 432)

All of the arguments rest on the realistic assumptions and observations, that many organisations (especially service firms) *interact with employees in a similar way to that in which they transact with external customers.*

(Pitt and Foreman, 1998: 25–36)

Marketers need to understand consumers first before addressing the complexities of organisational dynamics. The profession is being encouraged 'to get inside people's heads' by turning to the tools of ethnography and phenomenology for revelations of what a 'day in the life of the customer' is all about (Fournier *et al.*, 1998: 50). In effect, 'the foundations of our marketing work – our Western analytic research methods – have set us up to fail, time and again' (Fournier *et al.*, 1998: 49). However, even with a more comprehensive view of consumer behaviour, profitable opportunities greater than at present (presumably the driving force) may not be forthcoming. Up till now there has certainly been no evidence, in the internal marketing debate, of a willingness to unravel the working lives of employees. In fact just the opposite. The language of internal marketing has been that of management technology in which it is 'seen as something which the firm (in totality) does to its employees (in totality)' (Pitt and Foreman, 1998: 26). Such transparency is in stark contrast to the view that 'internal marketing, in essence, recognises that all employees are customers of managers' (Harrell and Fors, 1992: 300). This is typical of the thinking expressed in the 'upside-down' organisation in which employees are led to believe that management works to serve them and everyone works together to serve the customer. On the surface, it appears attractive as it portrays management as servant rather than authority figure engaged in an 'insidious act of management control'. It follows that interactions with employees are different in nature from transactions with external customers. The objective, externally, is to encourage and meet, in large part, aspirational needs. Consumers are engaged in a process of 'bettering themselves' through acquisition and consumption of goods and services. The status and future prospects of many service employees (jobs rather than careers) means that marketing cannot engage them in the way that it does externally. The employees' position, internally, may be likened to the poor and disadvantaged, externally, for whom marketing has shown little interest.

What is being bought and sold?

Of the 4Ps, product evokes the most comment. The job (as against career) still commands mention but not exclusively so.

The product in the internal marketing mix is a *commitment* on the part of staff to the idea of total customer service. The firm wants to *inculcate* in its employees a long-term view that if customers are treated properly, they will keep coming back. It involves encouraging the staff to *internalise a set of values* that incorporate greater concern and caring for the customer. It involves attention to detail and generally requires both *attitude and behaviour change on the part of most employees* (Barnes, 1989: 18).

Internal marketing can be defined as the *promoting of the firm and its product(s)* or product lines to the firm's employees (Greene *et al.*, 1994: 5).

Asking people to be brand ambassadors is almost like getting them to be internal customers. It means thinking like a marketer. But instead of having fizzy drinks or crisps as the product, *the product is the organisation, and its goals and its people are the target market*. So, just as with external marketing, you have to know what makes them tick, and what motivates them. Why would they buy the goals and objectives? (Gilbert, quoted in Mazur, 1999: 22).

The internal product comprises the marketing strategies and the marketing plan and *needs to be sold to employees as the value, attitudes and behaviours which are needed* to make the marketing plan work effectively. These *internal products* that employees are being sold may be *unwanted* or may have a *negative utility* (Gilmore and Carson, 1995: 303).

At the strategic level, the *product can refer to marketing strategies*; what is sold are those values and attitudes needed to make a plan work. At the tactical level, the *product could include new performance measures, new ways of handling customers* (Rafiq and Ahmed, 1993: 223).

The product is clearly defined to meet the needs of the organisation. Employees must be customer conscious. Unlike their external counterparts, internal customers have no input to product development. Even where input is present cynicism will hinder its value. The technology of behaviour modification and personality control offers more potential. Through careful selection, training and motivation, employers will create the 'kinds of people who would make decisions that management will approve' (Leidner, 1993: 37). Where potential employees' values and personal characteristics are deemed unacceptable, they will be excluded (Teather, 1996; Mazur, 1999).

Satisfied employees → improved performance → happy customers

Marketing academics and practitioners seem keen to deliver (or at least debate) employee satisfaction on the basis that it improves performance and creates satisfied customers.

The concepts of 'customer satisfaction' and 'employee contentment' are gaining prominence. It is *very difficult to serve customers well when employees are unhappy* and disgruntled about some aspect of their job. Job satisfaction, therefore, becomes an important construct for managers of businesses since an increase in job satisfaction among a firm's front-line employees will undoubtedly have a carry over effect on customer care (Rogers *et al.*, 1994: 20).

As with failure or mediocrity, success applies both to employees and to customers. Broadened job designs are accompanied by training and empowerment practices that allow front-stage personnel to control quality. With more focused recruitment, more intensive training, and better wages, employees *are likely to be happier in their work and to provide higher quality, customer pleasing service* (Lovelock, 1995: 229).

Researchers have repeatedly demonstrated that when employee job satisfaction is high, customer satisfaction is high; when job satisfaction is low, customer satisfaction is low (Zemke, 1989: 199).

Specifically, Friedlander and Pickle studied the satisfaction of customers, stockholders, managers, employees and suppliers of more than ninety organisations to establish the magnitude of the agreement across these constituencies regarding their satisfaction. Their data showed a statistically significant *correlation between employee and customer satisfaction*...In a series of papers, I and my colleagues have substantiated the conclusion that *the way employees experience their work organisations is reflected in the perceptions customers have of the service quality they receive* (Schneider, 1994: 64–76).

Furthermore, the assertion that having satisfied employees leads to (greater customer orientation and hence) satisfied customers, is largely an *untested assertion*. In fact, where it has been tested the *evidence has been found to be weak* (Rafiq and Ahmed, 1993: 219–232).

Recent research from Warwick University (1998) suggests that happy workers do not make the most profit. This is in stark contrast to the much acclaimed and much publicised 'aphorism' from J. Willard Marriott in the 1970s that, 'you can't make happy guests with unhappy employees'. The Warwick research centred on a retail chain and management's explanation for the findings was simple: the most profitable stores are the busiest. It is much harder working in the most profitable stores, so the shelf stackers and the checkout operators are not as happy as elsewhere. According to the researcher, 'A key message is that simply evangelising about happy employees is not enough – it's too simplistic and it will just produce a lot of cynicism from employees and managers who are aware that the best units don't have the happiest employees'. Evidently, it is not true to say that unhappy staff make for higher profits, whilst it is true that higher profits make for unhappy staff. Where service organisations call, as they invariably do, for more output from less input it is not surprising that employees are unhappy. Internal marketing thought is some way behind as 'most researchers have relegated the notion of the happy–productive worker to the folklore of management, as an unsubstantiated claim of practitioners and the popular press. Because decades of research have failed to show a close link between job satisfaction and performance, the field of organisational behaviour has ceased investigating whether happier workers are also more productive' (Wright and Staw, 1999: 1).

Clinical and rather sanitised

Marketing's effervescence, vitality and creativity are self-evidently absent in internal marketing. Even though the language of external marketing is present, internal arrangements, operations and exchanges are anaemic by comparison.

> everybody should see himself as a customer of colleagues receiving *products, documents, messages* etc. from them and he should see himself as a supplier to

other internal customers. Only when the internal customers are satisfied – it is the satisfied customer that counts irrespective of whether he is external or internal – has a job been properly executed.

(Gummesson, 1987: 10–20)

Internal marketing is an impersonal, unemotional and hygienic process. It operates in a vacuum starved of controversy, power and conflict.

The many backstage steps involved in service delivery (which can be captured graphically by flowcharting) constitute a claim of *internal service transactions*, culminating in the 'moments of truth' front stage when contact personnel serve the firm's customers. At each step in the chain, one or more support staff members are suppliers to an internal customer, who is the next person on the chain; finally support staff supply contact staff *with the service they need* to serve customers well (Lovelock, 1996).

There is a linearity and technical rationality that characterises the process. The richness and diversity of interpersonal exchanges is missing together with the realities of organisational life. A workbook used by Federal Express adds weight to the clinical approach. As part of its quality improvement programme employees are trained to understand the notion of customer–supplier alignments. The workbook is designed to walk 'customers' and 'suppliers' through three key alignment questions:

What do you need from me?
What do you do with what I give you?
What are the gaps between what I give you and what you need? (quoted in
    Lovelock, 1996: 519)

Much of what is contained in these workbooks or manuals spells out in great detail tasks to be undertaken and procedures to follow. It is a form of quality assurance where the systems are said to be in place for delivering quality. However, the delivery of quality requires more than a manual. The approach by Federal Express gives consideration to what people need. Understandably, these will resonate with systemic needs, for example, accuracy, speed and reliability. What is not so easily documented and forthcoming are needs concerning trust, integrity and understanding. The impact of these needs, in terms of satisfaction/dissatisfaction, on the functioning of the overall system has not been properly addressed by internal marketing. The much quoted saying of the late Charles Revlon, 'In the factory we make cosmetics, in the drugstore we sell hope', evokes consideration of parallels with external marketing. Consumer needs were met not only on the basis of what an offering did (its functional value) but also for what it meant (its symbolic value). Internal marketing and internal customers/suppliers seem locked in the former and oblivious of the latter.

Other aspects of marketing, namely market segmentation, pricing and place are not well equipped for shedding light on employees as internal customers.

That, in itself, undermines the legitimacy of marketing in this area. Furthermore, there remains the unresolved matter of who internal marketing applies to and in what situations (Pitt and Foreman, 1998: 25–36). From the outset, front-line employees regarded as pivotal to success have been the focus for much of the thinking behind internal marketing. Even professionals in the front line have come within its remit (Rafiq and Ahmed, 1993: 222). Recent theorising (Pitt and Foreman, 1998: 25–36) suggests a prime role for internal marketing in organisations where there is goal congruence (mutuality of interest between employee and organisation) and high levels of performance ambiguity (difficulties measuring the performance of parties to an exchange). Industries evidently meeting these criteria are hospitality, financial and professional services, and consulting firms. However, hospitality and financial services are largely characterised by relatively low-status, low-paid jobs (low mutuality of interest) along with predictability from predetermined scripts and routinisation (low performance ambiguity). As for professional services and consulting firms, it could be argued that they are characterised by high mutuality of interest and high performance ambiguity. However, professional services in particular, and consulting firms to a lesser extent (depending on how they are defined), are hardly in need of marketing internally given the core values of respected professions (Crainer and Dearlove, 1998: 29–30):

- lofty ideals that transcend self-interest
- mastery of a craft or body of knowledge
- a body of knowledge based on sound reasoning, not dogma or unproven rules
- reasoning based on the ability to use language clearly and precisely
- high ethical and technical standards

Placed against such criteria, arguments for internal marketing appear unsustainable. This highlights a central point concerning internal marketing. The success of marketing externally is, in large part, obtained by meeting the needs of higher income, aspirational customers. They gain symbolic value that creates and cements their lifestyle. Companies, in turn, accrue increasing amounts of profit. Conversely, there is much less for marketing in addressing the needs of the 'less well-off'. Internally, it appears to work the other way round. The higher echelons do not need to be marketed to, whereas the 'lower orders' need to be cajoled, manipulated and generally 'encouraged' to perform at levels the organisation requires to meet its objectives. Therefore, internal marketing needs to delineate its boundary by addressing the following questions:

- How far back in the organisation should internal marketing go?
- How far up the organisation should internal marketing go?

The realities of organisational life

Internal marketing claims, as its overriding objective, to meet and satisfy the needs of employees in their role as consumers. It falters, however, in two respects. Firstly, it defines its target market, simply, as employees. Secondly, it fails to recognise the realities of organisational life, thinking of it rather as some kind of 'germ free' environment. As one commentator reflecting on the teaching of organisation studies, puts it:

> organisation studies ignores or, worse still, consciously hides that which is thought to be unacceptable in polite company. There is little mention of sex, yet organisations are redolent with it; little mention of violence, yet organisations are stinking with it; little mention of pain, yet organisations rely upon it; little mention of the will to power, yet organisations would not exist without it. Consider any of the major textbooks, let alone the Handy (1994) libraries of 'Thought for the Day', and you will see almost more of the underside of organisational life...To be pure and avoid the profane we have to hide the reality of the objects we study.
>
> (Burrell, 1977: 52–3).

Perhaps less visceral in substance and tone might be possible observations from employees qua employees, namely:

- no respect from management
- shortage of staff
- poor communications
- an obsession for efficiency
- constant monitoring and surveillance
- slow to praise, quick to reprimand

How would internal marketing address these issues? It would need more than a technical attractiveness to enable a response. Appreciation of social, political and moral dimensions would be a prerequisite.

Nevertheless, 'solutions' for the observations cited above are in abundance e.g. total quality management, empowerment and not least of all, corporate culturism. Empowerment, for example, part of internal marketing thought, has managed to withstand substantial criticism. The real goal of such an approach, it has been said, is to get workers to 'think and act like managers without, at the same time, sharing managerial power' (Fischer, 1994). It has, furthermore, been portrayed as an illusion.

> Managers love empowerment in theory, but the command and control model is what they trust and know best...Let us stop a moment and ask ourselves how there can be empowerment when there is neither guesswork nor challenges – when the job requirements are predetermined and the

processes are controlled. For employees operating in such a world, the environment is not empowering, it is foolproof.

(Argyris, 1998: 102)

Corporate culture has suffered a similar fate against a background of claims that a strengthening of it provides the key to securing 'unusual effort on the part of apparently ordinary employees'. Under its philosophy, organisations expect and require employees to internalise its values and to adopt and cherish them as their own. The end product is enhancement of organisational performance. Critics point to its moral significance and implications, characterising the colonisation of employees' feelings and thought as 'incipiently totalitarian' (Willmott, 1993: 516–17). By internalising corporate value, employees are deemed obedient and compliant. The delicate issue of trust is no longer contestable.

In fact, you have to learn to trust the people in the company and give them the power to solve problems. Easy to say, but often not so easy to do. For example, in one company, managers said to this that you cannot trust front-line operatives to give refunds or replace products because 'the kids would give the store away!' A test was set up; groups of managers and groups of front-line employees were given simulation exercises in handling customer complaints. At the end we compared who gave away most in solving problems – guess what, it was the managers.

(Piercy, 1997: 79–80).

Trust is a key ingredient for the achievement of effectiveness in interpersonal and marketing exchanges. In much of its conduct, marketing is believed to have forfeited customers' trust. It is generally agreed that the following conditions are considered to be important with respect to the nature and formation of trust at work (Butler and Cantrell, 1984: 19–28):

- Integrity: characterised by sincerity, honesty and truthfulness, and promise fulfilment.
- Competence: the technical and interpersonal knowledge and skills required to do one's job, decision-making and role performance.
- Consistent behaviour: behaviour that reflects, for example, consistency and fairness, predictability, discretion and good judgement.
- Loyalty or benevolent motives: associated with intentions, motives and shared values and goals, commitment to and willingness to protect and save face for a person.
- Openness or mental accessibility and availability; a willingness to share ideas and information freely and accurately.

A further condition has been cited by Clark and Payne (1997: 208), namely respect shown which relates to an individual's perception of the respect shown to him/her by the subject of trust.

From an internal marketing perspective two questions arise:

- How well can internal marketing accommodate these conditions?
- Does internal marketing need to accommodate these conditions?

If external performance is anything to go by, the answer to the first question must be 'not very well'. Internal marketing must not only market the concept of suppliers, customers and an internal marketplace but also ensure its practice adopts an enlightened approach akin to that increasingly argued for by critics of the external market. Internal marketing may appear attractive in principle but not in practice. When faced with actions designed to manipulate, distort and protect self-interest (organisational realities), internal marketing's dilemma is whether to cleanse or confirm.

> In relation with others, sincerity is highly valued but not implacably required. Tact, courtesy, and convention all temper sincerity as an ideal. Indeed, few of us would want to live unshielded from some of the sincere feelings of our associates... Although most adults recognise limits to the practicality of sincerity, they generally agree that it is dishonourable to disguise feelings, intentions, or characteristics in order to present oneself in an undeservedly flattering light or to put others at a disadvantage.
>
> (Leidner, 1993: 218)

While internal marketing struggles with the darker side of organisational life, recent emphasis given to technical rationality as a way of managing may save it the bother (answer to question two above).

> The essence of the application of technical rationality is that all processes, physical and social, can and should be rationalised; which means broken down into constituent parts so that they can be completely controlled. Technical rationality is adopted in organisations in regard to the concern for regulation and pursuit of productive efficiency. Whatever is capable of regulation and control can be conceived as rationally determinable.
>
> (Bowles, 1997: 791)

This process of standardisation and routinisation is known as McDonaldisation (Ritzer, 1996, 1998). It is much in evidence across a range of service industries, including education, health and travel. Its authors believe its irresistibility lies in 'four alluring dimensions, which offer consumers, workers, and managers efficiency, calculability, predictability, and control'. For internal marketing then, the way ahead appears 'clear' as the system is sanitised of its darker side.

> Yet, despite all of these rationalising practices, irrationalities will emerge, for two reasons: first, the ordered structures of bureaucratic rationality may clash

with the emerging disorder of post-modernist culture; and second, these means may subvert some of the very ends which they purport to achieve.

(Hartley, 1995: 410).

So, for internal marketing there is a choice: firstly, to be part of a system cleansed largely of its irrationalities where the marketing task is simply to maintain and contain; or secondly, to be a force for liberation and enlightenment as an antidote to conventional organisation theory which has 'suppressed whole categories of human beings and forced them to keep their heads down' (Burrell, 1977: 12).

Conclusions

The concept of internal marketing needs to be problematised to a far greater extent than has hitherto been the case:

> That techniques are typically taught with little or no questioning of the ends they might serve, or indeed the taken for granted beliefs and assumptions of those who might use them, further reinforces the lack of critical reflection. In sum, the danger of much technical management education is that it gives students the rhetoric of objective rationality both unexplored and unreformed. It encourages an escape from the potential perils of subjectivity rather than a full understanding of its creative possibilities and inevitable limits.
>
> (French and Grey, 1996: 61)

Internal marketing fails to address the feelings of employees about their jobs, their work mates and their managers, as well as their anxieties and aspirations. After all, they are now customers with needs where formerly they were employees subject to commands. The portents are not reassuring given the increasing surveillance of employees at work which marketing is party to, such as mystery shoppers and customer surveys:

> For instance, I've been in motorway service stations where customers are invited to put their thoughts about the staff in a comments book – which in practice ends up with a load of adolescent abuse about the table clearers. That's not a complaints system, its just a way of humiliating your employees.
>
> (Coughlan, 1999)

Looking after employees (Lewis, 1995: 59) is likely to be the subject of many debates in the years ahead.

Appendices. It is not often that the views of employees or their representatives appear in management textbooks. Appendices 1 and 2 are simply an account, from two trade unions, of employee conditions in a service environment.

Appendix 1: a view from the other side

Seldom can the UK financial sector have experienced such apparent success. Share prices of many financial institutions, particularly banks (including former building societies) stand at an all time high, and profits have reached the level in the larger institutions where they are expressed in billions. The cruel paradox is that other records are also being broken. The incidence of stress-related illness is rapidly increasing, long-term job security is at an all time low, fewer school-leavers are finding careers in high street banks and more and more is being demanded by employers for less and less in return.

The industry is run on the twin policies of greed and fear, as the relentless pursuit of higher and higher profit is ruthlessly maintained. The net result is rock bottom staff morale, with spiralling profits only being outstripped by the clamour for early retirement each time a voluntary severance package is announced. The industry has been asset-stripped with many of its middle managers being dumped in mid-career, and in most banks it is a rare phenomenon to find a managerial grade over the age of 45. All this is done in the pursuit of higher profit as sell, sell, sell becomes the slogan of modern day banks. Such policies undoubtedly have brought short-term success, but long-term sustainable growth cannot be built on such shaky foundations.

Most analysts would agree that prudent financial management is an essential ingredient for long-term success. In this respect the three Es are often quoted as the keystones, namely Efficiency, Effectiveness and Economy. No sensible person could dispute this philosophy. All workers aspire to working in an efficient organisation that gives an effective service and is run on sound economic grounds. However, the problems begin to arise when the sole measure of efficiency and effectiveness is how cheaply the job can be done, irrespective of the impact that may have on the quality of service to the customer or on the morale and well-being of staff. Sadly this Profit before People ethos is all too prevalent in the present day financial sector. In this connection City analysts must shoulder much of the blame. Increasingly, the viability of a company can be determined by the whim of the City, where cost–income ratios are often considered as being the single most important factor. Profits may rise spectacularly, but if this is accompanied by any upward movement in the cost–income ratio, the City reacts unfavourably and the call goes out to cut staff costs or face adverse market reaction. Such simplistic analysis cannot be allowed to continue. Staff must be recognised as an asset and resource and not simply as a cost. Sadly, that is a pious hope in the markets of today where long-term planning and investment are often sacrificed on the high altar of short-term gain.

Over the past few years, the whole concept of banking has changed dramatically and all changes have not necessarily been for the good of customers or staff. New technology is here to stay and has been embraced correctly by financial institutions, but the downside is that this has been paid for by large-scale branch closures and thousands of redundancies. Community banking is virtually a thing of the past and many customers find themselves forced to accept telephone banking irrespective of whether or not it meets their needs. De-regulation has also brought a myriad of problems, none more so than the conversion of banks to retail outlets. Customers may argue that competition cuts costs, but this is not borne out by the huge increase in profits enjoyed by all banks. Direct selling by telephone or mailshot is replacing traditional banking methods. With virtually all of the sales staff on performance-related remuneration packages, which are underpinned by very demanding sales targets, it is hardly surprising that many staff openly concede that meeting the target takes precedence over satisfying the customers' real needs. As a result, many customers are sold products not best suited to their particular circumstances.

Until recently, banking was looked upon as a secure career. Now, job security is top of any survey covering the concerns of bank staff. This position is played heavily on by the employers who rely on the 'aren't I lucky to have a job syndrome' to pressurise already overworked staff to work longer hours, often unpaid, to reach targets which year by year are increased in the relentless pursuit of profit. This growing insecurity is not helped by the merger mania currently prevalent in the financial sector. Staff live in constant fear of hostile take-over bids which inevitably lead to job cuts, synergies and rationalisation, much of which can only be achieved through redundancy. Few companies are prepared to offer re-training to existing staff; they would rather buy in the required expertise on a short-term contract. As a result, banks and other financial institutions are employing an increasingly casualised workforce, which does little for company loyalty or customer service. Flexibility is also becoming the established norm, with new starts and promotees being required to sign flexible contracts which bind them to being available for work seven days a week, with Saturdays and Sundays no longer attracting premium rates.

In recent years, much of the financial service revolution has led to a proliferation of call centre jobs being created. Many of these are short-term contracts, carry little or no job security, and are low paid and stressful.

Many new players in the financial services market are hostile to trade unions and operate under the philosophy that an unorganised workforce allows the company to maximise its profits. A whole new raft of health and safety problems has sprung up, and the Health and Safety Executive in England and Wales has recently decided to look into problems such as high noise levels, stress, shift patterns, back pain, seating arrangements and levels of humidity.

Raw exploitation is the hallmark of many non-organised areas. Rigid targets and quotas are set and a prison camp management culture puts relentless pressure on each worker to reach their target. The concept of teams is used to put additional pressure on staff by creating peer pressure that creates the belief that failing to get a target rebounds not only on an individual, but also on other team members. If demanding targets are met, then the thanks staff receive is to have them ratcheted up for the next accounting period. Often workers will work hours of unpaid overtime in order to catch up on the logging of calls and sending out letters, faxes and e-mails. Answering the call is always the priority for management.

This style of management philosophy can be no better summed up than by quoting the words of a managing director of a key call centre who recently stated:

> We have no need for trade unions. Staff here are happy and don't want them. In fact they are so happy and committed to the company that they come in to work on their day off and work for nothing just to achieve their weekly bonuses.

Instead of subscribing to the burn-out theory that staff are expendable by age 40, banks must realise that long-term success and sustained growth can only be built by attending to the needs of shareholder, customer and staff. Today, only one leg of this tripod is soundly founded. Service to the customer comes a poor second to satisfying the needs and, in some instances, greed for the shareholders, and the morale and well-being of staff does not even feature on most banks' agendas. Itinerant workforces hawking their wares from company to company cannot be the answer. Pride in the job and soundly based ethical standards need to be re-introduced into the financial sector before it self-destructs. Loyalty is very much a two-way process, and it is high time that financial institutions recognised the fact.

Sandy Boyle
Deputy General Secretary
Banking, Insurance and Finance Union
June 1999

Appendix 2: call centres – a trade union perspective

Trade unions recognised the importance of call centres early on – both to the service suppliers and customers – and also as a major employment opportunity. They perform a vital point of contact between the customer and the service provider, and call centre staff have an essential role in providing that link.

UNISON recognises the importance of call centres today – particularly in the area of the utilities where we are the leading union – and we want call centre staff to be properly represented and created.

We do not subscribe to the prevalent view that these jobs are somehow 'low-value'. Many call centre jobs are highly skilled and challenging, such as nursing advice and services. As the range of services provided by call centres increases, the status of the staff involved should increase accordingly. They should know what their rights are, what standards of good practice can be demanded, and how they can get the best conditions possible.

In short, we want companies to recognise the legitimate needs and concerns of call centre staff, to recognise the key role they have in the company and to treat them with the consideration to which they are entitled.

UNISON has pursued this agenda in call centres from the beginning, visiting call centres and surveying the working practices adopted, and using the results of that research to issue advice for negotiators dealing with call centres.

The results showed that both good and unsatisfactory practices and conditions existed. If call centres are not to become the battery farms of the service sector, it is imperative that working standards are raised to the highest possible level.

The increase in commercial competition, for example in the deregulation of the domestic gas and electricity supply industry, and the increasing number of service suppliers, has led to increasing pressure to produce ever faster, ever more complex responses to customers. In bad cases, such pressures can lead to increased pressure on breaks, general working arrangements and increased workload.

In particular, the UNISON survey found that main areas of concern were on pay and contracts, training and development, health and safety, fairness and equal opportunities, and recognition and collective bargaining.

Particular problems have been highlighted as far as health and safety are concerned. Sickness is relatively high in call centres. This is unsurprising given the nature of the job and the workplaces: an intrinsically stressful job in an open-plan office with easy germ transmission. The constant increase in the amount of calls and the areas dealt with, coupled with the demands for an all-hours quality service, will mean that the pressures on staff will increase and health and safety need to be in the forefront of the minds of both employers and staff.

Another area of concern is the provision of equal opportunities: it is indicative that although the vast majority (around 70 per cent) of call centre staff are women, these figures are not reflected in promotion to management. The position of black and ethnic minority staff is even worse.

In addition to dealing with this discrimination, there are sound business reasons for implementing equality at work not least the reduction in the sometimes frighteningly high turnover of staff – and UNISON negotiators have been raising the issues of childcare, flexibility and fair recruitment practices, throughout the industry.

Fair and equal pay rates are something that is noticeably more likely to occur in call centres with union recognition than those without, and demands for proper training and development plans for all staff are also commoner in companies with good employment practices.

It is UNISON's view (unsurprisingly) that the issue of recognition is a key one when looking at all the areas of concern connected with call centres. The facts of surveys and statistics seem to bear us out.

On Line Advice, a negotiator's guide to good employment practice in call centres, was published by UNISON (London, 1998).

Chris Barter
Communications Officer
UNISON Scotland
June 1999

References

Argyris, C. (1998) 'Empowerment: The Emperor's New Clothes', *Harvard Business Review*, May–June, 102.

Ashforth, B.E. and Lee, R.T. (1990) 'Defensive Behaviour in Organisations: A Preliminary Model', *Human Relations* 43(7): 621–48.

Barnes, J.G. (1989) 'The Role of Internal Marketing: If the Staff Won't Buy It, Why Should The Customer?', *Irish Marketing Review* 4(2): 14, 18.

Bartels, R. (1968) 'Are Domestic and International Marketing Dissimilar?', *Journal of Marketing* 32(July): 56–61.

Beckett, R. (1999) 'Trust Me, I'm a Marketer', *Marketing Business*, April, 30–1.

Berry, L.L. (1981) 'The Employees as Customer', *Journal of Retail Banking* 3(1): 34.

Bowles, M. (1997) 'The Myth of Management: Direction and Failure in Contemporary Organisations', *Human Relations* 50(7): 791.

Brown, S. (1995) *Postmodern Marketing*, London: International Thomson Business Press, London, 37.

Burrell, G. (1977) *Pandemonium: Towards a Retro-Organisation Theory*, London: Sage, 52–3.

Butler, J.K. and Cantrell, R.S. (1984) 'A Behavioural Decision Theory Approach to Modelling Dyadic Trust in Superiors and Subordinates', *Psychological Reports* 55: 19–28.

Clark, M.C. and Payne, R.L. (1997) 'The Nature and Structure of Workers' Trust in Management', *Journal of Organisational Behaviour* 18(3): 208.

Coughlan, S. (1999) 'Don't Get Mad – Complain', *Guardian*, 29 May.

Coulson-Thomas, C. (1992) *Transforming the Company: Bridging the Gap Between Management Myth and Corporate Reality*, London: Kogan Page, 78.

Crainer, S. and Dearlove, D. (1998) *Gravy Training: Inside the Shadowy World of Business Schools*, London: Capstone, 39–40.

Curtis, J. (1996) 'Down with Equality', *Marketing*, 4 April, 18–19.

du Gay, P. (1996) *Consumption and Identity at Work*, London: Sage, 60.

Fineman, S. (1997) 'Emotion and Management Learning', *Management Learning* 28(1): 20.

Fischer, F. (1994) 'Organizational Expertise and Bureaucratic Control: Behavioural Science as Managerial Ideology', in Fischer, F. and Sirianni, C. (eds), *Critical Studies in Organization and Bureaucracy*, Philadelphia: Temple University Press, 174–95.

Fournier, S., Dobscha, S. and Mick, D.G. (1998) 'Preventing the Premature Death of Relationship Marketing', *Harvard Business Review*, January–February, 43.

French, R. and Grey, C. (eds) (1996) *Rethinking Management Education*, London: Sage, 61.

Gabriel, Y. and Lang, T. (1997) *The Unmanageable Consumer: Contemporary Consumption and its Fragmentation*, London: Sage, 91.

Gardner, N. and Rigby, J. (1999) 'Salesmen Admit to Dirty Tricks on Endowments', *The Sunday Times*, 7 March.

George, W.R. (1990) 'Internal Marketing and Organizational Behavior: A Partnership in Developing Customer-Conscious Employees at Every Level', *Journal of Business Research* 60(January): 63.

Gilmore, A. and Carson, D. (1995) 'Managing and Marketing to Internal Customers', in Glynn, W.J. and Barnes, J.G. (eds), *Understanding Services Management*, London: John Wiley & Sons, 303.

Greene, W.E., Walls, G.D. and Schrest, L.J. (1994) 'Internal Marketing: The Key to External Marketing Success', *Journal of Services Marketing* 8(4): 5.

Gummesson, E. (1987) 'The New Marketing: Developing Long-term Interactive Relationships', *Long Range Planning* 20(August): 10–20.

Harris, M. (1981) *America Now: The Anthropology of a Changing Culture*, New York: Simon and Schuster, 39–59.

Harrell, G.D. and Fors, M.F. (1992) 'Internal Marketing of a Service', *Industrial Marketing Management* 21(4): 300.

Hartley, D. (1995) 'The McDonaldization of Higher Education: Food for Thought?', *Oxford Review of Education* 21(4): 410.

—— (1997) *Reschooling Society*, London: Falmer Press, 24.

Hochschild, A.R. (1983) *The Managed Heart: Commercialisation of Human Feeling*, Los Angeles: University of California Press.

Iacobucci, D., Grayson, K. and Ostrom, A. (1994) 'Customer Satisfaction Fables', *Sloan Management Review*, Summer: 93–6.

Kotler, P. (1972) 'A Generic Concept of Marketing', *Journal of Marketing* 36(April): 46–54.

Kotler, P. and Levy, S.J. (1969) 'Broadening the Concept of Marketing', *Journal of Marketing* 33(January): 10–15.

Leidner, R. (1993) *Fast Food, Fast Talk: Service Work and the Routinisation of Everyday Life*, Los Angeles, CA: University of California Press, 4.

Lewis, B.R. (1995) 'Customer Care in Services', in Glynn, W.J. and Barnes, J.G. (eds), *Understanding Services Management*, London: John Wiley & Sons, 59.

Lings, I.N. (1998) 'Implementing and Measuring Effectiveness of Internal Marketing', *Journal of Marketing Management* 14(4): 344.

Lovelock, C. (1995) 'Managing Services: The Human Factor', in Glynn, W.J. and Barnes, J.G. (eds), *Understanding Services Management*, London: John Wiley & Sons, 229.

—— (1996) *Services Marketing*, Englewood Cliffs, NJ: Prentice-Hall, 519.

Luck, D.J. (1969) 'Broadening the Concept of Marketing Too Far', *Journal of Marketing* 33(July): 53–63.

McKenna, R. (1991) *Relationship Marketing: Successful Strategies for the Age of the Customer*, Reading, MA: Perseus Books.

Majaro, S. (1977) 'The Many Faces of Marketing', *Marketing*, 20 August: 16–18.

Mazur, L. (1999) 'Unleashing Employees' True Value', *Marketing*, 29 April: 22.

Mudie, P.M. (1987) 'Internal Marketing: Cause for Concern', *The Quarterly Review of Marketing* 12(3–4): 21–4.

Piercy, N. (1997) *Market-led Strategic Change*, Oxford: Butterworth-Heinemann, 79–80.

Pitt, L.F. and Foreman, S.K. (1998) 'Internal Marketing Role in Organisations: A Transaction Cost Perspective', *Journal of Business Research* 44(January): 26.

Rafiq, M. and Ahmed, P.K. (1993) 'The Scope of Internal Marketing: Defining the Boundary between Marketing and Human Resource Management', *Journal of Marketing Management* 9(3): 222.

Reichheld, F.F. (1996) *The Loyalty Effect: The Hidden Force Behind Growth, Profits, and Lasting Value*, Boston: Harvard University Press.

Ridley, Y. (1999) 'Poor, Old, Disabled? Don't Complain', *Observer*, 21 February.

Riesman, D. (1953) *The Lonely Crowd: A Study of the Changing American Character*, New York: Doubleday, 305.

Ritzer, G. (1996) *The McDonaldization of Society*, Newbury Park, CA: Sage.

—— (1998) *The McDonaldization Thesis*, London: Sage.

Rogers, J.D., Clow, K.E. and Kash, T.J. (1994) 'Increasing Job Satisfaction of Service Personnel', *Journal of Services Marketing* 8(1): 20.

Rose, N. (1991) *Governing the Soul: the Shaping of the Private Self*, London: Routledge, 56.

Sasser, W.E. and Arbeit, S.P. (1976) 'Selling Jobs in the Service Sector', *Business Horizons*, June: 61–5.

Schneider, B. (1994) 'HRM: A Service Perspective: Towards a Customer-focused HRM', *International Journal of Service Industry Management* 5(1): 64–76.

Schneider, B. and Bowen, D.E. (1985) 'Employee and Customer Perceptions of Service in Banks: Replication and Extension', *Journal of Applied Psychology* 70(3): 432.

Shaw, R. (1998) *Improving Marketing Effectiveness: The Methods and Tools that Work Best*, London: Profile Books, 78.

Teather, D. (1996) 'Inner Strength', *Marketing*, 18 January: 23.

Thomas, M.J. (1996) 'The Changing Nature of the Marketing Profession and Implications for Requirements in Marketing Education', in Shaw, S.A. and Hood, N. (eds), *Marketing in Evolution*, London: Macmillan, 190–205.

Thomas, R. (1999) 'The "I" Society', *Observer*, 4 April.

Ungoed-Thomas, J. (1998) 'Shrinking Food Packs Conceal Profit Hikes', *Sunday Times*, 26 July.

Warwick University (1998) study by Silvestro, R., cited in the *Guardian*, 23 September.

Weatherly, K.A. and Tansik, D.A. (1992) 'Tactics Used by Customer Contact Workers: Effects of Role Stress, Boundary Spanning and Control', *Internal Journal of Service Industry Management*, 4(3): 4–17.

Willmott, H. (1993) 'Strength is Ignorance; Slavery is Freedom: Managing Culture in Modern Organisations', *Journal of Management Studies* 30(4): 516–17.

—— (1999) 'On the Idolization of Markets and the Denigration of Marketers: Some Critical Reflections on a Professional Paradox', in Brownlie, D., Saren, M., Wensley, R. and Whittington, R. (eds), *Rethinking Marketing*, London: Sage.

Winter, J.P. (1985) 'Getting Your House in Order with Internal Marketing: A Marketing Prerequisite', *Health Marketing Quarterly* 3(1): 71.

Wright, T.A. and Staw, B.M. (1999) 'Affect and Favourable Work Outcomes: Two Longitudinal Tests of the Happy-Productive Worker Thesis', *Journal of Organisational Behaviour* 20(1): 1.

Zemke, R. (1989) 'Auditing Customer Service: Look Inside as Well as Out', *Employment Relations Today*, Autumn, 199.

16 A broader conception of internal marketing

A social constructionist perspective

Richard J. Varey

Introduction

Much of the literature on internal marketing has arisen from the field of retail service management, particularly in the USA where it has been applied to bank, healthcare, and professional services marketing as an approach to improving service quality and profitability. Many writers have adopted this approach since the logic it offers is clear and attractive. However, there has been little examination of some of the major assumptions upon which this concept has been applied. Where critique has arisen, this has been concerned largely with imperialism or encroachment of marketing specialists into other management territory, such as HRM.

Re-examination of the early literature on internal marketing reveals a pervasive perspective on internal marketing, which is narrow and observably unhelpful due to its lack of clarity and poor fit with the realities of organisation and management. Conceptual development would be a greater contribution at this point in the evolution of the field than would continued attempts to operationalise 'best practices'. We have yet to satisfactorily answer the moral and political questions about 'why?', so it is premature as yet to put all effort into working out 'how?'

A number of aspects of the popularised concept of 'internal marketing' have been re-examined to consider their appropriateness, and some significant flaws in the commonly-held notion are revealed (Varey, 1996). Further work has examined the problem of the survival of an outmoded conception of communication in the marketing literature, particularly textbooks that reproduce the orthodoxy. A re-conceptualisation is suggested as a major development of internal marketing into a market-based management system.

The internal relationship management system

It no longer makes sense to treat internal marketing as a specialist functional approach. It really represents the convergence of a number of previously separate management technologies, such as human resource development, employee relations, strategic management, quality management, corporate communications and macro-marketing. It is recognised, increasingly, that managing a business effectively requires the close integration of these many functional specialisms, and that management is a continual and complex process and cannot be seen as a sequence of discrete steps or a set of discrete functions. The work of the manager is not compartmentalised into discrete areas but is a portfolio of skills which are not functionally distinguishable and which cut across the traditional functions: the manager as negotiator, resource allocator, information disseminator, and so on.

It is proposed that the basic ideas that have led to the proliferation of writing on internal marketing are fundamentally sound. However, it is suggested that in order to take into account the real problems of achieving a genuine 'value-for-stakeholders' orientation, be it through marketing orientation, TQM, stakeholder analysis, corporate communication (the emerging discipline of managed integrated business communication), or some other managerial approach, there is a need for managers to develop generalist skills and competencies based on the application of sound macro-marketing principles throughout the organisation. A particular form of internal marketing can provide the mechanism for the major re-orientation needed in so many corporations. However, the view that internal marketing is solely the domain of marketing, or human resource specialists, applying a micro-marketing concept and associated tools (the ubiquitous 4Ps) is too narrow and does not take into account the needs of all local stakeholders. In this respect, current interpretations of the internal marketing concept are too 'product' orientated, being based on the traditional conception of marketing, rather than being marketing orientated. Marketing thinkers must put their own house in order on this matter before they can hope to demonstrate the true worth of the internal marketing concept as a business management paradigm.

Major change programmes and plans clearly present problems and Mastenbroek (1991: 243) has suggested that continual internal and external marketing are more effective in bringing about organisational change than any short-lived programme of attention. This is supported by Johnson and Scholes (1989: 314) who argue that the consolidation of acceptance of significant change is vital and is achieved through communication: 'it is the political and cultural barriers to change that may well provide the major stumbling blocks to the implementation of strategic change' (1989: 46).

In extensive consulting work, Thomson (1990) has identified people issues and organisation issues within the context of the culture of the organisation. The former are concerned with maximising relationships within the organisation where individuals, teams, managers and leaders are seen as internal 'target' customers with needs which can be satisfied through the generation of internal 'products and services'. The latter includes practices, plans, structure, vision, mission and values, and is concerned with maximising (the effective utilisation of) resources.

The terminology is yet to develop fully to the point where a single clear understanding of the underlying principles of internal marketing is widespread among managers. Some strong resistance to the use of the term 'internal marketing' has been experienced amongst academics and practitioners, as it suggests that the mechanism of change management being described is the exclusive property of marketers, or there is a narrow perspective on the purpose and form of 'marketing'. The terms 'internal relationship marketing', 'internal relationship management', or 'internal social process management' are proposed as a development of other terms used by writers elsewhere. These new terms recognise the applicability of the marketing concept through the identification of (intra-organisational) exchanges in working relationships and between the organisation and its customers, since 'all employees are customers of managers who wish to carry out the firm's objectives' (Harrell and Fors, 1992). It also recognises differing goals of the parties to these exchanges, within the overall organisational goals of survival and prosperity, to be accomplished through profitable long-run customer satisfaction and loyalty, requiring demonstrated customer orientation. This is pursued in a planned manner by all organisation members as a means to achieving differentiation of the corporation for the purposes of attaining sustainable competitive advantage. Ulrich (1989) has argued that customer satisfaction is not sufficient and that differentiation must be sought in the conscious development of customer commitment, i.e. loyalty and devotion that transcends short-term 'feel good' relationships by building interdependencies, shared values and mutually beneficial strategies.

As yet, there is little empirical basis for the required theory of internal marketing as a change management concept. At the same time, there is empirical data to show that internal marketing, in various forms, is being practised as a viable response by managers to the real problems of achieving the objectives required by strategic decision-making. Internal marketing cannot be viewed as simply the application of (traditional mass market) marketing concepts within the organisation, nor is it the use of modified human resource management principles. It is, conceptually, a separate phenomenon that warrants further investigation and development. Further, much of the literature disregards the difficulty of the political processes, i.e. differing ideas, beliefs, and values held by managers, supervisors and front-line service providers (Dawson, 1994). This literature is too prescriptive and too narrow in trying to apply the marketing concept as it has developed as a response to (external) market relationships (Mudie, 1987 and private communication, 1992). It was thus a 'reform ambition' (Strauss and Corbin, 1990) which motivated the present continuing research project to develop a more appropriate theory of internal marketing which takes a wider view than that of the traditional economics-based marketing concept (see for example a recent popular textbook, Dibb *et al.*, 1994).

The necessary re-conception of communication

Buttle's (1995) review of the treatment of marketing communications in marketing textbooks showed that very few marketing specialists have attempted to produce comprehensive, integrative, theory for marketing communication at both the interpersonal and mediated levels. He found that of 101 texts surveyed, all attempted to provide some theoretical basis for the development of managerial strategies, but many did so only implicitly and did not explicitly recognise the theoretical grounds of their discussion. Buttle shows that the work of Wilbur Schramm (first published in 1948) has been, by far, the most widely adopted in promoting a set of communication practices designed to produce cognitive, affective, or behavioural outcomes among a specified internal or external target audience.

Schramm's work remains disproportionately influential and is still the main basis of the prevailing orthodoxy in the consideration of the communication aspects of marketing. Although Schramm did update his thinking (in 1971) to spell the demise of the earlier 'bullet theory of communication', he still retained the encoder–message–decoder model, and this has become firmly entrenched in marketing texts. In fairness, Schramm's thinking did shift to communication as 'a relationship, an act of sharing, rather than something which someone does to someone else' (1971: 8). This was a considerable development from the earlier view that communication was a 'magic bullet' that 'transferred ideas or feelings or knowledge or motivations from one mind to another' (1971: 8) (Klapper's (1960) term 'hypodermic effect' also become popular in mass communication studies). At last, communication was seen as the study of people in relationship. Indeed, Schramm claimed that all communication necessarily functions within a broader framework of social relations: the physical/spatial relationship between sender and receiver; the situational context; role expectations; and social norms. Yet, this conclusion and essential orientation has not yet percolated into marketing texts. Another problem remaining is that some marketing texts have taken either an interpersonal or mediated communication perspective, thus failing to cope with the diversity of activities that fall within the field of marketing communication.

Buttle (1995) concludes from his meta-analysis that marketing textbooks share, because of the common ancestry for their theories of communication, four themes and assumptions (Table 16.1). Buttle highlights the problem that the very themes and assumptions, upon which marketing and marketing communication textbooks are designed (he terms this normal marketing communication theory), have been questioned by contemporary communication theorists. It seems that these fields do not readily communicate! The wider communication literature can deal better with the weaknesses and omissions of popular (textbook version of) marketing communication theory. What resides in most textbooks is outdated, ill-informed, and in need of revision. Perhaps marketing communication texts should be (at least) co-authored by a communication scholar. Such a text is in preparation (Varey, 2001).

Proceeding from Buttle's end-view, we need an *abnormal* marketing communication theory. A social constructionist perspective, hinted at by Schramm but for some reason not picked up by subsequent marketing textbook authors, offers this improvement.

Social approaches to communication are in opposition to a psychological

Table 16.1 Critique of prevailing themes in marketing communication theory

Textbook theme	Critique
The individual is the appropriate unit of analysis	Marketing has communicative effects at household, family, institutional, and cultural levels, yet, in common with other fields of inquiry, there has been bracketing of human experience – the exclusion of some elements whilst including others – to simplify the complex situation to make it more accessible to explanation. This ignores the systemic character of the social world.
The principal concern is the effect of particular messages	Marketing communication has a pervasive, inescapable presence in our day-to-day consciousness. Consumers can find meaning in almost any publicly accessible information about corporations, product, people, etc. All elements of the 'marketing mix' are (at least potentially) communicative.
The intention of the source determines the meaning of a message	Assumes that the audience is passive and that the receiver is relatively powerless in how they respond to the content of a message to which they are exposed. Recent communication theory development has introduced the notion of interpretive community members deriving meaning by interacting with the content.
Communication is 'effective' when the receiver's decoding of message content produces the same meaning as intended by the encoder	Assumes that the content of marketing communication is closed, but accessible to a competent receiver. But people contextualise received messages – co-orientation and fidelity are unlikely once the message is released out into others' interpretive frames.

Source: adapted from Butler, 1995.

approach (see Britt (1978) as an example from the marketing field), and characterised as 'organic' rather than 'mechanistic', concerned with 'ritual' rather than 'transmission', and fundamentally 'interpretive' rather than 'scientific' (Leeds-Hurwitz (1995) provides a comprehensive collection of essays around this 'new paradigm'.)

Social approaches to communication describe events occurring between people in the process of interacting. This is in contrast to the reporting of how events are perceived through a single individual's understanding. Thus, communication is thought of as inherently collaborative and co-operative visible behaviour, rather than as merely personal cognition.

A particular definition of what constitutes communication is adopted. This focuses on process as well as product or outcome. For example, Carey (1975: 17) defines communication as 'a symbolic process whereby reality is produced, maintained, repaired, and transformed'. More will be said about this particular conception of communication in what follows.

Social reality is not seen as a fact or set of facts existing prior to human activity – it is created in human interaction (see Berger and Luckmann (1967) for the classic exposition of this view, and Gergen (1985)). Berger and Luckmann analysed knowledge in society in the context of a theory of society as a dialectical process between objective and subjective reality. They concluded that people interact and produce meaningful behaviour patterns that construct a shared reality. We create our social world through our words and other symbols and through our behaviours. Such an approach requires that we question the validity of traditional 'scientific' experiments. The business of the interpretivist is not to reveal the world to us but to create some part of the world for us. 'Inquiry is the professional practice of the social creation of reality' (Anderson, 1990: 14). Interaction is forwarded as a creative social accomplishment. Deetz feels strongly that 'if the study of human communication is not ultimately the study of how we *make* the world in which we have our human existence, then it is as trivial as our dominant "model" of it would seem to say it is' (1995: 130). Further, 'communication, then, is the process in which we create and maintain the "objective" world and, in doing so, create and maintain the only human existences we can have' (Deetz, 1995: 203). The dominant model will be critiqued.

The central problem attended to is how social meanings are created. The focus is on people not as passive rule followers operating within pre-existing regulations, but as active agents – rule makers within social contexts. Identity is seen as a social construction, and study of social role and cultural identity leads to study of power and what happens when particular identities are chosen or ascribed by others.

The concept of culture is central and is defined as the knowledge that people must learn to become appropriate members of a given society. Cultural contexts include the community in which particular communicative behaviours arise. Social approaches are mostly holistic; the study of interaction requires the whole picture to understand how the multiple components are related.

Reddy (1993) observed that our major metaphor for communication takes ideas as objects that can be put into words, language as their container, thought as the manipulation of these objects, and memory as storage. Thus, in this view we send ideas in words through a conduit – a channel of communication – to someone else who then extracts the ideas from the words. A consequence of this metaphor is that we believe that ideas can be extracted and can exist independently of people. We also expect that when communication occurs someone extracts the same idea from the language that was put in by someone else. Meaning is taken to be a thing. But the conduit metaphor hides all of the effort that is involved in communication, and many people take it as a definition of communication.

Mantovani (1996) heralds the obsolescence of the *old model of communication* as the transfer of information from one person to another. No longer should we be satisfied with an outmoded model which conceives of communication as 'the transportation of an inert material – the information that actors exchange with each other – from one point to another along a "pipeline"'. There is no account of the co-operation that stimulates reciprocal responsibility for interaction and the series of subtle adaptations that occur among 'interlocutors'. Nor does the old model consider that communication is possible only to the extent that participants have some common ground for shared beliefs, they recognise reciprocal expectations, and accept rules for interaction which anchor the developing conversation. The old theory of communication treats knowledge as an object (i.e. as a body of information as independent facts to be processed), existing independently of the participants, that can be carried through channels and possessed by a receiver when communication is successful. The *new, alternative, conception of communication* is of a common construction of meanings. Information is not moved from one place to another: it is always a means to an end, produced and used by social actors to attain their goals in daily life.

Why do so many of us retain this outmoded way of thinking of communication? The conduit metaphor of communication, Deetz (1992) shows, is thoroughly taken for granted in institutional structures and everyday thinking, aligning well with dominant power structures and liberal notions of democracy. It supports the view that the dominant group (i.e. the corporation is the management group) is accomplishing control over those they choose to subordinate. We retain a conception of the communicative process that gives liberal guidance to communicative practice – in the face of corporations as communication systems of control – we misconceive of how human perception and expression work. Yet, the denial of democracy is an everyday occurrence not necessarily done for the purpose of control. A web of strategic moves of asymmetrical power-based relationships is enacted through discursive practices. Managed (corporate) communication is needed to avoid managerialistic communication (the traditional 'corporate communication(s)'). In systematically distorted communication systems, managers become locked into praising each other, discussing the difficulties of the job, making endless agenda lists, inventing elaborate strategies, and trying to decide what to do, and yet they communicate in ways that inhibit resolution of problems and rarely say what they mean.

The contemporary everyday conception of interacting with others through effective communication is conceptually flawed as the basis for participatory democracy. Identity is fixed in distorted communication systems, and actors are denied the possibility of regaining the (constructive) conflict and self-formation that has been excluded. Counter to the common sense view, communication is not for self-expression but for 'self'-destruction. It is a social act to overcome one's fixed subjectivity, one's conceptions, and one's strategies. Identity, meaning and knowledge are opened to the indeterminacy of people and the external environment.

Our everyday work experience includes the self-deception that individuals are engaging in communication action in pursuit of mutual understanding, when they are actually engaged in concealed strategic action (even concealed from themselves), resulting from confusing the pursuit of mutual understanding with the pursuit of success. What is missing is a productive, rather than a reproductive, conception of communication as the fundamental process by which mutual understanding arises in regard to the subject matter rather than in the sharing of opinions. Conversation is the ongoing process of creating mutual understanding through the open formation of experience.

Most of us are still operating in outmoded instrumental-technical modes in pursuit of control. Communication is seen as a conduit for the transmission or transportation of expressions of self-interest (i.e. informational for understanding). These conceptions and metaphors no longer suffice. Information conceptions of communication only work in situations in which consensus on meaning, identities, construction of knowledge and basic values can be taken for granted: this is no longer a realistic view of our world! If we control through information systems, we are in danger of non-responsive self-referentiality. Hayek (1990) called this the 'fatal deceit': we do not ask questions because we think we have the answers. Some crucial questions are never asked. Imaginary worlds are misrecognised as real. Management practice distorts, manufactures (artificial) consent, excludes, suppresses differences; asymmetrical power relations suppress natural conflicts. Social divisions are assumed to be fixed and in need of promotion. Consensus over problems, personal identities, knowledge claims, norms of interaction and policies for directing joint action are assumed as the basis for interaction, when they need to be negotiated through interaction for creativity and to meet diverse stakeholder interests. When the 'corporation' is the management team, all other stakeholders are externalised as costs to be contained. Then, stakeholders are managed for the managers' benefit.

Most corporate communication systems are systems of corporate control, when participation is required. A corporate communication managing system as a corporate participation system has been proposed (Varey, 1998). The Corporate Communication Research Unit at the University of Salford is working in this field to bring the benefits (and values) of contemporary communication thinking into management (and marketing) practice.

We must shift from our general belief in liberal quasi-'democracy', and its adversarial expression of self-interest, opinion advocacy and persuasion, to a constitutive real participatory democracy of negotiated co-determination through interaction ('It's good to talk' is a moral stance). We need to move from controlling to stewardship. This requires a mindshift from self-interest to service; from patriarchy to partnership; from consent to co-ordination; from dependency to empowerment; from involvement to participation.

'Communications' are best understood as interaction acts, not as objects and artefacts. We communicate when we interact. Communication is best understood as constitutive. Interests should be understood as social products, often produced by decisions and opportunities.

We must often speak when we do not know: not knowing is a reason to talk with others! We can reach consensus if we interact. We need a *conversational model* of corporate life that we can apply in pursuit of dialogue before expression. Covey (1989) teaches us why we should 'seek to understand before seeking to be understood'. Such organised gossip can lead to serendipity, the repair of faulty mental maps, and productive 'inter-changes'.

The conversing corporation is full of natural talk, curiosity, discussion and questions. Conversing corporations can expect:

- more satisfactory goal accomplishment
- recognition of an important value in a pluralistic society in which a wider range of social values and lifestyle options are emerging
- equality in pay-in (contribution) and pay-out (benefit)
- fair representation of interests
- products and services that fulfil customers' needs and desires, and meet workers' needs for fulfilment and pride
- a self-correcting whole, promising genuine opportunity and progress
- people who have a voice

The moral question is, are all positions granted an equal right of co-determination? Morally, psychology pursues reflective autonomy (of the person), sociology pursues legitimate social order (of the collective), and communication pursues equal participation (in the social system). We need a communication theory of managing. This is largely a personal value decision, about why rather than how.

We no longer have cosmos (an ordered, predictable system); the (post)modern world is chaos (formless, utter confusion). There is no longer fundamental consensus on what things mean; interaction has become about values and differing meanings. We no longer have a stable, homogenous society. The problem of 'inadequate communication' is not merely one of divergent understandings but of divergent interests. We need real communication, not 'more' or 'better' communication. Interaction can no longer be the expression and transmission of meaning (an information process). It has become about the construction and negotiation of meaning (a communication process).

Marketing is theorised as participative, i.e. voluntary exchange (a negotiative constitution), but is mostly practised as strategic or consensual (a dominant constitution supported by systematic distortions). For example, advertising is almost always dominant expression and is selected as the means of communication because it is so. Yet, goals cannot be preconceived, but are co-determinate.

It is perhaps ironic that the field of marketing, with its emphasis on exchange and communication, has not been in close contact with the field of communication. A cogenerative relationship between these domains of knowledge can bring the premises of marketing theory and practice into a more contemporary form. Perhaps then a broadened conception of internal marketing will be thought more sensible in the future than has been the case in the past.

References

Anderson, J.A. (ed.) (1990) *Communication Yearbook*, vol. 13, Newbury Park, CA: Sage.

Berger, P.L. and Luckmann, T. (1967) *The Social Construction of Reality: A Treatise in the Sociology of Knowledge*, Garden City, NY: Doubleday.

Britt, S.H (1978) *Psychological Principles of Marketing and Consumer Behaviour*, Lexington, MA: Lexington Books.

Buttle, F.A. (1995) 'Marketing Communication Theory: What Do the Texts Teach Our Students?', *International Journal of Advertising* 14: 297–313.

Carey, J.W. (1975) 'A Cultural Approach to Communication', *Communication* 2: 1–22.

Covey, S. (1989) *The Seven Habits of Highly Effective People: Restoring the Character Ethic*, New York: Simon & Schuster.

Dawson, P. (1994) *Organisational Change: A Processual Approach*, London: Paul Chapman Publishing.

Deetz, S.A. (1992) *Democracy in an Age of Corporate Colonization: Developments in Communication and the Politics of Everyday Life*, Albany, NY: State University of New York Press.

—— (1995) *Transforming Communication, Transforming Business: Building Responsive and Responsible Workplaces*, Creskill, NJ: Hampton Press Inc.

Dibb, S., Simkin, L., Pride, W.M. and Ferrell, O.C. (1994) *Marketing: Concepts and Strategies*, Boston, MA: Houghton Mifflin Company.

Gergen, K.J. (1985) 'Social Constructionist Inquiry: Context and Implications', in Gergen, K.J. and Davis, K.E. (eds), *The Social Construction of the Person*, New York: Springer-Verlag, 30–180.

Harrell, G.D. and Fors, M.F. (1992) 'Internal Marketing of a Service', *Industrial Marketing Management* 21(4): 299–306.

Hayek, F. (1990) *The Fatal Deceit*, Chicago, IL: University of Chicago Press.

Johnson, G. and Scholes, K. (1989) *Exploring Corporate Strategy – Text and Cases*, 2nd edn, London: Prentice-Hall.

Klapper, J.T. (1960) *The Effects of Mass Communication*, New York: The Free Press.

Leeds-Hurwitz, W. (ed.) (1995) *Social Approaches to Communication*, New York: The Guilford Press.

Mantovani, G. (1996) *New Communication Environments: From Everyday to Virtual*, London: Taylor & Francis.

Mastenbroek, W.F.G. (ed.) (1991) *Managing for Quality in the Service Sector*, Oxford: Basil Blackwell.

Mudie, P. (1987) 'Internal Marketing: Cause for Concern', *Quarterly Review of Marketing*, Spring/Summer: 21–4.

Reddy, M. (1993) 'The Conduit Metaphor', in Ortony, A. (ed.), *Metaphor and Thought*, Cambridge, MA: MIT Press.

Schramm, W.A. (1948) *Mass Communications*, Urbana, IL: University of Illinois Press.

—— (1971) 'The Nature of Communication Between Humans', in Schramm, W.A. and Roberts, D.F. (eds), *The Process and Effects of Mass Communication*, Urbana, IL: University of Illinois Press.

Strauss, A. and Corbin, J. (1990) *Basics of Qualitative Research*, London: Sage.

Thomson, K. (1990) *The Employee Revolution: The Rise of Corporate Internal Marketing*, London: Pitman.

Ulrich, D. (1989) 'Tie the Corporate Knot: Gaining Complete Customer Commitment', *Sloan Management Review*, Summer: 19–27.

Varey, R.J. (1996) 'A Broadened Concept of Internal Marketing', unpublished PhD thesis, Manchester School of Management, UMIST.

—— (1998) 'Locating Marketing Within the Corporate Communication Managing System', *Journal of Marketing Communications* 4(3): 177–90.

—— (2001) *Marketing Communication: A Contemporary Introduction*, London: Routledge.

Part VI
Conclusion

17 End-view

Directions for management

Richard J. Varey
Barbara R. Lewis

As we near the end of this journey, we take time to reflect on the stopping points we have encountered. We try to find out why internal marketing has yet to deliver widely on its potential as a structure for economic democracy. We hope that this analysis will consolidate the body of work currently available, and catalyse further developments among students of management, marketing, and corporate communication.

The conception of internal marketing

The broadened concept of internal marketing as a management framework, and not merely a marketing practice, has a number of implications for the management of an enterprise. A shared set of beliefs about the meaning of customer orientation is required. This will require the promotion of a particular interpretation of the marketing concept and the systems and tools to achieve its objective, i.e. delivering value to customers at a profit in a responsive and responsible manner within a stakeholder network. The managers of such an approach will focus on the understanding and acceptance of a 'corporate ideology' while planning locally for appropriate activities to operationalise it. Conceptions, skills, and attitudes for communication and service will be central requisites.

Repositioning the manager role

The role of the manager will be shifted from that of overseer and controller to that of organiser and supporter, i.e. co-ordinator of effort and steward of value-creating resources. 'Employees' and 'managers' will have to understand and agree on what is in the organisation's long-term best interest and how they individually gain from, and contribute to, this.

Internal marketing helps to redefine the role of managers and the relationships between members of the organisation. It provides a way to structure the 'percolation' of the marketing philosophy through the organisation and to emphasise customer orientation in a meaningful way. It assists the demonstration of the integrative role of marketing management in practice by ensuring market-led organisation of operations to create and maintain an adaptive, responsive and responsible business. The internal marketing process brings more members of an organisation into a market-like environment and provides greater legitimacy for management decisions (as distinct from the decisions of managers) and collaborative working practices. Gilmore shows that relational and communicative competencies are needed for the sustained and constructive operation and development of an internal marketing approach to network managing for collective enterprise. Participation must be sought over and above mere involvement. 'Poor communication' is widely seen as a problem caused by expression of own interests or by holding back information. More substantially, this is a problem of avoidance of participatory situations and processes for co-determination. Perhaps internal marketing has the capacity to resolve this weakness in corporate management thinking. Strategic gossip as genuine conversation to co-construct the enactment of the business environment can be created within an internal marketing framework that gives structure to, and conceptualisation of, the process by centring interaction and exchange. In contrast, Stauss and Hoffman take a traditional informational conception of communication to analyse a range of *communication gaps* that can be treated and closed efficiently with the installation of live Business Television as a new medium.

Conception of communication and the politics of communication practices

Much of the internal marketing discussion has, to date, emphasised a narrow conception of (promotional) communication, i.e. the outmoded 'marketing is selling and advertising' misconception. This is too limiting, mechanistic, and only tactical.

Flipo raises a political perspective on the relevance of traditional marketing thinking in the workplace. This resonates with the notion of systematically distorted communication practices. This calls for a reconception of communication as constitutive and not only expressive. When internal marketing is adopted in its narrow conception, based on marketing as a managerialistic technology, it serves only the interests of the promoter by manipulating the attitudes and actions of 'targeted' others. When a conduit of communication is wielded in support of the 4Ps, Mudie has good cause for concern. In contrast, the broadened conception of IM offers a system for participation in productive, cogenerative activity and purpose. Marketing is to be a mechanism of exchange, not a bundle of co-ordinated techniques for mass manipulation.

Communication will be seen as the *mode* of organisation, rather than the *means*. The achievement of goals will be seen as occurring within relationships rather than in discrete transactions of discrete individuals or groups. This interactional perspective will balance economic (monetary) and non-economic values through a co-operative management system. Above all, there will be a removal of the submissive, subordinate, working relationship at least at the local (team) level. Collaboration will mean the self-regulation of relationships and obligations at work. People will no longer be required to work under the duress of directing, order-bestowing force. Because the system is ambition-driven, their work will be a free act of obedience to their own purposes, which will be widely (publicly) understood and balanced with the collective purposes.

New possibilities for ways of communicating continue to become available and accessible. Stauss and Hoffman show an application that seems to help in closing certain gaps in corporate communication systems. But, we should not be beguiled by shiny technologies, we must still ask: 'why communicate?' Information and communication technology supports ways to communicate but cannot tell us how to do so. Dunne and Barnes's urge is to not lose the 'human moment' by adopting technologies that separate rather than communicate.

The broadened internal marketing concept is part of an emerging paradigm shift in which the very nature of management and organisation is being recast within a participatory corporate communication framework, constructed on the desire for symmetric communication for co-operative working amongst multiple stakeholders. Internal marketing is internal communication since marketing is simply a special case of a human communication process.

Voima helps us to realise that in Western society our transactional conception of communication differs markedly from the relational conception of Eastern thinking.

Focus on relationships, not merely outcomes

In the era of virtual corporations and relationship marketing, we should be focusing more strongly on relationships. Indeed, Gummesson shows us that, when the business enterprise is organised as a flexible network, there is no 'internal–external' boundary to straddle. There is an operating environment in which to manage productive working, and a range of differing relationship forms to contend with and to take into account. If internal marketing is cast as *relationship-oriented management* (Ballantyne, Voima), this will foster recognition of 'other' as well as 'self' and the growing need to co-operate and collaborate. Voima shows that marketing thinking, embodied in internal marketing thinking, is only now beginning to shift from the orthodox view of exchange as expression through transaction, to exchange as more about relation through interaction. It is intriguing for Westerners to realise that Eastern philosophy has always held that the self is defined in an interdependent, communal, connected sense, with prime concern for affiliation and co-operation. We need relationships in order to define a positive self-concept (Dunne and Barnes).

Internal marketing seen as internal relationship management is an integrative process within a system for fostering positive working relationships in a developmental way in a climate of co-operation and achievement. The *internal customer relationship management system* has a number of key features:

*   the 'voice' of the customer is incorporated into product/service decisions;
*   customer commitment is earned in a 'social' contract;

- there is open exchange of ideas for mutual gain;
- customers are involved in product design, production, and service;
- there is close partnership between suppliers and customers;
- customers are viewed as individual people, as are 'value' providers;
- there is continuous interaction and dialogue between suppliers and customers;
- there is a focus on discovering, creating, arousing, and responding to customer needs – value is socially constructed in interaction;
- relationships are viewed as enterprise assets;
- there is systematic collection and dissemination of customer information (detailing and negotiating requirements, expectations, needs, attitudes, and satisfaction).

The broadened concept could replace TQM or HRM as a *service delivery system* concept (Ballantyne, for example, identifies internal networks with marketing goals towards customer consciousness), or internal customer management as a form of human relations management which has a broader purpose than purely economic transactions. Internal marketing is a process for incremental culture change in a self-organising (living) system. Dunne and Barnes argue that HRM must develop through the adoption of IM. What is essential, they suggest, is a process within which authentic human encounters will occur. Their approach centres people in the effort to organise and, thereby, to deliver service value – perhaps this is the only true source of competitive advantage.

The broadened internal marketing concept can help to mobilise corporate purpose by providing a mechanism for co-producing and deploying corporate values and ambition in a way that is meaningful to each member of the corporation. The adoption of an IM approach to managing a business enterprise could lead to participation based on exchange as a significant development over mere involvement programmes. Structurally, a system of co-operative working and negotiative communication would be installed. A market orientation and a marketing orientation would be modelled for all members of the corporate body. In the UK, according to Hogg and Carter, the Investors in People programme deals, in broad terms, with the day-to-day communication needs of the business enterprise that are essential for the health of the corporation as a productive social system.

With considerable consulting experience in this field, Thomson and Arganbright are convinced that the adoption of internal marketing can address the malaise in productivity and service orientation that has developed in many contemporary business enterprise systems. The pay-off is all too apparent for those who receive benefits from business performance, and many managers are open to be persuaded that IM is the 'right' approach to 'employee communications' as a business tool in modern times. The question remains, however, as to the real benefits to be experienced by the workers whose efforts contribute to that performance. If IM promotes for workers an authentic sense of meaning and identity with some higher purpose, then all well and good. If 'IM' is used to promote the need to do whatever it takes to satisfy the customer, then it is great for customers, but may not be a universal good for the business and all its employees. If we want *brands* to mark us and our products on *consumer consciousness*, then we should want to do the same among co-producers.

Marketing as a social process, not a managerialistic technology

Subscription to the managerialistic perspective on marketing management allows the ring-fencing of 'marketing' as a set of activities to be carried out by a department. A number of variables have to be selected and manipulated, but no commitment to a value-creation philosophy is required. This simplifies the perceived complexity of enterprise organisation and direction, and permits tribal empire-building. The resulting intra-organisation communication problems are perpetuated through attempts to manage via such a fragmented approach to organisation and management.

Most conceptions of internal marketing use the consumer marketing model of '4Ps' in which the marketer actively targets relatively passive consumers. We (the editors) believe that this is too narrow and that internal marketing is capable of application to any organisational adaptation and environmental responsiveness situation, in order to enhance organisational capability. Further, the macro-marketing conception of marketing as a social process does not limit the concept's application to only economic exchange; thus, it can (must) deal with relationships within the organisation. Internal marketing has particular value when seen as a social process that is not limited to economic exchange and is not dependent upon the existence of competition and choice. The management technology perspective on marketing is too narrow.

Holistic network management process

The functional distinctions of discrete marketing, personnel, quality and corporate communications management are becoming less helpful in understanding the complexity of strategic management of adaptive organisations. Internal marketing is not the property of a single functional specialism, but includes organisational behaviour, organisational development, strategic management and other areas that can contribute. Internal marketing, as Ballantyne shows, can be a parallel process for change.

Chaston examines relational and role competencies of small manufacturing firms in supply chains. Internal marketing is proposed as a framework for developing and investing in relationships for higher-order learning. In this manner, important performance gaps can be addressed, by shifting thinking away from transactional exchanges, and applying much more attention to exhibited competencies.

Operational internal marketing is an integrative activity throughout the organisation. It is decentralised to line managers but must include marketing managers because employees' skills, knowledge, experience, values and work are marketing resources and, along with their interactions, part of the value package bought and experienced by external customers. The *customer service function* merges marketing and operations management. A shift from strictly-maintained hierarchical organisation structure is necessary to facilitate mutually satisfying interactions between employees and customers.

The broader approach discussed here robs the functionalist/specialist of sole ownership of the territory, but the gain to the system when each individual is able to contribute to the whole enterprise is realisable in terms greater than mere 'market efficiency'. The needs and wants of the individual can be met as the means to achieving the organisation's success in conducting the business of the enterprise.

Halal has provided important evidence that the structure for this is a network of self-managing teams (or mini businesses) who serve each other, develop specialist knowledge, execute projects and sell to 'outsiders'. Internal marketing is the relationship and knowledge management required for the 'new organisa-tion'. The internal–external boundary becomes blurred as the traditional organisation form is dissolved. This 'marketisation' is characterised as:

- a flattened organisation;
- fluid arrangements;
- projectised work;
- temporary network membership;
- individual units aiming to own a market through better service;
- symbiosis with customers;
- pursuit of mutually satisfying work relationships.

The common research themes in marketing management and quality management are: barriers to success and critical success factors for implementing change in the structuring of organisations and their operations and the competen-cies and values required by their people, for sustainable competitive advantage.

Competitive effectiveness might be improved considerably by a good internal marketing management approach. By addressing the issues of strategic manage-ment, this would also draw in the ideas of employee involvement, participative management, and cross-functional team-based problem-solving for the contin-uous quality improvement and culture change processes that are discussed in the literature on total quality management.

Marketing as the central mode of enterprise management

Bureaucratic hierarchical power structures are increasingly dysfunctional. Halal offers a democratic enterprise based on an internal market mechanism as the way to ensure responsive, responsible corporate activity. Internal markets need internal marketing processes. Internal marketing links, dynamically, external to internal operating environments.

Much of what is presently described as internal marketing is manipulative in pursuit of performance (i.e. a 'push' strategy for management), whereas the broadened concept we offer is consciously a 'pull' strategy that is developmental in pursuit of progress. This fits well with the notion of *kaizen* (continuous improvement).

Internal marketing can ensure that the marketing concept and practice is not the sole property of a marketing department, and that functional specialists interact with marketers to form internal customer service-focused alliances. Internal networks can strive to achieve customer consciousness through marketing-like activity (Ballantyne).

The concept of internal customers first emerged in the quality management literature. Yet, management *for* quality is still largely operations-led and few organisations are truly marketing-led or market-led (customer-led), despite the urges of many management writers and educators over several decades. If marketers led quality programmes through the common link of customer-orientation, then internal marketing could be expected to be understood and acceptable more widely. But, as yet, this happens in only a few organisations. Rafiq and Ahmed integrate Berry's 'employee as customer' concept with Grönroos's notion of 'customer-mindedness' and the 'interactive marketing' concept to provide a framework for implementing internal marketing through focusing on employee attitudes to service quality.

Strategic planning must be catalytic in the strategic management process rather than managers simply adopting a product orientation by formulating strategy which must then be 'sold' to staff through memos, briefings and reports. Internal marketing should apply the marketing concept in driving and modelling a customer-oriented strategic management process in which business performance is the product (outcome).

Marketing specialists need to co-ordinate exchange processes across all business functions, and to disseminate process know-how and tools in the organisation. Chaston's study of SMEs is valuable in indicating the significance of IM in the development of corporate competence as a service provider that is able to learn from interactions with customers.

The transaction cost perspective developed by Foreman examines the notion of the corporation as a marketplace for transactions between employees. Focusing on performance ambiguity and goal congruence in the employee–employer relationship provides a more useful definition of the service deliverer as customer, and this in turn allows for the possibility of a more coherent economic explanation of employee contribution to profitable (external) market exchanges.

In a service economy, the people who interact with customers to co-produce the service are the principal marketers (Berry and Parasuraman). Successful competition in recruiting, deploying and retaining talented and contributing service producers may just be the most important responsibility of managers.

Knowledge gaps

An historical study, which traces the evolution of academic literature on marketing management, would be of value in highlighting the origins of the internal marketing concept in the early development of marketing theory and practice.

Internal marketing is widely understood on a basis of the 4Ps framework: a broader concept-in-use is not generally evident. Further, systematic, empirical work is needed to examine how the various forms of internal marketing can be operated in a variety of settings.

Empirical research is needed to reveal how internal marketing can operate as a (parallel) process or mechanism (or meta-structure) for change management in organisations, and to develop a framework that deals with the integration of marketing, quality management (in both product and service terms), and human resource management principles – all based on contemporary communication theory. A suitable terminology will be needed which makes sense generally to managers and not just to marketing specialists.

Mudie raises, rightly, the continuing problem of divergence among ideology, rhetoric, theory and practice. If IM is to be truly constructive, and not manipulative and exploitative, then those who deploy 'marketing' practices and are subject to them need to reflect on their value-based assumptions. This is a moral and ethical problem. Yet, perhaps our Western thinking of the self is a root of the problem. Our self-definition is of a bounded, autonomous, individualistic entity motivated to achieve through competition and self-expression. Eastern thinking has much to offer, it seems. The motive towards affiliation through co-operation, if adopted, gives a very different sense to the notion of 'communication'. In this collection of papers, we have begun a process of repositioning internal marketing by reconceiving of marketing from a communication perspective. Of course, this requires a reconception of communication.

Conclusion

If we were to adopt more contemporary theory to explain communication for the management of marketing with internal and external customers, particularly in respect of a social constructionist approach, a participatory conception of communication would enter managerial thinking. This could open up the prospect of a democratic decision-making system. Corporate communication could evolve from a closed control system to a balanced open system (with closed sub-systems) for participation. This new configuration would allow a broadened internal marketing framework to contribute to learning and development.

If internal marketing is to be socially valuable as a democratic, diversity-integrating, system for organisation and management, it must have a vocabulary that is acceptable to all 'specialist generalists'. Some reasons for the lack of clarity in the internal marketing concept are:

• marketing is equated, by many, with advertising and selling (i.e. with promotion and persuasion);

- words have more than one meaning; people may hold multiple, implicit, and possibly incomplete, models of internal marketing, based on assumed meanings;
- language used in one context has been adopted by some in different contexts; are the meanings people hold for them then the same?;
- academic terms relate to abstract concerns, thereby extending and multiplying everyday meanings of ideas;
- terms and concepts have political, economic, and social connotations that impact, often subconsciously, on our personal emotions, interests, and actions.

If control is the purpose, then an informational model of interaction is the constraining stance that denies that communication is about transformation, not information. Consequently, any thought arising from conflicting experience, interpretations and alternative choice possibilities is excluded from the corporate environment.

Internal marketing can evolve if we abandon outmoded and inadequate information-based bureaucratic notions of liberal democracy, advocacy and adversarial expressionism. The marketing concept can support a constitutive, negotiative and participatory democratic system of corporate communication (in the corporation as a collegial community), but will not prosper without it.

The marketing process needs a communication emphasis, but with a conception of communication as a social process by which meanings, psychological states, identities and social structures, knowledge and so on, are produced, reproduced and changed.

We have a body of theory and explanation of internal marketing that has survived considerable scrutiny, debate and criticism. The pressing need now is for learning more about internal marketing from trying to apply the framework into management thinking and practice. We should now look forward to a collection of case histories of successes and failures focused on this endeavour. We might also draw in Eastern influences as a way towards an even more sensible conception of internal marketing.

Index

Notes: Subheadings in bold type indicate contributions to this volume. Page numbers in italics refer to tables or figures Internal marketing has been abbreviated to IM in subheadings